THE OTHER SIDE OF TERROR

The Other Side of Terror

Black Women and the Culture of US Empire

Erica R. Edwards

NEW YORK UNIVERSITY PRESS

New York

NEW YORK UNIVERSITY PRESS
New York
www.nyupress.org

References to Internet websites (URLs) were accurate at the time of writing. Neither the author nor New York University Press is responsible for URLs that may have expired or changed since the manuscript was prepared.

Library of Congress Cataloging-in-Publication Data
Names: Edwards, Erica R. (Erica Renee), author.
Title: The other side of terror : Black women and the culture of US empire /
Erica R. Edwards.
Description: New York : New York University Press, [2021] |
Includes bibliographical references and index.
Identifiers: LCCN 2020055481 | ISBN 9781479808427 (hardback) |
ISBN 9781479808434 (paperback) | ISBN 9781479808403 (ebook) |
ISBN 9781479808410 (ebook)
Subjects: LCSH: American literature—African American authors—History and criticism. |
American literature—Women authors—History and criticism. | Feminist literature—United
States—History and criticism. | Terrorism in literature. | Imperialism in literature. | Racism
in literature. | African Americans in literature. | Literature and society—United States.
Classification: LCC PS153.N5 E345 2021 | DDC 810.9/928708996073—dc23
LC record available at https://lccn.loc.gov/2020055481

New York University Press books are printed on acid-free paper, and their binding materials are chosen for strength and durability. We strive to use environmentally responsible suppliers and materials to the greatest extent possible in publishing our books.

Manufactured in the United States of America

10 9 8 7 6 5 4 3 2 1

Also available as an ebook

For the insurgent ground

And in memory of Hampton Gilmore Edwards

CONTENTS

Color illustrations appear as an insert following page 182.

Introduction

What Was to Come

Velma Henry, the protagonist of Toni Cade Bambara's 1980 novel *The Salt Eaters*, is positioned on a stool, in the center of a healing circle, for nearly the entire duration of the 296-page text. She is in the hands of Minnie Ransom, who wants her to be well and who wants her to *want* to be well. But it is a decade after 1968, that bloody year of assassinations, that soaring year of Black aesthetics and Black studies, that helter-skelter year when "the familiar world spun out of control."[1] It is 1978, and Velma is a Black woman activist surrounded by fellow Black radicals— "veterans of the incessant war," Bambara calls them—and she has just suffered a breakdown that ended in her attempting suicide by putting her head in an oven. Now, Bambara writes, Velma "felt like she was in the back room of some precinct, or in the interrogation room of terrorist kidnappers, or in the walnut-paneled office of Transchemical being asked about an error."[2] She could be a domestic terrorist, or she could be the hostage of foreign terrorists, or she could just be a Black woman at work. Velma can imagine all of these possibilities alongside the possibility that she might return to her right mind only to shoulder the burden of life right back on this side of terror, where to be liberated gives way not to the glory of achievement but to a pain that is even deeper and even more mind-scrambling. It could be that nuclear disaster, the continued failures of Black politics, ever-resurgent white supremacy, or old-fashioned warfare will finish the work of Velma's suicide attempt or simply give way to new threats. She does not yet know it, but "what had driven Velma to the oven . . . was nothing compared to what awaited her, was to come"; her "next trial might lead to an act far more devastating than striking out at the body or swelling gas" (293–94). For now, Velma Henry sits on the healer's could-be terrorist / could-be hostage stool. She sits throughout a novel that Bambara, a master of short fiction who devoted her precious latter years to filmmaking, wrote in part to satisfy a cultural marketplace that kept Black women's literary labor, even in its most radical expressions, on spectacular display. To study with care Velma's position at the intersection of liberation, terror, and work is to take up the task of studying the full range of positions that Black women occupied in the culture that has justified and spread US imperialism throughout the late twentieth and early twenty-first centuries. Throughout this book, I call that culture the *culture of US empire*.

In this book, I analyze the relationship between race, gender, terror, and the making of US empire through the late Cold War technologies of counterinsurgency. I argue that throughout what I call the *long war on terror*, the culture of contemporary empire-building through the technologies of war, surveillance, and detention—the culture of "keeping America safe," of "securing our borders," of "defeating terrorism"—has transformed African American literature as a social field. The imprint of domestic and foreign counterinsurgency on Black women's writing in particular at a time when "the community of Black women writing" became, in Hortense Spillers's oft-cited words, "a vivid new fact of national life," was unmistakable in the clarity of both its inspiration (the blood spilled in Boston, Atlanta, Detroit, El Salvador, Guatemala, Lebanon, Nicaragua, Palestine, and Iraq in the name of North American security) and its imperative (to create and communicate ways of defending against what the US state was calling "defense" throughout the long war on terror).[3] The *long war on terror* is the large-scale, multipronged campaign of counterterrorism that escalated during the late Cold War period against organizations deemed domestic terrorist threats, such as the Black Panther Party for Self-Defense and the Black Liberation Army. Starting in 1968, I map the transformations of Black women's expressive culture against the campaigns of counterterrorism at home and abroad, beginning with COINTELPRO's efforts to contain Black radicalism and radical Black feminism and proceeding through Reagan-era counterinsurgency, and the wars in Iraq. If US empire-building throughout the long war on terror demanded a shift in racial gendered power, with Black women coming to occupy a central place in the late twentieth-century imaginary and iconography of global power, Black feminist writers predicted and tracked that shift. More than that, they crafted ways of surviving it. This is a story of state power at its most devious, at its most absurd, and, at the same time, a literary history of Black feminist radicalism at its most trenchant. If I follow Bambara's lead, the term "incessant war" might serve just as well as "long war." The "old-timers" who crowd around Velma in her healing room in *The Salt Eaters* are "Garveyites, Southern Tenant Associates, trade unionists, Party members, Pan-Africanists," united by their memory of "night riders and day traitors and the cocking of guns" (15). They are those for whom the sound of a door clicking into its jamb holds within it the sonic terror of anti-Blackness spinning through the generations, those who lack the luxury of literary critics' stubborn preference for discrete periods. They might know what was to come after all, and have an answer for it.

Black feminist expressive culture has taken as one of its central motives deciphering the tracks between anti-Black terror and the operations of late- and post–Cold War counterinsurgency, which have increasingly depended on Black loyalty to country, Black statecraft, what Gwendolyn Brooks decades ago referred to sneeringly as the "government men" with pretty brown faces, to spread the fiction of democracy around the world, in sentences of justification and with actual weapons of war.[4] My hope is that this work will broaden discussions of race, violence, and contemporary politics, pushing literary critics to engage how Black feminist writers have exposed the assumptions undergirding the long war on terror, while offering historians, political theorists, and gender studies and ethnic studies scholars a new perspective on race, gender, state violence, and cultural forms. As essential studies in the relationship between expressive culture and US empire-building have shown, we gain a clearer understanding of geopolitics, as well as our own role as beneficiaries of and dissenters to US foreign policy, when we approach our most beloved cultural objects with an appreciation for their role in protecting metanarratives of multiracial US secular citizenship.[5] Expressive culture gives us "performances of freedom" and "alternatives to ways of living under a routinized surveillance," as Simone Browne powerfully argues.[6] But expressive culture is also the very means by which the US nation-state "produces narratives of exception through the war on terror," consolidating national sentiment and consensus through the incorporation of "some, though not all or most," of its previously marginalized subjects.[7] The delineation between the some and the most, as I will argue, has been drawn along the lines of gender propriety and respectability. Black feminist literature deciphers the tracks between anti-Black terror and global counterinsurgency. It also analyzes the means—the very language—by which the state justifies security, performed both as "hard" militarized assault and as the "soft" power of humanitarianism, through the projection of an imperiled US power that calls on not only the white security mom or humanitarian but also the exceptional Black woman to prove its worth and its durability.[8]

Black Women and the Culture of US Empire

To read contemporary Black women's writing in isolation from the historical context of the long war on terror is to ignore the ways that the insurgent textuality and activist labor of Black feminist literary culture wrestled with the literal terms of the new world order. While studies of Black feminist literature and the wider field of Black women's writing have insightfully pointed to writers' critiques of intraracial hierarchies of gender, class, and sexuality, we have yet to fully grasp the ways that Black women's writing refracts the fantasies and applications of US foreign policy, particularly as these emerged in the context of anti-Arab counterterrorism and police actions and proxy wars in the Caribbean and Central America. But as recent work by M. Jacqui Alexander, Carole Boyce Davies, Shaundra Myers, Randi Gill-Sadler, Patricia Stuelke, Roderick Ferguson, Cheryl Higashida, Grace Hong, and others has suggested, when we cast our studies of Black women's writing in the context of the new world order that was shifting the geopolitical pressures on writing itself, we better understand the nature of power and its relation to race and gender difference.[9]

In addition, we cannot help but marvel at Black feminist writers' unrelenting attention to the linguistic code that situated Blackness squarely within power's new grammar: how, for example, Jordan used the term "white English" to refer to "the rhetoric about borders and national security and terrorism and democracy and vital interests" coming from the White House and the *New York Times* but also turned her eye to the "light-headed nigger behind his walnut, 'anti-poverty' desk" who couldn't help but hear "the Man talking that talk."[10] Of course, it is Audre Lorde who provides the paradigmatic instance of Black literary feminism's keen analysis of racial reform and late- and post–Cold

War US foreign policy when she writes of the "home girl" serving as the "american deputy assistant secretary of defense for equal opportunity." When home girl makes a speech in Lorde's poem "Equal Opportunity," published in 1986's *Our Dead Behind Us*, she speaks for the state—"as you can see the Department has / a very good record / of equal opportunity for our women."[11] When Black feminists critique the feminist movement's focus on the rights of middle-class, mostly white, women, therefore, we should notice how often those critiques center around the failure to account for *equality's* intimacy with the "sweetish smell of rotting flesh," as Lorde describes the Black dead in "Equal Opportunity." Alternatively, when Black feminists critique the sexism of ethnic nationalist movements, we should notice how often those critiques center around their failures to address those who work "to make the bread we waste" or those who provide "the energy it takes to make nuclear poisons" or those who "go blind assembling the microtransistors in our inexpensive calculators."[12]

My understanding of the culture of US empire is informed by critical studies of security and imperialism and, in particular, the contributions of Black, Arab and Arab diasporic, Asian and Asian American, indigenous, Latina, and transnational feminists to that body of work (even when it has not been understood in the precise terms of political theorists or international relations specialists) and to the many theoretical, artistic, and poetic experiments with alternative forms of security and protection.[13] For example, Angela Davis recounts in her 1974 autobiography a scene of anti-imperial instruction from below in the New York House of Detention, where she was incarcerated in 1970:

> One evening, after lock-up, a loud question broke the silence. It came from a sister who was reading a book I had lent her.
>
> "Angela, what does 'imperialism' mean?"
>
> I called out, "The ruling class of one country conquers the people of another in order to rob them of their land, their resources, and to exploit their labor."
>
> Another voice shouted, "You mean treating people in other countries the way Black people are treated here?"
>
> This prompted an intense discussion that bounced through the cells, from my corridor to the one across the hall and back again."[14]

a preoccupation with sound (handwritten margin note)

The embodied theorizing of imperialism as the geopolitical expression of anti-Blackness takes the form of Black women's voices bounding over concrete and bouncing off cold bars: a loud question resounding, speculations echoing.

Accordingly, this book centers Black feminist theories of power in its attempt to account for the domestic and foreign iterations of US imperialism. The premise I begin with is that the September 11 attacks hastened the construction of the legal groundwork and the affective scaffolding for the "counterterror state," a post-9/11 state formation that traded even the appearance of a "social commitment to building a prosperous collective future" for the unapologetic embrace of a long, unwinnable war for national security.[15] But the attacks were less a radical break than, in Nadine Naber's words, "an extension if not an intensification of a post–Cold War U.S. expansion in the Middle East."[16] I also argue, though, that this extension and intensification in the laws, popular culture, and military maneuvers of the post–Cold War state depended on the figure of Black gendered threat against which any notion of the prosperous, the collective, or the future has historically been articulated in the long history of US imperialism. I refer to 9/11 as a *catalysis* to capture the sense of a chemical agent accelerating a reaction that was already in motion. Not only did the official declaration of war against terror speed up the changes of the years immediately preceding the attacks, during which the United States expanded the field of the neoliberal economy through rising militarism in the Arab world and the 1991 Iraq War sparked intense anti-Arab racism, but it also expanded the repertoire of counterinsurgency that the US state had amassed as its response to its "crisis of legitimacy" when, as Jordan Camp recounts, "freedom struggles gained more significant moral and ethical legitimacy than the forces of Jim Crow capitalism."[17]

The continuum of this long counterinsurgency that I privilege in this book stretches from 1968 to 2012. Remembered as "*the* year of revolution and counterrevolution," 1968 saw urban rebellions in more than two hundred cities, student and worker uprisings in Mexico City and Paris, growing opposition to the US war in Vietnam, and a widening sphere of influence for global Black Power.[18] The counterrevolution brought military repression and increased police surveillance to US cities, along with the exponential growth of the prison-industrial complex, institutionalized "terror as a response to an unmanageable political economy," in Angela Davis's words. The prison, according to Davis, "has become the institution *par excellence* in the aftermath of the disestablishment of the welfare state."[19] In addition, the US state shored up its apparatus of counterterrorism through programs like COINTELPRO and the School of the Americas, so that hemispheric counterterror became the very apparatus through which anti-Blackness worked through the discourses of terrorism and communism to police Black radical internationalism. Throughout the late 1960s and 1970s, too, the US imperial program in the Middle East capitalized on the trope of "the terrorist" to breathe life into the nationalism that had been injured by the 1960s social movements, to recover from the shame of defeat in Vietnam, to suppress anticolonial leftist movements, and to expand US interests in the region.

The year 2012, on the other end, marked a shift into a new racial regime as the postracialism that enabled and punctuated the Obama era crumbled into a sea of loud, unbridled white supremacy that has been so untamable in its mission to destroy the Earth and the peoples who have built and bled into and shepherded it that I might have once or twice caught myself feeling nostalgic for the self-deluded hope of the multicultural years. I do not intend for these bookends to mark a period of exception but rather to function as useful brackets for capturing the essential features of Black women's culture that shaped itself in the crucible of late US empire. It was in this period that Black women were most visible in US political, popular, and literary cultures, as dangerous, disloyal, inscrutable threats and as quintessential, protective, caring national subjects. Therefore, I use these dates as heuristics for elucidating incorporation of racialized gender into the state's understandings and rationalizations of empire and the repeated, ardent refusals of that incorporation.

The work I discuss throughout this book unfolded against the backdrop of two particular imperial misadventures: the 1979–90 Contra war in Nicaragua, which was funded by the illegal sale of arms to Iran, and the wars, sanctions, and occupation in Iraq stretching from 1991 to 2011. These two campaigns were united by the post-1968 desire on the part of the US state to squelch the surge of democracy it saw rising throughout the Global South. They were also connected by the long history of what Timothy Mitchell calls "carbon democracy": the architecture of governance centering around the containment and management of the fossil fuels, particularly oil, that power industrialization and globalization.[20] Oil was lighter than its predecessor, coal, and easier to transport with pipelines and tankers. Because its infrastructure had fewer points of input and output, the system of extraction, refinement, and transport was less vulnerable to labor activism. Mitchell debunks the myth of oil's scarcity: through the twentieth century, oil corporations controlled the flow of oil by slowing down production, which allowed them to control oil prices and limit competitor fuels like natural gas. Such control of oil was indeed the "preeminent postwar foreign policy goal," and for the postwar US state, managing the flows of energy as well as the legitimacy and the spread of its limited understanding of democracy defined its strategies for both hemispheric counterinsurgency and war in the Middle East.[21]

The *long war on terror* is thus the term that I use to designate the assault on radicalism that escalated during the late Cold War period, against the rise of Black Power, student movements around the world, and resistance movements in Southeast Asia, Africa, and Latin America, and extended, in accelerated fashion, through the first post-9/11 decade. As Black feminist scholarship and activism have shown, terror's long *durée* extended into the current epoch the historical uses of Black women's flesh to imagine, experiment with, and ultimately prove the extent to which US law and policy could codify and glorify, even beautify, the gory avarice of capital. Davis writes in her foundational work of the brutal counterinsurgency aimed at defanging the radicalism of the Black woman, "the custodian of the house of resistance," during slavery.[22] These "terrorist methods" included burnings, hangings, executions on the wheel, and parading heads on poles.[23] For Saidiya Hartman, anti-Black terror during the antebellum period rested as much on these spectacular displays of "the shocking and the terrible" as they did on the recognition of the slave's humanity, and "reciprocity and recreation obscure[d] the quotidian routine of violence."[24] Both forms of terror—spectacular and diffuse—continued to take shape after what Hartman calls the "nonevent" of emancipation.[25] As Sarah Haley witnesses in her pioneering work on punishment in Georgia, for example, "Black women were caught in a violent abyss" of the early twentieth-century southern penal regime, which made Black female otherness a material resource to be plundered in the economic and cultural transition from planta-tion to industry.[26] *Gendered racial terror*, to use Haley's term, provided the grammar through which threat and punishment could be imagined throughout US modernity.[27]

Not only did Black women's unprotectability and hyperimprisonabil-ity smooth the transition to the industrial economy and make modern "progress" possible, but Black women also served as scapegoats when that economy was in decline at the other end of the century, when any pretensions that it might be put to work in service of social wel-fare became woefully untenable. Indeed, Black women captives on the home front—on the plantation, on the chain gain, in the prison yard or solitary cell, in the car, in the front-yard garden, at the airport, on the sidewalk—served as test cases for the techniques of surveillance and torture that would be exported after 2001, during the "high" war on ter-ror.[28] "Ultimately," Andrea Ritchie writes, "whether a woman of color is read as a drug user, courier, distributor, a disorderly person, an un-desirable immigrant, a security threat, or some combination of these, the war on drugs, broken windows and gang policing, immigration en-forcement, and the war on terror weave a web of criminalization that ensnares women in devastating ways."[29] So let the adjective "long" serve not as a cover for the ideology of a righteous nation caught in inevi-table, unwinnable, permanent war (as it did, for example, when Donald Rumsfeld gestured to the occupation of Iraq as a long war in which "they will succeed in changing their way of life or we'll succeed in changing theirs") but rather as an imperfect sign for the unmeasurable hell burn-ing four centuries of Black women's flesh into national amnesia/fantasy and into the government's and its genteel citizens' unquenchable thirst for punishment through detention and deportation, caging, torture, and outright murder.[30] What they called the war on terror, what they had previously called the war for democracy, was the war of conquest.[31] This country has never ceased its drumbeat of war. It has never faltered in its quest to penetrate, castigate, and domesticate Black female flesh. But neither has it been so brazen in its recruitment of Black women to hold its drumsticks.

Over the decades I study here, the culture of empire returned ob-sessively to narratives of Black exceptionalism even as it posited racial Blackness as, still, the exceptional—in the sense of unrivaled, in the sense of bigger-and-badder—threat to order. The official war on terror, which escalated after the September 11 attacks of 2001, accelerated and heightened the impact of imperial discourses of race and gender in the contemporary United States. Against the threat of a foreign enemy, public culture emphasized national unity across divisions of race, gender, and religion. While public discourses after the September 11 terrorist attacks emphasized racial unity, increased surveillance linked the threat of Islamic terrorism to a history of domestic counterterrorism aimed at containing Black activism. As scholars of race after 9/11 argue, the war on terror *exported* the technologies of surveillance and punishment historically aimed at Black people while *importing* the racialized figure of the Muslim enemy.[32] The result was a transformation in the relationship between Black gender and the culture of United States imperialism.

While anti-Black racism continued to link Blackness to criminality, domestic public culture also *affirmed* Blackness as the sign of enlightenment, with officials like Condoleezza Rice and Colin Powell announcing the nation's fitness as a world leader in multiracial democracy. This affirmation often rested on the cultivation of public personas that were in line with existing images of respectability, as Black officials and celebrities performed their own incorporability by conforming to gendered ideals of citizenship (with Rice, for example, embodying the virtues of a Black southern belle). Grace Hong emphasizes the function of respectability—with marriage, reproduction, and consumption being markers of assimilability and proper citizenship—in distinguishing between protectable life and ungrievable death in the context of neoliberalism, offering that the "neoliberal disavowal of gendered, sexual, and racialized precarity is so centrally predicated on respectability as the only avenue of security."[33] But crucially, the incorporation of Black representatives for US empire, not as every-once-in-a-while aberrations but as banal features of national life (the "new Black normal" is how I referred to it in an earlier essay), also depended on a cast of new characters crafted from the raw material of existing racial gendered significations that loosened and stretched the boundaries of respectable behavior: the crisis manager, the fixer, the president, the CEO, the diversity officer, interracial lover and the mixed-race child, the administrator, the golfer, the Mom-in-Chief, the talk show host, and so on.[34]

Films, television shows, and news stories completed this refashioning of racial gendered signification. In other words, as much as culture provides the material for liberation, imperial culture also manufactures consent to domination. In the wake of the 1991 Iraq War, Edward Said credited media dominance at the dawn of the information revolution as the force of cultural imperialism that would allow for the "twinning of power and legitimacy," the joining of brute force to consent.[35] Even anterior to the domination that might accrue through the manufacture and dissemination of the news is the media's capacity to represent "strange and threatening foreign cultures for the home audience, rarely with more success in creating an appetite for hostility and violence against these cultural 'Others.'"[36] If empire, as American studies scholars suggest, goes beyond economics to comprise a *way of life*, "not only for the 'foreign' subjects of domination but for the U.S. citizens who benefit from it, who are subjugated to it, and who resist it," one of our tasks as students of power remains querying how international relations shape domestic cultural expression and how culture in turn enables US imperialism.[37]

Still, as much as studies of empire have taught us about the practices of empire-building—structural adjustment, NGOization, support for dictatorships and puppet governments, war and occupation, support for Israeli settler-colonialism—*and* about the way cultural objects build consent among subjects of an empire that never projects itself as such, they have had relatively little to say about Black feminine gender as the highest symbol for the continual recalibration of imperial power and its structuring ideologies of protection. What does the Black woman do for this culture of empire? If Black Americans in the interwar period "ironically maintained a national identity that figured them as empowered on the global stage," how does the gaze affixed on Black empowerment on the imperial stage falter when it crosses with the Black woman's body, so filled to bursting with significations that it, as Daphne Brooks suggests, "remains the central ur-text of alienation in transatlantic culture" at the end of the twentieth century and beyond?[38]

To address this question and the questions it might in turn prompt for us—about our role as students, consumers, and producers of multicultural imperial culture and also about the role of cultural expression in documenting and generating livable realities in the belly of the beast—I turn to the contemporary history of African American literature and popular culture. While studies of twentieth- and early twenty-first-century African American literature have been dominated by analyses of "post–civil rights," "post-Black," "post-soul," and "post-post-soul" generational rifts, often based in masculinist notions of Oedipal refusal, closer attention to the political economic context of this literature reveals how it both reflects and ruptures the racial gendered discourses of twentieth- and twenty-first-century US empire. Analyzing works by Black women writers such as Toni Cade Bambara, June Jordan, Gloria Naylor, Danielle Evans, and Alice Randall alongside media phenomena such as the prime-time series *Scandal*, I argue that Black feminist literary culture exposes the war on terror not as a rupture with previous modes of dominance but, again, as a *catalysis*, a crystallization in which existing codes of race, nation, and security converge to reinvent duty and belonging and state legitimacy. I analyze Black women's role in the security regime, a role that developed from Black women's positions along the fault lines of competing (state and Black) nationalist projects, and I analyze the Black feminist literary project that has long been dedicated to exposing those fault lines and, again, crafting viable forms of living and creating among them.

I draw the title of this book, *The Other Side of Terror*, from Alice Randall's 2009 novel *Rebel Yell*. In her post-civil-rights epic, Randall's protagonist, Abel Jones, civil rights dream child, turns away from his upbringing in Nashville, where he grew up as the son of a protest leader at the height of the movement, to become one of the world's most powerful agents of counterterrorism. Disgusted by his father's softened civil rights masculinity, Abel prefers the hard armor of police force and torture, and state counterterror becomes the guarantor of his heteropatriarchal power. He becomes a political conservative, a spy, and a lexicographer at the Pentagon, where it is his job is to author and guard what I call the *imperial grammars of Blackness*. He spends his days analyzing and stretching definitions of torture to protect the United States' abuses of state power at Abu Ghraib, in the Philippines, in Martinique. On *this* side of terror—the side of security and espionage, perpetual detainment and touchless torture—Abel brings the skills that he learns as a young activist *object* of counterinsurgency to bear on his linguistic work as *subject* of counterinsurgency in the Pentagon. But when he collapses of an

A young boy dances in a counterformation of one in front of a line of law enforcement officers in a still from Beyoncé Knowles-Carter's "Formation" in her film *Lemonade*. (Parkwood Entertainment 2016)

asthma attack at a horse barn during a Confederate reenactment and the white paramedics, recognizing in his face the visage of his father, the civil rights activist, he crosses the line between anti-Black terror and state counterterror. "Then Abel Jones, lawyer for Abu Ghraib, crossed back over to where he had begun, the other side of terror," Randall writes.[39]

Since the late Cold War, Black women writers have surveyed the line that Randall writes of here, depicting Black intimacy with state-sanctioned terror through vocabularies of both complicity and resistance, intimacy and estrangement. On the *other* side of terror is the long history of state-sponsored anti-Black terror; on this side is the troubling reality of Black responsibility for the state-sponsored terror that keeps Black people in danger but also unleashes itself without predictable fealty to modern racial formations. For me, to stand on the other side of terror is not to cling to a "melancholy historicism" that locates a point of collective origin in the history of racial terror.[40] Neither is it to make anti-Black terror (or resistance to it) wholly determinative of one's political, intellectual, and sexual gratifications, as Abel does. It is, though, to recognize the maneuvers that transmogrify terror's object into terror's subject, to be on constant watch for those maneuvers, and to refuse the pull toward the security that is no security at all. I hold in my mind the image of a hoodied child dancing in front of a line of riot-geared cops in

"Formation" or, better, of the half-turned-back figure of Lorna Simpson's *Source Notes, 2019*. Draped and dripping in blue-blackness, adorned by a watchfulness "more powerful than skepticism," torso headed offward and leftward, she stares down the past (and you) while charting an unsecured path in an altogether different direction.[41]

I began writing this book with a sense that in order to fully understand the twenty-first century in African American literature, we needed a robust theory of how the literature reflects the changes in the nature of racial power ushered in by the war on terror. I wrote much of this book during the second term of Barack Obama's presidency, attempting to grapple with how public narratives of Black political success covered the rising tide of deportations that began with 1996's Illegal Immigration Reform and Immigrant Responsibility Act, accelerated after the September 11 attacks, and rose steadily through 2012. Many of the stories here are about that larger story of racial power: about African American literature's troubling embeddedness in public languages of security and about the way Black women writers, from this position of troubling embeddedness, call forth new languages, new practices, and new imaginaries of survival and safety. When I analyze Condoleezza Rice's memoirs, I discuss how she writes the history of late- to post–Cold War US power as a coming-of-age story in which the histories of racial violence and resistance to it are lessons in domination that the nation eventually comes to master. Linking her own coming of age and the nation's development to hard work and democratic ideals, Rice constructs the United States' global domination, and its overcoming of racism, as inevitable developments in its progress. When she writes of the ceremony in which she is sworn in as secretary of state, she glances up at a portrait of Benjamin Franklin and wonders, "What would he have thought of this great-granddaughter of slaves and child of Jim Crow Birmingham pledging to defend the Constitution of the United States, which had infamously counted her ancestors "three-fifths" of a man?"[42] Conjuring the history of racial exclusion only to expiate it, she writes, "Somehow, I wanted to believe, Franklin would have liked history's turn toward justice and taken my appointment in stride."[43] Turning to the history of coloniality to defend the post–Cold War operations of security, diplomacy, and preemptive war—as well as to affirm her own role in those operations as one of the architects of contemporary security policy—Rice ties

Lorna Simpson, *Source Notes, 2019*. Ink and screen print on gessoed fiberglass.

life-writing itself to the imperial enterprise. Rice figures herself as an American daughter both literally (a "child of Jim Crow Birmingham") and figuratively, as an inheritor of the Founding Fathers' promise. Given this entanglement of gender, nation, and form in a story that rewrites the racial history of the Cold War and its aftermath, Rice's memoirs can be said to render the imperial grammars of Blackness one of US empire's significant means of communication. This book developed as a way to make sense of those grammars and as a way, too, to examine and unsettle my own relationship to "Black" and "American" literary objects and, really, to my own job as a tenured professor in the US academy.

As the project progressed, I became more and more interested in how many of the writers I was reading were writing from Black feminist postures of *counterveillance* or what Browne calls "dark sousveillance"— postures from which you might get a long, hard look back at the power that is looking at you, postures that exposed the longer history of the war on terror as an imperial project that was articulated through both existing and newly invented codes of race, gender, and sexuality.[44] Black women's writing exposes Black women's intimacy with surveillance, policing, incarceration, and border security, where *intimacy* signifies a multiscalar, complex relation between military-industrial and personal-cultural forces.

Take, for example, Gloria Naylor, who rose to literary fame after the 1982 publication of *The Women of Brewster Place*. Twelve years later, Naylor sat paralyzed in her study, unable to write for fear that the computer she was writing on was being hacked or that the room she was writing in was bugged or that the voices she was hearing were not coming from inside her own head but rather were being projected through her bedroom wall by a microwave sonic device. Instead of writing the ambitious fourth novel she had hoped to write, she wrote a "fictionalized memoir" about how the National Security Agency targeted her with a comprehensive program of surveillance and intelligence experimentation.

Take, for another example, Nikki Finney, whose 2011 volume of poetry, *Head Off & Split*, surveyed the scene of the post-9/11 United States with mocking, ironic verse addressing, among other things, former president George W. Bush's "mission accomplished," Condoleezza Rice's mastery of the concerto, and the abandonment of Black New Orleans after Hurricane Katrina. In "Concerto no. 12: *Condoleezza Visits NYC* *{during hurricane season}*," Finney tells the story of how Katrina exposed the vast gap between Black vulnerability and privilege from the perspective of the shoes that Rice was shopping for during the hurricane. "*Back / and forth we wondered what it must have / been like just to float away in the gushing / arms of the ultimate separation—Left shoe / stranded forever from her Right*," the shoes say. And when Rice walks into Ferragamo, the shoes expose their own vulnerability before Rice and her Secret Service agents: "*They marched straight to the back of the store / knocking us off our stands and poking / their secret hands down our satiny private parts. / From high in the stacks we watched her shoeless / dillydally bringing up the rear.*" The shoes have just the right perspective to get an accurate view of the US state's capacity to put on the power of Blackness, and Blackness's capacity, in turn, to flaunt the power of the US state. Finney uses humor to expose the absurdity of it all. The left shoe says, "*She was pretty gay about it all but didn't come near / divine, sequined me. I still got a / good look. I remember commenting, privately, / of course, to my Right, 'Beautiful toes for a secretary of state.*'"

Black women writers took "good looks" like these throughout the long war on terror. Take, for further examples, the memoir of Shoshana Johnson, a US soldier who was captured in Iraq in 2003; Danielle Evans's short story about a returning Iraq War vet who suffers from posttraumatic stress disorder (PTSD); and Alice Randall's story of a former civil rights activist who spends his days parsing definitions of torture in the Pentagon. We will find Black women in the stories I address here serving as coauthors of a national script for imperial power, but we will also find them exposing the fictions of official protection that rationalize imperial power and writing stories of sabotage, poison, endurance, and abolition. My goal is not to present us with a bipartite cast of bad subjects who are seduced by US empire and good subjects who resist it. It is instead to clarify the troubled intimacy between any notion of "Black women" and imperial culture and to draw this clarification in the trenchant terms of Black feminist organizing and literature (movements that had their own troubled intimacy).

The story I tell about Black women and Black women writers in and alongside the culture of US empire begins in 1968, when the phrases "Afro-American literature" and "Black literature" and "Black Aesthetic" and even "Black feminism" were being wielded as the fighting words that carved out the critical discursive world that I now inhabit. That was then: when protests and assassinations, urban rebellions, and the declaration of war against urban Black communities with Richard Nixon's law-and-order campaign split time into an undeniable before and after, when what came after was not altogether new but was certainly an exaggerated, heightened convergence of the vectors of race, gender, and power. That was then: when writers and critics made explicit the political defiance that suffused calls to, for example, "let the world be / a Black poem," to make Black writing and criticism responsive and responsible to the revolutionary movements for independence and autonomy that were rippling throughout the African continent, the Middle East, the Caribbean and Latin America, the United States, and Asia.[45] And this is now: when the phrase "African American literature" rests neatly, unchallenged, in course catalogues, as a featured subcategory for online book shopping, or in polite conversation considering the latest best seller about slavery. During the five decades between then and now, texts by and about Black Americans surfaced in the most unlikely of places to do the weighty ideological work of building a domestic multicultural consensus to post–Cold War US foreign policy. Texts by Black authors bore the iconoclastic standard for revolutionary change at the same time as they were marketed to consumers in the multicultural classroom or bookshop or even daytime-talk-show audience as keys for understanding the other. In other words, the developments in the culture of Black books at times shook but at times shored up the ideological scaffolding of late–Cold War and post–Cold War US security. Black texts, in this way, played an important role in making the world that was being made safe for democracy *feel* democratic for American readers. This contradiction is most apparent when we turn to Black women's literature, which, because of the devotion of Black women writers, scholars, and activist, made unparalleled gains in innovation, aesthetic mastery, visibility, and marketability in the decades after 1968.

We have become accustomed to thinking of the world as anti-Black, of anti-Blackness as our atmosphere; we have become accustomed, too, to longing for the Blackness that weathers the long assault of the modern world.[46] Black gestures and habits of speech, as well as Black practices of making music, food, sport, dance, literature, and other forms of high and low art, bring into tangible expression a profound capacity to live and create in the context of a world that cannot imagine, but cannot resist, this creative capacity. That US governments, corporations, supper clubs, and schools might turn the authority that inheres in Blackness's creative endurance to their gain is nothing new. Since the first slave raid, Blackness has been the site of a permanent state of emergency, and white society has profited from its performance and consumption of cultural forms that bear witness to the Black's capacity to survive the end of the world. To be Black is to live on the jagged edge between terror and vitality—as Audre Lorde writes, we are the ones "imprinted with fear / like a faint line in the center of our foreheads," and we are the ones "learning to be afraid with our mother's milk"—and, also, to witness that generative power of living be constantly desired, diluted, commodified, packaged, and projected into the official stories of nation-states and corporations.[47]

Given the increased production and visibility of Black American women's writing over the decades during which white Americans were coming to grapple with terror and terrorism and began to face, on a large scale, the possibility of white civil society's dispossession at the hands of revolutionaries (in other words, the terror of a *generalized* state of emergency that was now to be unleashed from its singular association with Blackness), understanding the relationship between literature, late twentieth- and early twenty-first-century empire-building, and the racialized gendered regimes of mass incarceration and counterterrorism should help us clarify, and also interrogate and perhaps also indict, the motives we bring to Black (women's) literature. Contemporary Black women's writing testifies to the power of literature, like the Ferragamo footwear that told the story of Katrina in Finney's poem, to capture the beauty of a Blackness that was, against its own tendency to expose and explode US self-narratives of exception and goodwill, being channeled into state fantasies of protection.

This, then, is the story of Black women's writing as both the very material that the racialized gendered regime of security has circulated in its promotion of US multiculture and the material that Black feminists, and Black feminist writers in particular, have privileged in their experiments with Black radical internationalism. From state-glorifying memoirs and media to the books I teach as critiques of racial violence in classes that students take to fulfill curricular diversity requirements, the narratives I discuss in the following chapters tell the story of contemporary power's

Foucault

unfathomable reach, its self-aggrandizing lies, and, ultimately, its fallibility/phallibility. While I see the texts and writers I have gathered here as representing the diversity and scope of work that has imagined Black women on both sides of terror, and on the line between them, it is not exhaustive or definitive. I have attempted to gather a collection that includes various genres—fiction, memoirs, a fictionalized memoir, television shows, poetry, an unpublished play—and differing political perspectives and implications but that also offers a Black literary history of the long war on terror that begins and ends by taking into account the imprints of terror and counterterror on the writerly project. To do this meant making difficult decisions about which primary texts to include and which would have to await other elaborations. For example, I could see applications of this critical framework to Toni Morrison's *Home* or Claudia Rankine's *Citizen* or even Octavia Butler's *Parable of the Sower* and *Parable of the Talents*, but given the large bodies of work on these authors compared to the still scant criticism on, say, June Jordan or Gloria Naylor, I have decided to leave these important texts to previous and future studies.

The Other Side of Terror offers a new frame for reading, teaching, and writing about contemporary Black cultural expression. Rather than analyzing this varied body of work within generic or generational terms such as "post-Black," "post-soul," or "post–civil rights," I argue that in order to fully understand contemporary African American literature, we need a detailed history of the way it reflects changes in the nature of racial power throughout the long war on terror, with the culture of US empire. This requires an analysis of the relationship between race, security, US empire, and literary culture through the period I cover here. Black women's writing has been the scene of this convergence: of Blackness's imperial incorporation and its anti-imperial maneuvers of collective preservation. *Collective preservation* is what I call the movements of defense that are, more than attempts to free oneself from the constraints of the current order, efforts to reconstitute a collectivity, to "preserve the ontological totality granted by a metaphysical system that had never allowed for property."[48]

This book joins a body of work that has been rethinking the basic understandings of belonging and historicity that have driven understandings of African American literature. As Aida Levy-Hussen compellingly argues, contemporary African American literature is often marked not by a return to the past but by "stubbornly presentist, anti-cathartic, everyday experiences of race and racism," by a refusal to look back in order to inform the future.[49] Christopher Freeburg offers, "By reading the horizon of racial conflict and black aesthetics solely in terms of black collective politics," we miss Black aesthetics' focus on the *personal form*: "the ongoing moments where black artists repeatedly invoke and dramatize questions like how am I, what do I value, where do I find community," and so on.[50] The personal form is what Freeburg calls, after Anna Julia Cooper, a kind of "living *into*," rather than in resistance to, the modern world's accumulation of horrors. This of course follows Kevin Quashie's moving meditation on quiet as the metaphor for "the full range of one's inner life."[51] And Stephen Best offers the field a historicism that "accepts the past's turning away as an ethical condition of [one's] desire for it," that uproots the "traumatic model of black history, in which the present is merely an endless, Oedipal repetition of slavery and Jim Crow."[52] As Best suggests, it has become customary to conceive of the contemporary moment as continuous with the history of slavery. At the same time, the "posterizing" of African American literary studies suggests the 1960s as a break within a larger imaginary of history that it still wants to see, in some sense, as continuous. That is, contemporary scholars argue both a historical continuity with slavery and a generationality that posits contemporary Black literature as a rejection of the supposed dogmatism of the Black Arts Movement and Black Aesthetic criticism.

This is an attempt to more carefully link literature and terror in the contemporary period and, in so doing, to rethink contemporaneity beyond the terms of genre—with "contemporary" signifying post–Black Arts innovations in various forms and the upturning of the formal strictures of the Black Arts Movement—and generation.

Without Care or Cure

I use the term *imperial grammars of Blackness* to refer to the codes of cultural production and public discourse linking the rationalization of US imperial violence abroad to the US public sphere's manipulation and incorporation of Blackness as the sign of multicultural beneficence. It has been through the verbal and visual language of Black achievement,

Black suffering, and Black resistance that the United States has justified invasion, occupation, perpetual detainment, and the other military-carceral modalities of counterterrorism. If we use the term "grammar," after Spillers, to signal the ruling episteme's "dynamics of naming and valuation,"[53] or a treasure chest loaded with the inventions that swirl around "Black male" and "Black female" or "Negro family," we might extend the foundational intervention in "Mama's Baby, Papa's Maybe: An American Grammar Book" to probe the gendered proscriptions of what Spillers later terms the "systemic and systematic replay of gestures of *empowerment* of an ascendant Black class."[54]

A grammar organizes and communicates knowledge. Black subjection is the grammar of US power. White civil society is rendered intelligible through "the vernacular and semiotics of pure force, directed against the body of the Black incorrigible"; and state violence is "the common language of American white civil society's order," as Dylan Rodríguez argues.[55] But at the same time, the national fantasy-language of white civil society incorporates the signs, words, sounds, and images of Blackness to authorize, empower, and sanctify its preemptive attempts to guard its survival through the counterterrorism, security, surveillance, and data-gathering that perpetuate states of emergency for the vast majority of us.

If Blackness has served throughout the late- and post–Cold War periods to rationalize US imperial adventures, with the histories of enslavement, emancipation, civil rights, and post-civil-rights political power erupting in public political discourse to prove the United States' fitness as a world leader in democracy, Blackness has also continued to function as the radical ground for imagining a kind of social life that refuses the imposition of militarized security as the necessary precondition of human being-together. This a dynamic that Black feminist literary culture has exposed since 1968. If it was the glorification and performance of Black heteropatriarchy that smoothed the incorporation of Blackness into the signs of empire and, in turn, lubricated discourses of US exceptionalism, Black feminists have long honed a collective critique of what Candice Jenkins calls "the salvific wish," not only because they/we had to create models of intimacy that better suited Black women's needs and realities but also because that critique would prove essential in understanding and refusing the invitations of US empire.[56] It is for this reason, I suggest, that Black feminist writers were uniquely poised to de-velop ways of communicating and organizing knowledge that exposed, and then scrambled, the imperial grammars of Blackness throughout the long war on terror. They "invented new grammars," Ann DuCille argues.[57] These inventions yielded a collection of communication prac-tices that Black feminist writers developed to imagine and enact a world without militarized and carceral safety, ranging from linguistic primers to creative uses of speculative verb tenses (the subjunctive, the modal verb, the future conditional) to innovations in punctuation like the Black feminist backslash/blackslash.

To illustrate this point, let us return to Bambara's 1980 novel *The Salt Eaters*. *Salt* positions its protagonist at the nexus of security, nuclear threat, and Black political progress in the post-civil-rights years. Over the course of the novel, it becomes clear that Velma's suicide, were it suc-cessful, would have only finished off the destruction that *progress* after the civil rights movement, in the age of nuclear warfare, had already wreaked on her person. Velma is literally hanging on by her fingernails after she helps to organize a protest march that exposes the fractures within her town's Black movement culture. Depicting the scene of the march, Bambara conjures a scene of ruin in which Velma struggles to remain upright:

> The banners were still drooping, missing a string in one corner, the PA system only just arriving and two cables split, the bathrooms locked and boarded up and no food, no food. Just one lone pot of field peas and chicken backs a couple from the country had hauled up there in their pickup to feed the multitudes. Velma had leaned against a tree and tried hard not to look at her feet. Two pairs of rubber thongs left on the highway, a ragged pair of sneakers abandoned by a lard can and a patch of sunflowers on some railroad crossing, her reserve pair looped around her neck, feet too swollen to torture further. The mar-shals draggin themselves around trying to draw people in from the trees toward the flat-truck platform. The children crying from fatigue. The students singing off-key, ragged. The elders on the ground massag-ing knots in their legs. And Velma clenching her thighs tight, aware that a syrupy clot was oozing down her left leg and she needed to see about herself. (34–35)

Bambara's catalogue conjures the disarray of a post-1960s Black community organizing in its fictional town of Claybourne. Velma, debilitated by the exhaustion of a protest culture that overdepends on women's social reproductive labor—and pained by menstrual cramps on top of everything else—walks on tottering legs to the nearest Gulf station just as the protest rally gets under way with the appearance of a charismatic leader:

> And rounding a bend, the dulcet tones of the speaker soaring out overhead, she'd spotted the Gulf sign and knew beforehand that the rest room would be nasty, that just getting past the attendant would call for a nastiness she wasn't sure she could muster but would have to. Knew beforehand that she would squat over a reeking, smeared toilet bowl stuffed with everything that ever was and pray through clenched teeth for rain. Some leader. He looked a bit like King, had a delivery similar to Malcolm's, dressed like Stokely, had glasses like Rap, but she'd never heard him say anything useful or offensive. But what a voice. And what a good press agent. And the people had bought him. What a disaster. But what a voice. (35)

The juxtaposition of menstrual blood, shit, and the speaker's preacherly cadence exposes the intraracial violence of gender that catalyzes Velma's mental breakdown. Bambara's civil rights novel is gothic; it bloodies what my earlier work referred to as the "charismatic scenario" to interrogate what Robert Patterson calls "Exodus politics," the expectation that some Black male leader will appear, as if by miracle, to lead the journey to the promised land.[58] It is one that tarries in the ruins of social movement culture. As Carter Mathes suggests, Bambara crafts the novel with a "hinge-like quality operating across the temporal expanse of the text"; and as Bambara crafts the bloody scene of 1970s Black politics, the "nonlinear movement of images, ideas, and ultimately sounds reflects Velma's lived experiences and her awareness of subjection moving between dimensions of race and gender."[59] Later, when Velma leaves the encampment of protestors to go to a nearby hotel to make phone calls, find a doctor, fetch aspirin, and call in press notices, Bambara pictures her as, again, the one who pays the price for racial progress. "She was hanging on to the counter with both hands, nails splitting, hands swollen, the phone too heavy to consider handling without a deep intake of breath and resolve. She could barely stand up, much less focus on the clipboard and flip pages. And behind her the easy laughter, that familiar voice. Oh those dulcet tones. . . . The speaker and his cronies and the women, those women, coming down the corridor" (38).

I am returning to *The Salt Eaters* not to add to the brilliant body of work on Bambara and her craft but rather to fill a gap in thinking, on the one hand, about work by Black women writers on terror and counterterror and thinking, on the other hand, about the global sociopolitics of racialized gender.[60] These two vectors meet in Velma's bodily form. Bambara's juxtaposition of menstrual blood, excrement, and the dulcet tones of the speaker that can be heard overhead as Velma relieves herself expose the intraracial violence of gender that catalyzes Velma's mental breakdown. At the same time, it interarticulates Black protest culture, the promise of multicultural inclusion, and the scramble to control the resources of the Persian Gulf region. The filthy sanctuary that Velma finds is the Gulf Oil station, whose disrepair in the novel corresponds to its decline after the 1973 "oil crisis," which I will elaborate in chapter 1. As Courtney Thorsson points out, Velma is crossing enemy lines, as Gulf Oil was the target of a Black-led boycott in protest of its operations in Angola. But more than indexing what Thorsson reads as the novel's "vague connection to Africa," the Gulf station also appears as an index of 1970s discourses of "foreign oil."[61] And in *The Salt Eaters*, Bambara charts the violence of the postmovement era by scaling up from the intimate and bodily—Velma's oversoaked tampon—to the terrorist threat and planet-level nuclear devastation that is imminent. As Velma comes to sit on the healer's stool where she will remain for the entire length of the novel, she, again, "felt like she was in the back room of some precinct, or in the interrogation room of terrorist kidnappers, or in the walnut-paneled office of Transchemical [plant] being asked about an error." The novel hints that while Velma works at the chemical plant as a successful programmer who often takes government contracts, she may only be working there undermining its mission by hacking and by organizing labor. In this case, doing triple work for racial protest, corporate upward mobility, and what dark sousveillance—again, after Browne, the repurposing of surveillance technologies to facilitate survival and escape—Velma meets her limit and attempts suicide.

Something happens in *The Salt Eaters* that occasions Bambara's inquiry into the grammar of global security. It is a quake or explosion or nuclear attack, a cataclysmic rupture that shifts the narrative into the future conditional:

> Many years hence, when "rad" and "rem" would riddle everyday speech and the suffix "-curies" would radically alter all assumptions on which "security" had once been built, many would mark the beginning of it all as this moment. This moment, this light, this place, these strangers. All would be fixed more indelibly on the brain and have more lasting potency than circumstances remembered of that November day in '63. This moment, heart jarred and lungs starved, would supply the answers to the latter-day version of "What were you into when they wiped Lumumba out?" Or, "Did you ever go past the Audubon Ballroom after they gunned Malcolm down?" Or, "Where were you when the news came of King? Of Ho? Of Mao? Of Che? Of Fannie Lou? Were you wearing a fro the time they were hounding Angela across country? Did you raise funds for Mozambique, Angola? Were you part of the Movement? In D.C. in '63? Did you help pull the U.S. out of Vietnam, Eritrea, South Africa? Did you wear a Fair Play for Cuba button? Did you send defense funds for Joanne Little, for Inez Garcia, for Dennis Banks, for Russell Means, for the Wilmington Ten?" One would ask and be asked, "When did it begin for you?" (245–46)

The proleptic leap into the future conditional (*would*) is the linguistic sign of a temporal collapse; it lets us know that, just as 1968 "split time into an irrevocable before and after," as Spillers suggests, the explosion in the novel marks a new beginning.[62] In Cheryl A. Wall's illuminating analysis of the novel, she posits the event, a thunderstorm, as an announcement of the "descent of spirits" who make spiritual renewal possible; and Bambara's scene of cosmological, environmental, and personal transformation places it in a tradition of African American writing that moves through Zora Neale Hurston's *Their Eyes Were Watching God*, Audre Lorde's *Zami*, Paule Marshall's *Praisesong for the Widow*, and Gloria Naylor's *Mama Day*.[63] Indeed, the explosion makes possible a kind of collective altered consciousness that contracts space and time after the 1960s assault on radicalism. But in *The Salt Eaters*, this miraculous coming-together also raises the specter of nuclear annihilation.

That Bambara's half-miraculous, half-apocalyptic event reorganizes language, introducing "rad" and "rem" into everyday parlance and proliferating chemical compounds marked "curies," is significant. "Security," from the Latin *securitas*, is the condition of being free of care, that is, taken care for or taken care of. "Security" shares its root, *curer*, with the verb "to cure," also, "to care for." And the suffix "–curies," named after the Curies, names a unit of radiation. In the radical altering of security that Bambara writes of here, "security" might come to be understood as the condition of being both without *care* and without *cure*. The regime of security that is the long war on terror ends here in *The Salt Eaters*, in 1978; and here begins a new world not in which women like Velma are *secured* by a government that cares but rather one in which Black artists and organizers resignify care itself, inventing, to return to Browne, ways to endure life under routinized surveillance.

Even the radical care of the healer, in the end, is not enough to save Velma from the world; we cannot forget that what she has survived is "nothing compared to *what was to come*." Still, Velma emerges radiant at the end of *The Salt Eaters*. Her encounter with the healer in the center of a radical medical community leaves her literally floating on air, emitting that other kind of radiation that Bambara describes when she writes of Velma's "glow aglow and two yards wide of clear and unstreaked white and yellow" (295). As many studies of *The Salt Eaters* have argued, Bambara enacts a "textual healing" by beginning with the individual body and then radiating wellness outward.[64] But as Thorsson points out, even at the center of the healing circle—inside a "geometry of infinite horizons"—Velma enacts something other than "an atemporal, romantic vision of Black women as sites of healing."[65] We do not know what or who comes for Velma, but we know who, under the pretense of providing protection, came for Angela Davis, Safiya Bukhari, Assata Shakur, Eulia Love, Eleanor Bumpurs, Marissa Alexander, Sandra Bland, Korryn Gaines, Atatiana Jefferson, Breonna Taylor . . . The terror that Velma could imagine from her stool—the terror of policing, of terrorist kidnapping, of anti-Black corporate culture—makes necessary, and at the same time insufficient, the only real safety that *The Salt Eaters* can offer, the same kind that Toni Morrison's Baby Suggs offers her granddaughter when she urges her to know that there is "no defense" when she leaves her house and then to "go on out the yard" anyhow.[66]

Black women's literature gives us an unromantic picture of endurance amid the continuing onslaught, what Freeburg terms a "readiness for a new mode of living amid an accumulation of horrors—'living into it' in spite of them."[67] I consider these anti-imperial grammars of Blackness central to Black feminist literature's contributions to our understanding of the catastrophes of the contemporary moment. Black feminism, and Black literary feminism in particular, makes available a *reperiodization* of the War against Terror, a reperiodization that stresses, on the one hand, the continuities of counterinsurgent violence from the end of the 1960s to the present and, on the other hand, the modes of touching, watching, writing, teaching, and surviving that compose the negation of security as a global political project to save capitalism.

Unsecured Safety

"The other side of terror," as I noted earlier, is a phrase that brings into view the intimacy between anti-Black terror and Black agency for the evisceration that proceeds under the name of security. It is a term that might allow us to appreciate the how the global war against terror gathered the imperial grammars of Blackness into its symbolic arsenal and, at the same time, shifted the terrain of Blackness in contemporary literature. What follows is the story of this shifting.

Throughout this book, I argue that Black women's writing refracts the shift in racialization that occurred over the late- and post–Cold War decades, from 1968 to 2012. To understand this refraction—a process of reflection and discombobulation, wherein radicalized and gendered discourses and images of state protection meet their mirror and their breaking point—we must turn to the racial history of the late–Cold War US state by way of Black feminist writers' figurations of domestic counterinsurgency, foreign counterterrorism, surveillance, oil and proxy wars, torture, the rise of neoliberalism, the fall of the World Trade Center, and the failed promise of the multicultural. Black women's books, I argue, tell the story of their capture within and their flight from the discourses of postracial culture that normalized and naturalized the national security state and the global security industry.

This story begins in part 1, with a Black feminist cultural history of the long war on terror. In chapter 1, I discuss the three phases of counterinsurgency in the period between 1968 and 2012 that restructured the grammar of postwar US imperialism. As state and military agencies incorporated gestures of Black empowerment into the speech modes of counterinsurgency at home and abroad, Black feminist writers like Audre Lorde, Angela Davis, Assata Shakur, and Toni Morrison studied and contested that incorporation. In chapter 2, I offer a Black feminist cultural history of the Iraq wars to explain how narratives of the "new world order" called on existing ideologies of Black gender deviance and also made room for the production of new, exceptional, acceptable, patriotic performances of Black gender difference. I offer an analysis of Condoleezza Rice's memoirs and the ABC television show *Scandal* in chapter 3, suggesting that these two texts help us understand the Cold War reorganization of power that rewarded the performance of new Black femininities and culminated in the public positioning of Black women's power as both the perpetual threat to US security and the vehicle of its survival and redemption.

In part 2, I turn more deliberately to the ways that Black women's writing refracted the dreams of late empire and invented grammars of insurgent care against the rise of emergency preparedness and preemption as modes of power. Chapter 4 argues that texts by Black authors played a significant role in lubricating the shifts in postwar racial formations and that, indeed, the university was an important site for this smoothing. Because Black literature, especially by Black women writers, bore the mission of diversity training as it passed through post-1968 classrooms, it is important to consider how Black feminists' critiques of racial essentialism based in the manly literary value was as much an intraracial critique of Black nationalism as it was a critique of institutions' cannibalization of Black writing to fulfill market imperatives. In chapter 5, I turn to June Jordan's unpublished 1979 play, *The Issue*, and the poetry and essays she published after her trip to Nicaragua in 1983, to offer that Jordan's inquiry into what she calls the "perfect grammar" of empire articulates Black literary feminism as a code for insurgent care in the era of the late Cold War. Chapter 6 brings this analysis to twenty-first-century fiction. I analyze Black feminist literature after 9/11, with particular emphasis on Alice Randall, Danielle Evans, and Gloria Naylor, within the complex of race and identification during the "high" war on terror. I end with an afterword that discusses the implications of this work for future studies of the culture of empire and for the hard work to hasten what I am most assured will be its aftermath.

Many recent scholars have discussed Black feminism as a theory of, and answer to, neoliberalism.[68] Indeed, one could make the argument that Black feminism as we know it flourished during the late Cold War as a critique of both liberalism and ethnic nationalism, that racial/neoliberal multiculturalism is the racial regime that Black feminism is articulated against. But I would also argue that Black feminism is the imagination of a new world built on forms of relationality based not in capitalist exploitation or competition or the hierarchies of race, class, gender, and so on but rather in the generative practice of liberation that begins with bodily vulnerability. These Black, queer, feminist ways of relating are grounded in the unsecured, insecure forms of safety that I track in the chapters to come: the "deep water possibilities" that accompany June Jordan's spending the night in a canoe with Nicaraguan revolutionaries dodging assaults from helicopters and alligators; the Black female POWs' disorientation upon returning to the "homeland" in Shoshana Johnson's Iraq War memoir; the ontological vulnerability that calls forth racialized, gendered constructions of emergency statecraft and self-mastery in Condoleezza Rice's memoirs and *Scandal*; and the dark silence in which Black characters live when they forgo the patriarchal protections of the wartime state, the silence from which Black feminine characters stage conditional, subjunctive, noncathartic acts of survival.

The forms of unsecured safety that emerge in Black women's literature make the craft of surviving terror inhabitable and imaginable, but not in any straight(forward) way. Indeed, I would follow Candice Jenkins in arguing that safety is a racialized entitlement from which Black Americans are excluded; Black subjects experience the "doubled vulnerability" of socio-epidermal and personal-sexual exposure, and, accordingly, the work of many Black feminist writers who work against the respectability-based tactics of protecting Black life "can be understood as attempts both to limit such exposure *and* to create a kind of hyperprivate black space within which the vulnerability of intimacy is once again possible."[69] Sylvia Chan-Malik likewise uses caution with the term "safety," mobilizing the Morrisonian term "safe harbor" to discuss Islam as a temporary space of safety in which women of color find respite and solace while knowing how ephemeral such spaces are.[70]

At the same time, I want to posit safety not as a private entitlement—as something that one can *have* or *enjoy*—but as a redistributive goal of abolitionist transformative justice, as a collective craft. BYP 100 activists, for example, mounted the She Safe, We Safe (#shesafewesafe) campaign to develop noncarceral responses to gender-based violence and to reallocate funding from the police to community-based justice programs. Likewise, Black feminist experiments in outrunning and outliving the terror of late empire might be understood in the most unromantic terms as possible: as acts of working through cultural forms to imagine and invite abolitionist practices of doing safety, such as holding and beholding another, holding on and holding out, caring from below and carrying across, calling out to call in, and going dark when enlightenment beckons.[71] I therefore consider this a work of literary-cultural inquiry in the Black feminist mode of abolition. Black women's intimacy with US empire's inward modes of containment and outward modes of expansion and resource extraction should continually awaken us not only to literature's radical potential but also to its inextricability from power's carceral motives and movements. This may mean that our task as theorists of culture, keenly attuned to the proximity between the upward and downward mobility of Black women's texts and lives, to Black women's premature death and Black women's agency for premature death, is to be attuned, too, to the opportunities for the abolition of the violent preconditions of our own laboring. My hope is that this work somehow aids in that attunement.

PART I

Imperial Grammars

1

Inform Our Dreams

Black Women and the Long War on Terror

When June Jordan, the twentieth century's most prolific Black, leftist, feminist writer, wrote in 1969 of the urgency of Black studies—not simply as a field of knowledge but as an open laboratory for ongoing experiments in radical democracy ("Life Studies" is what she preferred to call it)—she stood on the wrong side of a line that was darkening before the world's eyes, the line that separated the *terrorists* from those worthy of the shaky protections and promises of liberal democracy. Writing about the struggle for open admissions at the City College of New York, she turned her attention from the work in the university to the state violence that secures work in the university, keeping white life safe on and off campus while exacerbating the conditions of premature death for Black and brown people. The study of life, then, was the study of Black resilience and the study of security as an epistemic object occupying the space between what an empire knows and what it shudders to imagine.[1] In a linguistic analysis that was characteristic of her work, Jordan wrote, "We have learned to suspect and to beware the culture belied by phrases such as 'the two-car family,' or 'job security,' or 'the Department of Defense,' or 'law and order.' A nation of violence and private property has every reason to dread the violated and the deprived. Its history drives the violated into violence and, one of these days, violence will literally signal the end of violence as a means. We are among those who have been violated into violence."[2] Twenty years later, after the Black studies revolution, after Black Power, in the last days of the Cold War, and on another US campus, Audre Lorde, too, situated student activists on the other side of the line between the good life and terror, articulating the same commitment to life studies. Lorde, like Jordan, wed a commitment to survival to an abiding awareness of the violence necessary to secure US life and the gendered definitions of bourgeois propriety that have undergirded distinctions between "terrorist" and "citizen." "We are citizens of the most powerful country on earth," she said in an address at Oberlin College. "We are also citizens of a country that stands upon the wrong side of every liberation struggle on earth. Feel what that means. It is a reality that haunts each of our lives and that can help inform our dreams."[3] Analyses of the entanglement of Blackness, study, and empire in writings like these encamped in Black feminist writing after 1968—over the decades of the long war on terror, the years during which to call yourself a "Black feminist" could get you a job or could get you killed (or sometimes it could get you a job that would kill you).[4]

The violence enacted in the name of North American security informed the dreams, to use Lorde's terms, of the Black feminist writers who rang the alarm about the dangers of counterinsurgency, nuclear proliferation, oil-driven war, and counterterrorism throughout the decades during which they were being hailed as the very proof of the success, or at least the promise, of the US democratic experiment. In the years that separated Jordan's missive, penned from a social movement that was set to turn Harlem's magisterial City College upside down, and Lorde's speech to Oberlin graduates, the world that was poised to make sense of Black feminist writing underwent a definitive transformation. During the 1970s, at the height of late twentieth-century Black feminist politics and culture, autonomous Black feminist organizations and Black feminist literary activism created whole new vocabularies of breakdown and regeneration for Black women writers whose political aims ranged from liberal reform to third-world revolution. In the decades that followed the 1970s surge of radical textuality, Black women writers continued to draw necessary links between counterinsurgency abroad and policing at home, between selling books and selling out, between the canon wars and the drug wars, and between the war on terror and the war against Black radicalism.

Contemporary Black women's literature is more than a mimetic archive of Black women's lives in the crucible of anti-Blackness and gender violence, more than a body of work exposing the masculinist limits of the Black Arts and Black Power movements, more, even, than a collection of exercises in the experimentation and innovation that would invent brand-new genres for exploding the English language. Contemporary Black women's writing also exposes the long war on terror as a racial gendered regime that gathers up literary production and literary knowledge as tools for reproducing the cultural logic of security. It exposes, that is, a cultural logic for which it has proliferated objects. That cultural logic, solidified in the multicultural discourse of institutions as wide ranging as the Department of State and the English department and the megabookstore, promoted Black women's books, and at times Black women themselves, as the shiny objects of a new world order that unleashed an arsenal of counterinsurgent, counterterrorist technologies while using the cover of an emerging postracialism to authorize the incessant war against Black, indigenous, and brown people in North America, Latin America, Africa, and the Middle East.

In this chapter, I offer a brief history of the long war on terror as a racial gendered regime of state protection that linked the project of racial reform to the project of defense through what I call *imperial grammars of Blackness*. After elaborating on the term *long war on terror*, I describe three phases of counterinsurgency in order to provide a critical context for understanding Black women's expressive culture of the late twentieth and early twenty-first centuries: first, the years between 1968 and 1980, during which public policy, popular culture, and political speech racialized terror through the figures of the Black radical and the Arab / Middle Eastern terrorist; second, the construction of the "new world order" in the waning years of the Cold War and the years after the fall of the Soviet Union (1980–2001), which tied the urgency to establish global military domination through new technologies of war to diversity imperatives and to the continued containment of the US Black population through drug policing and welfare "reform"; and, third, the post-9/11 era (2001–12), which saw the apex of postracialism and the uncanny collision, as I refer to it, of US political innovation with regard to racial representation and aesthetic innovation in Black literature and literary studies. Through each of these phases, politicians and policy makers sought to restructure the grammar of postwar US imperialism. So did Black women writers.

American Grammars

When President George W. Bush addressed the nation in a televised speech on September 11, 2001, hours after the attacks on the World Trade Center and the Pentagon, he spoke the grammar of an exceptional multiracial democracy under the threat of terrorism. Collective nouns followed by plural possessives signaled that the country that had just been attacked was so exceptional as to exceed the bounds of the single possessive "its": "America and *our* friends and allies" would now "stand together to win the war against terrorism." Single antecedents gave way to plural pronouns: "*America* was targeted for attack because *we're* the brightest beacon for freedom and opportunity in the world." The pluralization of the subject "America" was no doubt a construction that aimed to reflect a national unity that was more essential than ever. "This is a day," Bush said, "when all Americans from every walk of life unite in our resolve for justice and peace." Even if the grammar was wrong, it was right. And Bush's primer was, contrary to all appearances, no new grammar book.

Bush was authoring a revisionist history of the dispossession and death-making captured by the word "America" and, at the same time, authorizing new state projects of military incursion. His speech was drawn from the same grammar book that Hortense Spillers wrote of in her definitive 1987 work, "Mama's Baby, Papa's Maybe: An American Grammar Book." This is a symbolic order that began with the linguistic, ecological, political, and cultural ruptures of the Atlantic slave trade. It was predicated on the foundational signs of Black (un)gender: mother-dispossessed, son-disinherited, flesh-unprotected.[5] During the three decades that preceded the September 11 attacks, the grammar of US power expanded its range of uses, such that Blackness could be called on as both threat and promise in the linguistic performances of national unity; this revised grammar book was founded on the updated symbology of Black ungender. One of the primary aims of this book is to offer a genealogy of this expansion. In later chapters, I discuss the critical moments of crisis and transition—the institutionalization of Black studies, the early intrahemispheric wars of the early 1980s, the Iraq wars, the September 11 attacks—that called forth new terms for calibrating racial power. I detail, in turn, how the work of Black women writers both lubricated and interrupted that calibration of power's grammar. Here, though, I would like to offer a brief analysis of the historical situation—the long war on terror—that created an inescapable intimacy between Black women's writing and the US security regime. I have elsewhere written about how post-9/11 fiction *refracted* the war on terror: just as shards of glass *refract* reality, throwing reflection out and around, what I earlier called the "new Black novel" breaks and breaks open the spatial logics of the long war on terror, throwing into light how the culture of permanent war reorganizes codes of race, at once *informing* and *unforming* existential questions about Blackness, art, and being. I would like to elaborate on that point here by stressing the continuities between pre-9/11 and post-9/11 discourses of national protection and the ways that Black women's writing has surfaced and ruptured those continuities through their attention to the imperial grammars of Blackness.

As I pointed out in the introduction, I use the term *imperial grammars of Blackness* to refer to the codes of cultural production and public discourse linking the rationalization of US imperial violence in the late- and post–Cold War years to the US public sphere's manipulation and incorporation of Blackness as the sign of multicultural beneficence. It has been through the verbal and visual language of Black achievement, Black suffering, and Black resistance that the United States has justified invasion, occupation, perpetual detainment, and the other military-carceral modalities of counterterrorism. If the term "grammar," after Spillers, signals the ruling episteme's "dynamics of naming and valuation" and can be used to refer to the treasure chest loaded with the inventions that swirl around "Black male" and "Black female" or "Negro family," we might extend the foundational intervention in "Mama's Baby, Papa's Maybe" to query the gendered proscriptions of what Spillers later terms the "systemic and systematic replay of gestures of *empowerment* of an ascendant Black class."[6] To endow Black gestures of empowerment with the magic of state sanction, or to take them over altogether, has been a primary strategy of neoliberal governance. Imagine: a white marine singing the Negro spiritual "Go Down Moses" days before Christmas in 1979, at a demonstration in support of the hostages being held captive at the US embassy in Tehran.[7] Imagine: Condoleezza Rice performing "His Eye Is on the Sparrow" accompanied by John Ashcroft on the piano in an impromptu tarry service at Camp David, days after 9/11. Or remember: Colin Powell, the first Black national security adviser and first Black chairman of the Joint Chiefs of Staff, carefully laying out the case for preemptive war in Iraq a year after the Bush defense adviser and Shakespeare scholar Kenneth Adelman referred to that proposed mission as a "cakewalk."[8] Or recall: Barack

Obama's preaching the values of nonviolent protest to Egyptians under the authoritarian rule of Hosni Mubarak.[9] As Cynthia Young argues, efforts by the US state to "interpellate Black Americans into US empire-building projects" during the war on terror *"borrow the language"* of the Black freedom struggle "in the name of US imperialism."[10] Dragging the sonic and linguistic labor of global Black rebellion into the offensives of US counterinsurgency required carefully contained performances of Black gendered propriety. The aggressive erasure of Black insurgency was in this way routed through the tightly contained, cisgendered Black body on the world stage.

Of course, these gestures of empowerment have a significant prehistory in the post-1945 scaffolding of racial-national power. The imperial grammars of Blackness are the linguistic structures through which the United States recalibrated post–World War II racial power as it projected global power through essentially nationalist iconography and ideology and tethered that globalized nationalism to the demands of military defense. World War II intensified *both* the liberal and radical strands of Black activism and political organizing (it was during the war that, Cedric Robinson argues, "Black Americans experienced the most profound Americanization of the collective social conscience since the beginnings of the Civil War"); and it also transformed the US government's relationship to Black activism and politics.[11] As Mary Dudziak's well-known study argues, US governmental agencies like the United States Information Agency and the State Department circulated images of Black liberation struggles in order to promote the image of US democracy after World War II.[12] During the Cold War, the government's granting of formal rights of citizenship to Black people was part of a larger foreign-policy strategy of image management. This meant, though, that the vocabulary with which one could speak of Black liberation was tightly contained: while President Lyndon B. Johnson might say, after the assassination of John F. Kennedy, that the "time has come for Americans of all races and creeds and political beliefs to understand and to respect one another," anticommunist initiatives and discourse also endangered the Black Left and enforced models of racial reform and conciliation based on performances of mutual respect and understanding rather than structural change and, most certainly, rather than socialist revolution.[13] Official antiracism quieted radicalism, diluted class consciousness, and shored up the moral rationale for the United States' global influence. Cold War discourse, in this way, linked the project of racial reform to the project of defense.

Official antiracism was not just public relations; it was a strategy to legitimize the political authority of the sovereign security state after seemingly irreparable rupture. Members of the liberal-conservative intellectual elite posited that the "excess of democracy" that the 1960s antiracist, anticolonial, and antiwar movements had unleashed had dampened US public approval for defense and had led to demands for spending on public services. They blamed the failed war in Vietnam on the overpowering antiwar sentiment of the people, which limited the authority of the state to act aggressively. They urged a "moderation" of democracy, a contraction of "the democratic principle."[14] In 1968, the Harvard political scientist Samuel Huntington, who later chaired the Democratic Party's Foreign Policy Advisory Committee, served in the Carter administration's National Security Council, and served as an adviser on security to P. W. Botha in apartheid South Africa, observed, "Marginal social groups, as in the case of the blacks, are now becoming full participants in the political system. Yet the danger of overloading the political system with demands which extend its function and undermine its authority still remains."[15] For Huntington, whose *Political Order in Changing Societies* (also published in 1968) provided the terms of order through which crisis would be understood and managed by political leaders, assimilation was key to political order. Modernization "brings into existence and into political consciousness and activity social and economic groups which either did not exist in the traditional society or were outside the scope of politics in the traditional society. Either these groups are assimilated into the political system or they become a source of antagonism to and of revolution against the political system."[16] Proper assimilation would prevent revolution; it was one strategy for restoring the authority of political leaders who had fallen prey to the "egalitarian ethos of the times."[17]

The worldwide insurgency of 1967–68 weakened the perceived authority of the security state—people "no longer felt the same compulsion to obey those that they had previously considered superior to themselves"—and the "democratic distemper" of people in the United States demanded the expansion of governmental activity (public services) and the contraction of governmental authority.[18] Welfare thus became a security problem, and the increased demand for the government to provide services was of course laid at the feet of the Black matriarch and the "startling increase in welfare dependency" caused by the pathological Black family.[19] It was of course Huntington who later promoted the myth of the "clash of civilizations" to define threat as cultural or civilizational rather than geopolitical. The clash of civilizations thesis brought the cultural pathology thesis into foreign affairs, with faulty social reproduction being the link between the 1960s social movements and the "warfare between Arabs and the West" that Huntington predicted would become more virulent.[20]

As intellectuals like Huntington realized how close they were to losing their war of conquest, they devised ways to recover authority. Collective power could be physically suppressed through counterinsurgency, and it could be repressed through the kind of co-optation that overwhelmed collectivist visions for the future with individualist dreams of success. It is for this reason that when Cedric Robinson wrote of the political scientists who deified order and demonized chaos, disorder, disintegration, and disorganization, his goal was to expose the academic discipline's role in prescribing "*ordered rather than democratic* states."[21] Robinson pointed out, too, that the Right's "naked class warfare," which turned anticommunism into "race discourse on the rule of law," was a response to the crucial coming-together of the Black liberal tradition and what he called "Black communitarianism." The 1960s saw the radical and liberal strands of Black organizing—an ascendant and hyperpublic Black liberalism, an insurgent and often underground Black radicalism— "tangentially touch" as "liberalism exploited American patriotism and national unity for its agenda in race relation and the democratic tradition insinuated its concern for liberation into working-class militancy." The struggle for governmental legitimacy, that is, made use of the gulf between the "liberal theater" of Black achievement in government, higher education, corporate management, and public service; it also made use of the connections between the same.[22] The wager that Huntington, Moynihan, and other policy makers made was that the promise of social visibility and cultural recognition could force a trade between the demands of revolution and the quest for individual distinction.[23] It is for this reason, too, that we must understand the exhausted figure of the Black woman organizer and the exalted figure of the Black woman writer as twin problems for thought.

The grammars of race and power changed as the racial regime of white supremacy gave way to several successive racial regimes over the course of the late Cold War. These were the racial regimes of the long war on terror: the Negrophobia subtending law and order in the 1970s, multiculturalism and colorblindness in the 1980s and 1990s, postracialism in the 2000s, and the "return" of bold, unbridled white supremacy after the 2016 election of Donald J. Trump. During and after that campaign season, of course, we witnessed the rejection of melting-pot discourses by both white supremacists, who vowed to restore a prelapsarian American greatness, and antiracists, who asserted, against the gush of colorblindness, that racial particularities mattered. What we witnessed with the first Trump election was indeed a shift from one racial regime to another: not a wholesale break with a previous order but a moment of crisis followed by a resettling and further crisis. I borrow the term "racial regime" from Robinson, who used the term to capture the "lived multiplicities" that relations of power necessarily entail and that scholars often have a difficulty reconciling in theories of domination. Racial regimes, Robinson is careful to note, are unstable systems of racial meaning that may falter "under the weight of their own artifices, practices and apparatuses; they may fragment, desiccated by new realities, which discard some fragments wholly while appropriating others into newer regimes."[24] If racial regimes are essentially unstable, in the first place, because the invention of racial difference masks other "shared identities," such as class, and in the second place, because regimes are cultural machines that set off "fugitive, unaccounted-for elements of reality," they require constant maintenance.[25]

Michael Omi and Howard Winant posit that the global discrediting of the racial regime of Jim Crow after World War II produced a "racial break," a shift away from the government's formal sanctioning of white supremacy. But they point out that that break was incomplete and that the period following the formal outlawing of Jim Crow might be understood as a racial "interregnum" in which white supremacy coexists with official antiracism. In a sophisticated revision of Omi and Winant's racial break thesis, Jodi Melamed goes so far as to argue that the racial break of the post–World War II era was complete and that the US state and its ideological apparatuses—including philanthropic foundations that supported contemporary literature—initiated a whole "new worldwide racial project" founded in the official recognition of difference. Now "formally antiracist, liberal-capitalist modernity" could "partner with" white supremacy "without replacing or ending it."[26] Through three phases of postwar racial reordering—racial liberalism, liberal multiculturalism, and neoliberal multiculturalism, US state and state-funded agencies *rationalized* the violence of late racial capitalism, carefully controlling knowledge about race, racism, and antiracism to make the economic, political, and social hierarchies that persisted through the post-civil-rights era appear "as the result of fair competition."[27] For Omi and Winant, the Black activist organizations that brought the US state to crisis in the 1950s and 1960s fragmented: "entrists" built organizations aimed at political reform while socialists and nationalists continued to push for radical transformation in defiance of mainstream political organizations. "Once the organized Black movement became a mere constituency" within US politics, they write, "it found itself locked in a bear hug with the state institutions whose programs it had itself demanded, while simultaneously isolated from the core institutions of the modern state."[28] The break with Jim Crow, that is to say, required a certain intimacy between Black politics and state politics. The sedimentation of the post–Jim Crow racial order ran parallel to, and at critical moments in tandem with, the solidification of a *worldwide* racial order that coded "democracy" and "freedom" as white and enlightened and "communism" and "totalitarianism" as dark and dangerous and in need of militarized sanction.[29] When Bush drew from that same old grammar book to declare war against terror in 2001, then, it was as much to pronounce a new military-political order as it was to dramatize a racial order that had been solidifying through successive regimes during the post–World War II period. These successive regimes not only depended on state and cultural institutions' incorporation of minority difference as a strategy of depoliticizing the global Black freedom struggle but also rested on racialized, gendered significations of terror and terrorism.

The Racialization of Terror: 1968–80

(radicalization) / (incorporation)

The intimacies between the domestic racial project of reform and the geopolitical project of securing the world for unregulated capitalist growth deepened over the latter years of the Cold War, particularly as the carceral technologies of racial control in the United States coincided with the practices of foreign counterinsurgency. In the 1960s and 1970s, especially after armed resistance definitively entered into the public's imagery and imagination of the Black struggle in 1967, the line between lawful citizen and unlawful terrorist (the very line June Jordan crossed when she situated herself and the student activists she followed "among those who have been violated into violence") blackened. That is, the specter of armed Black resistance, or Negroes with Guns, on the fields of civil rights struggle and, eventually, at the California state legislature in May 1967, hastened the racialization of terrorism through the very initiatives of domestic policing and intelligence that the state rationalized through appeals to democracy and public safety. The appearance of the Black Panther Party for Self-Defense, in particular, changed the terms through which the US state would understand and confront, and in turn represent, Black struggle. As Kara Keeling argues, armed Black resistance punctured the public narrative of racial reconciliation that had become dominant: "If the civil rights movement secured the Black's full citizenship, why did he pick up the gun? How could slavery, share-cropping, silent suffering, gospel singing, Aunt Jemima, Uncle Tom, Topsy, 'We Shall Overcome,' cotton picking, illiteracy, 'massa lovin,' cannibalism, watermelon-seed spittin', white-woman chasing, nonviolent resisting, Mammy, and Jezebel give way to Blacks with guns?"[30] The appearance of armed Black radicals in intelligence documents, in newspapers, and on television screens ultimately revealed "the precariousness of the State's claim to represent Black people," effecting a "profound crisis in the hegemonic construction of reality that secures consensus to State power."[31] The response to this puncturing, which was further effected by the organization of underground groups like the Black Liberation Army and by the urban rebellions in 1965, 1966, 1967, and 1968, most memorably in Detroit, Los Angeles, Harlem, and Newark, was what Jordan called an "escalated phase of white war against Black life."[32]

If the 1960s marked the apex of what has been called the Second Reconstruction, the two decades that followed could arguably be called a second nadir for Black people in the United States. Punctuated by a series of dissolutions and death campaigns—the Attica massacre in 1971, the Nation of Islam's split in 1977, the Jonestown massacre in 1978, the Atlanta child murders beginning in 1979, the serial murder of Black women in Roxbury in 1979, the MOVE bombing in 1985—the twenty years after 1968 saw the state escalate its repression of radicalism through the mushrooming death industries of policing, incarceration, intelligence, and security. At the same time, the shift from protest to institutional politics, embraced by Black liberals and leftists alike, meant that the more radical challenges of Black activists would have to be bracketed in favor of more liberal, politically efficient goals.[33] Incorporation came with inevitable compromises and losses. But incorporation was only one mode of containing Black radicalism. Surveillance, incarceration, and police violence were also key in criminalizing and discrediting the Black freedom struggle. As Vesla Weaver argues, there were two stages of "frontlash" after the opponents to civil-rights-era social change were defeated. Republican lawmakers expanded punitive crime policy between 1958 and 1974. This was not backlash, a short-lived and impulsive reaction to the civil rights victories, but rather a concerted effort that was "strategic, alive, complex and sophisticated" in its aim to code Black freedom making—even nonviolent civil disobedience—as lawless and to criminalize legitimate grievances.[34]

A key case study in the way counterinsurgency played offense rather than defense—to criminalize freedom making, to offer hypercarceral solutions for endemic social and economic problems—is Detroit. In postwar Detroit, automobile companies moved their factories out of the city center, automated production, and cut jobs. Between 1948 and 1967, the city lost over one hundred thousand manufacturing jobs, with deindustrialization disproportionately affecting Black workers and entrenching the city's already stark segregated geography.[35] The summer 1968 rebellion in Detroit, which prompted President Lyndon B. Johnson to deploy nearly two thousand paratroopers, "turned the world upside down," according to Jordan Camp.[36] "There were hundreds of urban rebellions, but this one occurred in the context of a deeply politicized and concentrated Black working-class community in Detroit's ghetto and factories," he writes.[37] Bolstered by the racial liberal framing of the Kerner Commission's *Report of the National Advisory Commission on Civil Disorders*, which linked the Detroit uprising to disorder stemming from Black familial pathology, the state increased its surveillance and incarceration. What makes Detroit key in the history of the long war on terror is that it served as a laboratory for testing domestic warfare as a response to the crises created by the contradictions inherent in capitalism, as the Motor City was the proverbial canary in the coal mine that was the global economic crisis of the 1970s; and further, it was a theater for live connections between foreign counterinsurgency and domestic policing. Nikhil Singh quotes Johnson's national security adviser Walt Rostow, who wrote to the president after the Detroit rebellion, "At home your appeal is for law and order as the framework for economic and social progress. Abroad we fight in Vietnam to make aggression unprofitable, while helping the people of Vietnam and all of free Asia build a future of economic and social progress."[38] The counterinsurgency in Detroit, which led to the exponential rise in the Michigan prison population over the decades after the 1967 rebellion, proved the extent to which anti-Blackness could function as the glue for global counterinsurgency, with the surveillance and policing of Black workers drawing hard lines of state violence between points of so-called disorder, from the US Midwest to Saigon.[39] During this phase of the long war on terror, US power "collapsed the distance between places like Cortland, Saigon, and East Lansing, [Michigan,] not only through transportation logistics and applications of massive military force but also through the diffusion and dissemination of distinctive repertoires of racialized governance," according to Singh.[40] These repertoires, shared by way of think-tank documents, field manuals, academic theories, military policies, intelligence communiqués, and other cultural products and performances of war, united the "inner war" of domestic policing and the "outer war" of counterinsurgency.

Detroit was a single point of intensity in a national, even global, expansion of repression. "Police were everywhere," wrote Assata Shakur about her capture on the New Jersey turnpike in 1973. And "every radical activist had learned [by the 1970s] that our public meetings were subject to routine police and/or FBI surveillance."[41] As Ruth Wilson Gilmore explains, after the disruptions of 1968, when opposition to the US war in Vietnam, anticolonial and antiapartheid movements throughout Asia, Latin America, and Africa, and the US Black Power movements posed a radical challenge to the Western world powers by reinvigorating the connections between liberation projects in the "first" and "third" worlds, "the state responded to radicalism by distilling radicalism into 'singular instances of criminality.'"[42] Policing was a way to domesticate anti-imperial Black politics and to depoliticize radicalism. The turn to policing and caging as forms of social control culminated in the 500 percent increase in the prison population between 1970 and 2000. These developments constituted what Dylan Rodríguez calls "White Reconstruction," a protraction of postbellum white supremacy that was "instantiated through white civil society's awakening to the possibility of its own political disarticulation at the hands of Black and Third World insurrectionists and revolutionaries."[43] It is important to note that buildup of what Beth Richie calls a "prison nation" drew on significations of pathological Black gender, with the figure of the Black male rapist and the unfit Black mother rationalizing the state's aggressive pursuit of problem men and deviant women.[44]

Throughout the 1970s, US intelligence agencies, including the FBI, the State Department, the CIA, and US embassies, continued to contain Black activism on both the domestic and international scales. The arrests, raids, and assassinations targeting Black radicals in the late 1960s and early 1970s systematically thwarted post-civil-rights Black radicalism. The FBI, through its counterintelligence program (COINTELPRO), worked with local police departments to coordinate a full-on assault on Black radicalism. This culminated in the death of at least twenty-eight members of the Black Panther Party for Self-Defense, the imprisonment of many others, and psychological and permanent physical damage to hundreds more.[45] Angela Davis writes in her autobiography of a heavily armed raid of the Black Panther Party headquarters at Forty-First Street and Central Avenue in Los Angeles in December 1969. She writes of armed officers "creeping snakelike along the ground" and "swarming the entire area."[46] What she witnessed was the debut of Los Angeles's Special Weapons and Tactics (SWAT) team. Bombs were detonated; a tank was called in for reinforcement. Six Panthers were wounded. Davis then describes a surprise attack on participants in a vigil at the site of the bombing days later. Again, police cars are "creeping by," and Davis mistakes the agents peering at her and her comrades as features of "normal surveillance":

> But at that moment, I saw a swarm of the black-suited cops who had executed the attack on the office the day before, and some of them were about to converge on us.
>
> I had been facing the crowd. I turned quickly, but before I could break into a run, I was knocked to the ground. I hit my head on the pavement and was momentarily stunned. During those seconds of semi-consciousness, I felt feet trampling on my head and body and it flashed through my mind that this was a terrible way to die.[47]

Davis later referred to the 1969 offensive as the first collaboration of its kind between local law enforcement and the FBI. "At the time," she said, "we were aware that the LAPD was training Vietnam veterans in counterinsurgency."[48] COINTELPRO formally dissolved in 1971 after its three-year reign of terror against Black radicals and the New Left. But COINTELPRO was no exception to *normal surveillance*: it was an expression of the FBI's routinized quest to quell Black radicalism.[49] Perhaps more importantly, limiting our understanding of antiradical repression to the activities of COINTELPRO both overestimates the role of US activists in the transnational movements of Black Power and underestimates the global network of surveillance, harassment, police violence, and infiltration that repressed and archived those movements at and across national borders.[50] That counterinsurgency has had a prolonged and geographically extensive reach since the formal dismantling of COINTELPRO is evident in the fact that by the late 1970s, over two million Black Americans were arrested every year; at least thirty thousand civilians had been killed in the CIA-backed war against the Sandinistas in Nicaragua after the 1979 revolution; and Operation Urgent Fury left hundreds dead in Grenada in October 1983. And the FBI keeps the Black Liberation Army activist Assata Shakur on its list of "Most Wanted Terrorists." The sharp bifurcation of Black life that crystallized during the 1970s, that is to say, cannot be isolated from the culture of intelligence and the industries of knowledge that contained leftist activism through ideological consent and brute force throughout that entire decade (and afterward).

While I have taken pains to describe the repression of the 1970s, I want to note that narratives of Black radicalism's retrenchment often disappear the unstoppable force of radical Black feminist and women-of-color activism, which surfaced in organized collectives such as the Combahee River Collective, the Black Women's Revolutionary Council, and the Third World Women's Alliance as well as in looser, more ephemeral collectivities gathered in protest against nuclear proliferation, South African apartheid, and the occupation of the West Bank and Gaza Strip well into the 1980s. Black feminists of the 1960s and 1970s shaped postwar activism in ways that we are still trying to understand or that, with rebellions to police violence that swelled between 2012 and 2020 and privileged Black feminist critique, we are perhaps beginning to grasp. Black feminists worked in and between Black Power and feminist organizations to analyze the overlapping oppressions that structured their lives and to fight against those oppressions throughout the postwar period, even in the face of increased repression and surveillance.[51] Even more importantly for us, the narrative of post-civil-rights defeat and retreat downplays or neglects altogether the organized, productive rupture that Black feminists forged in print culture in the late 1970s and early 1980s, a point to which I will return shortly.

It was perhaps anti–Vietnam War activism that brought the various in-print and in-person modalities of Black feminist protest culture together most powerfully. Antiwar sentiment catalyzed artistic creativity throughout the Black Arts era. And while Black women do not often feature in histories of Black anti-Vietnam activism, as Nadine M. Knight argues, "they were of course participants in the war, victims of its efforts, and keenly attentive to the ramifications of the war's effects on black communities."[52] Black feminist creative writers like Toni Morrison and Ntozake Shange incorporated the figure of the returning Vietnam veteran to expose "just how ravaging American wars were for black men—and thus, in turn, for the black women expected to support them as they attempted to return to a civilian life with grievously inadequate (social) services for black veterans."[53] (The male veteran's surfacing to expose the state's narratives of patriarchal protection and the featuring of Black women in those narratives is a trope that Black feminist writers returned to decades later, during the US war in Iraq, a point I address at length in chapter 6.) Toni Cade Bambara, as Linda Janet Holmes chronicles, joined a feminist delegation to meet the Viet Nam Women's Union in Hanoi. Smuggling in her suitcase an anticonvulsive medication that could treat women exposed to Agent Orange during childbirth, Bambara wrote afterward of the women revolutionaries who had first "experienced two thousand years of feudalism under the Chinese, the Mongols, the Chinese again," then "80 years of colonialism and foreign aggression under the French and then later the Japanese in '45 and the French again," only to survive "a fantastic war with the most powerful military machine, the most powerful counter-revolutionary force in the world, the United States."[54] For Black feminist writers and activists, the struggle for independence in Vietnam was perhaps the most important front in global anti-imperialism. Print culture was a crucial stage for this struggle, not only in works like Shange's *for colored girls* but also in radical journals such as *Freedomways*.[55]

Despite the radical commitments and furious optimism that Black feminists brought to the streets and to paper, the indicators of material deprivation and political defeat in post-civil-rights Black communities were undeniable. While a Black middle class was slowly growing, the Black working class and the Black poor struggled to live with increasing rates of substandard housing, unemployment, and premature death due to unreliable health care, substance dependency, and homicide.

The 1970s was an era of both advance and retrenchment for Black peoples and politics in the United States; it also constituted a crucial moment in the production of *terrorism* as a category of knowledge and as a foil for US nationalism. The increasing presence of terrorism narratives in US news and popular culture after the 1967 Arab-Israeli War, the 1972 Munich Olympics (during which ABC News provided live coverage of an attack carried out by Black September, a strike force for the Palestinian Liberation Organization), and the 1973 Arab-Israeli War provided avenues for rehabilitating US nationalism, which had been put to the test by the 1960s social movements and by the United States' declining international power (epitomized, for example, by the defeat in the Vietnam War). A "rising media fascination with Middle East terrorism," Melanie McAllister argues, was linked with the valorization of the state of Israel as a model for defense. After Vietnam, and after the Israel Defense Force's rescue mission, which on July 4, 1976, freed hostages held by the Popular Front for the Liberation of Palestine–External Operations at Entebbe Airport in Idi Amin's Uganda, "Israel became a prosthetic for Americans; the 'long arm' of Israeli vengeance extended the body of an American nation no longer sure of its own reach."[56] The long war on terror, then, began to coalesce as a global war for capitalist hegemony in which the government used racialized narratives of vulnerability to justify foreign invasion and domestic caging. Political discourses of the 1970s made Blackness the criminalized threat to the national family and made the "Muslim terrorist" a scapegoat for the United States' financial precarity at the end of the Fordist economic system.

We cannot appreciate the connections between the counterinsurgencies of the post-1968 period without a clear understanding of what Timothy Mitchell calls "carbon democracy." The Western imperial powers, Britain, France, and the United States, controlled the resources of the oil-producing nations, their Middle East client states, through doctrines of civilization, protection, and self-determination. For example, the Arabian American Oil Company, initially Standard Oil of California, entered into a concession with Saudi Arabia in 1933, controlling the price and quantity of oil production. The company extended the segregation that bloodied US soil to the oil fields of Saudi Arabia, erecting a labor hierarchy that outfitted American and European workers with air-conditioned homes with swimming pools and civil services while confining Arab workers to ramshackle and crowded housing, low wages, and no access to social mobility. As Robert Vitalis offers, "The record of life in the Aramco settlement at Dhahran and of the clash of cultures on the Arabian oil frontier provides scant support for conventional periodizations and truth claims about a unique American form of *empire-lite*."[57] Throughout the 1940s and 1950s, the alliance between the US government, the CIA, and the company eventually known as Aramco nourished the rule and hegemony of Abdulaziz ibn Saud, one contender of many for the Arabian Peninsula. These forces, along with British colonial rule that preceded them, quelled dissent at every turn. The transition to the US sphere of influence coincided with a resurgence of resistance and a rise of leftist movements and decolonial struggle, from Algeria to the Arabian Peninsula to Yemen. When Abdulaziz's successor, Saud ibn Saud, succeeded his father in 1953, he courted leftist politics, which included a broad array of socialists, communists, and pan-Arabists, who succeeded in challenging Aramco's hegemony. In most historical accounts and in

Arab nationalist narratives, Saud's brother, Crown Prince Faisal, is celebrated for his ostensible pan-Arabism. As Rosie Bsheer has shown, it
was Saud who courted populist politics and was deeply aligned with the
pan-Arabist and Third Worldist Egyptian leader Gamal Abdel Nasser.
US state and corporate power backed his opponent, Crown Prince
Faisal, eventually helping to push King Saud out of power in 1962. Faisal
then established a reactionary, authoritarian regime that enjoyed the
support of the US state and Aramco.[58]

As the case of Aramco and Saudi Arabia shows, the US government
and US corporations had a vested interest in squelching resistance,
in keeping oil production under the control of foreign corporations
rather than local states, and in establishing military bases in the Middle East region. These patterns built on earlier patterns in the Middle
East and beyond; authoritarian governments struggling to keep rising European political and economic hegemony at bay would fall into
the trap of "defensive development," accruing debt and selling their
countries' resources to the highest bidder.[59] In Iran, these dynamics
of debt and concession were at play since the early twentieth-century
concession between the Qajar regime and the corporation that would
become British Petroleum. In the second half of the twentieth century,
the US stepped into the fray by coordinating with British intelligence
and corporations the overthrow of the democratically elected and decolonial parliamentarian Mohammed Mossadegh, who had national-
ized Iranian oil (and suffered the ensuing trade embargo). The United
States later infused over $500 million in military aid to Mohammad
Reza Pahlavi's authoritarian regime, which consolidated its power in
the wake of the 1953 coup.

It is in this context of carbon democracy that we can understand the
"crises" in the Middle East that, in addition to the fires in US streets, legitimated the long war on terror. As movements in Iran and Saudia Arabia—indeed, throughout the Middle East and North Africa—loosened
the grip of foreign corporations in the late 1960s and 1970s, the United
States waged a war of "savage development," in which elites backed authoritarian regimes in order to enforce neoliberal economic policies.[60]
On the domestic front, neoliberalism was a form of governance—
market rule—that emerged as an alternative to democratic deliberation,
and oil fueled the new conception of the economy both as "an object

that could grow without limit" and as "an alternative project to defeat the threat of the left and populist democracy."[61]

The discourses of "crisis" and "foreign oil" reached a peak in the years between 1967 and 1973. I see this as a crucial conjuncture for understanding the shape of postwar US imperialism for three reasons. First, the Arab-Israeli War of 1967 was a turning point for the United States and its Middle East foreign policy. The six days of war culminated in an overwhelming victory for Israel, which occupied the remaining Palestinian territories of the Gaza Strip and the West Bank, as well as seized Egypt's Sinai Peninsula and Syria's Golan Heights.[62] This cemented Israel's regional hegemony as a superior military force. It also extended the Palestinians' losses of 1948, known as the Nakba, *the catastrophe*, when an estimated 700,000 Palestinian people were expelled from their homes, with the remaining 150,000 becoming "citizen strangers."[63] In 1948, the "fledgling Israeli government overturned the social and human landscape of Palestine," Sherene Seikaly suggests, and the settler-colonial program rested on "the Zionist emphasis on the lack of a politically coherent and distinct people in Palestine who deserved to make claims to the land on which they had resided for hundreds of years."[64] The 1967 war escalated what Seikaly calls "a politics of deferral," renewing the 1917 Balfour Declaration's designation of the Palestinians as people who were not quite prepared for self-governance.[65] Israel became the preeminent military power and, for the US elite, a model of defensive power that would be an antidote to the "Vietnam Syndrome," the idea that the US military suffered loss in the Vietnam War because of the state's lack of authority and nerve. It was also during this period that Black cultural politics self-consciously aligned with Palestinian freedom. The year 1967 represented, in that way, both the threat of Afro-Arab coalition and the promise of neoliberal rule secured by a hyperdominant US military that was allied with Israel.

Second, what was called the "oil crisis" in 1973 was a response to the October 1973 war, when Egypt and Syria launched a coordinated attack on Israel in an attempt to regain the territory that was lost in 1967. The Arab oil-producing states declared a boycott on the shipment of oil to the United States and the Netherlands, a crucial port of distribution to the rest of Europe. Then they announced a decrease in production and distribution. Panic ensued. Countries scrambled to secure oil from other sources. Prices soared. The Organization of Petroleum Exporting Countries (OPEC) raised taxes on oil production—in response to increased US support for Israeli defense—which led to the fourfold increase in the price of oil in the United States. Occluding the question of Palestine that was at the heart of the embargo, President Nixon encouraged US oil consumers to exercise moderation. The oil corporations and the state used the embargo to their benefit, as Mitchell argues. The crisis "enabled Washington and the oil companies to move to a system of higher energy prices, and also gave a boost to something else that was increasingly associated with the price of oil: militarism." For the United States, which had supplied arms to Israel, it was proof that "with the right equipment, tactics, and training, contrary to the lessons of Vietnam, large conventional armoured battles could be fought and won."[66] The US state's promotion of "democracy" pivoted on military aid. While the United States historically provided Israel with the lion's share of this aid, it forged much of its policy around military armament in Iran and Iraq and throughout the Arabian Peninsula. The oil wealth, particularly after the windfall of 1973, was funneled into armament. US corporations and the government were direct beneficiaries.

Third, these two crises provided the language and the repertoire of maneuvers for the conservative resurgence in the United States, which tied the upward redistribution of wealth to the discourse of antiterrorism. This is especially the case after the Iran hostage crisis of 1979–80. As Sohail Daulatzai argues, that crisis was represented on the nightly news as "a narrative in which an innocent America was under siege from ruthless and maniacal Muslims," and now US film and television ramped up portrayals of "terrorism," drawing on a reservoir of significations of Black criminality. According to Daulatzai, the internal threat of the Black "criminal" and the external threat of the Arab/Muslim "terrorist" were the "twin pillars" of US state formation in the post-civil-rights era. Blackness, indeed, has historically shortened the rhetorical distance between the domestic "criminal" and the foreign Muslim "terrorist," as the Black American Muslim is constructed as a fundamental threat to national identity and racial harmony. Over the latter decades of the twentieth century, Daulatzai argues, the "racialized discourse of empire" eventually produced "a subject where the foreign and the domestic collapse upon themselves, as the fears of 'terror' are conflated with 'Black criminality,' gangs, prison culture, and urban violence."[67] Importantly, Black radicalism and struggles for Arab and Muslim self-determination were not only linked through counterinsurgency but also linked through the "geographies of liberation," those spaces that Alex Lubin refers to when he writes of the Black internationalist comparative framework that, for example, led the Student Nonviolent Coordinating Committee (SNCC) and the Black Panther Party to break with the mainstream civil rights organizations and define and challenge Zionism and the United States' investment in the "security" of the State of Israel as expressions of racial capitalism and imperialism. As Lubin explains, no US organization "was more directly responsible for creating a geography of liberation linking Palestine and urban black America, and in developing an ideological position on third world solidarity, than the Black Panther Party."[68] I will return to the fissures that the question of Palestine created within Black progressive organizations, especially among Black feminist collectives, in chapter 4, and to the internationalist geographies of liberation that led to important innovations in contemporary Black writing about Palestine, particularly June Jordan's, in chapter 5. Here I simply want to note that the armed self-defense and self-determination of both the Black Panthers and the Palestinian Liberation Organization, and the solidarity forged across sites of repression in the United States and Middle East, drew together the domestic terrorist and the foreign terrorist in ways that continue to inform and provoke US counterinsurgency.[69]

The development of counterinsurgency during the 1970s, which mobilized anti-Blackness and anti-Arab, anti-Muslim sentiment to weave a web between domestic and foreign terrorism, had specific ramifications for Black women in US public life. The Black women writers who were organizing to make literature a radical form of critique during the 1970s were doing so in a national context in which state and cultural institutions were ready to pounce on their work for the sake of "public trust" or "inclusion" or "diversity" or "progress" or "race relations."

Indeed, it was at this precise moment, when foreign and domestic versions of racialized unpredictability and threat were collapsing in the figures of the radical and the criminal and the terrorist, that at least one Black woman's gestures of empowerment saved the nation from political crisis. Texas senator Barbara Jordan became a guardian of the public trust when she defended the impeachment of then-president

Richard Nixon in her July 1974 address to the Congress on behalf of the House Judiciary Committee.[70] Defending Nixon's impeachment, Jordan claimed herself as an "inquisitor" whose responsibility it was, as the *Federalist Papers* specified, to guard the public trust from abuse and violation. Claiming her authority to do so on the basis of power granted by the Constitution, Jordan said, "My faith in the constitution is whole; it is complete; it is total. And I'm not going to sit here and be an idle spectator to the diminution, the subversion, the destruction, of the Constitution."[71] For Brittney Cooper, these words signaled "a different moment: one in which Black women were asked to step into the national imaginary as a keeper of the public trust and an arbiter of the nation's moral conscience."[72] As congressional law and order stepped in after the Watergate scandal to depose one of the very architects of the post-1968 carceral regime, it was Jordan's impeccable rhetoric that, on the one hand, enlarged the imaginary of the nation-state and reclaimed law and order from its blood-hunt for Black radicalism and, on the other hand, gave evidence of a "different moment" in which Black women were being hailed as arbiters of a national fantasy of righteousness. Jordan's speech defending her own position as a guardian of democracy might be understood not only as a signal of the contradictions of the post-1968 era, which at moments saw Black women emerge as keepers of the nation and at others saw them exposed as the most dangerous threats to democracy, but also as an indicator of Black women's capacity, nurtured on steady doses of resistance to white terrorism over at least decades, to bear and embody these contradictions in their persistent efforts toward liberation.[73]

All the mechanisms of state surveillance in the 1970s—from beat patrols to infiltration and agent provocateurism to espionage and wiretapping to the unexpected visit from a social worker from the welfare agency to the protocols of the routine performance review—caught Black women in the net of an intelligence-gathering enterprise that was the domestic iteration, if we want, of a global project of counterinsurgency. At the same time, of course, Black women were a resource that might be drawn on in a range of media to teach the country how to guard against internal and external threats and, too, to teach the country how to survive in the case of an emergency that was, now, always already imminent.

Black Women and the New World Order: 1980–2001

(imagining otherwise)(defanging the radicalized)

Black women have filled a central position in the explanatory frameworks of the global security apparatus that emerged over the course of the Cold War and spun a web of containment and detainment throughout the long war on terror. From Rosa Parks, Angela Davis, Assata Shakur, and Shirley Chisholm to Lani Guinier, Marian Wright Edelman, Condoleezza Rice, Anita Hill, Michelle Obama, and Kamala Harris, Black women have featured in postwar US political culture *both* as threats to the nation-state and as harbingers of democratic promise vis-à-vis multicultural inclusion. The *racial* break that I described earlier—from the exclusions of Jim Crow to this inclusion of a domestic civil rights agenda that splintered antiracism, anticolonialism, and internationalism—was also, that is, a *gender* break that rewrote metanarratives of politics, intimacy, bodily sovereignty, and sexuality, in part through the spectacular picturing of Black women in positions of marginalization and exclusion, on the one hand, and power and achievement, on the other.[74]

That Black women were both the targets of state defense initiatives and authors of a national narrative of democratic righteousness meant that they were positioned along the fault lines of competing nationalist discourses. For in the Black nationalist imaginary throughout the 1970s, 1980s, 1990s, and 2000s, Black women were responsible for reproducing the nation and, at the same time, the bearer of every pathogen—social, political, biological—imagined to be the source of a larger, cultural pathology. Black nationalism frames racism as an emasculation to be addressed, or redeemed, in a contest between Black and white men. In this context, Black women can only fulfill one of two functions in the struggle: the loyal supporter in a struggle that essentially belongs to the Black man or the betraying Jezebel literally in bed with power. As Toni Morrison wrote in 1997's *Paradise*, if Black nationalists were after racial, or at least political, purity, "everything that worries them must come from women."[75] If Black nationalism in its everyday instantiations—as a narrative of collective identity, as a system of aesthetic value, as an ideology of liberation, as a general way of talking about what "we" need to do to survive the everyday terror that overwhelms life with death—depends on ideals of racial and political purity in which Black female desire functions as the source of corruptibility, heteropatriarchy is the bargain that "the Black community" made in the name of post-civil-rights progress. The Black woman, at turns idealized and demonized (but in both cases emptied of a political subjectivity of her own), was the centerpiece of that bargain. Black women, then, personified the unpredictable threat that must be contained (Assata Shakur's "police were everywhere") and, at the same time, upped the ante on US democracy (Barbara Jordan's "I'm not going to sit here and be an idle spectator").

Accordingly, the story that we must now tell about gender violence in US politics and Black politics is still more complex than I imagined when I wrote, in my first book, of the violences embedded in the ideal of charismatic leadership. Now, ideals of political representation that took root in gendered ideologies of value and giftedness within the *intraracial* community also project onto the mainstream justifications of US imperialism. Not only does Black heteropatriarchy diminish the gender and sexual heterogeneity of Black life or circumscribe the scholarly and popular histories of social movements or limit the imagination of resistance to anti-Black terror. It also dampens the critical capacity to address the deep intimacy between Black cultural forms and state violence. This is the very capacity that Black feminist literature has exercised throughout the late twentieth-century racial regimes.

My goal here is not to add to the brilliant body of work critiquing the politics of racial uplift; rather, I follow Cooper in reading beyond the analytical frame of uplift, to foreground substantive engagement with Black women leaders and intellectuals during the very decades in which, after the assassinations, incarcerations, and co-optations, Black leadership was in a prolonged, heightened state of crisis.[76] Here, I would like to ground that engagement in a brief history of the second phase of the long war on terror, which spanned the 1980s and used Central and Latin America and the Caribbean, as well as US cities, as laboratories for counterinsurgency.

Public narratives of danger and defense in the 1970s constructed white US civil society as perpetually threatened by revolutionaries and terrorists (and revolutionaries *as* terrorists). Through the 1980s, the rise of the New Right capitalized on public consent for militarized policing and defense. This consent was secured by public narratives of Black and Arab-Muslim criminality. Nixon's War on Drugs, formalized in 1970 and increasingly, by the end of the century, cast in terms of defense and security and "street terrorism," inaugurated what became a 500 percent increase in incarceration. The War on Drugs also normalized militarized law enforcement as a presumed necessity for public safety. Because of new legislation to control drugs and gangs, Gilmore argues, "crime was objectively and subjectively different" after 1980 than it was before. "Politicians of all races and ethnicities merged gang membership, drug use, and habitual criminal activity into a single social scourge, which was then used to explain everything from unruly youth to inner-city homicides to the need for more prisons to isolate wrongdoers."[77] The militarization of state police departments and the mushroom of carceral legislation not only built on the foundation of counterinsurgency laid years earlier by projects like COINTELPRO and SWAT but also allowed the state and the prison and policing industries to capitalize on the anxieties of Black lawmakers and spokespersons from hard-hit Black urban areas. Donna Murch's history of the War on Drugs shows how it helped build the grammar for the war on terror, with state rhetoric turning "police into soldiers—not civil servants or guardians of the community order"—and winning over Black lawmakers' support.[78] The figure of the drug dealer–terrorist rationalized the intense, militarized policing of everyday Black life.

Military and carceral buildup through the 1980s was also catalyzed by anti-Arab/Muslim racial panics and by state rhetorics of economic and political freedom. In late 1979, in response to US intervention in Iran, Iranian students overtook the US embassy at Tehran and took sixty-five American hostages. The Iran hostage crisis amounted to a media spectacle and a public humiliation that lasted 444 days, took over the evening news, induced a failed rescue mission, and left Democratic president Jimmy Carter appearing impotent. It was what Junaid Rana calls a "racial panic," the public surfacing of intense affect that connects a perceived threat to the social order to a global racial system that constructs the "dangerous Muslim" as a racial category.[79] One of the most widely covered stories in US television history, the crisis prompted a shift in US foreign policy and discourse. President Carter, for example, identified "the free movement of Middle East oil" as a key priority for security in his 1980 State of the Union Address—proof of a long-term strategy of development that targeted the Middle East as pivotal in the making of

US global hegemony. The hostage crisis even inspired what amounted to an early declaration of war on terror.[80]

When Ronald Reagan was inaugurated as the US president the following year, in January 1981—coincidentally, on the very day that the hostages were freed—he connected the economic imperative of neoliberalism to the social imperative of multiculturalism and the political imperative of counterterrorism, all of which would help to rationalize the exponential military buildup over the next sixteen years. In that speech, which famously declared that "government is not the solution to our problem; government is the problem," Reagan promised "a healthy, vigorous, growing economy that provides equal opportunities for all Americans, with no barriers born of bigotry or discrimination." The nation was personified as a strong man, *homo economicus*, throwing off a shackling government and the threat of financial ruin and terrorist attack. "Ending inflation," Reagan noted, "means freeing all Americans from the *terror* of runaway living costs" (emphasis added). At the end of a speech that announced the neoliberalization of financial markets and US life and that drew on the terms "equal" and "opportunities" to justify the diminishment of public goods and services, Reagan vowed to restore the country as the "exemplar of freedom" and the "beacon of hope for those who do not now have freedom." Promising, finally, protection against the "enemies of freedom," he rejected (presumably, the Carter administration's) "reluctance for conflict" and "failure of will" and promised action in the interest of national security: "Above all, we must realize that no arsenal or no weapon in the arsenals of the world is so formidable as the will and moral courage of free men and women. It is a weapon our adversaries in today's world do not have. It is a weapon that we as Americans do have. Let that be understood by those who practice terrorism and prey upon their neighbors." I quote Reagan's first inaugural speech at length because its rhetorical moves exemplify how by 1981, terrorism had "come to carry an 'excess of meaning'" for US nationalism.[81]

In the intra- and interhemispheric wars of the 1980s that the United States supported or initiated, Reagan's hard, preemptively oriented antiterrorist policies drew on the high rhetoric of freedom and defense to gain consent for and cover for invasions and occupations. In 1983, he authorized "aggressive self-defense" for the US marines stationed in

Lebanon as a "peacekeeping" force; when they were attacked in the marine barracks, Reagan drew on the latent discourse of anticommunism to connect Lebanon and Grenada: "Not only has Moscow assisted and encouraged the violence in both countries, but it provides direct support through a network of surrogates and terrorists."[82] Operation Urgent Fury, the invasion of Grenada that took place two days after the marine barracks bombing in Lebanon, was described by Reagan as a "rescue mission" that would help restore "conditions of law and order," a necessary incursion into a "Soviet-Cuban colony" that was preparing to be a "major military bastion to export terror and undermine democracy."[83] Two years after the Grenada invasion, Reagan referred to the Contras who were fighting the Sandinistas in Nicaragua as "democratic forces" and "freedom fighters" who were deserving of Americans' support. During the 1980s, the United States assembled its late–Cold War power with a combination of military and rhetorical flourishes: from the *freedom fighters* in Nicaragua to the twenty-six thousand "heroes" who invaded Panama in December 1989 to *restore democracy*, the wars of the 1980s allowed the Reagan administration to rid the government and military of the Vietnam Syndrome and to rebuild the Cold War consensus that had fractured after the war in Vietnam.

The Sandinista revolution in Nicaragua was, indeed, a test case for the Reagan regime's shadowy network of global counterinsurgency. The 1979 leftist revolutions in Iran and Nicaragua "added up to a grim prognosis for the dream of a global free market."[84] The United States had supported right-wing dictatorships in Nicaragua since 1936 and, too, supported authoritarian rule in Iran. After the Iranian Revolution, which ended in the fall of Shah Reza's regime, which the United States had supported through military aid since World War II, the United States began shipping arms to Iran via Israel. Reagan's officials also believed that the arms trades would free Hezbollah's hostages in Lebanon. They used the money to pay mercenaries, the Contras, to reverse the revolution in Nicaragua. The head of the CIA, William Casey, and a member of the National Security Council, Oliver North, oversaw the transnational network of trades. This network tied together two targets of destabilization.[85] Profits from arms sales in Iran allowed Reagan and his administration to subvert the congressional ban on action in Nicaragua. Like the 1980s assaults on Guatemala, El Salvador, and Grenada, the

Contra war was an opportunity for the United States to test new technologies of war and prepare for nontraditional low-intensity conflict. "Mass slaughter became a crucial instrument of U.S. foreign policy" in the intrahemispheric dirty wars.[86] As Black radicals were test cases for the technologies and practices of intelligence, so did war in the Central American nations help transition the practice of US power from the domestic countersubversion tactics of the early Cold War to the practices of remote warfare, torture, and rendition that became the legacy of the Iraq wars.

The wars, sanctions regime, and occupation in Iraq further exemplify the connection between permanent warfare, the racialization of Islam, and the reconstruction of authority after the 1960s. The Iranian Revolution left the United States without an ally in either Iran or Iraq; it put an end to the United States' previous policy of dual containment, courting both Iran and Iraq for political leverage. When Iraq invaded Iran in 1980, the United States began to support Iraq more aggressively while working against a UN resolution to penalize Iraq for starting the war and to require reparations. The United States, again according to Mitchell, "seized the opportunity to weaken both countries" and "helped to keep the war going for eight years, at a cost of more than a million people killed and wounded in the two countries."[87] The United States hoped to foster a dependency. Saddam Hussein's invasion of Kuwait in 1990, though, dealt a blow to that strategy. The invasion was an attempt to solve the financial crisis that the earlier war with Iran had caused. The US-led Coalition, protecting US "interests" in the Middle East and avenging the invasion of Kuwait, deployed more than nine hundred thousand troops in Operation Desert Storm. It was also, President George H. W. Bush argued, to "protect the sovereign independence of Saudi Arabia."[88] The victory of the United States and its allies was a display of unprecedented military might, and celebratory coverage of the war saturated twenty-four-hour news coverage. Between sixty thousand and two hundred thousand Iraqi soldiers are believed to have been killed; civilian casualties are estimated between one hundred thousand and two hundred thousand. Coalition casualties were in the hundreds.[89]

Significantly, the victory in the 1991 war in Iraq shored up the legitimacy of the US war machine. As McAlister explains, the Right took the win as proof that the US military defeat in Vietnam and the failed rescue of the hostages in Iran "had been caused by the failure in national leadership to authorize the use of adequate force and allow the military freedom of action"; the "failures of the 1960s and 1970s could be blamed on the lack of political will to use the military force available."[90] The war was followed by the UN sanctions regime, which, ostensibly designed to disarm Iraq, destroyed Iraqi infrastructure and prevented restoration after the damage of the war, caused the death of between five hundred thousand and one million Iraqis, mostly children, and impoverished the country for years.[91] The Oil for Food Program, established in 1996, allowed Iraq to sell oil on the world market in exchange for food and medicine. Sanctions also made the population more dependent on the authoritarian Ba'th regime for rations. When Madeleine Albright, the Clinton administration's ambassador to the United Nations, was asked by a *60 Minutes* correspondent if she thought the "half a million children" who had died were worth the price of sanctions, she responded affirmatively: "the price is worth it."[92]

When sanctions and covert operations failed to bring down the regime, the militarists in the George W. Bush administration began planning for war against Iraq. The September 11 attacks provided an opportunity to justify the second Iraq War, which began in March 2003. Using the now firmly established Manichean rhetorics of counterterrorism and emphasizing the threat of weapons of mass destruction, US government officials argued that deployment to Iraq would bring democracy to the Middle East. The "shock and awe" invasion by a US-led coalition gave way to an ongoing occupation that produced a neoliberal regime of reconstruction in Iraq. For H. L. T. Quan, the juridical infrastructure of the occupation "codifies legal protocols and relations to privilege the foreign corporate body over that of bio-personhood." The remaking of Iraq amounted to "no less than a corporate insurrection."[93] A character in Sinan Antoon's novel *The Corpse Washer* captures the absurd brutality of life under occupation when he says, after surviving an aggressive search by US soldiers when he is on the way to bury a man who died during a 2003 aerial assault, "Looks like these liberators want to humiliate us."[94]

My point in offering this sketch of the convergence of crisis and capitalism in the 1980s and 1990s is not to suggest that the US state or the corporations with which it enjoyed a relationship of mutual beneficence or the United States' allies in defense held a monopoly on violence. To

be sure, the violence and deprivation caused by both authoritarian regimes and militant claimants on power also amounted to uncountable
atrocities and casualties. I do want to suggest, though, that the discursive
architecture of counterterrorism served as a cloak for the neoliberalization of US foreign policy, which left a trail of human death and broken
infrastructure, over the decades of the long war on terror. Multiculturalism was a bright thread in that cloak.

Building credibility for US foreign policy and public favor for increased interventionism, the invasion of Grenada, the stationing of marines in Lebanon, the militarization of El Salvador and Honduras, the
covert war against Nicaragua, the Iran-Contra conspiracy, the School of
the Americas, the 1989 invasion of Panama, and the wars and embargo
in Iraq were test cases for an emerging post–Cold War national-security
doctrine that gradually shifted from unilateral anticommunist containment toward multilateralism and, in the 1990s, "military multiculturalism."[95] This consensus building reached into the farthest domains of
US culture, including ours: the university, the English department, the
Office of Multicultural Affairs.

With the fall of the Soviet Union, the end of the Cold War, and the
1991 war, the discourses of democracy and diversity were firmly linked
to provide justification for the war for domination, the "new world
order," that continued to be fought on multiple fronts. As Nadine Naber
recounts, after the dissolution of the Soviet Union in 1991, "the full
possibility of a full-scale U.S. military intervention in the Middle East
opened up," and foreign policy shifted toward strengthening military
expansion as well as economic neoliberalism.[96] This produced, in effect, a new racial regime. The "new world order," as George H. W. Bush
identified it in a joint session of Congress, was an alliance of the government, the military, and corporations aimed at protecting Americans in
a "still dangerous" world. As M. Jacqui Alexander argues, Bush's naming
the period was a way of gaining consent and legitimizing the state's rule:
his gesture to "troubled times" was "an appeal, intended as much for the
joint session and members of the corporate class as it was for the 'American people,' that amorphous, necessary grouping in whose name and on
whose behalf a great deal has been undertaken."[97]

Two symbols, in particular, helped galvanize patriotic support during the first Iraq war: the US woman soldier "chosen as the loyal marker

of emancipated modernity" against the Orientalist imagination of a veiled, oppressed Arab/Muslim woman, and the Arab-Muslim fanatic exemplified by Saddam Hussein.[98] This is to say nothing of the internal enemy, exemplified by Willie Horton, against whom the war on crime proceeded unchecked. But as television coverage of Operation Desert Storm emphasized the US military's technical mastery and sheer power, it also highlighted the racial diversity of the troops deployed to Kuwait. Thus, representations of the first Iraq war in the news and in popular culture extended and revised the racial logics of modern nationalism, and the "military multiculturalism" of the 1990s mobilized the diversity-management strategies of corporations to fashion the military as a modern, liberating, democratizing force.[99] While diversity became the desideratum of corporate and political organizations, the late 1990s saw the expansion of military control over the everyday lives of Black and Latinx peoples in the Americas. The Clinton administration virtually destroyed whatever shreds of a safety net might have been by rolling back welfare, withholding benefits from undocumented workers, denying access to housing for people convicted of federal drug offenses, building up the fence along the southern border, increasing drug arrests and speeding up mass incarceration with 1994's Violent Crime Control and Law Enforcement Act, structurally adjusting labor and farming with NAFTA, and deregulating banks.[100]

While military multiculturalism during and after the first Iraq war made specific use of the image of the Black male soldier as the ideal warrior and patriot who could transform the threat of Negroes with Guns into the very picture of national protection, it also authored a new phase in the US government's relation to Black women in the postwar era. It was not simply the Black male soldier or general who appeared as the exemplar of the new world order. Indeed, in the 1990s and 2000s, the culture of multiculturalism transformed the military as well as counterinsurgency agencies such as the State Department, the NSA, and the CIA, making Black women new subjects of counterinsurgency. As US popular culture witnessed an explosion of images of Black men as police and military officers, it also increasingly figured Black women's subjectivity through policing, prosecution, and protection throughout the 1990s and 2000s. Against the emergence of new, post–Cold War forms of threat, Black femininity surfaced in popular and political culture to bring the new modalities of US empire-building—preemption, surveillance, containment, preparation for disaster—into contact with post-affirmative-action diversity initiatives. Black women writers have wrestled with this conflation of Blackness and protection throughout the contemporary era; it is, of course, what Lorde stridently refuses when she writes of our "home girl," the assistant secretary of defense for equal opportunity and safety, swimming "toward safety / through a lake of her own blood."[101]

Black literary feminists in the 1980s and 1990s were on constant watch for the way terms like "terrorism" and "security" provided cover for the rehabilitation of racial power and the protection of white life; they were alert, too, to the way liberal reform was defanging Black radicalism with its felicitous invitations to soften one's speech and sit down behind a walnut desk. The catalogue of sticks and stones that Spillers offered at the beginning of "Mama's Baby, Papa's Maybe" found a companion in *Assata: An Autobiography*, published the same year, in which the fugitive Black Liberation Army operative recounts her capture by New Jersey state troopers and her subsequent incarceration in prose that uses a process of Black Power substitutions (in which, for example, "court" might become "kourt") to collapse the distance between the judicial institution and the Ku Klux Klan. Reproducing the text of a July 4, 1973, audiotaped missive "To My People," Shakur repeats variations of the phrase "They call us" to expose the material violence that made necessary the linguistic violence of the state:

They have called us gangsters and gun molls. . . . It should be clear, it must be clear to anyone who can think, sees, or hear, that we are the victims.

They call us murderers, but we did not murder over two hundred fifty unarmed Black men, women, and children, or wound thousands of others in the riots they provoked during the sixties.

They call us kidnappers.

They call us bandits.

They call us thieves and bandits.

> They call us thieves, but we did not rob and murder millions of Indians by ripping off their homeland, then call ourselves pioneers. They call us bandits, but it is not we who are robbing Africa, Asia, and Latin America of their natural resources and freedom.[102]

Shakur's catalogue of misnomers is a requiem for the dead and a litany, as Lorde would have called it, for survival. Activists like Shakur bridged revolutionary conceptions of the world, radical activism, and book culture and, besides that, bequeathed an archive of Black study to the coming generation of post-*Bakke* college students. As Stephen Dillon astutely points out, cultural expression was a way that fugitive activists like Shakur and Angela Davis "deployed culture to theorize the changes to global capitalism and incarceration happening around them"; they used cultural forms like the autobiography to indict power and to imagine postcarceral ways of being.[103] Even as this was so, Black women writers also used culture to call attention to culture's very intimacy with those forms of violence it was cataloguing. "How many of these gentle people have I helped to kill just by paying my taxes?" wrote June Jordan in an *Essence* magazine article on the US-backed war against the Sandinistas of Nicaragua.[104] "Washington [DC] might well come out the winner every time I opened my mouth," wrote Paule Marshall in her memoir's recounting of a State Department tour she took in 1965, a tour that just might prove "that the country was truly a democracy committed to respecting the First Amendment rights even of its most vocal detractors," including accomplished writers such as herself.[105] I will return to this point, and the complications it poses for Black feminist thought and African American literary studies, shortly.

Black feminist writers were tracking the changes in the way racial power entangled with military might throughout the long war on terror; they were making the literary text responsive to progressive transnationalism in an age marked by leftist despair. The attacks of September 11, 2001, brought an increased urgency to the Black feminist politics and poetics of radical protection, which continued to expose US imperialism and the forms of acceptable Black gender on which it bestowed recognition and invitations for liberal democratic inclusion.

Uncanny Collisions: 2001–12

(multiculturalism) / (de-essentialization)

Again, the pronouncement of war against terror in 2001 was a single performance in a larger drama of racialization that proceeded over at least three decades. So, as we understand the global war on terror as a military, governmental, and cultural formation that expanded and reorganized the security state, we should also understand it as a dynamic system within a much larger set of political and cultural-political processes that redefined threat and defense after 1968. Still, the September 11 attacks were an important point of catalysis, an acceleration in which existing codes of race, nation, and safety came together in new ways to reposition the United States as a global power.

Claudia Rankine signaled this catalysis in her 2004 *Don't Let Me Be Lonely*, a collection of lyrics that surveyed the domestic scenes of the global war on terror. Rankine uses the question mark to punctuate the shift in public grammars of safety and belonging that was catalyzed by the September 11 attacks. Looking back on the previous decade, she begins with questions that hark back to the prosperity of the Clinton years—questions that can only be read as cynical given the extending reach of US imperialism—and introduce readers to the grammars of a new now: "To roll over or not roll over that IRA? To have a new iMac or not to have it? To eTrade or not to eTrade? Again and again these were Kodak moments, full of individuation; we were all on our way to our personal best. America was seemingly a meritocracy. I, I, I am Tiger Woods. It was the nineties. Now it is the twenty-first century and either you are with us or you are against us. Where is your flag?"[106] In Rankine's lyric, the triple first-person pronoun "I" refers to the pluralization of the US multiracial subject embodied by the professional golfer Tiger Woods, whose performance on the barely desegregated greens and whose self-conscious performance of racial amalgamation on the *Oprah Winfrey Show* (when he referred to himself as "Cablinasian") paved the way for Nike Corporation to claim him as an icon of both individual self-determination and multicultural promise in its 1996 advertisement. The ad, "I am Tiger Woods," featured a progression of still and moving images ("Kodak moments") of phenotypically Black, white, Asian, and Latinx children walking through urban intersections pregnant with danger, then passing through pastoral golf courses, then turning to the camera, each in turn, saying, "I'm Tiger Woods." The Wieden+Kennedy agency's advertisement vivified the project of turn-of-the-millennium multiracialism. This was a project that, as Jared Sexton argues, reinforced "the idea of biological race" by "negatively 'purifying'—which is to say *quarantining*—racial Blackness in particular as the centerpiece of a vaster re-racialization of U.S. society in the post-civil rights era."[107] Blackness was not simply disappeared; it was sanitized and shined, then called on to be the "centerpiece" of the new American plural subject.

This positioning of Blackness at the center of the multicultural pluralization of the triumphant individual is what Paul Gilroy worried about when he published *Against Race* in 2000. Gilroy argued then that "the world of racialized appearances has become invested with another magic." The digital manipulation of visual images now "added a conspicuous premium to today's planetary traffic in the imagery of Blackness. Layer upon layer of easily commodified exotica have culminated in a racialized glamour and contributed an extra cachet to some degree of nonspecific, somatic difference." As a result, the hypervisibility of Blackness had become a "signature of corporate multiculturalism in which some degree of visible difference from an implicit white norm may be highly prized as a sign of timeliness, vitality, inclusivity, and global reach." Blackness was not simply a "badge of insult" but also an "increasingly powerful but still very limited signifier of prestige."[108]

The events of 2000 and 2001 exposed the clash between leftist Black activism and a US nationalism that transposed the multiculturalization of the 1990s onto the imperatives of total military dominance after the 9/11 attacks. Throughout the late 1990s, progressive Black activism had persistently challenged the police violence and mass incarceration, the privatization of public schools, and other processes by which the state managed and extended the racialized subjection of the Jim Crow state while adhering to the demands of official antiracism. Critical Resistance and the Black Radical Congress were founded in 1997; and the reparations for slavery movement gathered momentum as many Black Americans "no longer nurtured hopes that they could rely on traditional governmental remedies to redress racial injustices."[109] After the November 2000 election, when tens of thousands of voters were disenfranchised before the Supreme Court installed George W. Bush as the president, Bush gathered one of the most diverse cabinets in US history, appointing Condoleezza Rice as national security adviser and Colin Powell as secretary of state. These appointments did little to quell political outrage. The transnational movement for reparations reached its height in 2000 and 2001, spurred in part by regional events sponsored by the United Nations in advance of its World Conference Against Racism, Racial Discrimination, Xenophobia and Related Intolerance (WCAR) in Durban, South Africa, which began in late August 2001. The Bush administration reluctantly sent a small, low-level delegation to that meeting, but the United States and Israel staged an unofficial walkout out of the conference, denouncing calls for reparations and condemning defenses of Palestinian human rights and critiques of Israeli policy. The *New York Times* reported from Durban that Black Americans "took to the streets here, chanting 'Shame, shame, U.S.A.'"[110] As Sylvanna Falcón chronicles, the 2001 conference, like the previous UN world conferences against racism in 1977 and 1983, "demonstrated how out of touch the United States had become in regard to the global human rights movement against racism."[111] The United States' failure, though, did not detract from activists' sense that Durban would be a turning point in global antiracism.[112]

Three days after the conference in Durban concluded, the terrorist attacks of September 11 drowned the cries of political outrage and demands for reparations in a cacophony of fear, patriotism, and confusion. Representative Tom Lantos of California went so far as to suggest that the terrorist attacks of September 11 had spun out of the "abyss of international hate, discrimination, and indeed, racism" of WCAR.[113] A "new racial domain" is what Manning Marable termed the post-9/11 period: "As in previous times of war, the vast majority of Americans . . . immediately rallied behind the president, demanding retribution," but, at the same time, many Black Americans "were deeply troubled by the immediate groundswell of patriotic fervor, national chauvinism and numerous acts of violence and harassment targeting individual Muslims and Arab Americans."[114] After the attacks in Washington, DC, and New York City by the Islamist militant group Al Qaeda, Marable suggests, the "political universe" abruptly changed.[115] Since then, the image of Black agents of counterinsurgency has become necessary for the redemptive image of a "home front" united against evil.[116]

If, after 9/11, the equation of Blackness with enemy exercised a certain flexibility, such that diffusion and dispersion of threat both authorized the further criminalization of Blackness and, at the same time, demanded the increasingly spectacular equation of Blackness with safety—Colin Powell's 2003 speech at the UN Security Council selling the war in Iraq, Condoleezza Rice's appointments as national security adviser and secretary of state, Barack Obama's acceptance of the Nobel Peace Prize—the shifting relationship between Blackness, terror, and safety had meaningful reverberations in literature by Black American writers. In fact, we cannot begin to understand twenty-first-century African American literature without a full sense of the history of post–Cold War counterterror, in which Blackness came, paradoxically enough, to brighten the face of US empire.

Post-9/11 discourses of patriotic duty and security synthesized the production of new racial subjectivities and new forms of racial classification and violence with rationalizations of neoliberal economic policy and exercises of global expansion through military and carceral domination. The state's expanding capacity to preemptively counter what it deemed as illegitimate violence with its own violence opened up race to the callous caprice of post–Cold War power. Effectively, as Singh argues, "even though such violence may be mapped along the lines of existing social cleavages and (racial) differentiations, it also produces differentiating effects at the point of its application."[117] The state's shift from welfare to warfare increasingly, since 1945, demanded the multiplication of racial significations, such that the application of racial preference and racial violence at once clung to and loosened its grip on determinations of value based solely on skin color or other bases of racial identification. As Aihwa Ong argues, neoliberal economic policy transformed the norms of good citizenship such that "the most worthy citizen is a flexible homo economicus. In our age of globalization, the figure of entrepreneurial prowess is increasingly multiracial, multicultural, and transnational."[118]

If market values recoded citizenship, making citizenship a function of economic performance, the shift to permanent warfare also intensified the relationship between citizenship and the active demonstration of patriotic duty after the Cold War and in the lead-up to the war on terror. That is, one not only had to demonstrate the capacity and willingness to take private ownership for one's own social, political, and economic welfare but also had to demonstrate one's willingness to go to combat for the country's most sacred ideals. The national and the global, then, came together in the body of the neoliberal citizen who, on the one hand, could prove its fitness and fitfulness for global rule and, on the other, could present this fitness as a willing sacrifice to the security of the nation-state. As Deepa Kumar puts it succinctly, "The good neoliberal working-class subject is one who accepts precarious labor, shops at Walmart, and volunteers in defense of the homeland."[119] What Kumar calls "security nationalism" self-consciously adopts multiculturalism while nonetheless alerting the imperial citizen "to those 'bad' people of color with 'different cultures' who are capable of terrorist violence."[120]

In this sense, September 11—not the attacks themselves but the discursive complex through which the attacks became and continue to become knowable within frameworks of citizenship, safety, and national belonging—represents an important flashpoint along the continuum of racial projects that have advanced US empire-building since 1898. September 11 was not so much a sea change as a *catalysis*: a moment in which the processes of racialization that were already in motion *accelerated* to structurally adjust life as we know it to the dictates and demands of what David Harvey calls the "new imperialism."[121] This catalysis can be understood to have been sparked at the nexus of four related historical developments of the post-9/11 era:

1. The calls to and performances of patriotic duty that were linked to both everyday performances of wartime national identification (such as "play" with terrorist playing cards or the donning of the yellow ribbon signifying support for the US military) and wartime consumerism (Bush's decree to get back to the malls)
2. The imperial articulation of domination through endangerment, what Anne McClintock calls "imperial paranoia," US empire's capacity to discursively "cohere as a collective community around contradictory cultural narratives, self-mythologies, practices, and identities that oscillate between delusions of inherent superiority and omnipotence, and phantasms of threat and engulfment"[122]
3. The culture of surveillance that created and policed the "terribly broad" racial category of the "Arab–Middle Eastern–South Asian–Muslim," allowing for the scandal of misreading Sikhs as Muslims that exposed US ignorance[123]

4. The larger narrative of race and nationality, that is, the public fantasy of US postracialism, that held these developments together as signs of national righteousness and power rather than as indicators of jingoism, rogue statehood, or hypocrisy

The discursive production of 9/11 as an emergency requiring closure around conservative notions of homeland in infotainment, film and television, policy speeches, and other sites of knowledge production changed the definition and experience of threat. McClintock argues that what was "genuinely new" about the post-9/11 period was that "for the first time, control of the technologies of the image-world had swiveled in orientation: instead of the West looking at the rest of the world through the God-eye of modern visual technologies, it was as if the globe had swung on its axis and the ex-colonized world was now gazing at the West with technologies of vision believed for centuries—by the West—to be under the West's control." That is, "a wounded United States was looked at, watched, and surveyed during a moment of great exposure, devastation, and loss."[124] The nexus of patriotism, imperial mythologies, surveillance, and postracialism articulated itself in the increasing representations of Black people protecting and soldiering on behalf of and in intimate relation to the state—many of which representations I discuss in the next chapter—and also in the *browning* of threat. As Carmen Lugo-Lugo and Mary Bloodsworth-Lugo point out, anti-Latinx fears regarding the "browning of America" that coincided with late twentieth-century demographic shifts and a growing Latinx population coincided with post-9/11 fears to make browning a "dialectical and self-supporting process in which the same bodies marked as threats are rendered in need to constraint."[125] In this context, Black people, Latinxs, Central American immigrants, Middle Easterners, and South Asians could at once ignite the public imagination of the ideal patriot—and, by extension, a postracial future—and call up fears of treason, invasion, and mass violence. It is with this post-9/11 browning of already-Black threat in mind that we can comprehend 2005's Hurricane Katrina as another front in the Gulf war, a perfect storm of the state's callous disregard of Black people, capital's cannibalization of disaster, and the drama of border patrol and detention.

In this context, the relationship between the browning of threat and anti-Blackness took on new dimensions of complexity. It was not that Arab became "the new Black," taking the African American's place as the racial identification most targeted for policing, violence, and political exclusion, but rather that September 11 *intensified* categories of racialization while recalibrating racial hierarchy to incorporate the production of the "Arab–Middle Eastern–Muslim" into preexisting codes determining the distinction between livable life and disposable life.[126] That is, 9/11 magnified how the unprecedented consolidation of carceral and military power at once exported the technologies of surveillance and capture that have historically played out on the domestic field of anti-Blackness and "brought home" the racialized figure of the Muslim enemy; this simultaneous digging-in to preexisting racial classification and opening-out to taxonomize new racial formations sifted multiple identifications (the "Arab–Middle Eastern–Muslim," the "terrorist," the "enemy combatant," the "illegal," the "gang member," the "freedom fighter") through a post-9/11 racial project focused on quarantining, torturing, and otherwise punishing elements deemed enemies of the state, that is, enemies of a globalizing, forward-looking, multicultural United States.[127] One example of this double-sidedness is the Black woman TSA agent who performs the power of the state to see and search, however fleetingly and precariously, while embodying the very threat that she is tasked with screening out. As Simone Browne points out, Black women by the turn of the millennium had the highest likelihood of being strip-searched at an airport and were, more often than not, marked as more threatening and unruly than others; therefore, the Black woman who might staff the airport security checkpoint after 9/11 "might not be able to access the very thing she is tasked with protecting": movement across borders.[128]

But perhaps nothing exemplifies this double movement of racial power more than the election and administration of Barack H. Obama, which brought us the drone attacks, digital surveillance, and cyberwar that were a prelude to the Trump administration's "overtly barbarous and protofascist recombination of 'fire and fury'" along with so many eloquent disquisitions on peace and perfect unions intoned by the man whose face was pasted next to Martin's and Malcolm's and even Harriet Tubman's on posters lining Black folks' entryways and kitchens.[129]

(Obama replaced the term "war on terror" with "Overseas Contingency Operations"—we can add this bureaucratic phraseology to our Black imperial grammar book—as he escalated the drone war in Iraq, Afghanistan, Somalia, Yemen, Libya, and Pakistan.)

The changing nature of threat in the post–Cold War period demanded a loosening of norms of race and gender at the same time as it allowed for a practical tightening of the apparatuses of policing and capture that disproportionately affected racialized populations and made racialized gender ripe for both resignification and co-optation. I will return to this point in my discussion of Condoleezza Rice's memoirs and *Scandal* in chapter 3. After the September 11 attacks, the United States' history of anti-Black violence and antiracist protest was articulated as both the ethical ground of a new Americanism in whose name the wars against Iraq and Afghanistan might be waged and as the excess of that new Americanism, the ghostly subject of a different ethical positioning.

For example, the author Walter Mosley said in an interview with *The Guardian* that "Black people know that most Arabs and Muslims are good people, that their beliefs are just as valid as Christian beliefs, that they have been at the receiving end of American so-called foreign policy for years. As a people of colour, we know how America treats other people of colour—with suspicion or disdain. What I am saying is that because of our unique position, we should be at the forefront of a new peace movement that starts the process whereby Americans start to see the world, and themselves, differently."[130] Mosley's attempts to bring the significations of "Arab" and "Muslim" into the ethical terrain of "valid" "Christian beliefs" solidifies the fictions that secure that terrain in the first place: he articulates an acceptance of Arab/Muslim difference that only serves to shore up the secularist and sectarian logics that rationalize the United States' preemptive invasion of Iraq and Afghanistan in the first place. If secularism is a political rationality that functions not as the dissolution of the relationship between church and state but the rearrangement of that relationship to make it "more congruent with a certain mode of liberal political rule," it equates proper religious expression with rational assent while deeming Islam (offered in this case as synonymous with Arab) in need of policing and surveillance.[131] That Mosley is serving in this interview as one who atones for the United States' original sin against Black people becomes clear when the *Guardian* journalist turns to Mosley's own accounts of his Black characters' rage. "Hate and rage simmer beneath the surface of all seven Easy Rawlins novels," the reporter writes. The analogy between Black Power and political Islam, in this case, places Black authorship in the position of mediation: if Mosley, by way of his expertise as a Black writer and his authority as an expert on Black rage, assuages the reporter's fear of a global world war sparked by Islamicist terror, he does so in a way that announces Blackness as the promise of a new United States redeemed of its genocidal, colonial sins.

Of course, this claim, that Black people have a special destiny within the United States, echoes earlier statements of Black giftedness. But it also makes a connection that is particular to the post-9/11 era, in which the construction of US exceptionalism gained new coherence in the circulation of stories and images of collective woundedness and vengeance. A certain *sexual* exceptionalism subtended rationalizations for preemptive war after the September 11 attacks, as the incorporation of queer sexual subjects into the national imaginary of familial wholeness and national wellness proved the country's progress toward social, political, and philosophical enlightenment. If, as Jasbir Puar argues, the "*convivial relations*" between queerness and the machineries of the war on terror reveal how "new normativities" are in circulation in the twenty-first century, these new normativities, too, set in motion—and solidified—old and new narratives of excellence and exceptionalism based in racial conciliation and the success of racial minorities in the spheres of politics, corporate power, entertainment, and the arts.[132]

Ideas and ideals of Black exceptionalism infused not only public discourses of security and threat after 9/11 but also discussions of Black expressive culture. During the post-9/11 years, the ethos of gentrification—the commodification of racialized objects of food culture, art, and design and the concomitant expulsion of working-class and poor racialized peoples from the places where their foodways and folkways are put on display—has infused, too, public talk regarding Black cultural production in the literary arena. Take, for example, the screenwriter John Ridley's infamous February 2007 essay "The Manifesto of Ascendancy for the Modern American Nigger," published in *Esquire*, which uses the representation of Black authority in the 9/11 complex as a basis for a larger set of claims about the post-racial-uplift project of African American literature and film. Drawing a stark line between the "niggers, the oppressed minority *within* our minority," and "Black Americans," Ridley writes, "It's time for ascended Blacks to wish niggers good luck." This argument, an elitist rejection of an ethos of linked fate, draws as its primary evidence Colin Powell and Condoleezza Rice's role in crisis management after the 9/11 attacks: "We need to burn into our collective memory the event that marked the beginning of our new timeline: an event from early in this millennium that seemed, for its moment in time, auspicious but that is now all but forgotten. It was lost in the ash of fires in Over-the-Rhine. Buried in the rubble of 9/11. But I for one will not let it go, won't let it get dumped into a potter's field of U.S. politics. It was too important. Far too significant. It was eleven days when two Blacks ran America."[133] Citing Powell and Rice's leadership as the example of Black American ascendancy, Ridley's reactionary rant follows liberal proclamations about the death of the nigger, marking the emergence of the *new* Black as classed projection of enlightened subjectivity and political community. Ridley brings the history of Black agency for counterterror after 9/11 to bear on a classed projection of Black achievement; the power to enforce policies of protection is thus linked to the power to create narratives of Black success. These are two uplift projects that both proceed by cleansing from Blackness the threat of the nigger, which is the threat of insurgency (central to Ridley's essay is the demonization of "Blacktivists") as well as the stain of the abject, the slave, the one who *is* overcome versus the one who *has* overcome. One the one hand, Ridley's rant can be dismissed as an anti-Black conservative tirade. But given that Ridley went on to win an Academy Award for the screenplay of *12 Years a Slave*, the adaptation of Solomon Northup's 1853 fugitive-slave narrative, we would have to ask how Ridley's new racial progress narrative provides the script for a kind of Black expressive culture that has been projected through a *liberal* frame of official antiracism. We would also have to interrogate how closely this liberal narrative of overcoming resembles similar post–"New Black Aesthetic" manifestoes that emphasize a certain gentrification of African American literature, such as Trey Ellis's "New Black Aesthetic" or Charles Johnson's "The End of the Black American Narrative" or Nick Chiles's "Their Eyes Were Reading Smut."[134]

What draws Ridley's notion of ascendancy together with Mosley's articulation of New Black Power is each author's fetishization of the "new Black" within a post-9/11 global regime of race that resignifies the complex relation between racial otherness, class position, nationality, and criminality: the racialization of Islam, at once anti-Black and Islamophobic, increasingly links diasporic Arabs, Muslims, and Southeast Asians to Blackness and associations of Islam with Black criminality; Black leadership over military, security, and governmental operations furthers the "legend of America as a liberalizing force in world affairs"; the nation's security, and the rationale for expansion through perpetual warfare, rests in the open embrace of racial difference at the same time as it depends on the deletion of reference to racial hierarchy.[135] The increasing visibility of post-civil-rights Black leadership in government, the military, entertainment, and athletics, against the backdrop of the post-9/11 racialization of Islam, thus interarticulated Blackness as promise of safety and threat of danger. If the Arab/Muslim became "the new Black" at the same time as the African American became "the new Black," what were the terms in which writers came to represent Blackness and its relationship to the articulation of new American identity in the years following the September 11 attacks? What was generated by the uncanny collision between writerly calls for innovation against essentialist prescription and public culture's commodification and circulation of postracialism as the cultural logic of the security state?

The global war on terror both called on new grammars of racial subjectivity and sociality produced by the neoliberal marketplace *and* collapsed, or flattened, them, replacing a liberal imaginary of individuated *I*'s endowed with the magic of beauty, liveliness, and unlimited potential for success in a global competition for resources with a conservative imaginary of a flagpinned *us* that transposed the optimism of the multicultural 1990s onto an idealized, but threatened (or idealized *because* threatened), national unity. In Rankine's new now, this post-9/11 fusion of patriotic duty and security ("Are you with us or against us?" morphs into a suspicious "Where is your flag?") synthesized the production of new racial subjectivities with rationalizations of neoliberal economic policy and exercises of global expansion through military and carceral domination. To define and refuse and offer alternatives to that new now are tasks that in part defined Black women's writing throughout the long war on terror.

To stand sentinel and rooted in the bloodied ground on the other side of terror, to be violated into violence, to inform our dreams, to refuse the *us* that increasingly pried itself open to claim Black people as its own: these were the projects of Black women's writing after 1968. In this chapter, I have presented the history of the long war on terror through the vantage point of these projects. My point in doing so is not only that Black feminist literature links counterinsurgency to the too-long onslaught against Black women's flesh—when were Black feminists not trying to alert us to "what was to come"?—but also that it asks us to deepen our attention to how Black feminist theories of power have tracked the prehistory of the security state. Could not Toni Morrison's 1997 *Paradise*, originally titled *War*, with its story of defense turned offense, be read as a theory of contemporary counterinsurgency or its walled-in all-Black town as an analogue to an Israeli settlement? Did not Octavia Butler's *Parable of the Sower*, with its world on fire and its weary band of travelers, expose the false security of the gated community and insist on the unsecured safety that would have to be crafted daily by fugitive slaves and motherless children, thrown-away women and heartbroken, middle-aged men? Was not her *Parable of the Talents* warning enough that the imperialism of the 1990s and 2000s would boomerang to the "homeland" as a vicious MAGA-style isolationism that would only worsen the earthwide impact of the wars, all the while adding to white supremacy's domestic death toll? Black feminist writers throughout the long war on terror refracted the shifts in racialization, military ideology, and political economy that brought Black women into deeper intimacy with state violence on either side of terror: the side of the terrorized-targeted and the side of the aggressor-apologist. I return to this story of Black feminist literature in part 2 of this book. But first, I would like to look more closely at the function of the imperial grammars of Blackness in three important institutions of contemporary power: the military, popular culture, and the university. In chapter 2, I argue that the figure of the Black soldier in US popular culture of the late 1990s and early 2000s embodied both the promise of multicultural democracy spreading through imperial war and the threat of armed Black uprising. The Black soldier's translation of the imperial grammars of Blackness, then, provides an analytic of double-sidedness that will prove useful as I continue to analyze the two sides of terror shaping Black women's writing of the contemporary era.

2

The Imperial Grammars of Blackness

Iraq War Circuits and the Picture of Black Militarism

You are watching a young woman flutter around a beige and white, mostly updated, kitchen. A second ago, your eyes were on an old-school calculator and the ballpoint pen twirling in your brown right hand. The calculator is—that is, *you* are—drowning in bills. It is 2005. It is breakfast time. Or perhaps the cereal you are eating for dinner is a reminder of just how tired you are, how little you have tucked away in a college fund, how fresh produce and boneless skinless chicken breasts are luxuries that you cannot afford. "Look, Ma," this woman, fresh-faced and brown with a ponytail full of relaxed hair, says as she grabs a box of Corn Flakes and crosses toward you. She sits down at the table and looks at you dead in your eyes. She is about to get real with you. "If I still want to be a doctor when I get out, I'll have had four years of experience as a nurse or an X-ray tech or an OT specialist"—she clasps her hands together to emphasize this—"working with *real* patients." Breathless now, she says, "That's why I want to enlist in the military." Her eyes narrow, and your eyes move from her face to the refrigerator plastered with photos and other signs of your would-be good life. When you look back at this woman, she says, "It'll be good for my career." Now she is squinting at you, waiting on you. She asks, "What do you think?" You can barely hear a door shut somewhere to your right, and a smallish woman, also brown, is walking toward you. You only get a second to see her. Turning back to the girl before you can think too much about this other woman, you watch her plead, "Ma?" not to the woman who has just walked in but to you yourself. She bites her lip and waits for you to respond. Just as it is getting uncomfortable, white titles letting you know that it is "YOUR TURN" fade in front of this scene, and an authoritative-sounding voice is encouraging you, "Make it a two-way conversation. Get the facts at TODAYSMILITARY.COM." The mother is you. And this means that you are Black and possibly (probably) single and that you are possibly (probably) grateful that your woman-child is making the choice to be all that she can be.

The Department of Defense's October 2005 marketing campaign for the US military was intended to position viewers in the empathetic positions of guardian, coach, and caretaker. Created by Mullen Advertising, the commercials produced in the series that included "Mother Daughter," the advertisement whose melodrama I have just narrated, were designed to convince parents and young adults alike that military service was a wise choice even as the casualties in the war in Iraq mounted and as recruitment for the war dropped off.[1] The commercial is a sentimental product of the three-way relationship among corporate advertising, military recruitment strategy, and film culture, and it followed other similarly maudlin advertisements for the US Army and US Navy that called on Black actors and/or directors to sell the country's military campaigns abroad, particularly in the Persian Gulf. As Paul Gilroy noted at the turn of the millennium, "easily commodified exotica" and "racialized glamour" endow racial difference in advertisements and in other visual media of consumer culture with "magic"; the hallmark of corporate multiculturalism is that "some degree of visible difference from an implicit white norm may be highly prized as a sign of timeliness, vitality, inclusivity, and global reach."[2] In this case, the Black woman enlister, a figure of irreducible racial difference, embodies the allure of the bourgeois good life, the enticement of US power secured through multicultural belonging, and the overall sense that "today's military" is as bright-eyed and fresh-faced as the brown girl in the camera's frame. And the proper mother, the one whom the daughter addresses, is positioned against the woman who emerges as a shadow, appearing on-screen only long enough to conjure thoughts of babymamas and welfare queens. This projection of three simultaneous figures of Black cis-femininity draws Black female being into the visual frames of the war on terror to perform the critical tasks of recruiting soldiers and winning favor for an unfavorable war. Indeed, the campaign proceeded with the faith that Daniel Patrick Moynihan professed in the military's ability to perform the miracle of saving the Black family by offering warrior masculinity as an antidote to Black matriarchy or, in this case, by making over the Black woman into the image of cool, rational patriot-caregiver.[3]

If Black gender is the ultimate target of the long war on terror, as I have suggested, it is also at the heart of the state's ultimate fantasy of imperial protection. Black Americans in US visual culture have been pictured at the forefront of the US defense strategies, defeating the threat of terror through preemptive war and holding highly visible positions of power in the Pentagon, the White House, and the Capitol. This has especially been the case since the September 11 attacks. The scenes of Black state representatives on *this* side of terror—becoming perpetrators and avid supporters of US imperialism rather than targets of state-sponsored and/or state-sanctioned violence—range from Colin Powell's 2003 address to the UN Security Council supporting military action in Iraq to Condoleezza Rice's shoe-shopping on the evening news after Hurricane Katrina to President Barack Obama's spearheading the US military campaign in Afghanistan and committing to drone strikes there and in Pakistan and Yemen even as he accepted the Nobel Peace Prize. These scenes echo in US mainstream entertainment media of the post-9/11 years, in which Black actors have protected the planet from the threat of annihilation and taken the lead as spokespersons for a reborn, self-righteous, postracial nation.

The visual representation of Black soldiering has most definitively told the story of US multicultural promise throughout the long war on terror. In television advertisements, recruitment posters, print ads, films, and television shows, Black soldiers do the martyring work of twenty-first-century empire-building while disappearing the anti-Black violence of the long war on terror. Therefore, *Black military visuality*, a term I am using to connote US visual culture's continual citation of Black soldiering to construct the war against terror as a freedom struggle as well as to refer to the staging of Black soldiering as a shorthand for freedom-making within the history of Black expressive culture, is one significant terrain for working through the fraught relationship between Black creative expression and the racial and gendered logics of US imperial power. The term refers to the set of aesthetic maneuvers, within cinematic and televisual texts in particular but in mass culture more broadly, that position the Black soldier-patriot as the figure who secures a liberal ideal of homeland by achieving greater and greater intimacy with the military processes of empire-building, giving proof to the United States' capacity to perfect racial democracy and at the same time bringing with him into each frame a history of anti-Black terror that, too, has to be rehearsed in order to be worked through. The intensification of Black military visuality's circulation throughout the post–Cold War period, during the first and second Iraq wars, draws the terrors of slavery, colonialism, and Jim Crow into intimate conversation with the terrors of US counterinsurgency and military aggression abroad, particularly in the Middle East.

The Black soldier's interpellation within various modalities of imperial visual culture—militainment, recruitment posters, film, television news—brings the threat of terror invoked by the new US wars into intimate relation with the violence on the *other* side of terror that continues, even now, to haunt Black film, Black fiction, and Black life narratives: the nightmares come to life of restless souls tossed and driven in the Atlantic; chains chafing against narrow wrists and ankles; Black lungs collapsing under the strain of asphyxiation; lunch-counter humiliations and the everyday deprivations of Jim Crow; and soft, brown human flesh bloated and buoyed on flood waters. In what follows, I provide an analysis of Black military visuality that twenty-first-century Black-authored texts take as a primary point of inquiry. Reading representations of the Black soldier in texts as varied as Spike Lee's 2008 World War II film *Miracle at St. Anna*, the 1990s sitcom *A Different World*, and the HBO drama *In Treatment* before turning to my analysis of Shoshana Johnson's 2010 military memoir *I'm Still Standing* (2010), I read Lee's film and Johnson's life-writing against the conventions of post-9/11 US television and film, which have persistently aimed to make permanent war not only acceptable but riveting and to make the appearance of armed Black insurgents not the apocalyptic announcement of the end of the world but the messianic arrival of a whole new one. These dislocations allow the protagonists of the film and the memoir to end up not at home but rather in some place in which and from which readers and viewers might begin to literally see Black cultural texts of the long war on terror differently.

Black Military Visuality and the Performance of Refusal

You are drifting toward a tattered armchair, where an aging, brown-skinned man sits watching the D-Day invasion of Normandy unfolding before his eyes in *The Longest Day Ever*. Floating toward the darkened corner of this Harlem walk-up, you pause to take in a poster of Joe Louis, triumphant. The poster mocks the older Black man in the corner, who hunches over in his easy chair, squinting through his thick glasses while the light from the television bounces off his head, which is bald except for the tight white curls that hover above his ears. "We fought for this country too," he tells the television, tells John Wayne, tells you. Moments later, you are puzzled when this man, now at his workstation in the post office where he works as a clerk, pulls a gun from his top drawer and shoots the white man in front of him in the face, point blank.

The opening scene of Spike Lee's 2008 film *Miracle at St. Anna* is an extended meditation on the relationship between Black military service and the cinematic. A self-conscious revision of the war-film genre, Lee's *Miracle* opens with a scene of Hector Negrón, a Nuyorican veteran, "going postal" and shooting the Italian partisan who shows up at his post-office window asking to buy a twenty-cent stamp. To explain the murder, the film goes back in time and space, to 1944 in Italy, where the Ninety-Second Infantry Division of the US Army, also known as the Buffalo Soldiers, is fighting the threats of Nazism, fascism, and communism abroad while fighting white supremacy at home. Here, four men of the George Company—Second Staff Sergeant Aubrey Stamps (Derek Luke), the highest ranking officer among the four; Sergeant Bishop Cummings (Michael Ealy), the con artist and womanizer; Corporal Hector Negrón (Laz Alonzo), the Puerto Rican "outsider"; and Private First Class Sam Train (Omar Benson Miller), the oafy Christian farm boy—are stranded behind enemy lines and take refuge in the Italian city of Colognora. A war-on-terror-era film about Black soldiering in US visual culture, *Miracle at St. Anna* reveals how Black cultural production functions not only to reveal the intimacy between Black visuality and the Iraq wars but also to destabilize it. If the reinvention of racial terror after World War II transformed the appearance of Black state authority over the past five decades, making Negroes with Guns over into symbols of state beneficence, Black American expressive culture, particularly film, has documented that transformation even while, at times—sometimes in unexplainable, estranging moments—disidentifying with it. Understanding Lee's film within a genealogy of such disidentifications helps us grasp how the forms of Black military visuality that surfaced between and after the Iraq wars index both US culture's incorporation of Blackness into the imperial grammars of the post-1945 world and the open circuits of terror in which the appearance of the Black soldier disrupts the national narratives of US militarism.[4] In this section, I construct that critical genealogy of war and of the Black soldier's interpretation of its imperial grammars of Blackness.

The Black soldier in US visual culture reflects and manages collective racial anxieties and fears of invasion, penetration, and castration by a foreign, racialized enemy. The apparatus of mass-distributed film, in particular, has served as a privileged site for this reflection and management. Since World War II, Black soldiering in US film has been linked to three disparate but related articulations of the function of US military forces: (1) that the US military is the arbiter of global democracy; (2) that the successful integration of Black soldiers into the US Army, Navy, Marines, Air Force, and Coast Guard proves the myth of US multicultural beneficence; and (3) that enlistment is a form of social protest that attests to Black soldiers' capacity to fight on behalf of US freedom (or the freedom of capital) *and* their capacity to reserve the force of violence to act on behalf of their own freedom. The terror and the promise of the image of the armed Black person thus subtends efforts on the part of the mainstream corporate film industry and on the part of Black filmmakers, filmgoers, and race leaders to promote and manage the appearance of Black soldiers in mass-distributed film.

The Negro Soldier, a 1944 propaganda film produced by the War Department as part of its *Why We Fight* series, is an important case study in the way varied investments in the political usefulness of Black military visuality converged to change US film's representations of racial difference. *The Negro Soldier* was the product of a four-way collaboration among liberal Black advocacy groups like the NAACP, which saw World War II as the time to press for a "double victory" against fascism in Europe and racism at home; the War Department, which had begun financing film producer Frank Capra's *Why We Fight* series in 1942 in order to train soldiers and manage public perceptions of Black enlisters; the corps of social scientists in the Army's Information and Education Division, who were interested in measuring the impact of film on relations between white and Black soldiers; and the Hollywood film industry. Taking place in a decorous Black church, *The Negro Soldier* begins with a preacher, Reverend Moss, extolling the virtues of US war and recounting the glorious role that Black soldiers have played in securing the democratic way of life. Using documentary footage, the film shows several scenes of valiant Black soldiering, confronting the stereotype of Black soldiers as cowards, promoting racial pride, and encouraging racial tolerance in the Army ranks. "The calculation underwriting the film," writes Vaughn Rasberry, "is that imagery of black achievement would supersede or smooth over the erasure of slavery and segregation and the ambiguous role of blacks in U.S. imperialism."[5] This is a gamble that US filmmakers made throughout the twentieth century.

After *The Negro Soldier*, the fantasy of Black military participation as an antidote to both domestic racial crises and domination by a foreign enemy continued to take shape throughout the post-1945 era in US film.[6] *The Negro Soldier*'s influence on later films is particularly significant in the history of racial representation. According to Thomas Cripps and David Culbert, the film "represented a watershed in the use of film to promote racial tolerance," leading to the production, promotion, and eventual demise of "race films" targeted specifically to Black audiences.[7]

Another key text for considering the history of Black soldiering on film is *The Home of the Brave*, a play by Arthur Laurents adapted by Carl Foreman, a writer from Capra's unit. *Home of the Brave* centers around a Black protagonist, Moss or "Mossy" (named after Foreman's friend Carleton Moss, who helped write the screenplay for *The Negro Soldier* and played Reverend Moss on-screen). Moss is suffering from amnesia and paralysis following a mission in the Pacific. As he undergoes psychoanalysis, flashbacks in the film suggest that his real sickness is racial consciousness: first hurt by his longtime friend and comrade, who nearly calls him a "nigger"—he does not get the whole word out, so we might say he literally calls Moss the n-word—he feels guilty because he later feels elated that it is this friend rather than himself who has been captured and tortured by the Japanese. Moss has to be convinced that the neuroses he suffers are not racially derived but rather endemic to war. As David Marriott explains, Moss "is oppressed because he is sensitive, and sensitive because he is oppressed."[8] Thus, the goal of *Home of the Brave* "was not only to counter the widely held belief that Negroes make cowardly soldiers, but to answer the political, fascistic fantasy of Black inferiority with the assimilationist fantasy of white liberalism."[9]

The World War II film has served, in this way, as a textual ground for the articulation of racial liberalism and as a particular mode of fantasizing about the capacity of the United States to "move beyond" its own racial catastrophes and to dominate the planet through free trade. *Home of the Brave* was also, of course, the film that Frantz Fanon was thinking of when he wrote against the notion of racial sensitivity as a sickness or the equation of Blackness and disability: "I refuse to accept this amputation. I feel in myself a soul as immense as the world, truly a soul as deep as the deepest of rivers, my chest has the power to expand without limit. I am a master and I am advised to adopt the humility of the cripple." This refusal is an awakening: "Yesterday, awakening to the world, I saw the sky turn upon itself utterly and wholly. I wanted to rise, but the disemboweled silence fell back upon me, its wings paralyzed. Without responsibility, straddling Nothingness and Infinity, I began to weep."[10] Not only is *Home of the Brave* the film that "made a grown man cry," as Marriott puts it; it also announces Black military visuality as both one of racial liberalism's key modalities *and* a ground for the Black radical refusal of racial liberalism.[11]

Black American World War II narratives that emerged in print over the decades following *Home of the Brave*, such as Charles Fuller's *A Soldier's Play* (1981) and James McBride's novel *Miracle at St. Anna* (2002), capture the complexities of Black enlistment during Jim Crow segregation, presenting Black soldiers alternatively as war heroes, dissenters, Uncle Toms, crusaders for civil rights, and racial peacemakers. When these two particular texts were adapted for film, their perspectives on canonical World War II films differed vastly. *A Soldier's Story* (directed by Norman Jewison, 1984) capitalizes on many of the tropes that *The Negro Soldier* and *Home of the Brave* set in motion: the impassioned interracial embrace between men; the army as the advance guard of desegregation; and the Black man's adopting the "humility of the cripple" as an antidote to racial sensitivity and a substitute for racial justice. On the other hand, *Miracle at St. Anna* manipulates the images of canonical World War II cinema to intervene in the racial liberal imagination of the Black soldier. If Lee's *Miracle at St. Anna* weds a Fanonian refusal of racial liberalism to a critique of Black military visuality in the context of the Iraq wars, it situates World War II as a significant point of retrieval for both Black radicalism and racial liberalism. This makes that earlier war the ground of an epistemological battle more treacherous than Lee's veteran intimates when he cries, "We fought for this country, too."

Miracle at St. Anna departs from the formula of the World War II racial problem film in important ways. Its departures become quite clear when we consider how it differs from *A Soldier's Story*, released over twenty years prior. *A Soldier's Story* is a murder mystery about the killing of a Black noncommissioned officer at a Jim Crow army base. Set in 1944 at a fictional base named Fort Neal in Tynin, Louisiana, the action begins when a Black officer, Sergeant Vernon Waters (Adolph Caesar), staggers home after a night of drinking at a bar on the base and is murdered on the street. Viewers are first led to believe that Waters has been murdered by white supremacists who will not tolerate the sight of Black men in uniform. The initial suspects are Lieutenant Byrd (Wings Hauser) and Captain Wilcox (Scott Paulin), the two white servicemen who meet Waters on his drunken stumble back to the base and allegedly brutally assault him with racial slurs and kicks to the gut. But when Captain Richard Davenport (Howard E. Rollins Jr.), a Black, Howard University–educated lawyer, arrives from Washington to conduct an investigation, the film reveals that the killing was the product of not interracial but *intra*racial hostility, a three-way collision between Black soldiers.

In a poignant soliloquy that anchors the film's surprise discovery of intraracial political difference, Sergeant Waters is shown rationalizing his hatred for CJ Memphis (Larry Riley), an officer whom Waters calls a "geechee," a backward, bumbling, southern fool who must be exterminated in the name of racial progress. CJ is, interestingly, a character type that becomes a staple in Black military films: in 2002's *Antwone Fisher*, Leonard Earl Howze plays "Pork Chop"; and in 2008's *Miracle at St. Anna*, Omar Benson Miller plays Private First Class Sam Train, "the biggest Negro you've seen in your life," who peppers the film with moral platitudes and "premodern" superstitions. CJ, like these others, is an oversized southern farm boy who plays foil both to northern cool and to the blues/folk hero. While CJ is depicted as something of an innocent, an unwilling hero who loves justice and hates war, he ignites Sergeant Waters's animosity and self-hatred. Waters relates his ire for CJ to his own service in World War I, when white soldiers paid a Black solider from the South to "run around half naked making monkey sounds":

"White boys danced that night, passed out leaflets with that boy's picture on it. Called him 'Moonshine, king of the monkeys.' My daddy told me we gotta turn our backs on his kind. . . . Close our ranks to the chitlins, collard greens, cornbread style. *We're men. Soldiers.* And I don't intend for our race to be cheated out of its place of honor and respect in this war because of fools like CJ. You watch everything he does. Everything." As this confessional soliloquy—an acting out of the talking cure— reveals, intraracial violence based in the sergeant's pathological inability to let go of racial violence and racial shame is to blame for a murder that was initially blamed on anti-Black hostility. Motivated by his memory of coerced minstrel performance in World War I, by his father's advice to "turn our backs on [CJ's] kind," and by his duty to protect Black bourgeois military masculinity, Waters frames CJ for the shooting of a white officer. CJ is then locked up in the military prison.

Demanding justice for CJ, Private First Class Melvin Peterson (Denzel Washington) murders Waters, punishing the senior officer's accommodationist response to white supremacy. The figure of model soldier, Captain Davenport, becomes key to this 1980s civil rights film. He seals the film's project of literally domesticating Black protest. With his mod style and self-composed cool, Davenport disposes of all three types to articulate a post-civil-rights Black masculinity stripped of anger and the threat of retribution. In the final scene, the Black officers finally receive word that they are being deployed to fight in Germany; as they proceed out of Fort Neal, Davenport makes his way back to Washington, and all the Black men move forward into history, saluted by white senior officers as they go off to war. The film thus stages Black incorporation into the US military regime as the advance guard of national progress in "race relations," offering a now familiar celebration of modern Black political-military masculinity as a model for post-civil-rights Black subjectivity and politics. *A Soldier's Story*, in this way, uses white supremacy as a red herring and surprises the viewer with its climactic scene of Black-on-Black violence, retraining 1980s multicultural audiences to unsuspect white supremacy and to welcome neoliberal multiculturalism's individualist rhetorics of race and power.

Importantly, Lee's appropriation of the genre of World War II film reverses course on this triumphalist World War II narrative. The celebration of Black incorporation into the military, particularly in the context of the first Iraq war and the post-9/11 war on terror, has been a crucial part of US public culture's formula for utilizing Black visuality in the articulation of the aims, logics, and affects of empire. This formula is an uneasy fit with Black American cinema, a cultural constellation at once productive of and at odds with mainstream representations of Black masculinity. Lee's *Miracle* preserves a space for Black discontent with US progress at a moment that demanded visible Black assent to war against the so-called Axis of Evil. Both the novel and the film are recuperative projects aimed at enlarging canonical histories and narratives of US war. James McBride states in his prefatory note to the novel, "[What] follows is real. It happens a thousand times in a thousand places to a thousand people. Yet we still manage to love one another, despite our best efforts to the contrary."[12] While the film follows up on the novel's promise to offer a fictional account of World War II in the realist strain of postmodern narrative, it sidelines McBride's liberal recovery project by countering the novel's universal love message with a critical historiography that centers white-supremacist terror and refuses to offer interracial love as an antidote to the violence that has accompanied US empire-building since World War II.

Miracle projects military exertion through the audiovisual language of diasporic loss and anti-Black terrorism. The film's picture of Black death and diasporic trauma is clearest in its battle scenes. The third scene of the film is a battle scene lasting fifteen minutes, and it culminates in the onslaught that separates the four main characters of the film from their company and lands them behind enemy lines. Here the influence of Italian neorealism on Lee's aesthetic is evident. Italian neorealism is "characterized by its use of on-location shooting, long shots, natural lighting, nonprofessional actors, working-class protagonists, nonliterary dialogue, and open-ended narratives about World War II and its aftermath."[13] This is the genre that Lee referred to when he called *Miracle* an "homage to Rossellini, De Sica, and those cats."[14] *Miracle* recounts a fall 1944 campaign at the Serchio River during which the Black soldiers of the Ninety-Second Division, in spite of the fact that they were inadequately trained and ill equipped, were thrown onto the front lines of combat against deeply entrenched German forces. The Ninety-Second was "always moving in full view of the waiting enemy, attacking frontally in many instances in the face of overwhelming fire from several directions, . . . [plunging] forward as ordered," despite the hostility with which white commanding officers such as General Edward "Ned" Almond treated Black soldiers and the intense vulnerability that marked the Black soldier's experience in Italy.[15] Shot on location in Tuscany, *Miracle* retells the story of the Serchio Valley campaign in order to expose the myth of Black cowardice and to reveal the racism that exposed the Ninety-Second Division to overwhelming German force.

In Lee's interpretation of the Serchio Valley campaign, the scene opens with a close-up shot showing a muddy puddle trampled by an army boot, with soldiers, shot from behind, in the background. Next is a close-up of an intricately woven spiderweb among tall ground brush, behind which one of the four main characters, Aubrey Stamps, comes into view. The focus on the terrain through which we see Stamps and the other characters creeping toward the German line lends to the film's neorealist aesthetic and emphasizes attention to the small, the local, and the intimate. One fearful soldier's cry interrupts the sounds of boots through mud and the melancholic, suspenseful notes of Terrence Blanchard's score: "Kill me now! Kill me now! I want to go home to my mama!" Throughout the scene, the advance is interspersed with scenes showing the Nazi forces broadcasting propaganda via loudspeaker, with "Axis Sally" asking the Buffalo Soldiers, "Why die for a nation that doesn't want you?" It also focuses on the interaction between a white captain and a Black lieutenant, both positioned a mile away from the battle, during which the captain forces the Black officer to fetch him fresh water and chastises him for acting like an "uppity Negro." In this way, the film captures the irony of Black enlistment, emphasizing the everyday means by which Black soldiers waged the Double V campaign, against both fascism and Jim Crow.

The explicit depiction of death and dismemberment in this scene links the action in Italy to the history of Black pain and dispersal. As the men cross the Serchio River, Nazi soldiers begin their assault with sniper fire and artillery. While some men make it across the river and take cover, others go down in the water and on the banks. This is a massacre that prefigures that later massacre at St. Anna di Stazzema, where Nazi soldiers kill 560 innocent Italian civilians. Here the soldiers crawl through the shallow water; they cry for help; they scream in agony; they absorb the impact of bullet after bullet. There are losses on both sides,

GIs float face down in a battle scene in Spike Lee's *Miracle at St. Anna* (2008), recalling the flooding of Black New Orleans that Lee captured with *When the Levees Broke*.

but the camera draws the viewer's attention to the losses in the river. In a series of close-ups accompanied by the crescendoing score, the camera lingers on bloodied bodies lying first face down, motionless, then face up, legs wide open. One shot shows a soldier from the waist up, lying still in the water while his helmet floats past him. Another shows clear water turning dark red around the head of an officer whose eyes stare beyond the frame. The image of dead Black men floating in water, accompanied by Terence Blanchard's mournful trumpet, recalls Lee's 2006 *When the Levees Broke*, marking *Miracle* as a kind of requiem for fallen Black soldiers and as a part of Lee's post–Hurricane Katrina project of interrogating US domestic and imperial containment.

Miracle disrupts the project of closure that the interracial war film pursues not only by overwhelming the triumphal appearance of the Black soldier with the history of white-supremacist terror but also by loading Black military visuality with the bloody sight of Black abjection and Black loss. The requiem that surfaces at the beginning of *Miracle* brings the history of racial terror—as middle passage, as historical erasure, as broken levees—into articulation with and through Black military visuality. This is, after its in medias res beginning in Hector Negrón's apartment, a second preface that lays out the conditions on which the film's history of Black involvement in World War II will come to be known. And these conditions are those same conditions of middle passage that the water here hints at: exploding guts, spattering blood, severed limbs, the irresistibly disgusting sight of Black people abandoned by, and to, white power. Black death thus functions as an open circuit on-screen. An electric circuit through which a current cannot flow because the path is broken or interrupted by an opening, an open circuit turns energy backward. This is a story of defeat and humiliation that, in the tradition of neorealism, resists resolution and recuperation.

Miracle is a story of unexpected fidelities and unforeseen betrayals. Loyalty happens, and unhappens, in strange places. At the center of the story is Sam Train, who is one of the four main characters who survive the assault in the Serchio River. Train is a farm-bred innocent from Alabama who rescues an orphaned Italian child named Angelo. When Sam rescues Angelo, the young boy mistakes the oversized American as both "a chocolate giant" and a monkey, licking his face to see if he tastes like Hershey's chocolate and asking, "Where is your tail?" While Sam's fellow soldier Bishop tells him that he has no responsibility to care for the orphaned child, who, we later find, has "miraculously" survived his parents in the massacre of Italians by German soldiers at St. Anna, Sam insists on playing the role of caregiver. Sam plays the stereotype of the naïve soldier-buffoon. Hyperemotional and hyperreligious, he carries with him the large head of the statue of the Trinitá, the statue from the church at St. Anna, believing it to be a charm that makes him invisible. Effeminized as a kind of mother figure to Angelo, Sam nurtures the child's injuries, feeds him, carries him along the refugee route from the Cinquale Valley to Colognora, teaches him to communicate through a sophisticated tapping system, tells him about salvation, and passes on charms and superstitions. He is responsible, that is, for social reproduction through a kind of motherly nurturing and is the one character charged with keeping Angelo in line and alive. This image of Black queer Madonna and child at the center of the film thus anchors its explorations of intimacies frustrated and fulfilled, of unanticipated fidelities and unexpected betrayals.

The film stages most of its betrayals and fidelities through sex between Black men and white women or the Black man–white man buddy plot, playing out familiar US cinematic formulas of personal and political desire. There is the frustrated love story between Stamps and Renata, a Colognora native, which dissolves when she prefers the suave and crass Bishop to the good-natured and well-behaved Stamps. There is the unexpected "miracle" of a Nazi defector telling young Angelo to run as fast as he can from the German soldiers carrying out the massacre at St. Anna. There is Rodolfo, the Italian partisan who betrays the people of Colognora when he refuses to warn them of the Nazis' imminent arrival, the very traitor whom Hector recognizes and kills four decades later in a Harlem post office. There is the Nazi sergeant who hands a gun to Hector Negrón, the only survivor of the George Company, and tells him, "Defend yourself." And, finally, there is the "miracle" at the very end of the film when Angelo, now an adult, posts bail for Hector Negrón and meets him on a beach in Nassau, Bahamas, the surprising last intimacy in this epic war film.

The fidelity-betrayal plot is mapped onto relationships both between individuals and between the George Company and the US state. *Miracle* is an allegory of the frustrated love story between Black men and the post–World War II United States. This frustrated love story is key to the film's rejection of racial liberalism's interest in Black military visuality. At a narrative turning point, Bishop and Stamps argue about whether to obey their commanding officer's orders to capture a German POW for intelligence while they are themselves vulnerable to attack. Here Stamps articulates the master narrative of military integration: "They said we couldn't fight . . . but the Ninety-Second proved we can fight. This is our country too. We helped build it from the ground up. I'm here for my children and future grandchildren, Bishop. This is about progress!" Refusing this triumphalist narrative of Black American progress, the film offers, in flashback, a scene that reminds both Stamps and the viewer of the historical context for Black men's "integration" of the armed forces during World War II. The film offers a flashback showing the men's humiliation at a lunch counter back at their army base back in Merryville, Louisiana. Here the young trainees attempt to relieve themselves of the Louisiana heat by buying ice slops. When they see German POWs eating at the very restaurant where they are refused service, they leave the store, only to return in protest. Using their military uniforms and revolvers to demand justice, they stage a militant protest that, intertextually speaking, revises the scenes of Black upward mobility in *The Negro Soldier*, of impassioned interracial embrace in *Home of the Brave*, and of conciliation and the scapegoat of Black-on-Black crime in *A Soldier's Story*'s Louisiana.

That the film retrains viewers to see Black enlistment not as the romantic fulfillment of US multiracial democracy but as that which exposes its contradictions is evident in its staging of the soldiers' refusal of the liberal frame that has historically constructed the World War II racial problem film. After the flashback, the film stages a moving portrait of Black resistance to US racism and military dominance. The four soldiers, now inculcated in the life of the Italian village of Colognora, where the Germans have posted Nazi propaganda depicting Black men as apes and monsters, stand in a line, as if posing for a picture, while staring at the Nazi propaganda posted on the town wall. Posed with rifles at the ready, they are both looking and looked upon; as they stare into the camera and at the wall of racist propaganda, the looks on their face communicate disgust, disappointment, and disillusionment. Breaking through the fourth wall of cinema to confront viewers' assumptions of US military history and to insert themselves into the collective memory of World War II, the characters stare the camera down before finally leaving the frame one by one, Bishop spitting on the ground before he swaggers away. Whereas the posing might initially be read, in an earlier cinematic framework, as a visual grammar of imperial Blackness, a staging of Black complicity with US militarism and a nonverbal plea for inclusion into the national narrative of military heroism ("We fought for this country too!"), the exits from the portrait in *Miracle* might be read as visual signs of national disidentification and transnational identification. The moving portrait stages the characters' plea for recognition as war heroes *and* their disavowal of that very recognition. In this way, the film brings them into US military history only to offer them an exit route. The George Company decides to stay in Colognora with the Italians when the Ninety-Second comes to "rescue" them, effectively going absent without permission. It is here when they are attacked by Germans and all are killed except for Hector and the young Italian boy, Angelo, whom the soldiers have taken in their charge. The surviving two escape by miracle.

In fact, the moving portrait visualizes the long history of Black soldier resistance. This history, which stretches back to the runaways who joined the Seminoles and the "contrabands" in the Union army, includes great instances of unpermitted absence that we might understand, following Avery Gordon, as an important form of anticapitalist, anti-imperial resistance. Writing about soldier desertion, Gordon points out that during

Black American World War II soldiers stationed in Italy stage a moving portrait of armed Black resistance to Jim Crow and imperialism, in Spike Lee's *Miracle at St. Anna* (2008).

World War II, forty thousand US soldiers went absent without leave during only three years of direct combat. In Vietnam, there were one and a half million "AWOL incidents," with one hundred thousand US soldiers being discharged for absence offenses, to say nothing of the over sixty thousand draftees who fled or hid to avoid conscription. Soldier desertion, Gordon argues, is an example of "being in-difference," a disposition of refusal that we will all have to adopt if we hope to abolish the global security apparatus on which the permanent war economy toddles. Desertion is the very process "by which militarism and the disposition to war is abolished."[16] The moving portrait is thus a performance of desertion, a recapitulation of abolitionist history and an invitation to run away.

I have spent so much time with *Miracle* because its visual grammar of suffering and refusal—the language through which it pictures Black pain and militant Black protest—refuses the narrative of service to country captured by the affirmative-action-era plot of *A Soldier's Story* and the integrationist plots of *Negro Soldier* and *Home of the Brave*. This refusal helps us understand the competing claims that the Black enlister and Black veteran manage in contemporary expressive culture. Rather than demanding national fidelity, *Miracle* revises the canonical war story to depict the complex of complicity *and* disavowal that is the Black vet's legacy after segregation. In this way, it can be read as a distinctly post-9/11 text that, like other contemporary Black war stories by Black women, such as Alice Randall's novel *Rebel Yell*, Danielle Evans's short story "Someone Ought to Tell Her There's Nowhere to Go," and, most importantly here, Shoshana Johnson's Iraq War memoir *I'm Still Standing*, is constituted by the narrative problem of Black intimacy with state violence.

Miracles and Militants

The teenage dance film might be the version of the interracial war film made just for people like you, who became Coco or Leroy each time you hopped up on the sofa with your sister and your cousin from Cleveland, the three of you belting your hearts out while learning to fly and perhaps living forever. You eventually settled for latecomers to the genre like *Save the Last Dance* (if nothing else because the Black South Side highs schoolers teaching the white girl to dance were teaching your ass something too). Imagine your surprise when the miracle you so needed then grows up to be the miracle that can only be aggressively disbelieved now.

Miracle ends with a kind of cinematic epilogue that refuses narrative closure around the kind of interracial intimacy necessary to secure the image of a benign, multicultural United States fighting terror around the globe. Hector Negrón, who has been arrested for the shooting of the Italian betrayer in the post office, is now in court for his arraignment, and when Angelo, now a wealthy capitalist, posts bail for him, he leaves the country. In the final scene, Hector walks onto a beach in Nassau, Bahamas, where he runs to meet Angelo and the two embrace. Crucial in this exchange is Zana Wilder, played by Kerry Washington in an uncanny prediction of the role of fixer she will come to play on ABC's *Scandal*. Wilder is an executive lawyer for Exxon who mediates Hector's liberation by Angelo, who has now grown wealthy selling safety devices like seatbelts. Here, as Wilder facilitates the final miracle of the film, she plays both the Black lady overachiever who has been incorporated into structures of power (indeed, we are to read her as what the soldiers died *for*) *and* the infiltrator saboteur who emasculates those very structures of power. When the judge in the courtroom calls Wilder to his bench after she informs him that Hector will post the $2 million bail in cash, he tells her he is suspicious of Exxon's interest in this

Zana Wilder, a Black woman lawyer for Exxon played by Kerry Washington, defends the Black soldier deserter in Spike Lee's *Miracle at St. Anna* (2008).

case. "Exxon buying the US Postal Service?" he asks her. "I smell a rat." To quiet his objections, Wilder threatens him, suggesting that he "cover [his] nose" if he wants to be reappointed. This scene calls attention to the self-consciously visual construction of US juridical power. As the camera pans from the elaborate stained-glass dome to the wall-to-wall renderings of fourteenth-century European painting, the viewer is asked to see Zana as a figure who, in Nicole Fleetwood's terms, "troubles the visual field."[17] In a scene filled to bursting with visual signifiers, the image of the Black woman as corporate lawyer and defender of global capital that overlays the image of her coming to the Black war hero's rescue captures the competing narrative impulses of post-9/11 Black cultural production—the plot of intimacy with global capital and the project of resolidifying Black solidarity. The appearance of the Black woman is, in other words, the apocalyptic sign of a narrative collision of corporate imperial power and Black filial love.

The film ends in riddles. Hector stands on a Nassau beach, looking beyond the surf. He wears a bright white guayabera, and a man wearing a crisp white suit walks up to him from behind. Now the score offers major chords and the soothing melodies of a violin, making the viewer ask, *Is this heaven?* The man reintroduces Hector and Angelo, the film's last survivors, after offering a speech that articulates a disavowal of security apparatuses and, perhaps, the ideological underpinnings of the national security state. Referring to Angelo, he says, "Your friend has learned there's no control in life. Wherever you go, wherever you hide, there's risk. Your friend understood that and turned that knowledge into invention: seatbelts, safety devices, and so forth. And your friend made a fortune. People pay for control, even if they have none. Safety is the greatest risk of all because safety leaves no room for miracles. And miracles are the only sure thing in life." Angelo's wealth, based in the illusion of safety, secures Hector's flight from home. This is a story of transcendence vis-à-vis Black first-world ascendance: two Black Americans facilitate Hector's second escape from the frame of World War II liberalism. In this scene, the postcolonial island is a site of play, fantasy, and metaphysical union between men, faith, and nations. Hector runs to Angelo and kneels in the sand, where lies the head of the statue of the Trinitá that graced the cathedral at St. Anna. Angelo removes a rosary from around his neck and places it around Hector's neck. As the two hold each other's hands and cry in mutual recognition, the camera offers a close-up shot of their hands, clasped around each other and holding the crucifix of the rosary. The head of the statue is centered in the frame behind their interlaced hands, and Hector repeats the name of the angel, "Angelo," three times.

As *Miracle* ends with this meditation on safety and risk followed by Hector and Angelo's tearful embrace, it returns us to the history of the World War II racial problem film. Just as *Home of the Brave* ended with the interracial embrace, so too does this film offer to the Black veteran the dubious miracle of racial equality and offer up, in turn, the Black veteran *as* a miracle of historical redress. But here, there is no return home; rather, Hector and Angelo's embrace is a meeting of exiles, of those who remain, in the end, outside the national narrative of World War II heroism. Given the film's earlier flights from this narrative—in the scene of river crossing and in the exits from the war heroes' portrait—we can read the film's conclusion as the refusal rather than the promise of home and safety.

If the island at the end of *Miracle at St. Anna* is a site of fantasy and metaphysical affirmation, it is also a site of excavation. As Hector stares out at the Atlantic, the film replaces the official history of World War II as a war for democracy with the visual assertion that, in Derek Walcott's famous words, "The sea is History."[18] As Hector stares out at the sea, this body of water becomes the monument to the Buffalo Soldiers who were earlier seen splayed out in the Serchio River and to the sixty million and more who were taken by the sea in the middle passage, in exercises of colonial domination, in wars and greater wars. Following up on the film's earlier disavowal of Black war heroism, punctuated by the exits from the portrait, this final scene disrupts the connections between the proper channeling of Black militant energy and the solution to the "Negro problem," between an integrated military abroad and a united populace at home, between the stability of the American family and the soldier returning home. These are the very connections that were forged in US diplomacy, foreign policy, and popular culture as the country rose to global hegemony after World War II.

If we read this wartime film in the context of its historical present, we can understand its narrative as a kind of prehistory of perpetual war, a prehistory that situates anti-Black racial terror, and Black resistance to it, at the center of a meditation on US military, corporate, and juridical power. Hector, alone on the beach, staring into the sea, communicates loss and displacement. The sea is a symbol of erasure and a site of insurgent retrieval. Holding the histories of Black experience on the *other* side of terror, it disrupts the homeward impulse of the World War II film to tell a story of dislocation and homelessness in a world now structured by security apparatuses, safety devices, and a never-ending war to protect the fantasy of a multiracial homeland. That colonial fantasia serves as the premise for this disruption only indicates how the film remains circumscribed by the very apparatus it critiques. With this contradiction in mind, I turn to the stories about Black Iraq war enlisters and their cultural armor; the disruptions they effect are, too, limited but significant.

Gulf Triangulations

The camera captures snapping fingers and wriggling hips as Whitley Gilbert, Kimberly Reece, and Jaleesa Vincent offer you a surprise performance of "Boogie Woogie Bugle Boy." It is January 10, 1991, a Thursday night. Operation Desert Shield, the build-up phase of the what was known as the Persian Gulf War, is about to give way to Operation Desert Storm, a five-week naval and aerial bombardment. Upwardly mobile Black folks are must-see TV, and these Black collegians have kick-ball-changed into living rooms all over the United States on Cliff Huxtable's heels.

In "War and Peace," an episode of the *Cosby Show* spin-off *A Different World* (January 10, 1991), Blair Underwood guest stars as Zelmer Collier, a PhD student and army reservist who is visiting his alma mater before deploying to Saudi Arabia for the 1991 Iraq war. The characters, students at the fictitious HBCU Hillman College, come to accept and celebrate Zelmer's deployment in the face of protests against the war and against the sense that Zelmer in particular should be spared because he is so close to finishing his dissertation and joining the small elite of the Black doctorate. The episode revolves around Zelmer's longtime friend and *A Different World*'s leading male character, Dewayne Wayne (Kadeem Hardison), who refuses to accept Zelmer's mission or participate in the farewell party that culminates in the "Boogie Woogie" performance. A mind is a terrible thing to waste, after all, and Dewayne looks up to Zelmer, calling him a "genius" and his "brother." Zelmer, too, wavers in his resolve and eventually asks the Hillman math professor and veteran Colonel Taylor (Glynn Turman) to help him find a way out, crying to Taylor, "I'm a Black man in the prime of my life!" The end of the episode is mournful yet resolute. Zelmer accepts his mission and arrives at Dewayne's apartment to say good-bye. Dewayne, now resigned to Zelmer's fate, sets the timer on his camera, points it at Zelmer, and places it on the television. He joins Zelmer on the sofa, and the men proceed to wrap their arms around each other. They half smile, a shutter clicks, the image freezes, the credits roll. Behind the credits, the photograph shrinks and is framed with a white border, as in a family album or scrapbook, so that the photograph takes on the status of "real" artifact.

Like *A Different World*'s episode about the AIDS epidemic or the one about divestment from South Africa or the one about the Rodney King riots, "War and Peace" showcased the sitcom's commitment to exploring the pressing social and political questions facing what could then, in the late 1980s and early 1990s, still somewhat innocently be called "the Black community." The photograph brings gravitas to that commitment. The omission of the closing-credit music that ends each episode turns the conclusion of this episode into a moment of silence during which you might even expect the kind of televisual memorial that often flashes before the credits to honor the life of a deceased producer, director, or actor. It is a futural memorial for those who will fall in the Iraq war and a visual cry that echoes, so to speak, the calls for "peace in the Middle

East" that permeated 1990s hip hop culture and provided, at their very best, what Fred Moten terms a "refreshment" of radical solidarity for Black scholars and writers.[19] The diminishing photo captures the manifold and conflictual identities that Zelmer Collier embodies: patriot and race man, scholar and soldier, lone wolf and sacrificial lamb.

The Black Iraq war soldier is a figure that contemporary Black feminist theorists have turned to in critical histories of post–Cold War power. M. Jacqui Alexander, for example, argues that the United States gained consent for the 1991 Iraq war by projecting images of hypermasculine soldiers of benevolence. These soldiers were usually racialized as white in media circulated abroad, but they were "sometimes racialized as black" in domestic media "to signal a dutiful return to family." In the years that separated the invasion of Kuwait in 1991 and the invasion of Iraq in 2003, partly as a result of the September 11 attacks, the United States became more invested in promulgating the war against terror as the reason for the security state's being and the primary ideological basis for protecting the security state's class interests. For Alexander, the nation's drive to expulse or cordon off the internal threat of the (dark) naturalized citizen or immigrant and, at the same time, to conquer the threat of an external enemy was so urgent that, she wrote, "there is no task that can legitimately rival this in terms of enormity; no ideological boundary that will not be contravened in its service."[20]

Indeed, the appearance of the Black soldier in the visual culture that circulated through the era of the Iraq wars, sanctions, and occupation is proof of the enormity of the security state's task of gathering to itself narratives of national family that were expanding their race and gender boundaries. As Wahneema Lubiano argues in her reading of a New York Times photograph of a Black soldier returning from the 1991 war to the United States and embracing his daughter, the image of the Black Iraq war soldier not only calls attention to the disproportionate representation of Black people in the US military but also invests pleasure and moral rectitude in the sight of Black soldiering in, or against, the (Muslim) third world. She writes, "That photo and that pose evoke the 'Black family' in all of its distorted and pathos-filled narrative glory. There he stands: the 'missing' Black father aesthetically and sentimentally inscribed on the full page of the New York Times with his child." The Black soldier "steps into both patriarchal and warrior glory."[21] Black military visuality thus follows up on the intensification of anti-Black policing that progressed throughout the second half of the twentieth century and presents itself as one medium in which we can watch what Lubiano refers to elsewhere as the state's "aestheticized disciplining" of Black gender and sexuality, or "the aesthetics of state repression dressed up in Blackface, in slogans of responsibility, in increased attention to Black self-help, in Black military or militarylike trappings, in the valorization of Black male self-assertion predicated on the silencing of women, of Black gay males, of anyone who falls outside of the parameters of the Black nationalist 'family.'"[22] Commercial films of the 1990s followed up on this articulation of state power through the same valorization and habituation of Black masculine military cool that suffused commonsense Black nationalism throughout the post-civil-rights era. In *Glory*, *The Siege*, *Rules of Engagement*, *Three Kings*, and *Courage under Fire*, the Black soldier speaks for home and homeland, converting the energies of protest captured by the appearance of Negroes with Guns into labor on behalf of US empire.

In "War and Peace," Zelmer Collier joins this mission of projecting consent for the war in the Gulf through the frame of commonsense values of familial and military honor associated with certain strands and tenets of Black nationalism. He also foresees the mission and imperial ethos assigned to Black soldiers in US visual culture in the war on terror: to exemplify the righteousness of US military action in Iraq, in the Afghanistan-Pakistan borderlands, and in North Africa by extending projections of heroic military masculinity onto an ever-widening array of racial subjects and to perform this symbolization not exclusively but especially in visual media. Black Americans were positioned as ideal patriots throughout the years of the George W. Bush administration, during which the war on terror proceeded as what Bush called "a war to save civilization itself."[23] As Cynthia Young argues, "From the onset of the 'war on terror,' Black Americans have been front and center in foreign policy debates, in televisual representations, and in military troop depictions, positioned as charismatic US ambassadors."[24] These real-life ambassadors (Colin Powell, Condoleezza Rice) and their fictional analogues in counterterrorism television series (characters like David Palmer on Fox's *24* and Jonas Blane on CBS's *The Unit*, both played by Dennis Haysbert) "call up the pain and violence of slavery and segregation only to disavow its continuing salience and justify a post-9/11 racial order that discriminates against Arabs and Muslims."[25]

As US visual culture relied increasingly on Black representatives of counterterrorism to embody the promise of US multicultural democracy, the Black soldier surfaced over and again in film, television, photojournalism, social media, and ephemera to dissimulate the racialist frame of the war on terror. As Sohail Daulatzai argues, the war on terror replayed "the unresolved racial dramas of U.S. power," projecting the benevolence of US democracy through the appearance of Black achievement and Black agency for foreign policy.[26] The increasing production of symbolic Black first-world power after 9/11—reaching its apotheosis in the election of President Barack Obama in 2008—extended the strategies and concessions that Black liberals forged during the Cold War, when "the rhetoric of 'anticommunism' birthed a heightened American nationalism" as "influential Black liberals who sought to gain concessions on domestic civil rights supported violent American foreign policy throughout Africa and Asia."[27] Black American agency for the war on terror, best displayed by Colin Powell's 2003 speech before Congress justifying the invasion and occupation of Iraq but also evinced by the more mundane performances of Black enlistment and war-making in the media and public sphere—the woman pleading for your maternal assent to her choice to enlist; the reluctant warrior revealing that his postgraduate years are weighted with a deadly debt to family, community, and nation—reinforce "the philosophical basis of 'color blindness' by promoting an American triumphalism in which a pan-racial enemy (the Muslim) threatens a multicultural America."[28]

The interpellation of Black military performance into the epistemological framework of the war on terror, hinging on the racialization of Islam and Islamism as the imperial West's mortal enemy, was part of an epistemic shift—again, a catalysis—in racialization following the 9/11 attacks. The rhetorical displacement and representational triangulation of Black and brown domestic populations within an "Axis of Evil" required their reconceptualization as foreign threat via a strategy that scholars such as Melanie McAlister and Daniel Widener refer to as "military multiculturalism," a legacy of the Cold War, a structure of feeling advanced by media representations of a color-blind military. Such representations, as Widener argues, give ethical justification for the war against terror.[29]

Journalism, television, and film worked to create affective attachment to new policies and practices of surveillance, detention, interrogation, invasion, and occupation after the September 11 attacks.[30] These same media forms foregrounded Black statespersons, police officers, and military personnel, endowing war stories with a liberal-humanist gravitas. Films such as *Antwone Fisher* (dir. Denzel Washington, 2002) and *The Hurt Locker* (dir. Kathryn Bigelow, 2008); television series such as *The L Word* (Showtime, 2004–9), *Army Wives* (Lifetime Television, 2007–), *In Treatment* (HBO, 2008–10), and *Empire* (Fox, 2015–); and advertisements such as "Mother Daughter," "For Myself" (a US Army commercial in which a young Black man confesses to his father that it is time for him to take responsibility and "do something" for himself), and the public service announcement in which Michelle Obama and Jill Biden visit Sesame Street to urge viewers to support military families all conflate projections of multiculturalism, with the Black character serving as a beacon of new US power, and the everyday imaginary of Black military achievement that, *along with* representations of innate Black criminality and maternal pathology, anchor post-civil-rights public and visual discourses in the United States. The Black soldier-patriot enacts a crucial series of makeovers: Negroes with Guns become protectors of first-world freedoms; menaces to society become noble grunts; fatherless sons become dutiful patriarchs; the diasporic dispossessed become hometown heroes; would-be welfare mothers become marriageable, upwardly mobile sisters and daughters; and soul brothers and soul sisters become patriots fighting for the soul of America. If, as Frank Wilderson suggests, "*Antwone Fisher* begins by assuming that Black masculinity *is* the law (naval officers and ensigns) rather than a void created by the force of law," the larger post-9/11 cinematic field in which the fictional Black solider appears throws into relief, indeed, the shift in racialization within the larger political field that makes such an assumption not only possible but immanent and necessary.[31]

This reconstitution of the global racial order did not spontaneously transform over the decade between *A Different World*'s "War and Peace" capsule episode and the September 11 attacks. The changes in the articulation of racial power that culminated in hyperpublic performances of Black agency for US imperial domination had been churning since World War II, as I noted earlier. First, over the post-1945 period, the

US government codified in law the extension of the protections of citizenship to Black people even as it engineered the largest growth in the industry of human cages in history, which resulted not only in mass incarceration for the US Black population but also in the banalization and militarization of everyday modes of surveillance, harassment, and capture. Incorporation into the formal democratic processes of state and capital, that is, was accompanied—and monitored—by the intrusion of militarized state and capital into every area of Black life.

Second, Black enlistment could be used to bolster the narrative of the military as the advance guard of desegregation and multicultural democracy. Black employment in the military, of course, provided one of the few paths to the federal civil service. With the construction of the permanent war economy and the sprawling military-industrial complex after World War II, the US armed forces became a "mercenary army of the poor," in Gordon's words, with the military being "the wealthiest and only functional (and popularly legitimate) social welfare department of the United States."[32] By the time Zelmer Collier had survived the tax cuts, unemployment, and rising poverty level of the 1980s, he would face a stark choice: don a government-issued uniform with its government-issued weapon or adapt to a life of "saturation policing" on the home front.[33] Indeed, since the beginning of the "all-volunteer" military in 1973, Black enlistment rates have topped Black population rates, reaching a high of 28 percent in 1979. While this rate dropped in 1990–91 and continues to decline, Black people still enter the armed forces at higher rates than white enlisters.[34]

Third, the development of the intellectual and political institutions of the Far Right and the rise of Black conservatives like Colin Powell, Ward Connerly, and Clarence Thomas provided the script for the imperial grammar that organized knowledge about the permanent security war that became the official war on terror. Colin Powell, in particular, emerged as perhaps the most important intellectual and military figure providing support and rationale for the Iraq wars. As a Vietnam War veteran, Powell was an ideal spokesman for the promises of the casualty-free, asymmetrical warfare that would correct the failures of the earlier war. At the same time, he drew on the practice in briefing that he earned as a young major in Vietnam, where he investigated the mass rape and massacre at My Lai and covered it up, writing up a report suggesting "relations between American soldiers and the Vietnamese people are excellent."[35] As Young offers, it was Powell's "stagecraft" as a public speaker, his self-presentation as a "reluctant warrior," his self-cultivation as a "black Horatio Alger" that made him the "ideal ambassador to an international (and national) audience suspicious of US Empire."[36]

As public grammars of multiculturalism and colorblindness obfuscated the state's surveillance, incarceration, and extermination of Black people, which proceeded by targeting racialized, gendered figures of deviance—the drug dealer on one hand, the welfare mother on the other—they dissimulated the reproduction and reracialization of the category of *enemy*, which occurred in tandem with a number of Cold War and post–Cold War military actions: in Cuba in 1961, in the Dominican Republic and Vietnam in 1965, in Argentina in 1973, in Grenada in 1983, in Panama in 1989 (when General Colin Powell, as Bush's chairman of the Joint Chiefs of Staff, supported the attack and also helped to develop the administration's public relations strategy), in Kuwait against Iraq in 1991, and so on.[37] Consider the statements of the Tuskegee fighter pilot and Air Force general Daniel "Chappie" James, quoted at the beginning of the military pamphlet *Black Americans in Defense of Our Nation*, first published by the Office of the Deputy Assistant Secretary of Defense for Equal Opportunity and Safety Policy in 1982: "My mother used to say: don't stand there banging on the door to opportunity, then, when someone opens it, you say, wait a minute, I got to get my bags. You be prepared with your bags of knowledge, your patriotism, your honor, and when somebody opens that door, you charge in."[38] The spectral presence of the Black mother that accompanies the portrait of the patriotic Black soldier signaled the intimacy between the picture of Black soldiering and state scripts for "safe" Black femininity. As Lubiano argued in 1996, "In the dominant imaginary, the United States is threatened from within by Black men and the drug trade and by Black women and their culture of poverty. The threat from within prepares the ground by which the American public recognizes the threat from without."[39]

The fundamental change in the nature of threat over the course of the late–Cold War period meant that policing and other forms of racial violence mounted in the name of security were built on modern paradigms of racial differentiation but also depended on the production of new racial subject positions, namely, positions invested with *both* irreducible racial difference and exorbitant state power, the magical combination that rendered Condoleezza Rice, Colin Powell, Barack and Michelle Obama, Susan Rice, Kamala Harris, and other Black law- and policy makers exemplars of triumphalist discourses of US democracy. ("Only in America," Barack Obama would repeat with near-obsessive frequency, "is my story even possible.") Given this transformation in the social and political value of racial difference, according to Nikhil Singh, "forms of past racial ordering are only partially predictive of racial (or nonracial) futures."[40] And, more importantly for us, Singh argues, "If Blackness has been the principal figure and ground for defining and enacting a racialized *inhumanity*, particularly in U.S. history, it has also proven to be at once analogically flexible and only one part of a heterogeneous repertoire of racializing motifs that have in turn informed the creation of a heterogeneous military-policing apparatus at home and abroad."[41] That 9/11 was a "trigger event" in this resettling of the global regime of race is evident in official narratives of the September 11 attacks. By the tenth anniversary of 9/11, for example, the chairman and president/CEO of the NAACP could write that in retrospect, "the magnitude of what we faced allowed us to put our personal differences—race, class, culture and faith—into context and stand together for common values: Freedom. Justice. Love." And now, "Ten years have passed since that fateful day. Life has returned to a new normal for our country, and mercifully, we have gone back to our daily lives. But we are different now, changed. Our September 11th experience allowed us to see and feel a higher unity, however briefly. This is the lesson we must never forget."[42] The NAACP's new Black normal, a political position in which racial difference is sublated to universal values of the European Enlightenment to which the first-world Black patriotic subject can now claim unproblematic access, is premised on identification with "our country" ("*however brief*") and the elision of the misery of the global majority. The Black soldier, as a historical and fictional figure, enmeshed identification with country; in the Iraq wars, the Black soldier became a major player in the racial "war of position" that Omi and Winant theorized in 1986, emerging as important coauthor in the discursive regime of neoliberal multiculturalism.[43]

One way to register this coauthorship is to interrogate how popular culture engaged the fictions of Black military agency. When HBO's original series *In Treatment* premiered in 2008, for example, Blair Un-

derwood played Alex Prince, an elite Navy pilot who undergoes psycho-
therapy after bombing a school in Iraq. I want to briefly comment on *In
Treatment* as a way of further exposing the relationship between terror,
visuality, and race that the Black soldier in the war on terror literally
brings into view. The half-hour serial ran five days each week for three
seasons. Starring Gabriel Byrne as Dr. Paul Weston, the series revolves
around Paul's psychoanalytic sessions with his patients—among others, a middle-aged immigrant from Calcutta who is grieving his wife,
an architecture student struggling with lymphoma, and a young doctor
named Laura who declares her love for Paul early in the series—and his
sessions with his own analyst. In Alex's first Tuesday-morning session
with Paul, Alex confesses that he is a pilot who killed sixteen Iraqi boys
at a school on the outskirts of Baghdad when acting on possibly faulty
naval intelligence identifying the religious school as a safehouse for insurgents.[44] Prior to therapy, Alex suffered a heart attack after pushing
himself and his gay friend and running buddy Daniel to run a much
longer distance than their usual six to ten miles ("He wanted to stop.
Little bitch. But I wasn't going to stop."). Alex collapses at twenty-two
miles, dies, and is revived. He starts therapy shortly afterward, seeking
support for two major decisions: to return to Iraq to visit the site of the
ambush, and to leave his wife.

That the analytic encounter is precipitated by Alex's acting out a stock
scene of Black American masculinity—John Henry against the steam
shovel, or *Run, nigger, run*, or *Keep this nigger boy running*—means that,
in some way, Alex comes to Paul to work through the very fact of his
Blackness or, perhaps more specifically, the complications of gender, of
sex, and of trauma that issue from the Black soldier's intimate experience of Gulf combat. After eight sessions, during which Alex discusses
his return to Baghdad, his separation from his wife, his sexual relationship with Paul's patient and love interest Laura, his fear that he might
be gay, and his childhood trauma, he dies under suspicion of suicide. In
season 2, Alex's father (Glynn Turman) visits Paul seeking restitution for
Alex's death, which he blames on therapy.

In Treatment offers a troubling example of the way Black agency
within stories of empire globally embed and circulate anxieties about the
Middle East. Based on verbatim translations of the Israeli series *BeTipul*,
known for its shoot-and-cry motif, *In Treatment* adapts the character

Yadin, a fighter pilot who seeks treatment after bombing a Palestinian apartment complex, for Underwood's Alex Prince. Alex is not the innocent, reluctant warrior heading off to war that Underwood captured with his earlier performance as Zelmer Collier. Here he is the war-worn master pilot returning "home" with the burden of a PTSD that issues not only from front-line combat in Iraq but also from the history of homegrown terrorism against Black people. Alex's therapy begins with a question that reveals *In Treatment*'s interest in the relationship between overlapping terrors of anti-Blackness and counterinsurgent warfare through Black male gender-sexual panic and competition. "Do you recognize me?" he asks Paul. The question is a practical one—Alex wants to inform Paul that he is the infamous "Madrassa Murderer" that has been featured in the news—but we could also read it as an existential inquiry.

Alex's question announces the ocular basis of racial subjection, as, for example, Fanon describes in *Black Skin, White Masks* when, following Hegel, he asserts that it is on recognition by the Other that one's "human worth and reality depend" but insists that mutual recognition is impossible for the Black in the first place because he is "an object in the midst of other objects" and in the second place because the abolition of slavery proceeded without the violent struggle necessary for mutual recognition. "There is not an open conflict between white and Black," Fanon writes. "One day the White Master, *without conflict*, recognized the Negro slave." For Fanon, the former slave needs a challenge to his humanity; the slave desires to "*make* himself recognized."[45] By triangulating the Iraqi in the Western racial encounter, *In Treatment* reimagines the Fanonian "racial primal scene," a scene of intrusion "in which the Black subject comes into self-knowing through the traumatic recognition of its utter objecthood in another's eyes."[46] Here, crucially, the question of recognition enacts the same interruption, or redirection, of Black visuality that post-9/11 visual culture imagines over and again. By staging a neocolonial encounter between Alex and an Iraqi in US-occupied Baghdad, *In Treatment* reimagines the relationship between Black visuality and the US racial regime: no longer *simply* a phobic imago, the image of the Black man, in particular, offers assurance and protection. As Young puts it, "We feel good about the nation because we feel bad about America's white supremacist past, and we feel good about antiterrorist violence because we feel good about antiracist self-defense."[47]

Alex, played by Blair Underwood, tells his psychiatrist about exchanging looks with an Iraqi civilian after bombing his village, in *In Treatment*, season 1, episode 7 (2008).

This is a complex equation that *In Treatment* stages on the ground of triangular recognition.

Alex is not *recognized* when he engages in a battle with a white master—although the physical fight he later has with his analyst may leave this open to debate—or *misrecognized* when he is hailed by a frightful white child on a crowded street in Lyon. Rather, he opens up the question of recognition, "Do you recognize me?" when he returns to Iraq to face, literally, the damage he has wrought. Alex returns to the madrassa that he bombed, this time with a church group, in order to see things up close, to see if he can feel anything. After his return from Baghdad, he confesses to Paul that at the site of the bombing, he felt numb. When Paul asks Alex to recall a moment when, there in Iraq, he thought he should have feelings but could not access them, Alex tells him about an encounter he had on the street where he dropped the bomb:

> I don't know if this is what you're looking for. But there was a moment when this old man came over to me. He had been burned. His arm was bandaged. He kept looking at me with a strange little smile. [*Speaks in Arabic*] *Ana ba'rafak.* Which means, "I know you. I know you." I ignored him at first but a couple minutes later, he was back. "I know you. I *know*

you," he kept saying. For a second, I thought he did recognize me, but I didn't really believe that. I doubt he'd ever seen the internet, but in some deep, intuitive way, he knew. He knew I was the man that destroyed the whole street we were standing on.[48]

The Iraqi looking back at the Black, the Black looking back at himself: Alex tells Paul it was "like a totally bizarre dream" and that the old man was "kind of amused, kind of friendly"; meanwhile, he himself stood there frozen, and a crowd gathered around them until one of Alex's cotravelers pulled him away. The moment of transfixion that Alex describes pictures the scene of ruin in Baghdad as the terrain of an emergent Black subjectivity. The quadruple repetition of "I know you," which Alex himself translates, performs this emergence for Paul, giving Paul, Alex hopes, "what [he is] looking for." In Alex's performance of the scene for Paul, the old man sees through him, and Alex sees through the old man. This picture of intimacy, premised on a mutual transparency that hinges on Alex's embodying both captor-subject (he is the looking subject who comes to survey the damage he has caused) and captive-object (he is caught within the diegetic *and* extradiegetic Negrophobic gaze), projects Iraq as a cypher for racial play. The street scene that Alex recounts is an acting out, or at least a rehearsal, of new scenarios of global racial formation.[49]

While the terrorist Arab-Muslim did not replace domestic Black men as the primary target for surveillance and capture, post-9/11 culture effected a layering of significations in the way that *In Treatment* does, in effect reminding the audience that the United States was once victorious in domesticating the threat of destruction vis-à-vis Black nationalism. Alex's performance of being "known" as an author of violence in Iraq, that is, invites the audience to gaze on him not with the fear of a white boy on the street (*Look, a negro!*) but with the interested curiosity, and the intention to pet, with which one approaches a horse or an elephant one has tamed. Alex's capacity and willingness to exert violence on the ungrievable lives of the Iraqis sanitizes the fear of his acting out that violence on the white family.[50] Alex's translation of "I know you," then, is a projection of Blackness's imperial grammar, a reminder that he has already been known and, accordingly, endowed with the power to visit violence on the still-unknown terrorist.

Blackness in the frame of the war against and occupation of Iraq makes visible how the metanarrative of the wars in the Middle East resignify what counts as livable life by filtering racialized significations of criminality and deviance through new scenarios of discovery and recognition.[51] As Judith Butler notes, "grievability is a presupposition for the life that matters." And notions of the human inscribed in the very perceptible reality that media organize establish which lives are grievable and which are not: "The field of perceptible reality is one in which the notion of the recognizable human is formed and maintained over and against what cannot be named or regarded as the human—a figure of the non-human that negatively determines and potentially unsettles the recognizably human."[52] Given how perceptible reality demarcates the human that can be grieved and the life that cannot, the various forms of photography that have represented the post-9/11 wars within the Western English-speaking world have traded on the photograph's "distinctive capacity to establish grievability as a precondition of a knowable human life."[53] For Butler, for example, the detainees who were tortured at Abu Ghraib "do not readily conform to a visual, corporeal, or socially recognizable identity; their occlusion and erasure become the continuing sign of their suffering and of their humanity."[54] In the scene of looking that Alex describes, two subjects at the edge of the human gaze upon each other at empire's new frontier. This gazing ultimately preserves humanity for the white consumer (or analyst, in this case) on whom the ultimate decision about who is deserving of human life belongs, but the white analyst's humanity cannot be protected without the *fantasy* that the Black soldier and the Iraqi civilian can both be known and mastered.

The scenario of recognition in *In Treatment* transforms the armed Black man into a magical character who transfigures terror. Here, terror cannot be the seared-apart or popped-open flesh of the African captive or the burned metatarsals hanging from a branch pulled downward by its corpulent mass; it cannot be sensed in the bloated nonbody that viewers could not bear to see but could not bear not to see as they filed past the open casket at that South Side church or opened that summer 1955 *Jet* magazine; it cannot be what you might have heard when the incarcerated persons at the Metropolitan Detention Center banged their hypothermic fists on walls and windows and bars; and it certainly cannot be what you might feel if you are Black and there is a police cruiser in your rearview. In this scenario of recognition, the anti-Blackness that has been synonymous with terrorism is displaced by Alex's—and the HBO viewer's—liberal regard. The encounter on the Baghdad street, in which Blackness becomes knowable both to the old Iraqi civilian and to the US viewing audience, surfaces Alex's humanity as that which occludes what Calvin Warren refers to as the Black's "ontological insecurity."[55] The picture of the Black soldier who is known by the known Iraqi, who is penetrated by the analyst, who is sympathetic to an American television consumer, in this way, colludes with the long war on terror's tendency to put Blackness on display both as a target of suspicion and as a glamorous cover for the anti-Black terror that must be actively *un*known.

We see Alex see himself seeing the Iraqi who is seeing him. This is a chain of looks that ties Black intimacy with global warfare to the viewer's faith in the curative value of racial difference within the (therapeutic) scene of nightly television. In war-devastated Iraq, *In Treatment*'s Black analysand comes face-to-face with the worst of himself: his capacity for brute violence against potential "terrorists." This capacity makes Alex knowable to the old man on the street. But it is also the entry point into his own self-recognition and, importantly, the audience's recognition. As Alex describes the scene on the street, the camera pans toward him from the lower right, establishing a tight close-up. Slow piano music accompanies his description of the encounter in Baghdad, drawing the viewer into the scene sonically. The music sounds so much like the new-age music of meditation tapes and massage salons that Paul's response to Alex—"You could be describing a mystical experience, like a dream"—confirms the sonic mood of otherworldliness.

The intimacy that the camera establishes with the close-up empha-sizes how Alex's agency is inextricably bound to his capacity to act au-thoritatively on behalf of the US state and then to confront the emotional fallout of that capacity. The careful construction of this intimacy in turn establishes him as a sympathetic character for the series. Alex, in other words, is a subject not only of imperial grammar, where he occupies the second-person "you" who must be reseen and reknown if empire is to prevail, but also of Black imperial agency, where he feels and desires the nation's imperial domination in his heart of hearts. The compassionate Black warrior, that is, invites identification in the place of Negrophobia.

When Alex explains that the way the Iraqi on the street looked at him approximates how his father looks at him—"like he knows my secrets, like no matter what I do, I can't hide from it"—he recognizes himself not only as captor-subject but also as captive-object; he is "frozen there," as he remembers, trapped in the Iraqi's gaze. The recollection in this way offers a crucial revision of the "specular intrusion" of the street scene that Fanon describes in *Black Skin, White Masks*.[56] Here the fear that in Fanon's analysis belonged to a white French boy, the fear that he would be eaten up by the Black man, is transfigured into a meeting of vulnerabilities, a staging of shared precariousness, wherein both the Black analysand and the Iraqi object of analysis, even while acting out a scene of mutual recognition, are offered up for consumption by an audience hungry for both protection from terror and sanctuary from the guilt that the nation's own history of terror induces.[57]

In the context of the war on terror, in which the cinematic appearance of the Black soldier is tied to the political rationalities of counterinsurgency (the policies and practices of containing insurgency) and counterterror (which is the civilizational struggle against fear itself, which shows up both in counterinsurgent actions and in the everyday forms of surveillance and crisis management both abroad and at home), visual media play a major role in making over Negroes with Guns—the specter of armed Black soldiers that has haunted the national imaginary since the Civil War—from armed threat to armed protectorate. As Young argues, the representation of Black soldiers as compassionate warriors "pretends that Black, male bodies are no longer vulnerable to random and systematic attack. Consequently, antiterrorist violence maps onto antiracist resistance in a way that validates US Empire and Black equality simultaneously."[58] Significantly, Alex's guilt, which smooths the way for viewers' compassion just as Powell's performances as the reluctant warrior smoothed the way for the devastating occupation of Iraq, is a substitute for what would certainly be righteous anger and what could certainly be a political response.

In Treatment's format aids the excavation of the emotional vulnerability of the Black male soldier that actually covers over his existential vulnerability. Therapy sessions in *In Treatment* are structured mainly by two-shot sequences composed of medium close-ups, and the major innovation of the show's "modular" format was that it was aired five days a week, creating the illusion that the viewer was accompanying Paul in his everyday work as a therapist. The camera language is mimetic—unobtrusive and unselfconscious—and it is meant to give the audience members the sense of being in the room, ourselves in treatment for what ails us. The diegesis is occupied, almost singularly, by Paul's home office (one exception being when Paul leaves the office to attend Alex's funeral). Even as *In Treatment's* attempt to mimic the scene of the talking cure as closely as possible constrains nearly the entire diegesis to two-shot sequences that take place in Paul's office, the show's display of the Black male subject's hostility and vulnerability draws on a history of US racial terror in order to bring the war on terror into an ethical and epistemological frame based in norms of recognition and grievability. In this way, *In Treatment* enlists Black military visuality to provoke an innovation in television programming. (One reviewer described how Underwood "smolders and brims with intensity.")[59]

The positioning of Blackness in the frame of the Iraq wars stages a series of ghostly encounters like the one Alex recounts in *In Treatment*, in which one subject/object of terror faces another. Given US visual culture's obsession with Black men's failed paternity, and the show's psychoanalytic premise, one could predict what happens when Alex likens the old Iraqi's piercing eyes to his father's. Paul, of course, asks his patient why the old man reminds him of his father. Alex tells him that his father killed his grandfather with his bare hands, explaining that his father was doing labor-organizing work in Oklahoma in the 1950s and that when a lynch mob attacked his father's house, they shot Alex's uncle and aunt. When Alex's father and grandfather hide in the boiler room, Alex's father accidentally suffocates his grandfather while trying to quiet his wheezing, hacking cough. Alex's father goes undetected by the mob and survives. The accidental death in the boiler room and the encounter on a desolate Baghdad street, projected against an analytic encounter that is structured in Paul's fear of Alex's sexual prowess (the competition over Paul's patient Laura), constitute Alex's two most formative traumatic experiences: one, a Black-on-Black patricide forced by an intruding white mob, and the other, a crucial revision of the "Fanonian moment" in which the Black man is indeed "known," or recognized, in a triangulated racial formation rooted in the structures of feeling of the post-9/11 world.[60]

If the Black soldier appears on the glossy and glassy surfaces of twenty-first-century media—television screens, Oscar-nominated films, recruitment posters—to announce the war on terror as a civilization-scale struggle to protect a multicultural way of life, this appearance redirects colonial formulas of identification. As Deborah Poole pointed out in her 1997 *Vision, Race, and Modernity*, modern power was constructed through visual technologies. "Racial theory built its classifications by comparing individuals with other individuals," she writes, "and then classifying them accordingly. Within each category or 'race,' individuals were considered equivalent to others as representatives of their kind. Across racial categories, individuals were compared for the purpose of assigning both identity and relative social worth."[61] This had particular implications for Black gender. As Maurice Wallace carefully recounts, for example, the emerging photographic technologies of the nineteenth century were guided by a "willful blindness" through which the looker could only see a spectral, virtual image of Black masculinity.[62] This "spectragraphic" attention to Black masculinity, which both invisibilized and hypervisibilized the Black (masculine) body, was the foundation for the "voyeuristic propensities" of the FBI, or FBEye, as Wallace calls it, in the late twentieth century.[63] In the global racial project of modernity, the sedimentation of racial categories based on phenotypical difference thus designated the ocular as a crucial terrain for the iteration of racial violence.

But if modern power announced its scopic function through the taxonomies of racial difference, neoliberal power is as invested in maintaining racial hierarchies as it is in puncturing them, that is, in making racialized subjects more and more intimate with war, accumulation, deregulation, and other processes that exacerbate conditions of premature death and in projecting that intimacy onto screens, large and small. As Jodi Melamed explains, "Privileged and stigmatized racial formations no longer mesh perfectly with a color line. Instead, new categories of privilege and stigma determined by ideological, economic, and cultural criteria overlay older, conventional racial categories, so that traditionally recognized racial identities—Black, Asian, white, or Arab/Muslim—can now occupy both sides of the privilege/stigma opposition."[64] The Black soldier, in this context, has emerged as the visible sign of neoliberal meritocracy: they inherit "the just deserts of multicultural global citizens while representing those neoliberalism has dispossessed"—including those who occupy the racialized categories of "criminal," "terrorist," or "enemy combatant"—"as handicapped by their own monoculturalism or other historico-cultural deficiencies."[65]

Yet, if the Black soldier occupies the center of contemporary "frames of war," marking out the lines of grievability, they situate the *ontological* question of grievability on the *historical* field, calling up overlapping histories of racial terror with their every appearance. These overlapping histories route Black militarism through the open circuits of terror: as when an electrical circuit lacks a complete path between its origin and its terminus or when the path of an electrical current is broken by an opening, the Black soldier's appearance on the scene of US imperial warfare disrupts official stories of counterterror by recalling the terrors and tortures of the Middle Passage and antebellum slavery, of broken promises and diasporas within diasporas, and of the white-supremacist violence that closed the psychic and political distance between lunch counter and lynching tree.

In this sense, the Black soldier's appearance both heralds the neoliberal project of a warfare state and promises that project's undoing. That appearance had been heralded since the early wars of empire and had even been trumpeted by the same deputy assistant secretary of defense for equal opportunity and safety policy whom Lorde, with tongue in cheek, referred to as a home girl. (In a letter to the reader prefacing the 1985 edition of *Black Americans in Defense of Our Nation*, Deputy Assistant Secretary Donna M. Alvarado saluted the Black Americans who "have contributed so much to the heritage, progress, and defense of our Nation.")[66] We could say that the Black soldier is an image of *common sense* that might set affectivity to work in the service of *good sense*: whether in a kitchen eating Cheerios, ogling Whitley Gilbert in a college bachelor pad, or retrieving traumatic memories on the therapist's couch, the Black soldier conjures the fantasy of violence either, or both, on behalf of or against country and Man.[67] Black military visuality has been mobilized, and continues to be articulated, through an ever-proliferating series of still and moving images of war pictured by and through uniformed Black subjects on this side of terror, projected onto and through Black eyes fighting to secure the "homeland." It fractures the texts that call on it to do narrative work, in effect mimicking the movement of trauma: making story fail and pushing history to the surface of the nightmares of the subject broken by wars both at home and abroad.

The Journey Home

You could be hearing the thuds of bodies against desert sand and the clang of hand grenades against metal right alongside the whisper of your fingers against the pages of an as-told-to memoir. You might then hear loud shots and the protestations of a sister crying out in pain from the Gulf desert: "I'm hit! I'm hit!" she yells.

The opening cries of *I'm Still Standing*, a 2010 memoir about US Army private Shoshana Johnson's detainment as a prisoner of war in Iraq in 2003, signal the relationship between the Iraq wars and visual culture that I am arguing might serve as the basis for our thinking about the appearance of the Black soldier in post-9/11 US culture and the various forms of post-9/11 Black diasporic expression in literature, television, and film. After the initial exclamations, Johnson writes, "It was like a line in a movie. But I was saying it."[68] Johnson had the distinction of being the United States' first Black female prisoner of war when she was captured by Iraqi rebels in the first weeks of the Iraq War, and the memoir's repeated returns to the movies—"We were all in some deep shit, the kind of shit you only see in the movies," Johnson writes three pages later—betray the memoir's desire to make its subject marketable within the complex of wartime spectacle and infotainment. Beginning in medias res, with shouts of anguish, the memoir draws the reader, from the first page, into a multisensory imagination of war that approximates, that begs to be, a screenplay. *I'm Still Standing*, doubly subtitled *From Captive U.S. Soldier to Free Citizen—My Journey Home*, is a cinematic text that probes the relationship between Blackness, war, media, captivity, and the eruptions of diasporic trauma into the narrative of the war against terrorism. It brings Black military visuality into the world of postmodern Black life narrative, provoking us to consider the open circuits of terror that splinter Black American literature and film and that rattle the stories of US freedom premised on the anti-Arab and anti-Muslim violence that flooded post-9/11 US culture.

I'm Still Standing is the result of a collaboration between Johnson and M. L. Doyle. Doyle, a former army soldier and fiction writer whose Master Sergeant Harper Mystery Series revolves around Lauren Harper, a Black American career soldier who finds herself in dangerous situations around the post–Cold War world. The memoir was the first of Doyle's two coauthored memoirs. Her other memoir, *A Promise Fulfilled: My Life as a Wife and Mother, Soldier and General Officer*, coauthored with Julia Jeter Cleckley, is a first-person narrative of the first African American woman to be promoted to flag officer in the Army National Guard. *I'm Still Standing* might be read alongside Doyle's other fiction and memoir as attempts to bring into literary expression Black women's achievements in the US military. But *I'm Still Standing* is unique in its attempt not only to bring an untold story to light but also to *correct* the gaps and errors within existing media stories of women in the US military. In Doyle's preface to the memoir, she recalls seeing Shoshana Johnson on *The Tonight Show with Jay Leno* while she was stationed in Germany. "She was beautiful, poised, bright, and articulate. She seemed so normal, so approachable, someone everyday Americans could relate to, and I wondered, like so many others did, why Jessica Lynch had been shoved before the cameras and not this brave, intelligent woman" (ix).

I'm Still Standing is an attempt to get Johnson's story *straight*, to represent Johnson as the "normal, approachable, good-hearted person" that appeared on Doyle's television (ix). To do this work, *I'm Still Standing* self-consciously indexes and self-consciously reimagines the media of US war. Like the first sentences, which position the reader, in medias res, as a visual and auditory witness in the scene of the ambush, Shana's recollection of "the movies" here writes *I'm Still Standing* into a larger cultural complex of war stories that includes not only Doyle's other texts about Black women in the US Army but also the mass-mediated visual texts that *I'm Still Standing* confronts throughout its recollections of Shana's captivity: war films, news coverage of combat, photographs of Jessica Lynch, US talk shows, and more. Indeed, Shana often imagines herself as a character in a narrative that is playing out on television. When she feels an explosion in her prison cell, she thinks, "I imagined what that huge explosion must have looked like and the damage it must have caused. During the First Gulf War, like everyone else, I had been fascinated watching CNN and the huge clouds of fire and smoke that billowed over Baghdad while we bombed the city. I imagined something like that had just happened, the geysers of flame and glowing sparks that flew in great fiery arches" (148). *I'm Still Standing*'s attempts to both intervene in and incorporate Johnson into readers' perceptions—*visual* perceptions—of the Iraq War drive the memoir's attention to both the norms of military/prison practice and the norms of visual framing. If, in Judith Butler's words, our task with respect to the photography of contemporary war is "to understand the operation of a norm circumscribing a reality that works through the action of the frame itself," our attention to *I'm Still Standing* might help us understand how Black women's framing within US war stories shifts the ground on which the categories of human and nonhuman are articulated and grasped.[69]

I'm Still Standing is structured by a split plot: a heritage plot that tells the story of Shoshana's growing up as a second-generation Panamanian immigrant, and the captivity plot that narrates her enlistment, her basic training, her deployment in Iraq, her capture by Iraqi rebels, her detainment, her liberation by marines, and her homecoming to Fort Bliss in Texas. The first twenty chapters of the memoir alternate between these two plots, shifting the focus from the desert ambush in chapter 1 ("A POW") to Shana's swearing in at twenty-five years old and her familial history in chapter 2 ("The Oath") to her being taken into custody by "wild-looking men" in chapter 3 ("Into Custody") to her giving birth to her daughter in chapter 4 ("Alone") and so on. These are short chapters that build readerly sympathy, emphasizing that Shana is a "normal" and "approachable" woman whom "everyday Americans could relate to," as Doyle pointed out, and, at the same time, that Shana's experiences as the "first" Black female prisoner of war make the story an exceptional one.

The double plot of *I'm Still Standing* depicts Shana as the noble grunt soldier, the innocent abroad who, like the US citizen-consumer, has little control over war policy or military tactics but bears the weight of war's consequences.[70] The memoir opens with a narrative of innocence. As Shana describes the scene of the ambush in the Iraqi desert, she describes the men and women in her unit as "lost lambs" who had "wandered into their killing field"; they are "trapped animals" in a pen (2). But as much as it emphasizes American innocence, the memoir calls attention to the contradictions of the war and the folly of Shana's deployment. Shana confesses that she did not know if the Iraq War "was the right thing to do"; "I didn't see the point," she says (37). A cook in the 507th Maintenance Company, Shana is deployed with a unit that maintains and repairs Patriot missile systems. She tells the story of ambush and capture from the perspective of surplus labor; as her unit's meals are either MREs or prepared by a civilian-operated dining facility, there is not much work for a cook to do. "I kept thinking that at some point, someone would figure out I wasn't needed in the heart of Iraq," Shana says, "but that never happened" (86). Shana's confessions of innocence and superfluity highlight her distance from military decision-making and offer the reader the illusion of innocence. If "the grunt soldier is innocent at the war's outset," Marita Sturken argues, "then the American public can identify through him with a sense of betrayal—we didn't know, we believed."[71] Against the backdrop of a highly contested war, the grunt soldier in fictional texts allows for the reader's cathartic release of anger and resentment issuing from this betrayal, a "cathartic absolution of guilt" that in turn actually mollifies antiwar sentiment.[72]

Johnson's memoir depicts Shana as the grunt who is, in some sense, every American; the narrative motor is the assumption that "everyday Americans" can relate to her. This assumption, though, is not grounded in the logic of sameness but rather in the magic of racial and gender difference. The text's attention to Shana's unique positioning as a respectable Black working-class woman from an immigrant army family projects the war against terrorism as a goodwilled US war to secure women's freedom and global, multiracial democracy. *I'm Still Standing* does nothing to contest the feminist master narrative of the war against terrorism, which has been "stubbornly focused on the ills of Taliban rule" but silent on US financial and arms support for the mujahideen, which amounted to "the largest covert operation in U.S. history since World War II."[73] Like *In Treatment*'s story of Alex Prince, *I'm Still Standing*'s exploration of Black enlistment triangulates racial sentiment such that the Iraq encounter allows for a revisiting or *visitation* of anti-Black terror. *In Treatment* exposes an originary racial-Oedipal drama that is then reinscribed and writ large as an imperial scene of Fanonian (non) recognition with the Iraqi on the street, whereas in Johnson's memoir, the adventure in Iraq, rendered through the Christian symbolics of redemption, calls up the history of US racial violence to clear a path, again, for absolution.

This cleansing proceeds through the memoir's driving binary between US and Iraqi gender ideals. Shana joins the army in pursuit of domestic stability. She enlists as a cook because she wants to become a pastry chef; and she explains, "I imagined that I could settle down on a military installation somewhere, cook great meals, have a nice apartment, save money, and maybe even go to school in the evenings" (11). She would be "surrounded by men," she imagines, and she "might meet a nice guy" (11). The memoir brings Shana's experiences as a single mother into the frame of the domestic good life that the army promises. The narrative of her parents' acceptance of her choice to become a single mother at twenty-seven—"They needed to let me know how disappointed in me they were, but after that initial anger, they have always been loving grandparents"—follows up on the memoir's attempt to wed Shana's single parenting to a politics of respectability (21). Shana's enlistment, too, extends a family tradition of military service. Central to the memoir's heritage plot is the story of migration; Shana recounts her family's move from Panama to California when she was five years old, explaining that her father was a fireman in Panama and that he enlisted in the army upon arrival to the United States. Afterward, the family relocated to Fort Lewis, Washington, then to Los Angeles, then to Fort Carson, Colorado, then to Fort Bliss, Texas, and then to Germany. The army is the family business, and Shana's enlistment is brought into the memoir's frame of domestic idealism and immigration in pursuit of the American dream.

Shana's respectability, secured through the promise of upward mobility that the army offers as well as through the depictions of her upbringing in a stable two-parent household, is thrown both into crisis and into relief when she is deployed in Iraq and shortly thereafter taken prisoner by Iraqis. One important terrain for this tension is hygiene and grooming, which symbolize femininity and respectability within the memoir's liberal feminist frame. Shana explains that she prepared to deploy by getting her hair braided, thinking she would be able to apply a curl relaxer to straighten her hair once she got settled in Kuwait or Iraq. When she and the other POWs are freed after twenty-two days of captivity, she complains to her mother on the phone about how unkempt her hair looks in the photograph of her that was circulating on the internet, which was taken shortly after the rescue. "That picture is going out all over the world, Mom. Worldwide, and I look like THAT! Hello!" (218). Shana's preparation for deployment also includes a trip to Victoria's Secret: "I had several matching girlie-looking bra-and-underwear sets and lots of lotions and bath gels. When you wear a uniform and combat boots, it's nice to have things that make you feel like a woman, things to remind you of your feminine side" (64). These are the "goodies" that Shana stocks up on. The memoir's attention to Shana's grooming and adornment—her hair, her lingerie, the tattoos intricately described in a chapter titled "Body Art"—emphasizes Shana's estrangement from US ideals of femininity. The text repeatedly displays her "feminine side," stripping her down to reveal her tattoos and nipple rings, to confess her affair to a married man, to show us her goodies. These details betray an anxiety about femininity, an anxiety for which the confessional mode of the life narrative compensates. The memoir also emphasizes Shana's bodily adornment as a Western freedom.

If *I'm Still Standing* exposes Shana's body to make her human, to make her woman, it keeps the women in Iraq and in Kuwait, where Shana is first stationed at Camp Virginia, hidden from sight altogether. As Shana leaves Camp Virginia for the first time, on a mission to retrieve equipment from the port and then return to Camp Virginia, she notices, "Some cars had curtains over the backseat and rear windows and I knew women were hidden behind them" (85). Shana's later experience as a POW is filtered through this framing of the Middle East as a gender-backward region in need of US intervention. When a uniformed Iraqi whom Shana has never seen comes to the small room in a storage facility where she is being held, asking if she is married in an "angry, almost accusatory tone," Shana fears her fate: "What if they simply handed me over to some man to keep? Would they force me to stay here as someone's wife? The idea was too awful to contemplate and I tried not to think about it" (186). Within a liberal feminist frame in which the Middle East represents gender and sexual deviance, turning out actually to be a liberal sexist frame, the memoir's depictions of Shana's wild hair and tattoos function as confession and penance—offering pictures of wayward femininity that the text assimilates in order to assert Shana's respectability as a Black American woman—and as symbols of Western women's agency, freedom, and choice.

If the memoir depicts Shana as an exemplar of Western freedom on whose behalf the Iraq War might be waged, though, racialized histories of forced passage, compulsory labor, and sexual violence haunt its depiction of her service to country. Take, for example, the memoir's recounting of one morning in captivity when Shana and the other POWs are served a breakfast and Shana is commanded to serve the male prisoners, or its account of how when Shana is rescued along with the other prisoners, she is forced to ride in the armored vehicle in the prone position: "I crawled on my hands and knees into the tiny space, moving as quickly as I could to the front. . . . Immediately the guys loaded into the LAV behind me so fast I didn't have time to sit up. I could only lie there, face-down in the back, my face in my arms" (203). The memoir's renderings of Shana standing on battered legs pouring tea and riding face down out of Iraqi captivity emphasize her unique position as a woman POW.

These renderings of Shana as a woman POW also present her body as a surface for inscriptions of both futural projections of US dominance and phantasmagorical markings of slavery. After she and the five other POWs are freed from Iraqi detainment, Johnson undergoes treatment in Kuwait before being transported for further medical attention in Germany. Here, she writes of the beginning of her journey "home": "We boarded a C-141, a large cargo plane that was filled with wounded on their way to Germany and the large Army hospital there. The wounded were on litters attached to the sides of the aircraft stacked five or six high. Some were almost covered in bandages; many were amputees. . . . It was hard to look at all of those young people so horribly maimed. I was strapped to a litter, but my wounds were minor" (222). The uncanniness of the image of disfigured men and women in a cargo ship strapped in and stacked up on their way from Global South to Global North is immediately juxtaposed with a scene of felicitous national identification. Shana climbs out of her litter to use the restroom, and as she hops on maimed legs to the bathroom, she recounts, "Soldiers and Marines held their hands out as support, steadying me, helping me along. . . . 'It's great to see you,' some of them said. 'So glad you're free,' they said" (223). In immediately disavowing the historicity of the trope of the cargo hold, *I'm Still Standing* turns away from the image of the middle passage that haunts it, marking Johnson's post-9/11 memoir as a first-person account hardly identifiable within the genealogy of Black American life-writing as a protest genre. More importantly, the memoir's figuration of visual recognition—its revelation that the other military personnel *see* Shana *free*—emphasizes the memoir's values of citizenship, safety, and belonging in a post-9/11 world in which there are no predictable enemies or friends.

As Shana narrates her captivity and her liberation from the Iraqis, the memoir emphasizes the relationship between visuality, recognition, and grievability. In *I'm Still Standing*, as in Abu Ghraib, photography is a terrain for marking out proximity to and distance from the human, a form that distinguishes between knowable, grievable lives and unknowable, ungrievable lives. For example, when Shana and the other prisoners are first captured in An Nasiriyah, they are transported to Baghdad. Once there, Shana explains, "The Iraqis took pictures of us and someone brought out a video camera. They didn't ask us any questions. They each wanted personal photos for their scrapbooks of the American captives. It was surprising that they didn't put themselves in the pictures, like tourists standing next to a celebrity. 'Hey, take a picture of me with the American POWs!'" (74). Shana's surprise at the composition of the photographs in Iraq—she is surprised that the Iraqis *do not* pose with their subjects—places this moment in conversation with the photographs from Abu Ghraib, in which soldiers did indeed pose with the prisoners they tortured.

Shana's consciousness of herself as a photographic subject, as a surface for inscriptions of both Iraqi and US fantasies, persists throughout the memoir, as when, later, the marines who free the American POWs pose for pictures with them or when, after Shana is captured, she sees herself on television. "It was odd to sit there and watch myself," she writes, "see the pictures that had been dredged up from my past flash across the screen and listen to strangers talk about my condition" (223). In these picturings of captivity and rescue, Shana sees herself and also sees herself being seen. "Hi, Mom. Hi, Dad," she says as she later waves to a camera (224). And if the memoir is interested in the optics of Shana's military experience, it is also invested in the optics of Iraqi civilians' war experiences. At the end of the memoir, Shana opines that the "Iraqis want a good life, and yes, they have humanity" (275). This affirmation, situated just before the memoir lists the fallen members of Shana's unit in its closing paragraphs, bolsters the memoir's liberal frame, shoring up rather than destabilizing the war on terror as a racial gendered regime of knowledge production and military assault. As Evelyn Alsultany argues, sympathetic portrayals of Arab-Muslim humanity have the ultimate effect of reinforcing rather than disrupting stereotypes of the Arab world.[74] In *I'm Still Standing*, affirmations of the humanity of Shana's

Iraqi captors surface throughout the memoir, forming an important piece of the liberal frame that pictures Shana as both unlikely hero and undeserving victim in the war on terror.

In order to bring Johnson into the heroic stories of the Iraq War and the War in Afghanistan, the memoir follows the formula of American life narratives, charting a course of moral uplift and national belonging won through personal struggle and positioning "the suffering body as an origin for U.S. citizenship."[75] But, like other military memoirs, it also registers disillusionment with the romantic image of war and depicts the protagonist as a victim rather than a hero.[76] These competing impulses of uplift and breakdown correlate to the memoir's fractured narration, which alternates between the heritage plot and the captivity story. *I'm Still Standing*'s use of photographs likewise captures the memoir's two competing aims of incorporating Shana into the master narratives of the US settler state and critiquing the particular strategies of US military operations.

In an analysis of the way the infotainment complex made Private Jessica Lynch a national heroine while representing Army Specialist Shoshana Johnson as unexceptional and unmarketable within the entertainment market, Rebecca Wanzo asks, "If we were to market a story about Johnson—African American, outside of traditional Western paradigms of beauty, with a biography as a Black single mother that automatically triggers criticism—how would we tell the tale so that she could be an object of sympathy and receive state and media attention?"[77] *I'm Still Standing* indeed is articulated on the ground of Wanzo's question; again, Doyle "wondered, like so many others did, why Jessica Lynch had been shoved before the cameras and not this brave, intelligent woman." As if to compensate for this absence in the mainstream visual culture of the war on terror, the memoir offers its own photographs. In the section of photographs that splits *I'm Still Standing* into two parts, pictures of Shoshana Johnson and her family and friends taken after her rescue lay beside photographs of Shana, her cousin Andre, and her father in army uniform. Here the image of Black agency for US militarism literally and figuratively splits the text in two. The images of Shana's celebration and homecoming—of the medical team that cared for her on her flight from Kuwait to Landstuhl, of her and her daughter at Disneyland, and of the Johnson family's annual Panamanian Fourth of July celebration—tell stories of recovery and perseverance after the folly of her deployment, while the photographs of the opposite page tell stories of faith in the promises of the army. "I'm all smiles when I pose for this picture," one caption reads.

Rather than ask why Johnson "could *not* function as an iconographic victim/hero of the war," my interest is in grappling with the implications that arise if we consider that Johnson *could* function as such a hero—or, at least, that she wanted to, or that we wanted her to—as well as with the assumptions that undergird that very desire: that Johnson should receive proper state and media attention, that the Black POW/vet should be a sympathetic character, and that Johnson's incorporation into the iconography of the war on terror should be an indicator of racial equality or racial justice.[78] These are assumptions that the memoir negotiates as it recounts Shana's journey "home." After she returns to her home in Fort Bliss, Shana embarks on a difficult recovery process that belies "home" and "return" as descriptors of her journey. She describes her struggle with PTSD and her attempts to claim proper benefits from the army after her return to the United States. She also recounts the "resentment and pettiness that made it nearly impossible to continue a life in uniform", describing how her growing celebrity and public recognition invited judgment from her peers and her commanding officers (243). She eventually requests a medical discharge from the army.

The publicity that Johnson receives after her return to the United States makes her the object of disciplining attempts to align the optics of Black femininity with anti-Arab and anti-Muslim sentiment in the post-9/11 US media. As she describes an event that she attends with Jesse Jackson, she describes how a photograph brings her into national political discourse:

> It was at one of [Jackson's] events in Chicago that I met Michelle Obama. Of course no one knew at the time that she would be first lady, but she and I were both on the agenda as speakers. I only met with her briefly, but later, I was in a group photo with her and several other prominent women. The photo became a big deal during the 2008 presidential campaign because Mother Khadijah Farrakhan, the wife of Nation of Islam leader Louis Farrakhan was also in the picture. Evidently, in some people's eyes, if you have your picture taken with someone, you must be in

total agreement with them politically. I'm standing right next to Michelle in the photo with a big grin on my face. (255)

As the memoir exposes the ways that public fears of Black radicalism and Islam often converged in suspicions of the Obamas, it positions visual material as a pivot between Shana's personal experiences of deployment, capture, and return and the public expectations for Black women as spokeswomen for US politics. In the memoir's final meditations on the Iraq War, the 2008 presidential election, and Shana's recovery process, its attempts to bring Shana "home" are tenuous. Shana's reentry into civilian life is marked by resentments and failures, PTSD and critiques of military strategy. We could read all of these disruptions of everyday life as specters of violence that bring the traumas of Black diasporic history into contact with the traumas of counterinsurgency warfare. The dislocations and relocations of racial capital are thus played out on the field of genealogical narration—first-generation Panamanian immigrant, second-generation soldier—and in the war theater and beyond, where scenes of felicitous national identification (all smiles!) play out alongside scenes of disidentification and breakdown.

The Open Circuit

In the advertisement I discussed at the beginning of this chapter, "Mother Daughter," the Black woman's kitchen table is the physical and ideological place where empire sentimentalizes and domesticates Blackness, with the fantasy of upward mobility through Black enlistment serving as the narrative of this domestication. Black military visuality during and after the two Iraq wars has served, as in the advertisement, as a reservoir for gendered national narratives of homeland, safety, and the good life. In the terms of electrics, the Black enlister is the conductor who carries along the redemption of the individual family—and, by extension, the national family—as the current that ideologically powers the war against terrorism. As Lubiano writes, "This is the U.S. State at its ugliest and most subtle," as "the military's exploitation of a racially, economically, and politically oppressed group is costumed into" the picture of Black familial wholeness.[79] At the same time, though, the Black soldier's appearance on distant shores, absent without leave, unclaimed and disinherited, calls up histories of dispersal and displacement that belie the tidy narrative of domestic and familial closure.

This history of dissolution is, indeed, the very living history that Nikky Finney captures with her poem "Florissant," written for LaVena Johnson, an eighteen-year-old army communications specialist who was raped and murdered by a fellow soldier in Iraq and whose death was initially covered up as a suicide. Finney attempts a fuller story, a rejection of the official story, that calls on the report of Johnson's father: "The Army man, the father / will tell you more, much more, / if you have the stomach for the details. / *If* your love for your country does not impair your higher affection for the facts."[80] The memory of the destruction disrupting Black familial integrity, a memory fiercely held in Finney's verse and in each picture of Black militarism, makes the Black soldier a faulty conductor for the transmission of national narratives of the Iraq wars, and the larger war on terror, as efforts to save humanity led by a multicultural military force.

Perhaps more importantly, each appearance of the Black soldier, armed or disarmed, calls up the specter of Negroes with Guns, that nightmare that haunts both domestic and foreign policies of counterinsurgency and security. This frame, which mobilized the language of civil rights liberalism to compel consent to a racial regime in which market logics of individualism and patriotism overdetermined antiracist calls for social justice, made it clear that, in Singh's words, the "nation-state has been a powerful mechanism for at once instituting racial division and domination and enabling universalistic visions of inclusion and opportunity."[81] The narrative frame of racial liberalism that made the long histories of Black protest over as the "short civil rights movement," and in turn rearticulated that movement as a triumph for US capitalism, was the same frame that powered myths of Black soldierly cowardice, that turned *Home of the Brave*'s Moss into a paralytic immobilized by his own racial sensitivity, and made intraracial violence an alibi for white supremacy in *A Soldier's Story*'s account of World War II.[82] And as the 9/11 attacks precipitated an idea of the United States that eclipsed racial particularity, the domestication of armed Black resistance in narratives of Black soldiering in Iraq and Afghanistan followed up on attempts to substitute images of relatively well-behaved Black citizens for visions of alternative Black pasts—histories of refusal, resentment, reprisal, retreat, and rebellion. If the soldier is one such relatively well-behaved Black citizen, the racial liberal frame of war travels cinematically, in scenes of model soldiering during World War II and in scenes of anti-Arab violence and surveillance in the Iraq wars.

The appearance of Black people with guns, then, is the nightmare come to life that racial liberalism, even in its instantiation in war films, in the cinematic imagination of the Black soldier, is meant to purge. But the Black soldier, again, is a faulty conductor for the transmission of national narratives of military multiculturalism. In *Miracle at St. Anna*, Hector's tour in Italy ends when he survives the Nazi attack on Colognora. Nazi soldiers pound through the town, at one point yelling in German, "Come on! Kill the Blacks! Those pigs. This way." Train, Stamps, and Bishop are killed, and Hector slumps to the ground after being injured. A Nazi soldier points a gun in Hector's face and tells him, in German, "Prepare to die." Hector survives because a Nazi officer pushes the soldier out of the way, orders the rest of the German soldiers away, hands Hector his gun, and instructs him, now in English, "Defend yourself." This is a strange reversal, one of many betrayals in *Miracle*, that returns to the war-film genre the ghost of Black militancy and armed self-defense that it is meant to exorcise. Hector, a man without country, is left with the gun. What are we to imagine will follow his return "home"? And if Hector has been stowing this gun in his desk at the post office until 1983, when the film opens, what are we to imagine lies beneath the veneer of Black first-world citizenship? One way to convert the threat of armed Black resistance into state power, to put it to work for the justification of world domination, is to dress Black military action in the visual language of patriotism, police power, and homeland protection. The living histories of Blackness on the *other* side of terror disrupt this conversion process.

If we understand the racial liberal frame of terror, again in the terms of electrics, as a circuit that uses the Black soldier to transmit the energies of permanent war—energies of multicultural ascent, patriotism, and a Manichean public aesthetics that announces a multicultural military as the embodiment of all that is good, true, and beautiful—it is an open circuit interrupted by the histories that the Black soldier shuttles into Black military visuality. In *Miracle at St. Anna* and in *I'm Still Standing*, dislocation effects a wrinkle in the universalizing narratives of US power during the Iraq wars. In *I'm Still Standing*, this dislocation takes the form of a fraught "journey home" that, as I have argued, belies "home" as a descriptor of where Johnson ends up. In *Miracle*, the dislocations are multiple: the recollection of the lunch counter, the exits from the portrait, the encounter on the beach, and the filmic avowal of Black self-defense. Each of these dislocations shakes the foundation of advertisements like "Mother Daughter" and demands attention to the work that Black characters perform in US culture, not only as idealized subjects of counterterrorism but also as those subjects who literally haunt state power, surrounding it, stalking it, shaking it, and keeping it awake at night.

While Johnson's 2010 memoir *I'm Still Standing* is rendered in quite a different style from much of the other work I consider in this book, it presents us with an opportunity to grapple with the way the imperial grammars of Blackness—the linguistic and visual codes giving identity to "America" and its new world order through Black figures and figures of speech—were the language through which the expressive culture of the Iraq wars tied Black freedom to global security. In Johnson's memoir, the Black female soldier proves the sheer *disciplinability* of US power: she serves up evidence of the very freedom and equality that authorizes her own disposability. In other words, it shows how Black women play a crucial but different role than Black men in the cultural-linguistic architecture of the imperial grammars of Blackness. As we continue to consider Black women's function in the culture of US empire, we must consider the ways that the very notions of *crisis*, *disaster*, and *emergency* called on Black women, and on significations of Black female sexuality, to construct the moral and political rationale for the development of the very post–Cold War US power that Spike Lee and Shoshana Johnson grappled with. I turn to this work in chapter 3.

3

"What Kind of Skeeza?"

New Black Femininity and the Seductions of Emergency

Over the decades of Cold War– and post–Cold War–era US empire-building, from 1945 to the present, Black women have played a central role in the imaginary of US dominance around the globe. Given how Blackness has functioned to justify the United States' narrative of itself as an exceptional, enlightened multiracial and equitable democracy, the work of racialized gendered subjects on this side of terror—as representatives for the government, the military, and the corporation who inflict pain on populations of color throughout the world, often in the name of counterterror—has been one of the most significant discursive inventions of our contemporary period. The "racial break" that effected a major transformation in US race relations after World War II—from the exclusions of Jim Crow to the inclusions of a domestic civil rights agenda that splintered antiracism, anticolonialism, and internationalism—was also, that is, a "gender break" that reformulated US metanarratives of citizenship, corporeality, and desire, in part through the spectacular picturing of Black women in positions of marginalization and exclusion and threat, on the one hand (on the FBI's most-wanted poster, for example), and power and achievement, on the other (in inauguration paraphernalia).

This chapter argues that the post–World War II reorganization of power, which coarticulated national security and putative racial equality through the joining together of diversity management and crisis management, has culminated in the public positioning of Black women's power as both the perpetual threat to US empire and the scandalous vehicle of its survival and redemption. Of course, the emergence of Black women's empowerment in the crucible of US empire has important implications for the way we read Black women's texts of the contemporary period, especially through part 2 of this book. If the imperial grammars of Blackness formed the systems of signification through which what I call the *new Black femininities* of the post–Cold War United States were introduced to new forms of threat, Black women writers both translated those grammars for the literary marketplace and invented whole other languages for imagining and enacting viable alternatives to the "protection racket."[1]

Even as US empire-building attached ideals of nationalism and citizenship to signifiers of Blackness, Black women did not figure in US public culture in any easy way as ideal citizens or model patriots. Rather, the images, ideas, and ideals of Black women's empowerment in the discursive regime of post-1945 US world-building have been squeezed from the very raw material that has shaped representations and projections of Black female identity, that is, the "signifying property *plus*" that has accrued to Black women in the West since slavery.[2]

This elaborate layering of significations of Black womanhood perhaps comes into view most clearly when we consider the representations, fascinations, and condemnations that configure around Condoleezza Rice. Rice, who served first as national security adviser to George W. Bush and then as secretary of state, serves as an avatar for the changes in the relationship between Blackness, the security apparatus, and contemporary codes of gender and sexuality that I have been discussing throughout this book. Rice has been featured in a wide array of cultural texts that attempt to account for her complicity with the Bush regime. For example, in Amiri Baraka's 2001 poem "Somebody Blew Up America," delivered weeks after the September 11 attacks, Baraka lists several Black officials in a catalogue of "American terrorists," which includes "the Klan," "Skin heads," and "David Duke or Giuliani." Delivered as a series of questions interrogating who the real terrorists are—"Who the fake president / Who the ruler / Who the banker / Who? Who? Who?"—the poem turns to Black conservatives in the US government after its catalogue of US imperial violence:

> Who do Tom Ass Clarence work for
> Who doo doo come out the Colon's mouth
> Who know what kind of Skeeza is a Condoleezza
> Who pay Connelly to be a wooden negro
> Who give Genius Awards to Homo Locus
> Subsidere[3]

Here Rice is figured as a Jezebel race traitor literally in bed with white supremacy. In fact, given how the internal rhyme of "Skeeza is a Condoleezza" is the only rhyme in a stanza whose primary modes of figuration are the homophone ("Tom Ass" in place of Thomas; "Colon" in place of Colin) and slant rhyme ("Genius" and "Locus"), the poetic, sonic, and performative force of the stanza hangs on the easy association of Rice with a kind of moral degradation and selling out that is never out of significatory reach in representations of successful Black women.

The sexualization of Condoleezza Rice's intimacy with the conservative regimes of the late twentieth and early twenty-first centuries actually diminishes her role in transforming state power during an epoch in which the aims of diversity management and crisis management were closely aligned. Rice rose to prominence as a security official at a crucial turning point in US history, at the end of the Cold War, which Christian Appy refers to a "competition over discourse."[4] During the Cold War, domestic discourses of race and foreign-policy-oriented discourses on colonialism combined to Americanize the abstract values of safety and freedom and to domesticate anticolonial resistance. And in the post–Cold War era, when the values of US freedom and security were jeopardized by the abandonments of the neoliberal state, which extended to white populations the insecurity long believed to be the exclusive province of the Black and Native and brown peoples of the global majority, security would become the occupation of the individual.[5] This required exceptional, securitized citizens who not only would bear the burden of filling in for the protection of the crumbled social welfare apparatus but would also securitize themselves, that is, internalize fear about external threats and take responsibility for security themselves.

As events like Hurricane Katrina exposed the weakness of the US government, Inderpal Grewal notes, the "waning of imperial power and its logic of security became visible globally through transnational media," and, as a result, the security state shifted exceptionalism from government to citizen: "In this neoliberal ideology, the claim is that what the state will not or cannot accomplish, exceptional American citizens will undertake."[6] Importantly, though, these exceptional citizens— the security mom, the humanitarian, the security feminist, the active shooter, the neighborhood watchman, the police-academy trainee—do not always conform to Grewal's racial schema, with white Christian men being exclusively "endowed with sovereignty to target black and brown Others . . . through modes of war that incorporate militarized humanitarianism and surveillance."[7] The security state most definitely needed Black people to do its saving, too. Even more significantly, the Black imperial citizens who changed the grammar of state power by translating the languages of Black freedom into the rallying cries of a flailing superpower after the Cold War were not simple pawns or ciphers for penetrative state power. They had their own universes of desire, their own theories of freedom, their own designs on power.

If Rice's exercise of state power made her vulnerable to suspicions of her selling out in the weeks and months after September 11, in the days during which she served as a key player in Bush's war cabinet as it launched what it called the "war on terror," she was even more susceptible to allegations of race treason after August 2005, when the *Drudge Report* released photographs of her shopping for shoes at Ferragamo and attending *Spam-a-lot!* on Broadway during the flooding of New Orleans that resulted from the broken levees in Hurricane Katrina's path. In an *Essence* magazine interview with Rice that ran a year later, in October 2006, the author reminds readers that on Rice's watch, "the war in Iraq has roiled on with no end in sight, weapons of mass destruction have not been found, and Osama bin Laden continues to send threatening messages, but we can't find him either. North Korea is defiantly testing long-range missiles, while back home, scandals and leaks rock the Bush administration, sending the President's approval ratings to a record low. And still etched in the consciousness of many of us are the thousands stranded last year in the flooded city of New Orleans." But even as *Essence*, a publication that served as a home for transnational Black feminist critique in the 1980s, about which I will say more in chapter 5—recounts Rice's responsibility for an unpopular war and for the drowning of Black New Orleans, the article assumes that underneath her façade lay a reservoir of racial solidarity: "Her words are carefully chosen, her defense of her boss unwavering. But her gestures—nods of agreement, ironic shrugs, even a deep scowl—reveal that she knows our questions have answers that are infinitely more layered than she may be willing to give."[8] Here loyalty to "her boss" is a narrative invention that depicts Rice as Baraka's "skeeza" does, intimating that deep down she knows better, even as it pictures her as a successful cabinet member who bears witness to the promise of US democracy. (An accompanying photo by Timothy White shows Rice poised on the red Victorian sofa in her office, staring out to the horizon, past the Lincoln Memorial.)

Just as the *Essence* article and Baraka's poem write Rice's record of public service into a narrative of Black women's deceitfulness on this side of terror, so do mainstream news accounts of her diplomacy trade in narratives that rely on the well-worn trope of the Jezebel–race traitor. In August 2011, an album featuring photographs of Condoleezza Rice was uncovered by rebels when they ransacked Libyan leader Muammar Gaddafi's Tripoli compound. US news outlets represented Gaddafi's treasure trove of Condi pics as evidence of his affection for the former national security adviser and secretary of state. NBC News reported Gaddafi to have said, for example, "I support my darling Black African woman. . . . I admire and am very proud of the way she leans back and gives orders to the Arab leaders. . . . Leezza, Leezza, Leezza. I love her very much," as it printed a photograph of Gadaffi's photo album being held open on a bare mattress adorned with pink roses.[9] If Rice is pictured here as an object of Gaddafi's affection, the photograph draws American readers into this barebones bedroom scene to bolster the narrative frame of the fugitive Libyan dictator's deviance and the West's moral and political purity. Like the photographs of prisoners at Abu Ghraib, the photographs of Gaddafi's compound redirected colonial formulas of identification toward post-9/11 representations of Arab, Muslim, Middle Eastern, and South Asian peoples as internal and external enemies. As Anne McClintock describes, these formulas depict photographic subjects as "historically 'primitive,' as animalized, as sexually deviant: the men feminized, homosexualized, or hypersexualized; and the women figured as sexually lascivious."[10] Rice's appearance in the photographs of the album triangulates this projection of deviant sexuality, on the one hand signaling a kind of contained sexuality (or *asexuality*) that throws Gaddafi's perversity into sharp relief and on the other serving as a target for readers' fantasies and fears of Afro-Arab relations in the shadow of what Sohail Daulatzai calls the "Muslim International": the internationalist alliances among Black Muslims, Black radicals, and anticolonial movements in the Muslim third world.[11] If Rice's projection as a paragon of ideal femininity draws a Manichean line between a democratic, multicultural US and the dark underworld of Gaddafi's

BEING CONDOLEEZZA

As the tensions between Hezbollah and Israel explode in the Middle East, the death toll rises in Iraq, and nations from North Korea to Iran remain defiant in their pursuit of nuclear weapons, the Bush administration struggles to regain the confidence of both foreign allies and citizens at home. And on the front line is a Black woman. Here in an exclusive interview, ESSENCE's Tatsha Robertson sits down with the secretary of state to ask the questions Black America wants the answers to

PHOTOGRAPHY BY TIMOTHY WHITE

ESSENCE 184 10.2006

An *Essence* feature shows Condoleezza Rice gracefully peering into the near distance while the Lincoln Memorial, a symbol of freedom and the promise of multiracial democracy, looms behind her reflection.

An album filled with pictures of former US secretary of state Condoleezza Rice was found in Muammar Gaddafi's compound on August 24, 2011. This photo appeared on NBC News's website *Photoblog*.

regime—made all the more perverse by the dictator's fantasies of *her*, of all people—Rice's Blackness no doubt shuttles into the photograph the very threat of the "primitive" that it is supposed to sanitize.[12]

When Rice's memoir *No Higher Honor* was published two months after the album was discovered, Gadaffi's admiration of her again became material for tabloid-style speculations about his sexual proclivities and Rice's implication in them. In the memoir, Rice writes of her 2003 visit to Tripoli: "At the end of dinner, Gaddafi told me that he'd made a videotape for me. *Uh oh,* I thought, *what is this going to be?* It was a quite innocent collection of photos of me with world leaders—President Bush, Vladimir Putin, Hu Jintao, and so on—set to the music of a song called 'Black Flower in the White House,' written for me by a Libyan composer. It was weird, but at least it wasn't raunchy."[13] Rice provokes and then deflects the reader's wildest flights of fancy, conjuring the possibility of—what? a porn video?—in the Libyan dictator's home only to deflate it. Further, the double meaning that accrues to "flower"—delicate nicety, sexual jewel—demands that Rice assure the reader that the gifts of the slide show and song are only "weird" tokens of diplomacy, not "raunchy" objects of foreplay. A writer for *Vanity Fair* captures the US media's lurid fascination with the story and the persistence of interest in Gaddafi's fantasy life, Rice's deflections notwithstanding. Celebrating the memoir's revelation of the "other side" of the Afro-Arab "love story," the writer intimates that in the memoir, the story "gets worse, by which we mean better": "What [Rice] doesn't know is that 'Black flower' is an Arabic colloquialism meaning 'foreign leader about whom I have sexy dreams, and I mean that in the most grotesque way possible.'"[14]

Rice's photographic appearance at the center of post–Cold War diplomacy and security as the exemplar of femininity at once idealized and racialized—"Black flower"—as well as at the center of Gaddafi's political arousal within media narratives of unruly Afro-Arab desire, begs us to consider how the appearance of Black women's (a)sexuality here secures the United States' self-representation as a beneficent multicultural democracy even as it conjures the layers of signification that tie Black womanhood to the deviant, the pathological, and the unruly. Together, these imaginings of Rice, along with countless other news stories and cultural texts that testify to Rice's magnetism as an object of public fascination, position Black femininity as that which both secures and threatens national security. Rice is a cold agent of security and diplomacy who faithfully fulfills the demands of her job in Washington while failing to protect the Black nation. At the same time, she is the hot object of fantasies and fears of Afro-Arab resurgence. In each case, *emergency* functions as a public feeling that correlates ideas about raced and gendered personhood and fears of extinction within a new script of US social-political relations, one that not only depends on Black deviance and marginalization but also demands Black achievement and exceptionality. If each of these textual events is understood in the moment of its emergence—after 9/11, after Hurricane Katrina, after the Arab uprisings of 2011—we could say that Rice exemplifies how throughout the first decade of the 2000s, across various crises, expectations for personal and public safety were tied to the imaginary of Black feminine power and agency on this side of terror. How do the practices, discourses, and images of the global security apparatus that was erected after the Cold War—especially in the realms of counterterrorism, crisis management, and emergency preparedness—thus depend on the fabrication, projection, and maintenance of power exhibited by Black women such as Rice?

The culture of emergency that permeated the United States after the 9/11 attacks ties the security apparatus to the gendered subjectivities of Black patriotism, achievement, representation, statecraft, diplomacy, and war-making. The Black citizen-subject's performance of achievement or excellence that seeks to assert, explain, or justify the classical liberal values of US sovereignty (freedom, equality, democracy) is one of the key means by which *Black imperial agency*—a term I am using to refer to the inner life of Black service on behalf of empire-building in the era of the high war on terror, which we began to see in chapter 2 with *In Treatment*'s returning veteran—has been tethered to the circulation of US power around the globe, not only in cultural forms such as memoirs, films, and novels but also in military operations, diplomatic talks, advisory memos, and board meetings. Accordingly, the suturing of Black women's achievement and mastery to the operations of *protection* (security, crisis management, rescue) and at the same time to the activities of *danger* (poor mothering, illicit sex, scandal, betrayal, and, potentially, rebellion) is one of the contradictions that shapes what I have been calling the imperial grammars of Blackness. More importantly perhaps, this contradiction points to the very unruliness of emergency itself as a basis for sovereignty and worldwide dominance.

In the sections that follow, then, I analyze the reformulation of Black womanhood for US empire through two primary figures of emergency preparedness and crisis management. I argue that the forms of protection and threat embodied by Black women in late imperial US culture make *emergency* visible as a raced and gendered logic of the security apparatus, one that positions Black women like Rice at the center of a new imaginary of US power in texts as varied as Rice's memoirs and the ABC television series *Scandal*. Reading these texts together, I argue that the seduction of US empire, shuttled through the irresistible fiction of US safety won though military and corporate dominance, coheres, and at the same time dissolves, in the tropology of the Black skeeza on this side, and on the other side, of terror.

Black Femininity at the Scene of Emergency

One of the most significant contradictions of contemporary US empire is its valuing of Black women's labor in the arenas of crisis management, national security, and counterterrorism in a historical context in which racialized gender, and Black women in particular, remain primary targets of surveillance, violence, incarceration, and disposal. In the culture of precaution that 9/11 both exposed and catalyzed, security checkpoints, see-something-say-something campaigns, renewed calls for civil defense, and everyday vigilantism were only the most visible indicators of the articulation of power that was necessitated by the Cold War's denouement. Further, the introduction of new, unpredictable threats to the West, not only in unexpected forms of attack (like planes flying into buildings) but also in the environmental disasters made inevitable by human disregard for nonhuman life, allowed for the continual recruitment of fear to produce consent for domination. Crises as varied as ecological catastrophes, mass protests, global financial crises, terrorist attacks, epidemics, immigration surges, and sex scandals in this context all came to be seen as uncontrollable risks in "a new social world in which technical expertise cannot calculate and manage the risk it generates."[15] And because threat—embodied in the suicide bomber or the wayward hurricane—is anywhere and everywhere, civilian life "falls onto a continuum with war, permanently potentially premilitarized, a pole on the spectrum."[16]

According to Andrew Lakoff, the political rationality of *preparedness* came to dominate US foreign policy and domestic security after the Cold War, when the country came to lack a stable, knowable enemy. The emergence of a "nonspecific enemy" after the fall of the Soviet Union demanded a change in security policy, away from containment and deterrence and toward emergency preparedness.[17] (One could argue, though, that the "revolution in military affairs" formalized what had to be consciously rationalized during the Cold War. The Cold War, indeed, justified a permanent arms race, with the mushroom cloud serving as the "organizing fetish" of the security state after 1945).[18] Western states and markets no longer "prioritize a stable-state vision of security"; as Brian Massumi argues, they now grapple "with the complexity of an uncertain, neoconservatizing environment in which risk is not only endemic but is inexpungeable and ultimately unknowable."[19] Jasbir Puar links the permanent state of emergency to temporality: "the frenzied mode of emergency is an alibi for the quiet certitude of a slowly normativized working paradigm of liberal democratic government, an alibi necessary to disavow its linkages to totalitarian governments."[20] Emergency dissimulates the United States' complicity with violent regimes abroad while aestheticizing the new nationalist identity formations that correspond to the regularization of risk and disaster. As Puar argues, homonationalism is one such identity formation; the Orientalist production of the terrorist "disaggregates U.S. national gays and queers from racial and sexual others, foregrounding a collusion between homosexuality and American nationalism that is generated by both national rhetorics of patriotic inclusion and by gay and queer subjects themselves: homonationalism."[21] But as homonationalism tied queer genders and sexualities to a cultural-political imaginary of national wholeness, so did idealizations of Black empowerment for subjects across the gender-sexual spectrum.

The fundamental change in the nature of threat necessitated a transformation in the categories of stigma and privilege and the processes of inclusion and exclusion that shape US racial power. In the context of what Massumi calls "ontopower"—an "environmental power" that responds to the everywhere of emergency by "counter-mimicking" the accident, by "returning to life's unliveable conditions of emergence in order to bring it back"—state power is no longer interested in the management of populations or the regulation of bodies as a way of reducing population-level threat. Now "the neoliberal tendency is not to mold to the norm, as do systems characterized by Foucault as disciplinary powers. Rather, its tendency is to *capture the exception and incorporate it* (in both senses of the word)."[22] If power operates on the presumption that catastrophes are to be endured rather than prevented, species endurance demands forms of emergency preparedness that aim not to make live and let die or even to make die and let live.[23] While "discipline regulates everything," security, as Foucault explains, "lets things happen." Security collates information and adds up details, and it approaches catastrophes as "necessary, inevitable processes, as natural processes in the broad sense."[24]

The security apparatus after 9/11, understood in these terms, aimed to protect systems and infrastructures in order to mitigate, not eliminate, vulnerability to threat. As Lakoff explains, "Preparedness organizes a set of techniques for maintaining order in a time of emergency. First responders are trained, relief supplies are stockpiled, and the logistics of relief distribution are mapped out. During the event itself, real-time 'situational awareness' is critical to the coordination of response. The duration of direct intervention by a preparedness apparatus is limited to the immediate onset and aftermath of crisis, but the requirement of vigilant attention to the prospect of crisis is ongoing, permanent."[25] The global pandemic caused by COVID-19 in 2020 gave us a myriad of examples of preparedness as a rationality: the scramble was to preserve financial infrastructure rather than human lives, and the state fantasy of order—the racial order of white supremacy, the financial order of savage capitalism—was the idol that crashed in street revolts by early summer. Importantly, the *norm* under the conditions of perpetual emergency is not a legal or moral imperative but "whatever proves to be consistent with generally liveable conditions, factoring in that the conditions are of continual variation."[26] Given that the survival of the species under the conditions of neoliberalism demanded a change in the very nature of governmentality, the functions of race, gender, sexuality, and so on as regulatory systems also underwent significant changes.

The relationship between Blackness and emergency preparedness is best understood when we consider the changing nature of threat, and threat's relationship to racial difference, in the post–Cold War United States. The forms of threat that were identified in the post–Cold War period and heightened in the post-9/11 years correlated with the widespread fear that the forms of bodily misery and collective pain that were historically experienced by racialized populations would now emerge, or erupt, indiscriminately. The form of threat was then "the suddenly irrupting, locally self-organizing, systemically self-amplifying threat of large-scale disruption." As Massumi points out, today's threat "is not only indiscriminate, coming anywhere, as out of nowhere, at any time, it is also indiscrimin*able*."[27] In this context, Hurricane Katrina would be likened to a terrorist attack; and terrorism, like the weather, came to be understood as a diverse and mysterious systematicity that might be loosely tracked but never fully known or adequately prepared for. In the context of the indifferent and *undifferent* emergence of threat— indifferent to human life and undifferent because "threat is only a threat if it retains an indeterminacy"—difference itself must be welcomed and known. The rise of "diversity management" in the 1990s coincided with the new forms of emergency preparedness and crisis management.[28] Avery Gordon noted in 1995, "Corporate culture links a vision of racial and gender *diversity* to its existing relations of ruling to produce what might be called multicultural corporatism." Importantly, "this vision of corporate multiculturalism has the potential to become an influential feature of the larger project, currently underway, of rewriting our nation's social contract."[29] This rewriting has involved, as I have been arguing, the introduction of imperial grammars of Blackness into the everyday operations not only of corporations but also of government agencies, universities, public services, and the military.

The incorporation of Black women into contemporary state power through the management of difference at the scene of threat's anywhere-everywhere emergence was thus not a spontaneous neoliberal invention but rather a legacy of the Cold War, what Jodi Kim refers to as "geopolitical scheme for making sense of the world," a "discursive cloak" obfuscating a decades-long race war.[30] While discourses of Black pathology and strategies of containment and capture dominated mainstream culture's response to twentieth-century Black radicalism and the threat of anticolonial resistance and third-world revolution as the United States rose to world dominance as an imperial power cum capitalist democracy, counterinsurgency also took the form of *productive* discourses of Black women's inclusion, reformation, and exemplarity. It was during the Cold War, of course, that state and cultural institutions invited and used objects of cultural difference—like area studies texts and novels and State Department tours of the latter 1950s—to win converts to capitalist democracy abroad and, in domestic contexts, to promote practical ways to achieve enlightenment on what was then called "the Negro Problem." Women like Leontyne Price, Marian Anderson, Maya Angelou, and Althea Gibson tested the diplomatic value of Black femininity on the world stage and tested, too, the Cold War state's strategies of incorporation. For example, when Angelou was offered a part in the State Department–sponsored tour of *Porgy and Bess*, she worried that she would not gain clearance: "I thought about the school I attended which was on the House Un-American Activities Committee list," she writes in her autobiography. The opera company assured her that they could "get a special dispensation."[31]

By the end of the Cold War and the solidification of the war on terror that was announced following the September 11 attacks, Black women's incorporation into the governing apparatuses of the state at higher and higher levels—eventually at the position of secretary of state, then in the role of First Lady, then vice president—led to the Black woman's serving as a figure for the government's readiness for disaster, which included its capacity to preempt nuclear war after the fall of the Soviet Union. Rice is a key example of this coalescence of Blackness and security. In fact, "condi-fi-cation" is the term that Carole Boyce Davies uses to refer to the "public positioning of oppressive Black conservatism and the normalising of the same while supporting amazingly offensive policies and politics, and masquerading them when convenient under a Black umbrella."[32] As we will see, the spectacle of Black conservatism is only one part of a larger tapestry of incorporation. US popular culture, especially in its liberal narratives of Black women's empowerment and even in its adaptations of Black feminist literature, has served as a formidable vehicle for the disciplining and repackaging of radical Black feminism. Since 1968, that is, Black women's *empowerment* has been framed as neatly compatible with US public policy aimed at dismantling the aims of the civil rights movement, the military-industrial complex and its structuring fictions of safety, bourgeois notions of Black women's roles in reproducing viable Black families, and the development of a US visual culture in which Blackness could be simultaneously valued as an aesthetic object and disarticulated from both US citizenship and radical challenges to the violence that secures it.[33]

If diversity management has since the early 1990s employed cultural difference in the service of governance, race and gender difference has been increasingly useful in crisis contexts. Several studies have shown that women and racialized minorities are more likely to be appointed to top leadership positions in poorly performing firms and firms in crisis. Michelle Ryan and Alex Haslam coined the term "glass cliff" to describe how, when women were appointed to leadership positions to FTSE 100 corporations in 2003, the appointments were often made to companies that were in financial crisis.[34] Later studies extended the glass cliff thesis to argue that the glass cliff persists because women are seen as possessing characteristics that are useful in a time of crisis and because racial-ethnic minorities are perceived as "suitable leaders under difficult circumstances where sensitivity toward people (warmth dimension) is deemed useful."[35]

The coming together of diversity initiatives and crisis management changed the face of national security after World War II, especially after the end of the Cold War. As Jasbir Puar and Amit Rai argue, counterterrorism solidified during the Cold War as an epistemological project, a "civilizational knowledge" that attempted to "taxonomize the terrorist's mind."[36] As a knowledge project, counterterrorism depends on a diversity of subjects of knowledge to match the diversity of objects of knowledge: as threat itself diversified after the fall of the Soviet Union, US institutions such as the military and the university would have to likewise recruit subjects of counterterrorist knowledge who represented a variety of ethnic, religious, and cultural backgrounds. Keith Brown discusses the use of anthropological knowledge in particular in the war against terror that began with Operation Iraqi Freedom in 2003. Whereas mainstream thought in the US Army continued to see culture as the "static, or slow-moving, property of a constructed 'other,' the Special Forces and the Marine Corps emphasized "a competing sense of cultural process as dynamic, interactive, and emergent."[37] The Marine Corps, for example, issued wallet-sized "Culture Smart Cards" to soldiers in Iraq in 2005 and Afghanistan in 2006. The cards were designed to help soldiers meet the enemy on the enemy's terrain, reflecting the Corps' strategy of incorporating knowledge of the enemy's terrain, increasing cultural sensitivity, and building cross-cultural connections.

If the war on terror is understood as another campaign in the culture wars—where terror, like culture, is "dynamic, interactive, and emergent"—it becomes clear why diversity-management practices were crucial in counterterrorist knowledge production and military training after the Cold War, in campaigns such as Desert Shield (August 1990–January 1991), Desert Storm (January 1991–February 1991), Enduring Freedom (2001–14), and Iraqi Freedom / New Dawn (2003–11). Indeed, as Melamed points out, "in a neoliberal-multicultural context where the United States describes its providential destiny to be the spreading of freedom, democracy and economic rights around the globe, the defense of America plays offense for neoliberalism."[38] The United States that military campaigns purport to defend, even when the United States is aggressor, was throughout the Cold War and post–Cold War years ideologically represented as a multiracial, multicultural democracy fighting to preserve itself as a bastion of equality and enlightened cultural sensitivity.

This military-ideological project rippled through the US surveillance and policing industries. The incorporation of Black agents of surveillance and defense into the armature of global security that solidified over the course of the Cold War was a key feature of what we have called the "post-civil-rights era." As Cathy Cohen argues in *The Boundaries of Blackness: AIDS and the Breakdown of Black Politics*, members of racialized groups "have acquired such relative privilege in part because of the connection to and authority within marginal communities."[39] Racial authenticity, that is to say, is not only assimilable but indispensable to governmental power: "In a changing world where demographic characteristics are evolving in conjunction with economic and political changes, privileged marginal group members, claiming authenticity within marginal communities as well as familiarity with dominant practices, find themselves positioned as necessary components for the continued functioning of dominant institutions." If racialized minorities are not only the "diversified workforce touted by private business and institutions" but also "the new Black police recruits in urban cities such as New York and Los Angeles" and the "case workers helping to implement workfare," diversity management and domestic security worked together to systematically adapt the itineraries of race and power during the global crisis posed not only by Soviet power in the Cold War era but also by internationalist mobilization throughout the Global South.[40] That is, if we understand neoliberal economic policy as partly a response to the fact that, as Cedric Robinson wrote in 1983, "the most formidable apparatus of physical domination and control have disintegrated in the face of the most unlikely oppositions (India, Algeria, Angola, Vietnam, Guinea-Bissau, Iran, Mozambique)," we can understand the successive racial regimes of the 1980s, 1990s, and 2000s as not only necessitated by the end of the Cold War but also driven by the strategy of incorporation after the mass antiracist and anticolonial movements of the 1960s, 1970s, 1980s, and 1990s.[41] As Cohen suggests, the incorporation of Black people into police forces and into agencies of social surveillance "should not be understood as the final breakdown of systematic exclusion, but instead as a process of further refining the mechanisms of power."[42]

Corporate multiculturalism did not simply transform "Blackness from a badge of insult to an increasingly powerful but still very limited signifier of prestige"; it also transformed the organizational cultures of security and counterinsurgency agencies, which were charged with managing unknowable and indeterminable threats on domestic and international fronts as the United States rose to imperial dominance over the second half of the twentieth century.[43] For example, a 2008 article in the *Black Collegian*, a quarterly periodical that was founded in 1970 to promote the recruitment of college-educated Black professionals by US businesses and to educate its readers about various career paths, discusses diversity initiatives in the CIA. In an interview with several CIA executives, the article educates readers about opportunities for Black employees in senior leadership positions. When asked why diversity in the CIA is important, Sue Bromley, deputy director for intelligence, explains to the interviewer, "We need the diversity that the world presents right here in our workforce. We must draw on different opinions and different experiences when we're trying to understand complex global issues."[44] The director for management, leadership, and diversity programs adds, "It is actually the key to our success." After discussing a mentoring program for midlevel minority managers, Bromley reiterates why diversity is a top priority for her office: "The global issues and situations we face are complex and we need to make sure that we are thinking about them in a sophisticated way, one that incorporates lots of different ideas and lots of different approaches. The way to do that is to constantly grow and evolve and take advantage of all the ideas that our employees can bring to the table. Our country's security is depending on doing nothing less."[45] Here the production of "sophisticated" knowledge about "complex" global problems places Blackness in necessary correlation to security, calling difference to the scene of threat's anywhere-everywhere emergence to produce intelligence, to manage crisis, and to prepare for life after sure catastrophe.

In the juncture that I have been discussing—the period of transition between the Cold War and the post-9/11 "high" war on terror—the coalescence of Blackness and security in US mass cultural forms like film and television made use of old racial-sexual tropes like the Jezebel and the Mammy but also loosened these tropes and invented new ones for Black female symbology. New Black femininities thus emerged, putting cultural and bodily difference to work for the varied discourses of emergency as empire-building. As Jayna Brown argues, for example, in post–Cold War dystopian US and British film and literature, the Black heroine emerges because slavery and colonialism were apocalyptic experiences, and Black populations' "routes of survival and exodus" became "emblematic of utopian possibility" amid fears of species annihilation that heightened after the Cold War.[46] In films like *28 Days Later* and *Children of Men*, Brown suggests, Black women hold "a mediumistic ability, a witchy access to otherworldly sources of power and information."[47] Black women's capacity to rebirth civilization in narratives of apocalyptic catastrophe opens classic figurations of Black femininity onto new territory; the centrality of Black women's agency and interiority, Brown explains, resignifies and redirects classic tropes of Black feminine pathology such as the Mammy.

Likewise, if the depiction of Black masculinity as hardcore state authority in US film articulated "some of the political, economic, and cultural conditions for a popular and lucrative antiblack Black visibility on a global scale" throughout the second half of the twentieth century and increasingly after 2001, so too was Black femininity's articulation through images of policing, prosecution, and protection a key feature of mainstream US popular culture throughout the 1990s and early 2000s.[48] These were the decades when US television introduced audiences to the Black female police officer and officer of the court: Marsha Warfield rendered her a wry and somewhat butch performance as the court bailiff Roz on *Night Court* (NBC, 1986–92), while previously, for one season, the great Paula Kelly as the public defender Liz Williams depicted a very different comic tone and presentation of professional Black womanhood (NBC, 1984). *Night Court* was a sitcom, though, and the drama of police work and the crime procedural eluded Black female actors and televisual representation until the era of diversity management. Lauren Vélez joined the cast of the urban police melodrama *New York Undercover* (Fox, 1994–98) to play the undercover agent Nina Moreno. Importantly, the depiction of Nina Moreno as a petite Black Nuyorican who wears makeup, sports long tresses, and becomes romantically involved with a fellow detective feminized the role of the female police officer by playing on stereotypical notions of Latina sensuality and availability. Quite in contrast to *Night Court*'s Roz and Liz, Nina is both subject of protection and object of heterosexual romantic and sexual interest in the workplace and on-screen. This would continue to be so for Velez when she joined the cast of the prison drama *Oz* as Dr. Gloria Nathan (HBO,

1997–2003). Later C. C. H. Pounder played Detective (later Captain) Claudette Wyms on *The Shield* (2002–8), District Attorney Tyne Patterson on *Sons of Anarchy* (FX, 2008–14), and coroner Dr. Loretta Wade on *NCIS: New Orleans* (CBS, 2014–); Anna Deveare Smith played National Security Adviser Nancy McNally on *The West Wing* (NBC, 1999–2006); Khandi Alexander played the chief medical examiner on *CSI: Miami* (CBS, 2002–12); Vivica A. Fox played a top FBI agent in Lifetime Television's *Missing* (2003–6); Sonja Sohn played the lesbian Baltimore detective Shakima "Kima" Greggs on HBO's *The Wire* (2002–8); Regina King portrayed Detective Lydia Adams on *Southland* (NBC, 2009; TNT, 2010–13); and, perhaps most importantly, S. Epatha Merkerson played New York Police Department Lieutenant Anita Van Buren during twenty seasons of NBC's *Law and Order* (1990–2010), appearing more frequently than any other character in the series. While Merkerson as Lieutenant Van Buren was "the boss" to a host of detectives throughout two decades, she was also a supporting character very much in the background, often removed from the scenes of male and criminal-juridical action. Of significance, and lasting across several early seasons, Van Buren's plotline highlighted a raced and gendered work-related struggle: she sued and lost against the NYPD for gender discrimination when she was not duly promoted.

Understood in this context, Kerry Washington's becoming the first African American woman to star in an hour-long network series with her 2012 debut on ABC's political thriller *Scandal* can be seen as either a logical extension of Black women's roles in crime and detective dramas or as a significant about-face. The televisual circulation of images of Black women as uniformed protectors, attorneys, and doctors in upper-echelon city and state agencies refuses the network of associations that have generally attached Black women to sexual deviance, to self-sacrificial nurturing, to poverty and illiteracy, or to explosive and emasculating anger. Crime and detective dramas depict a successful, agential, protective, professional Black femininity at the center of police power and juridical prowess. These television procedurals situate Black femininity in a critical position in post–Cold War knowledges of security, which construct threat as always already emergent, as the anywhere-everywhere of a terrorism against which a united and multicultural citizenry is perpetually at war.

The progressive feminization of images of Black women's protection made popular culture the scene of a makeover that was taking place in US political culture. At the scene of emergency, Black femininity brought post–Cold War modes of empire—preemption, surveillance, containment, preparation for disaster—into contact with post-affirmative-action diversity initiatives, in turn lining up emergency with not only the fear of Blackness as threat but also the celebration of Blackness as protection. The Black feminine woman's arrival on the scene of emergency to keep the United States safe and prepare for the worst-case scenario signals the very shift in racial formation that made George W. Bush's cabinet the most diverse in history at the time. If it is true that Black feminine figures in television, film, and public culture mark the multicultural promise of security—testifying, in real and simulated moments of emergency, to the United States' moral and political purity and its capacity to endure inevitable catastrophe—the narratives of women such as Condoleezza Rice and *Scandal*'s Olivia Pope show how the representational matrix of Black femininity refracts the coalescence of Blackness and security through figurations of emergency preparedness, crisis management, and counterterrorism. These narrative inventions—the securer, the fixer—bring Black femininity into view not only as resistant object of governmentality but also as self-conscious subject of it.

Birmingham, Bomingham, Buckingham

If the war on terror has been understood as a Manichean binary, with democracy and freedom on one side and terrorist militancy on the other, the new formulations of Black femininity have emerged in US public and popular cultures have cemented this binary. New Black femininities bolster the imaginary of democracy and freedom on one side of the binary and, on the other, call up the histories of Black antiracist resistance and anti-Black policing, surveillance, and containment. In this way, new Black femininities manage threat while serving as its residual embodiment. In this context, the narrative of protection vis-à-vis respectable Black femininity that Condoleezza Rice weaves through her two memoirs, *Extraordinary, Ordinary People* (2010) and *No Higher Honor* (2011), is seductive: trafficking in the affects of vulnerability and fear, the memoirs charge the traditional autobiographical values of self-reliance and triumph over adversity with the weight of the present, that is, the force of emergency.

Rice grew up in Birmingham, Alabama, in the 1950s and 1960s. She was a childhood friend of Denise McNair, who was murdered in the September 1963 bombing of Sixteenth Street Baptist Church. As a child of the Jim Crow South, Rice cultivated her talents at the piano and on the ice rink. She moved with her parents to Denver when she was thirteen. She enrolled in the University of Denver (then Denver University) at sixteen, eventually majoring in political science and becoming fluent in Russian and studying international relations with the Czech diplomat (and Madeleine Albright's father) Joseph Korbel. She did a master's degree at Notre Dame before returning to Denver for her PhD. Her dissertation was on party-military relations in Czechoslovakia. While in graduate school, she worked as an intern in the Bureau of Education and Cultural Affairs at the State Department, studying Soviet cultural programs in the third world. (There "was great concern that Moscow was making strides with young people throughout Africa and Latin America," she writes, "by sending the Bolshoi Ballet and the Moscow Symphony to these countries to perform.")[49] She did an internship, too, at the RAND Corporation and received a Ford Foundation fellowship in Soviet studies and international security. In 1981, she took her fellowship to Stanford, where she was subsequently appointed an assistant professor. As an expert on Cold War politics and military strategy, Rice was a key figure in late twentieth-century security culture, especially in the George H. W. Bush and George W. Bush administrations. In 1987, she served as an adviser to the Joint Chiefs of Staff; in 1989, she was appointed director of Soviet and East European Affairs on the National Security Council. She returned to Stanford in 1991 and was appointed provost two years later. As provost, her balanced budget demanded major cuts to student affairs and to the ethnic studies units—to those whom she refers to as constituents "who had felt privileged and untouchable." In 2001, Rice was appointed national security adviser by George W. Bush; she later was appointed Bush's secretary of state in 2005, succeeding Colin Powell.

Read together, Rice's two memoirs offer further evidence for one claim I am advancing throughout this book, that Black textuality in late US imperial culture paradoxically enough coheres in the structural tension between charting Black heritage ("a memoir of family") and tracking Black intimacy with the modalities of security: counterterror, counterinsurgency, policing, and detention ("a memoir of my years in Washington"). The first memoir, *Extraordinary, Ordinary People*, is a coming-of-age story that reveals a nation coming into its own as a global power over the course of the post–World War II era and as a young Black girl grows up the only child of a Presbyterian minister and a schoolteacher, striving to be "twice as good" as her classmates (3). Beginning in Birmingham in the 1930s and ending with the death of Rice's father weeks after the 2000 election, the first installment of the memoirs might be read as a story of Rice's rise to power and prominence within conservative scholarship, policy, and statecraft within a United States that is also rising to global dominance as the country asserts its global dominance through war, terror, and finance. This narrative of over-achievement and exceptionalism on two levels—the national and the personal—scripts terror as the motivating life force both of post–Cold War US hegemony and of Rice's perfectionism.

The memoirs position emergency as a narrative backdrop to highlight the values that shape Rice's upbringing in post–World War II segregated Alabama: refinement, self-control, self-reliance, hard work, composure, and cool rationality. These are the values, indeed, that mold the model Black feminine subject that the memoirs place at the vanguard of a post-9/11 imaginary of US dominance vis-à-vis crisis management and emergency preparedness. As Rice tells the fable of her paternal great-grandmother Julia Head near the beginning of *Extraordinary, Ordinary People*, she routes familial honor through the depiction of the armed protection of Confederate property. She explains that Julia was a favored house slave who "had run Union solders off the plantation and protected the horses during the Civil War. To the day she died, she would sit on her porch with a shotgun in her lap and a pipe in her mouth. Perhaps she thought she'd have to do it again" (13). If the tale of Julia's Civil War heroics stretches the construction of ideal femininity to accommodate self-defense and pipe smoking, Rice's recollections of her mother conform to Cold War constructions of gender roles. Angelena Rice is introduced as "an artist and a lady," a schoolteacher and pianist who "didn't really believe that women should play sports or, heaven forbid, perspire" (10). Even so, like Julia, Angelena is a paragon of strength. Rice remembers, for example, how an Easter shopping trip was interrupted by the prohibitions of segregation:

> We often shopped in Mountain Brook, a very exclusive white enclave outside of the city. At the Canterbury Shop for Children they didn't seem to care what color you were as long as you were willing to pay the exorbitant prices they charged. But on this day, we were downtown at Burger-Phillips and a clerk whom Mother did not know said that I would have to try on the dresses in the storeroom. . . . I remember it as if it were yesterday. Mother looked her dead in the eye. "Either she tries them on in the fitting room or we won't buy a dress here," she sternly replied. "Make your choice." The poor woman shooed us into the dressing room and stood guard outside, hoping that no one would see us. (86)

It is significant that the incident is related as a rare encounter with white supremacy in segregated Birmingham. Throughout the memoir, as in this passage, Rice is careful to turn stories of segregation away from victimization toward self-reliance, self-control, and strength. Here, as the saleswoman capitulates to Angelena's demands, Angelena's resolve, her grace under pressure, and her cool rationality connect the performance of Black femininity to the familial history of self-protection and self-reliance that the memoirs relate as the foundation for Rice's career in national security.

The heritage plot that excavates the history of the "extraordinary, ordinary people," the "middle-class folks who loved God, family, and their country," throughout the first memoir accomplishes two important tasks related to the post–Cold War construction of security through interracial cooperation (ix). First, it understates white supremacy and overstates Black achievement, minimizing iterations of racial violence *and* diminishing collective responses to racial violence. When Rice lists the accomplishments of the children involved in her father's youth programs of the early 1960s—the successes of people like the University of Maryland president Freeman Hrabowski III and Mary Kate Bush, who served as a Treasury official in the Reagan administration—she emphasizes, "These were just a few of the scores of teachers, doctors, lawyers, and other professionals who grew up at that time in deeply segregated Birmingham. They clearly took the right messages from their parents, teachers, and mentors such as my father and mother who emphasized excellence and hard work and never tolerated victimhood" (68). If antiracist activism is associated with victimhood, depictions of property ownership, educational achievement, and dignified self-comportment emphasize how the textual modeling of the exemplary bourgeois subject of the memoir is one of the overall strategies of racial liberalism, the favoring of "social development over directly confronting Jim Crow laws and institutions."[50] Rice recalls that her mother and her mother's siblings were never allowed to use segregated public resources: "'Wait until you get home,' they were told. And my grandparents always made sure that they had a car so that no one had to ride in the back of the bus" (8).

Second, as the memoir understates the effects of white supremacy and emphasizes individual rather than collective responses to Jim Crow, it also trivializes Black freedom struggles. Just as the autobiographical form of the slave narrative "required a literary narrative of the self-authoring autonomous individual to be distilled out of the heteronomous collective subjectivity of colonial slavery," as Lisa Lowe posits, this contemporary memoir requires that the heterogeneous collectivities that confronted everyday forms of terror in the Jim Crow South become invisible in Rice's narrative of career formation in the decades that succeeded the 1960s social movements.[51] While Rice writes that in 1962 segregation "was going challenged—and challenged hard—by the growing moment of the civil rights movement" (83), the memoir contains antiracist activism within a frame of racial liberalism in which "the dignity of suffering and the power of eloquent witness are the core lessons of the civil rights struggles" and "romantic notions of consensus across the color line obscure the real difficulties activists had in sustaining cross-racial alliances."[52] In this frame, what Charles Payne and Adam Green call the "Master Narrative of the civil rights movement," desegregation is represented as natural, as the inevitable course of US democracy.[53] "There were decent people," Rice writes, "many of them white, who were trying to do the right thing" (84). In this way, the first-person subject of *Extraordinary, Ordinary People* ties the heritage plot to the terms of civil rights discourse set during the late 1940s, when the "narrow boundaries of Cold War–era civil rights politics kept discussions of broad-based social change, or a linking of race and class, off the agenda."[54]

The memoir's understatements of anti-Black terrorism during Jim Crow and its overstatements of the merits of individual composure and strength tie the emergence of new Black femininity to counterinsurgency, security, and self-protection, suturing Black achievement to national security culture. *Extraordinary, Ordinary People* details how the Cuban Missile Crisis and the September 1963 bombing of Birmingham's Sixteenth Street Baptist Church traumatized Condoleezza as a young girl while also rationalizing the logics of security, tying them to the autobiographical values of self-reliance and achievement. In chapter 4, "Johnny, It's a Girl," Rice describes the family's purchase of their first television and the daily ritual of watching *The Mickey Mouse Club*. Rice interrupts the idyllic recollection of her first childhood home to relate her memory of October 1962: "But one of my most vivid childhood memories is the Cuban missile crisis in October 1962, in which the United States and the Soviet Union engaged in a tense standoff over the placement of Soviet missiles in Cuba. We were glued to the set every evening during those thirteen days. It was a very scary time" (38). Rice remembers witnessing television news reports that Birmingham was in the range of the missiles, and she recalls seeing "big arrows pointing right at us" on the television screen. Rice then realizes, "[This] was something my parents couldn't save me from. It was the first time that I remember feeling truly vulnerable" (38). Rice learns to take refuge in the promise of US military dominance: "Daddy explained that our country had never lost a war, and he was sure we weren't going to lose this one" (38–39). Rice renders the narrative of innocence lost as an object lesson in the importance of security, and she reassures readers of her stance on national security and her uncompromising intolerance for communism: "I once told an audience of Cuban Americans that Fidel Castro had put the United States at risk in allowing those missiles to be deployed. 'He should pay for it until he dies,' I said. Even I was surprised by the rawness of the comment" (39). In the recounting of the Cuban Missile Crisis, the performance of Black feminine vulnerability and protection—Rice's assurance that we are now safe but not rid of the threat of attack altogether—is tied to the threat of retaliation.

While the chapter on October 1962 represents the Cuban Missile Crisis as a formative scene in Rice's life, the chapter on September 1963, which recounts the atmosphere in Birmingham during the month after the March on Washington, deflects the vulnerability that Rice betrays in the earlier chapter. Here Rice recalls the bombing of Sixteenth Street Baptist Church that kills four little girls in September 1963, remembering how she and her mother were already at the church her father pastored when the bomb detonated: "Services hadn't begun at Westminster that Sunday, but the choir, elders, and ushers were already in the sanctuary. I was there with my mother as she warmed up on the organ. All of a sudden there was a thud and a shudder. The distance between the two churches is about two miles as the crow flies, but it felt like the trouble was next door. After what seemed like hours but was probably only a few minutes, someone called the church to say that Sixteenth Street Baptist had been bombed" (97). Rice's description of the September 1963 attack is written into a chapter that begins with a survey of 1960s Birmingham and ends with the Kennedy assassination, the passage of the 1964 Civil Rights Act, and a triumphalist declaration of the end of de jure segregation. Brief and anodyne, the recollection in Rice's memoir tells the story from the vantage point of strength and resolve, not fear and vulnerability. "Everyone was scared and parents just wanted to get their children home," Rice writes, diverting any feelings of fear, powerlessness, and despair into her very rejection of Black communal responses to the attack (97). For example, when the men of the neighborhood begin patrolling in self-defense, Rice remembers "feeling that they were really powerless to stop this tragedy"; when her grandmother reminds her that "the Lord worked in mysterious ways," Rice remembers "thinking that these mysterious ways were awfully cruel" (98). What frames the chapter, in fact, is a recollection of the "shock" of Rice's learning of the boycott of downtown stores during Christmas season. Here Rice remembers the boycott but also remembers her deprivation being ameliorated by the Christmas gifts brought to her by her aunt in Virginia: "Santa Claus . . . showed up as expected with a Charmin' Chatty doll that spoke multiple languages" (89). In this way, Rice's recollection of Bombingham is framed by the narrative of her early childhood achievements amid rare comforts.

Rice's recollection of the bombing is brief and unsentimental. Carolyn Maull McKinstry's 2011 memoir, *While the World Watched*, is a study in contrast. McKinstry fills several chapters of the memoir with a minute-by-minute eyewitness account of the bombing of Sixteenth Street Baptist, where she witnessed the bombing firsthand, and its aftermath. About the minutes following the attack, she writes, "Chaos ruled. Several church members stood outside with stunned expressions. Heads were cut and bleeding. Loved ones wiped their blood-wet faces. Mrs. Demand ran outside, her lower leg gashed by flying glass and her shoe filled with blood. Parents were frantically searching for their children."[55] McKinstry's peppering the recollection with adjectives—"stunned," "blood-wet," "frantically"—contrasts Rice's rendering of the event as a muted "thud and a shudder" sealed off in her memory. I am not suggesting that McKinstry's account is more authentic but rather investigating the different ways that trauma, or the withholding of it, constructs narrative meaning. If Rice's memoir depicts the post–World War II years as a "very scary time," it does so not by depicting anti-Black terrorism as a feature of everyday life in the Jim Crow United States but rather by tying the narrative's construction of Black femininity to the careful juxtaposition of vulnerability *and* strength that defined depictions of the United States' geopolitical position during the Cold War. In this sense, *Extraordinary, Ordinary People* is a Cold War memoir that throws US empire-building into light as a racial gendered project that depends on the careful production of knowledge about racial terror and racial resistance.

Extraordinary, Ordinary People situates emergency at the center of its heritage plot, which anchors the memoir of family in a narrative of extraordinary achievement and protection amid the crises of the post-1945 period. *No Higher Honor*, a second memoir, published in 2011, privileges a terror plot that redirects these themes toward Rice's defense of US foreign policy after 9/11. Recounting Rice's work as the national security adviser for George W. Bush and her service as secretary of state, the memoir draws on the heritage plot and the construction of Black femininity as at once genteel and defensive, vulnerable and armored, established in the first memoir to defend the strategies of preemption, detention, and rendition that have increasingly defined US security strategies since the 9/11 attacks. *No Higher Honor* exposes how the global project of counterterrorism is constructed not through the denial of racial difference or hierarchy (what is commonly referred to as "colorblindness") but through the affirmation of racial difference, the celebration of interracial intimacy, and the careful management of knowledge about antiracist resistance (what is referred to as "postracialism"). Here, as in

Extraordinary, Ordinary People, emergency comes into view as a narrative frame through which the memoir connects post-civil-rights Black achievement to US empire, announcing the Black feminine subject at the scene of threat's anywhere-everywhere as the ideal imperial agent.

No Higher Honor continues where *Extraordinary, Ordinary People* ends, narrating the 2000 election and Rice's first days as the national security adviser and then cataloguing the next eight years, giving readers an insider's perspective on the 9/11 attacks, the Bush cabinet, and the everyday demands of wartime diplomacy. Throughout the text, emergency functions as a thematic that holds together the sprawling account of Rice's everyday life in Washington. In the introduction, Rice begins by discussing her testimony before the National Commission on Terrorist Attacks Upon the United States (known as the 9/11 Commission) in 2004. Remembering her opening statement, she writes, "There was no silver bullet that could have prevented the 9/11 attacks. I concluded my prepared testimony by making the point that terrorists have to be successful just once, while the defender must be vigilant 100 percent of the time."[56] As she closes the introduction, Rice describes meeting with the Indian national security adviser after the Mumbai bombing in 2008, writing that he "had the same shell-shocked look" that she had in the days after the 9/11 attacks: "I took his hands. 'It's not your fault,' I said. 'I know how you feel. It's like being in a dark room with doors all around and knowing anything might pop out and attack again. But now you have to concentrate on preventing the next attack" (xviii). The memoir's staging of this scene of trauma and empathy places the reader first in the position of identifying with the victim of terrorist violence—first Rice, then M. K. Narayan—and then in the position of empathetic observer who absolves the national security adviser for any oversight or mistakes. The introduction closes by literalizing this projection of empathy, using the second-person singular to turn the reader into the embattled subject of emergency: "Protest as you might to yourself, to the nation, and to the world, you never get over the feeling that you could have done better. And you resolve never to let it happen again" (xviii). The juxtaposition of resolve and vulnerability and strength and fear through the narrative construction of empathy lends to the text an absolvent, even apologetic, tone—"A part of me wanted to apologize," Rice writes about her testimony to the 9/11 Commission—but at the same time, it appeals to the logic of sovereignty, naming the emergent terrorist attack as what Rice calls a "crack in time," or a cause for the suspension of normal protocols of executive, legislative, military, and judicial power (xviii).

Like the first memoir, *No Higher Honor* reveals the racial epistemologies of US empire throughout and after the Cold War, exposing a regime that makes global security contingent on the careful management of knowledge about racialized populations and those populations' forms of resistance to domination. When Rice discusses how she helped to prepare Bush to deliver the 2002 State of the Union Address, which outlined the Bush Doctrine and introduced the phrase "Axis of Evil" to identify the war on terror's shadowy targets, she writes, "We needed to drive home the point that the 'enemies of civilization' were of a different character than before. In the past, when the threats had come largely from states, there was some reasonable expectation that military preparations for attack would be visible. But terrorists operated in the shadows and could attack without warning—as they had on September 11. In light of this threat, limiting preemption to the occasions when we are sure an enemy is about to attack makes little sense" (154–55). The invocation of "enemies of civilization" no doubt casts the Arab Muslim world in shadowy opposition to the enlightened West, in Daulatzai's words, deploying the rhetoric of terrorism as a "proxy for race."[57]

The preemptive wars in Afghanistan and Iraq are thus justified by the nature of emergency within a post–Cold War epistemological frame in which the United States must eliminate threats to freedom and democracy. If Rice enlists the reader as the subject of emergency, projecting her own sense of responsibility *and* vulnerability onto the consumer of the memoir, emergent events such as the 9/11 attacks and Hurricane Katrina emphasize the memoir's construction of the scene of emergency through the epistemological frame of the war on terror as a racial regime. For example, Rice addresses how US security strategy sacrificed civilian lives: "I also found compiling lists of people who were individually targeted for 'kill or capture' disturbing, particularly because there sometimes seemed to be civilian casualties in such engagements. But that was the hand we were dealt after 9/11. I do not believe that we should have rejected options that were legal and necessary. I could not have forgiven myself had there been another attack. And had that happened, there would have rightly been a different kind of second-guessing as Americans asked, 'Why did you not do everything in your power to keep it from happening again?'" (121). The memoir casts the reader as the vulnerable American who *would* ask, as she faces future emergency, why *we* were not better prepared.

Rice explains the security regime's incursions on everyday life by appealing to the temporal logic of the security apparatus. As Foucault explains, security differs from disciplinary power in its concern for the population rather than the individual. With the growth of towns in the eighteenth century, Foucault explains, power became "a matter of maximizing the positive elements, for which one provides the best possible circulation, and of minimizing what is risky and inconvenient, like theft and disease, while knowing that they will never be completely suppressed."[58] In this context, governmental bodies aimed to halt epidemic phenomena, or population-level threats. "The town is seen as developing," Foucault writes, and "a number of things, events and elements, will arrive or occur. What must be done to meet something that is not exactly known in advance?" Security as a form of governance thus "refers to the temporal and the uncertain."[59] As Jodi Kim suggests, this is the mode of power that became dominant during the Cold War, when "the logic of the future anterior, or 'what will have happened' had not the United States deterred or opposed the Soviet Union's nuclear capacity, displaces the historical and materiality" of US military aggression throughout the third world. Kim also explains that this "imperial temporality" extended to the Iraq War, when "the notion of a 'preemptive war' against Iraq relies on a metaleptic substitution in which Iraq comes to stand in for al-Qaeda and its action and on a proleptic 'preemption' of future attacks against the United States."[60]

As Rice relates the events of 9/11, describing how she was interrupted in a meeting and then rushed to the White House bunker—she pauses the rushed account to meditate on the relationship between racial difference and US security. When Rice arrives to the bunker, she sees Norman Mineta, who was then serving as the US secretary of transportation. Describing him as "as decent a public servant as one would ever know," Rice points out that Mineta "is a Japanese American with one of those amazing personal histories of a family that remained loyal to the United States despite despicable treatment by the U.S. government during World War II" (73). This deliberately links the Bush Doctrine to the Cold

War, suggesting that just as the internment of Japanese Americans was a necessary, if "despicable," episode in the nation's history, so would 9/11 demand incursions on civil liberties and the ratcheting up of aggression. The memoir so links the imperial temporality of the post-9/11 era to its construction of patriotism vis-à-vis racialized difference.

As the memoir situates racial difference at the heart of its survey of US vulnerability and security in the post-9/11 era, it locates Black femininity at the scene of emergency not as a threat to national security but as the very guarantor of it. Central to the narrative framework of emergency preparedness is the construction of the authorial subject as a morally upright citizen who is both the rational, dispassionate stateswoman and the passionate defender of US ideals in the face of sure catastrophe. The memoir carefully manages the representation of Rice such that she emerges as both the vulnerable feminine subject in need of national protection and the strong representative of a powerful state whose dominance is inevitable. Rice explains, for example, how her position as the national security adviser distracted her from fear after 9/11: "I've been asked many times if I worried about my personal safety in the aftermath of 9/11. Occasionally, a scare like that one would remind me of my own vulnerability. But for the most part, such thoughts were buried deep behind the need to just get the work done" (102).

Solidifying the overachiever persona that surfaces in *Extraordinary, Ordinary People, No Higher Honor* depicts Rice as a self-made professional whose upbringing in the midcentury South is always on display in her poise and grace. Her self-conscious management of this persona is clear when she describes her preparation for her testimony before the 9/11 Commission: "I told myself to be conscious of how I entered the room (*with confidence*, I reminded the face in the mirror). Given the impact that a single picture—even a misleading one—can have, I even had to think about what the photograph would look like when I took the oath. (*You sometimes have a tendency to look wide-eyed*, I told myself. *Narrow your eyes*.)" (263). Rice's description of her own performances of poise, confidence, and assurance signals how the memoir affirms racial difference in the abstract even as it disappears specific forms of Black life, Black thought, Black activism, Black worship, and Black leisure. As Lisa Thompson points out, Rice "in part fashions her persona by making her sheltered southern Black middle-class childhood a central facet of her personal mythology. Her comportment recalls the image of the Black version of the southern belle."⁶¹

As Rice recalls visiting Buckingham Palace in November 2003, she refers to it as an experience that "had an almost fairy-tale quality" (252). "When we arrived, I was escorted to my room," Rice writes, "where my own personal maid waited to unpack my belongings. I instinctively started to help her. Seeing that, Colin Powell, who was there with his wife, Alma, . . . said, 'You're in her way. They've been doing this for three hundred years'" (252). Here Rice's mistake is more than a middle-class faux pas; it is a misreading of her role in a script of power relations inside a lived fantasy of imperial power. Powell's instruction is a lesson in the performance of power that compels identification with a royal "we" rather than a serving, laboring "they." That the woman unpacking Rice's bags is referred to in the third-person plural is significant. Without individuation, she stands in for an entire class and for a three-hundred-year history of domestic labor. Rice's slip in the script demands her meditation on her route from Birmingham to Buckingham as a Black feminine subject: "That night Colin, Alma, and I had a drink in the sitting room. What would our parents think? I thought. Then Alma and I drank a toast to her father and mine. Two little Black girls from Birmingham had come a long way. Then, as Prince Charles escorted me to the elaborate dinner as the orchestra played 'God Save the Queen,' I once again wished that I could tell my parents about this incredible experience. And so I did in a little prayer just before going to sleep" (214). The image of the Black princess in the royal palace completes No Higher Honor's fairy tale of imperial power, which rests on both the mythical fabrication of monarchical splendor ("God Save the Queen") and the mystical conjuring of two Black patriarchs from segregated Birmingham. In this way, the image of the Black southern belle sutures femininity to both vulnerability and mastery: Rice is both the little girl from Birmingham who hardly knows how to act in the palace and the powerful state representative who claims both a history of Black struggle and a future of global security and dominance.

As is evident in Rice's Buckingham prayer, religion manages the narrative tension between vulnerability and mastery, the tension that grounds the memoir's articulation of Blackness. As she describes the memorial service following September 11 at the National Cathedral, Rice remembers that the service was "cathartic": "I focused on the music and the extraordinary words of our great national songs. What had begun as a day of sadness ended, for me, with a sense of rising defiance. The last hymn was 'The Battle Hymn of the Republic.' . . . As the military choir sang the climactic 'Amen, Amen,' I could feel my own spirit renewed. We'd mourned the dead. Now it was time to defend the country" (83). Days later, at Camp David, Rice meets with Bush and his other advisers to decide on the course of military action after the attacks. Now "Attorney General John Ashcroft played spirituals on the piano and we all sang. . . . It was a deep, mournful moment. At dinner, the President asked me to say the prayer. 'We have seen the face of evil but we are not afraid,' I prayed. 'For you, O Lord, are faithful to us' (87). Recounting how Ashcroft plays "His Eye Is on the Sparrow" as she sings along, Rice depicts the impromptu tarry service as a pivotal scene in the Camp David retreat. A gospel standard made famous by Black women musicians such as Ethel Waters, Sister Rosetta Tharpe and Marie Knight, Mahalia Jackson, Jennifer Holliday, and Lauryn Hill, "His Eye Is on the Sparrow" surfaces in Rice's memoir to assure Bush and his advisers of divine protection on the eve of the war on terror. "That day," Rice writes, "the commander in chief worshiped with those whom he would soon order to defend our wounded country in a most distant land" (88). The memoir so calls on the history of Black cultural production not only to account for the logic of protection vis-à-vis preemption but also to smooth the narrative tension between innocence and vulnerability and mastery and aggression.

Rice's performance of "His Eye Is on the Sparrow" at Camp David shows how the language of Black suffering and resilience is assimilable into the imperial grammars of the post–Cold War United States. More importantly, Rice's self-representation as a spiritual authority within the Bush administration deepens the memoir's reliance on scenes of Black intimacy with Western empire. As Rice discusses a trip that she took with Bush to Baghdad in 2003, when the president surprised the troops stationed there, Rice relates how she led the passengers aboard the president's plane in praying with Bush before they landed: "There in the darkness on the presidential aircraft, we each offered a short prayer. When we returned to the cabin about ten minutes before landing, I closed my eyes to pray again. In my head I heard a voice say, 'and keep them safe from hurt, harm or danger.' They were words that I hadn't heard since my father died—the words of a prayer that he'd always uttered when someone was leaving on a trip. 'Thank you, Daddy,' I said softly to myself" (247). Rice, as when she sings "His Eye Is on the Sparrow," translates the languages of Black religious sociality—the grammars of Black song and Black prayer—into the vocabulary of empire. This is one significant way that the memoir, again, constructs counterterrorism not through the denial of racial difference but through the affirmation of racial difference, the celebration of interracial intimacy, and the careful management of knowledge about antiracist resistance. In this context, the memoir functions as a key work of translation, one that mobilizes the language of exceptionality for the very logic of the exception that powers the contemporary security apparatus. The imperial grammars of Blackness are the memoir's idiom and its mode of translation.

This work of translation becomes clearest as the memoir closes with Rice's meditations on the 2011–12 Arab Spring. Rice reminds readers that the United States, "more than any other country, should understand that the journey from freedom to stable democracy is a long one and that its work is never done": "After all, when the Founding Fathers said, 'We the people,' they didn't mean me. My ancestors were counted as three-fifths of a man in the deal that permitted the founding of this country. My father had trouble registering to vote in Alabama in 1952 due to poll tests and harassment of Black voters. And I didn't have a white classmate until I moved from Birmingham to Denver at age twelve" (731–32). Invoking the nation's histories of colonization, slavery, and segregation to discuss the difficult work of democratic nation-building, Rice also uses the history of Black antiracist struggle to bolster the myth of the United States as an exemplary Western power. She writes, "When Martin Luther King or Rosa Parks—one a recognized national leader, the other an ordinary citizen—wanted to challenge the status quo, they could appeal directly to America's own principles. They didn't have to ask the United States to be something else, only to be what it professed to be. That's the value of democratic institutions, even if their promise is not completely fulfilled immediately" (732). Black antiracism, in this way, participates in a grand discursive shift of the 1990s and early 2000s, one in which the history of Black freedom struggles is a powerful motor within the machine of US imperialism. The memoir writes the tale of US power as a coming-of-age story in which the histories of racial violence and resistance to it are both lessons in domination that the nation eventually comes to master. As Rice links her own coming of age and the nation's development to hard work and democratic ideals, she constructs the United States' global domination and its overcoming of racism as inevitable developments in its progress. When she writes of the ceremony in which she is sworn in as secretary of state, she glances up at a portrait of Benjamin Franklin and wonders, "What would he have thought of this great-granddaughter of slaves and child of Jim Crow Birmingham pledging to defend the Constitution of the United States, which had infamously counted her ancestors 'three-fifths' of a man?" (301). Conjuring the history of racial exclusion only to dismiss it, she writes, "Somehow, I wanted to believe, Franklin would have liked history's turn toward justice and taken my appointment in stride" (302). Again turning to colonial history to defend the post–Cold War operations of security, diplomacy, and preemptive war—as well as to affirm her own role in those operations—Rice ties life-writing itself to the imperial enterprise. Given this entanglement, her memoirs can be said to render the imperial grammars of Blackness one of US empire's significant means of communication.

New World Black Femininity

In this chapter, I have argued that one of the structuring contradictions of post–Cold War US power is the suturing of Black women's achievement to the operations of protection (security, crisis management, rescue) and at the same time to the activities of danger (abandonment, illicit sex, scandal, betrayal). The great irony, of course, is that the construction of the Black security class as a police force aimed at and sharpened against Black living occurred through the very decades that Black women built the movement that is now poised to abolish state-defined methods of protection. Rice's Bombingham was of course the childhood home of Angela Davis, the activist and intellectual whose writing and speaking has been so critical of security and incarceration, and so hopeful about its abolition, that it has rendered her image unavailable for use by the state. Speaking of Rice's memoirs, Davis told *Democracy Now!*'s Amy Goodman that whereas Rice left Birmingham with the mission to "be better than anyone else," her own formation in segregated Birmingham taught her "about the possibilities of community."[62] The intimacy between the two sides of terror that I have been surveying in this book is an intimacy that has lived, in other words, in Black women's neighborhoods and in our bodies, narratives, activism, and theories of justice. That the recruitment of fear and shame to smooth the transition to global empire could be so effective in some moments and so dismally weak in others should keep us on watch, not for traitorous Black women but for the capacity that protectivist narratives hold to penetrate our most informed dreams.

Condoleezza Rice is one highly visible public figure whose self-narrative helps illuminate this irony at the heart of contemporary power. Her memoirs might be read, at least in part, as an effort to redirect certain energies emerging from Black social life (common prayer, gospel music, etc.) and to redefine Black freedom struggles in the service of imperial protection. In the post-9/11 world, in which neoliberal financial policy, increased militarization and police violence across scales (from the block to the border), the mobilization of preemptive warfare, and the incorporation of minority difference into transnational networks of power combine in grand narratives of emergency preparedness, the Black woman has emerged as the political-sexual subject whose intimacy with state power authorizes her to enact global capital's fantasy of inclusion while embodying its most profound exclusions. The debut of ABC's prime-time political thriller *Scandal*, in this context, was revelatory and, in some sense, right on time. In the series, the Black woman protagonist, Olivia Pope, is a crisis-management expert whose affair with the Republican president is the scandal around which many others—blackmailings, terrorist bombings, election fraud, kidnappings—revolve. Under conditions of emergency, Black femininity in the series both secures and threatens national stability, situating *Scandal* along the same continuum of representations of Black femininity that Rice's memoirs occupy. In fact, given the picture of exceptional Black femininity that *Scandal* aestheticizes—the dream of being "twice as good as them to get half of what they have" is the lesson drilled into Olivia Pope by her father—one has to wonder whether her character fulfills producers' fantasies of who Condoleezza Rice might have been if she could have been invented. When Olivia faces potential exposure as the president's mistress, her father chastises her: "At the very least you could have aimed for chief of staff, secretary of state! *First Lady?!* Do you have to be so mediocre?" ("It's Handled," October 3, 2013).

Scandal was the third series to air on ABC that was created by the writer and executive producer Shonda Rhimes. Rhimes's first two series, *Grey's Anatomy* and *Private Practice*, both featured diverse casts and self-possessed, highly successful Black woman characters. *Scandal* is a fast-paced thriller set in Washington, DC. Each episode is composed of several short scenes that revolve around various scandals that the main character, Olivia Pope, and her crisis-management team at Olivia Pope and Associates (called "gladiators in suits" in *Scandal*'s first episode) are either fixing or engineering themselves. The liberal Republican president, Fitzhugh "Fitz" Grant, dominates the political scene and much of the show's narrative when viewers learn that he and Olivia have been having a romantic affair since she joined his campaign team and that Olivia, along with his other advisers, engineered the election fraud that resulted in his victory. Much of *Scandal*'s first season follows the story of Amanda Taylor, who threatens to come forward as Fitz's pregnant mistress. After Amanda is murdered, viewers learn that the audio recording of Fitz and an unidentified woman having sex was actually a recording of him with Olivia. While the first season features Olivia in her symbolic "white hat" fighting for good, managing crises, and saving political careers, the second season delves into her responsibility for election fraud in the Ohio town of Defiance and follows the administration's efforts to regain control after a mole is discovered and after Fitz is nearly fatally wounded by a sniper. The second season is also when viewers learn of B613, a black-ops division of the CIA that uses torture, blackmail, and murder to extract information necessary to protect "the Republic." In season 3, viewers learn that Olivia's father, Elijah "Eli" Pope (also called "Rowan"), is the director ("Command") of B613 and that Olivia's mother, Maya Pope, is a terrorist who has been in B613's possession since Olivia was a child. The show, then, revolves around the circulation of scandal across scales: the bodily/sexual, the personal/familial, the national/electoral, and the international/terrorist.

Season 2's episode 8, "Happy Birthday, Mr. President" (December 6, 2012), shows *Scandal*'s particular interest in representing the Black feminine protagonist as both the threat and guarantor of national safety. At the climax of season 2, Fitz is shot by a sniper as he and his wife, Mellie, arrive at his birthday gala. As the president undergoes surgery and remains in critical condition throughout the episode, flashbacks chart the ups and downs of Olivia and Fitz's love affair during the president's first thirty days in office. The early days of the Grant presidency also find White House Chief of Staff Cyrus Beene coming out of the closet and proposing to his boyfriend and Olivia reeling from the news that Hollis Doyle, who worked with the Fitz campaign and engineered the voter fraud in Defiance, is now responsible for creating a deadly explosion at the software company that made the chip for the rigged voting machine that was responsible for Fitz's victory. The episode, first airing on December 6, 2012, was part 2 of a three-part winter finale for *Scandal*. The three-part finale functions as a ratings booster (the first two parts created 10 percent and 14 percent spikes in viewership, respectively) and as a vehicle for expanding the characters' narrative past. As a single narrative is stretched over three weeks, the series can luxuriate in backstory. At the same time, it fabricates the temporality of emergency: brief scenes interspersed with flashbacks and "Breaking News" segments, along with cliffhanger endings to each episode, create the sensation that the viewer is hurtling toward the show's winter hiatus. Rendered in this way, as both diegetic and nondiegetic emergency, "Happy Birthday, Mr. President" beckons racial and sexual difference, firmly attached to the projections and performances of Black femininity, to the scene of emergency to manage threats to national security.

The episode opens with a special report in which a news anchor reports that shots were fired outside the birthday gala. Twenty-six seconds into the episode, the anchor is interrupted midsentence with news that President Grant may have been shot. As he holds his hand to his earpiece, he asks, "What? Where is the president? Why is he—?" After a moment, he looks into the camera and says, "I've just been told that the president has gone to James Madison Hospital. Why has he—? Okay, I'm getting a report now that confirms that President Grant was *not* wounded. He *was* wounded?" The absence of music in this scene, in a television series whose soul soundtrack and orchestral score punctuate even the most mundane of scenes, along with the anchor's broken delivery of the special report, mimics real-time news reporting, throwing the viewer into the episode's crisis temporality. Next there is a flashback to the shooting, and President Grant is shown falling to the ground amid screams from the crowd and the pursuant wailing of sirens. Quickly this bloody scene cuts to a third scene, which opens with a pan of a scene outside the hospital's emergency room. Two bright red "EMERGENCY" signs frame the shot, and a crowd of reporters is gathered, snapping photographs and buzzing around Secret Service agents. Olivia, dressed in a white sequined ball gown, comes into view as she is cleared for entry into the hospital by a Secret Service agent. Finally the opening sequence cuts to the inside of the emergency room, where Mellie screams at a nurse, "I'm fine. Stop! Get away from me!" and Olivia and Cyrus stumble forward as the background blurs and spins around them. A defibrillator whines, heart monitors beep, the camera zooms in on a puddle of blood on the floor. A voice behind a curtain yells, "Mr. President! Mr. President! Look at me. *Look at me.* You may not die. Do you hear me?"

It is significant that in this scene of chaos, Olivia and Cyrus are the central characters. Outside, they exchange long looks of concern; inside, they stumble through the hospital corridor together, and close-up shots of both characters make it clear that the scene is shot through their point of view. Olivia and Cyrus are the president's closest aides. They are also the characters whose minority difference seals the series's construction of a new United States, a country that not only affirms racial and sexual difference but also places racial and sexual difference—in this case, Blackness and gay coupling—at the center of its power structure. If, as I discussed earlier, the national scene of emergency after the Cold War called for the production of new racial and gender subjectivities— including new Black femininities—*Scandal* brings these new subjectivities into prime-time articulation.

The episode's alternating between real-time present-tense narration and flashback juxtaposes the two sides of Olivia's character around which the series, as a whole, constructs its narrative tension: the scandalous mistress who is weak for the president and the strong, competent, professional fixer who keeps her emotions in check. When the vice president, Sally Langston, takes over the president's duties, landing by naval plane on the White House's south lawn and setting up camp in the Oval Office, Olivia and Cyrus rush from the hospital and spring into action. Cyrus storms into the Oval Office and castigates Langston for her abuse of power ("Have you read the whole Constitution, or did you stop in rapture after the Second Amendment?!") and informs her that her taking over the president's duties while he is still alive is threatening the country's security. Meanwhile, outside the Oval Office, Olivia steps into the role she previously played as Fitz's communications director as she notifies White House staffer Jeanine that she is "back":

> OLIVIA: Hi, Jeannine. Go to my apartment. Secret Service has the address. Get me one gray suit, one blue suit, one black suit, six blouses, three pairs of shoes, some underwear, and my toothbrush. Bring them to me here.
> JEANNINE: Miss Pope.
> OLIVIA: Yes.
> JEANINNE: Does this mean . . . are you . . .
> OLIVIA: Back? Yes, I'm back. For as long as you need me. Everything *really is* going to be okay.

As Olivia commands Jeanine to assemble her wardrobe, she transforms from panic-stricken mistress to crisis manager. She protects, she assures, she rallies. As Olivia prepares to brief the press, the BNC News anchor reports, "The choice to hand the podium to Pope is unusual, but I am told that there's been a lot of chatter of support for Pope's display of patriotism in stepping up at this time of extraordinary crisis." That Olivia's performance is linked to her patriotism is key: this is one moment when *Scandal* self-consciously links Black achievement in the realm of state politics to Olivia Pope's performance of competence, self-sacrifice, and calm resolve. Olivia, in this way, fulfills post–Cold War expectations that Blackness will function as a sign of protection in fictional mass-media representations of emergency. The Olivia Pope character revises old tropes of Black women's sexuality in order to make Black femininity compatible with the production of what Olivia herself comes to call "a new world."

If Olivia bears Blackness as a signifier of protection and goodness—playing the good witch, dressed up in white, saving the day in episode after episode—the illicit interracial affair she has with Fitz further reveals how the series depends on Blackness to seal its narrative of a new America as the beacon of a new world. Throughout the episode, a flag pin that Olivia retrieves from the emergency-room floor serves as a symbol for this new nation and the sacrifices it demands. As Olivia first holds the lapel pin in her hand, the episode cuts to a flashback in which she gives it to Fitz before his inauguration. Telling him she bought it at an auction and that it once belonged to Dwight Eisenhower, she pins it on his lapel. Later the camera cuts to a scene after the inauguration, in the Oval Office, in which she attempts to end her affair with Fitz. Fitz insists, "You're the most important person in my life. I can't just stop. Can you?" Now Olivia pulls up her dress and pulls Fitz to her; the flag pin lingers in the foreground of the shot. The pin, embossed with the US flag, symbolizes the irony that Olivia embodies. Olivia's love affair with Fitz threatens the stability of Fitz's administration, but both Olivia's professional expertise and her intimacy with the president are central to the administration's success. At the end of the scene, a close-up of Olivia's hand reveals the pin, now splattered with blood, against the backdrop of her white evening gown. The pin circulates throughout the episode as the point of transfer between past and present and as a symbol of the relationship between the show's patriotic narrative of nationhood and its scandalous narratives of betrayal. In a later flashback, Mellie hands the pin to Olivia and reveals that she recovered it from Secret Service agents after Fitz lost it while out on a date with Olivia. At the very end of the episode, Olivia places the blood-spattered pin on Fitz's hospital bed as he lies there unconscious, and Mellie looks on from behind. In this way, the flag pin is a referent for the tangle of intimacies and betrayals at the heart of *Scandal*'s fashioning of national politics. More importantly, though, that episode so carefully tracks Olivia's handling of the flag pin signals that the (bloodied) country is, in some sense, in her hands.

Olivia's achievements as both chaste fixer and sexy mistress are instrumental in the program's refashioning of American identity. *Scandal*'s ethos, like that of *Grey's Anatomy* and *Private Practice*, is founded on the intersection of disparate trajectories of multicultural ascent, intersections expressed in scenes of interracial sex as well as in episodes of professional overachievement. In another flashback, Olivia helps Fitz prepare for his first State of the Union Address. She is shown meeting with his cabinet members at his retreat compound, wearing a light-gray suit and cautioning Fitz against emphasizing immigration reform in the speech. "The State of the Union Address is about the future," she says. "It should be a showcase of everything you believe." The scene in the wood-paneled meeting room quickly dissolves to a dimly lit bedroom scene. Now, as Olivia, naked, holds Fitz's head to her shoulder, she softly says, "Immigration is noble, but it doesn't light a fire." As scenes of the couple's lovemaking is intercut with scenes of the formal meeting room, Olivia convinces Fitz and Cyrus that the address should focus on giving college students tuition credits for volunteering: "Youth is the future. Youth is the next generation." Olivia wins this argument not only because of her professional expertise but because of her sexual prowess: shown overpowering Fitz in the bedroom, pushing him against the wall while she commands, "Stop running for president and start *being* president," Olivia here plays both political and sexual top to Fitz's bottom. This scene emphasizes Olivia's centrality in the early days of the Grant administration, and it draws a link between Black femininity and the show's imagining of a American future. That this future depends on the incorporation of previously excluded groups into the processes of governance is further accented by what follows in this same flashback. Olivia and Cyrus walk in the woods surrounding the retreat compound, and Olivia lets Cyrus know that the affair he has been having with a reporter is "the worst-kept secret in Washington." She counsels him, "You want to be with the man you love. Be with him." The story in the episode's backstory is one in which boundaries and borders are loosened in order to create racial and sexual subjectivities fit for a new United States. Just as Cyrus comes to affirm his queer sexuality, Olivia, too, has to affirm that the interracial intimacy she shares with Fitz is an expression of the promise of multiracial democracy rather than a legacy of its history of racial subjection.

This essential turn for the show's representation of Black femininity—from its associations with the past to its expressions of future glory—solidifies when Olivia raises the specter of slavery and sexual abjection. Angry at Fitz for bringing his wife to Olivia's room at the retreat compound and suggesting that his wife and mistress have dinner together, Olivia again tries to end the affair with Fitz, this time telling him, "I'm feeling a little, I don't know, Sally Hemmings–Thomas Jefferson about all of this. I have to go." If the Jefferson-Hemmings affair is the backstory of the show's backstory, the series deliberately reverses the master-slave relationship. It is later that evening, when Fitz confronts Olivia as she paces in the Rose Garden, that Fitz articulates precisely how the series's depiction of the affair is essential to its construction of a new America.

"You own *me!*" Fitz avers. "You control me. I belong to *you.*" Fitz refuses the connection that Olivia draws between Jefferson and his mistress and insists, "There's no Sally or Thomas here. You're nobody's victim, Liv. I belong to you. We're in this together." If interracial touch, according to Sharon Holland, "both sears the flesh and provides the opportunity for its suture," this scene opens up the taboo of interracial sex at the core of the nation's "wound" of slavery while also offering itself as a palliative.[63]

Scandal seals this resignification of interracial sex by revisiting the country's settler-colonial history. In a flashback later in the episode, Fitz takes Olivia to the National Archives, where he shows her the original document of the US Constitution and encourages her to touch it. "There are, like, six people in the last hundred years who touched the Constitution. Be the seventh," he urges. The couple is shot from behind, leaning over the glass case that holds the document. Two US flags flank the case, and the light glowing upward from the case infuses the scene with an air of magic. Olivia leans forward as a close-up shows her tracing the words of the preamble with her manicured hand.

> OLIVIA: Wow.
> FITZ: Wow. "We the People." That's just . . . That's . . . just . . . That's everything.
> OLIVIA: It's a new world.
> FITZ: It's a new world.
> OLIVIA: I love you, too. I'm in love with you, too.
> FITZ: So we're in this together?
> OLIVIA: We're in this together.

Olivia's hand on the glass is jarring, not only because it is so Black and beautiful but also because it appears in stark contrast to the gruesome scenes of torture—her associate Huck's drilling into people's skin to extract information, for example—that enable her to "fix" scandals.[64] Like Rice's memoir, the show symbolically touches the Constitution's "We the People" to affirm the promises of US democracy, promises that the Black protagonist, embodying both a history of Black suffering and a future of Black achievement, bears in her bodily form. Fitz's command to touch the document literalizes Olivia's intimacy with governmental power; as the two lovers' hands meet at the edge of the case, they

Scandal's Olivia Pope, played by Kerry Washington, caresses the US Constitution.

stare into the object of the past as if they are peering into history and into future at the same time. This symbolic copulation at the site of the Constitution results in the conception of "a new world," one in which the phrase "the people" undergoes a vast revision.

The juxtaposition of interracial sexual intimacy and the promise of federalism in this scene throws Olivia Pope into the same impossible position that public fantasies and fears of Condoleezza Rice created for Black womanhood. This is the position of the skeeza in bed with empire, a role based in the new articulation of Black femininity as both founded in overachieving professional coolness and inexorably linked to illicit, hot, promiscuous sex in places as austere as the Oval Office. The Pope-Grant affair is a threat to the nation that must be contained; as Olivia explains to Fitz, the Republican family ideal must be projected onto and through the office of the president. As Fitz pursues her in the Oval Office on the night of his inauguration, Olivia tells him, "Look around you. Look where we are. This can't happen, not anymore." *Scandal*, though, earns its name and its ratings by trafficking in this central contradiction: the affair is what threatens the structure of the presidency, but it is also what powers the show's narrative of new-world exceptionalism. As the lovers' visit to the National Archives shows, interracial sex is bound up with the show's rewriting the racial script of contemporary US power. Purged of its associations with racial subjection during slavery, the interracial touch in *Scandal*'s 2012 winter finale propels Black femininity into the new world, a world in which the Black woman symbolically rebirths a nation no longer marked by its history of racial exclusion but instead *touched* by the promise of multiracial governance. Diversity management meets prime-time spectacle at the scene of emergency, and Olivia Pope is the breath of fresh air that makes ABC's narrative of US empire-building irresistible.

Given these narrative expectations, Olivia has to manage an impossible double sacrifice: she has to maintain the show's investment in the interracial coupling and continue the illicit affair with Fitz, giving into the irresistible force of their union over and over again and sacrificing her desire to maintain the cool rationality that her job as a professional fixer demands; and she must end the affair, as many times as she succumbs to rekindling it, to protect Fitz's reputation and, by extension, the authority of the office of the presidency. This crisis of double sacrifice is one that the shifts in narrative time resolves: the backstory makes the new world birthed by Olivia and Fitz's coupling not only imaginable but irresistible, while each emergency in the narrative present feeds viewers' desire for Olivia's overachievement as a fixer, which in turn demands her spurning of Fitz's advances. Black women's power, in this way, functions as both the perpetual threat to US empire and the scandalous vehicle of its survival and redemption. Interracial sex exposes this conundrum for the show's protagonist, and *Scandal*'s narrative form resolves it, scene by scene, episode by episode.

If Olivia Pope fixes, even saves, the republic by playing hot sexual subject and cold overachiever at the same time, suturing the show's construction of new-world Black femininity to its construction of a US imperial imaginary, the heritage plot that unfolds in the series's third season, like that in Rice's memoirs, recalls Blackness's movements on the other side of terror. The link between the imperial grammars of Blackness and the history of Black anticolonial, antiracist resistance is solidified by the series's construction of Black familial intimacy, which rests on the story of Olivia's upbringing as the only child of two highly accomplished spies: a father who heads B613 and a mother who is a soulless "terrorist," one of B613's most dangerous prisoners. Olivia's parents straddle the line between this and the other side of terror: Eli Pope mobilizes (counter)terror to protect the nation, and Maya Pope conjures the association of Black femininity with unbridled rage against authority, capitalism, and democracy.

Maya Pope's surfacing as Eli's prisoner in season 2 awakens the history of policing and surveillance that has associated Black femininity with terrorism throughout the long war on terror, summoning the stories of Black women leftists and political prisoners such as Claudia Jones, Louise Patterson, Eslanda Robeson, Assata Shakur, Safiya Bukhari, and Angela Davis. Further, Maya Pope's escape from Eli's prison and her reemergence onto the scene of anti-American terrorism propels her into the same range of representations that Olivia tightropes through: representations of the Jezebel, of the overachieving Black professional, of the bad mother, and of the terrorist. In season 2's episode 9, "Yolo" (December 5, 2013), Maya escapes from Eli and greets Olivia on the street outside her apartment, emerging from the shadows. When Olivia and her team later secure Maya in their safe house, Maya tells Olivia that Eli imprisoned her because she was planning to fly to London and tell a reporter there about B613's clandestine abuses of power. But after Olivia's team arranges for Maya to be flown to Moscow and Maya boards the plane, Olivia suddenly recalls Maya having used her alias, Marie Wallace, when she was younger. Olivia and her team now realize that Maya is not Eli's innocent victim but rather a threat to national security. In the next episode, "A Door Marked Exit" (December 12, 2013), Olivia gets Marie Wallace's criminal record and learns that her mother was born in East London to parents who were associated with an organization called the Marxist Liberation Front and that she later became a spy who stole classified documents from the CIA—that is, from Eli—and sold them to various anti-American groups. Having entered the United States in 1972, Maya arrived on domestic soil just in time for the decimation of Black Power, for the escalation of surveillance and incarceration first via COINTELPRO and later under the banner of the War on Drugs, and for the post-civil-rights emergence of a Black professional class that was tasked with managing and containing the threats posed by antiracist organizing. With aliases like Marie Wallace, Margaux Bouvier, Hannah Stuart, Ines Bassir, and Saafi Ali Farah, Maya Pope is pictured in her criminal record in photographs with insurgents in Paris, Germany, Somalia, and Tunisia. As Olivia's team observes, Maya is a "woman without a country" who clings to "no ideology whatsoever." Olivia's mother is a figure for pure betrayal and treason, and whatever knowledge she has of radical politics (say, from her parents' involvement with a Marxist organization) is transfigured into indifferent and undifferent anti-American subterfuge and perfect greed ("She sold whatever she could get to the highest bidder"). With the introduction of the terrorist mother to *Scandal*'s plotlines of crisis management, the series calls Black femininity to the scene of emergency to represent danger and unbridled infidelity to the nation-state.

Maya Pope's outing as a radical turned mercenary "without a country" reveals *Scandal*'s representations of Black femininity as both directed toward a new-world expiation in which interracial sex rebirths the nation and connected to the symbolics of terrorism and insurgency that have historically attached to Black femininity. And of course, the associations of people of color with domestic terrorism and insurgency always cover over the histories of anticolonial, antiracist organizing on the other side of terror. As Daulatzai writes, "In the cacophony that masks itself as reason about the establishment of democracy and the fighting of 'terror,' much is made about the coalitions of the willing that have rallied around these causes. But do other kinds of solidarities exist? . . . [What] about other kinds of alliances, those built on anti-racist and anti-imperialist struggles like the ones at Bandung 50 years ago?"[65] *Scandal*'s conjuring of these "other kinds of solidarities" through the circulation of the Black female spy-terrorist clothes protection and threat in the same costume.

In the final scene of "A Door Marked Exit," Maya calls Olivia from Pennsylvania Avenue, where she stands outside the White House after having hijacked the plane that was supposed to fly her to Moscow. Scenes of Olivia at home, wearing a long, white cardigan and sipping red wine, are intercut with the scene of Maya menacingly occupying the dark sidewalk outside the White House. More significant than the dialogue here—Olivia simply repeats, "Where are you, Mom?" and Maya refuses to answer—is the wardrobe. Maya is dressed in a long, white, wool trench coat and light-gray leather gloves, and her hair is styled, like Olivia's, to cascade, straightened, below her shoulders. Dressed in power whites and muted lights, Maya appropriates Olivia's style. This suggests that, as much as Maya is Olivia's mother, she is Olivia's alter ego. "Don't worry, sweetheart, I'll see you real soon," Maya coos before hanging up the phone, throwing it away, and exiting the frame. As she leaves, the camera pans up to the flag atop the White House, signaling that this is, in the end, Scandal's "new world": a nation in which the demands of crisis management and emergency preparedness draw Black femininity into intimate relation with governmental power, so dangerously intimate that the line separating this side from the other side of terror is as tenuous, and as threatening, as the shaky connection between terrorist bad mother and estranged good daughter, between 1972 and the present, between the skeeza and the lady, and between freedom fighting and "terrorism." The show's scene of emergency, in this way, creates a narrative context in which new-world Black femininities can emerge even as it keeps in motion Black femininity's relationship to the kinds of solidarities that locate a "door marked exit" from the strictures of country and capital.

Scandal so reveals the seductions of emergency in contemporary narratives of US empire-building. Like Rice's memoirs, the series reimagines Black femininity—apart from, and at the same time *in the range of* its associations with illicit sexuality, subjection, and antiracist resistance (resignified as "terror")—in order to rearticulate the racial and gendered logics of post–Cold War US power. Scandalous though it may be, Black femininity arrives at the scene of emergency not only as a threat to national security but as its author and protector.

If the United States' rise as a superpower in the post–World War II decades effected a racial break, a reinvention of racial formation, Black representatives of the government, corporations, sports teams, and popular culture over these same decades announced and embodied this racial break, tying the rise of US empire to a liberal civil rights agenda that depended on the incorporation of minority difference into US power to justify global expansion. Crisis management, in this context, emerged as a professional discourse that tied together lingering (if loosening) disciplinary standards of individual comportment, the increasing human vulnerability to environmental power, and the persisting social ideas governing race, gender, sex. As I have shown throughout this chapter, the post–Cold War symbolics of crisis management and emergency preparedness charted new narrative terrain for Black femininity, prompting us to consider how Black women's sexuality and textuality are articulated in the projections of late twentieth- and early twenty-first-century US empire as well as how Black femininity remains a site of anticolonial, anti-imperial threat. From Baraka's rhetorical question, "What kind of skeeza is a Condoleezza?" to Rice's memoirs' constructions of US security as the legacy of a Black southern belle, to *Scandal*'s positioning of interracial sex at the vanguard of a new world, the resignifications of Black femininity in the post-9/11 era revealed the way that Blackness circulates within and around US imperial aspirations.

The activation of emergency powers called for the loosening of racial and gendered codes of governmental power—which allowed for the inclusion of heretofore excluded social subjects in the authoring and circulation of global power—and the tightening of those same codes, which provided for the continued surveillance and containment of the bodies, ideas, and movements of women of color. The Black feminine subject who arrives at the scene of emergency thus reconfigures the imperial and anti-imperial grammars of Blackness, mastering the languages of empire while keeping in motion the association of Black women's liberatory labor with the lexicon of Black women's stigmatization: "terrorist," "whore," "mother." In this chapter, I have analyzed that reconfiguration in an attempt to make good on my promise to reckon with the relationship between US empire-building and Black women's expressive culture throughout the long war on terror. In part 2, I turn to the ways Black women writers and critics effected this reconstruction of imperial and anti-imperial grammars within and beyond the literary institutions of the security state, including universities' English departments.

A young boy dances in a counterformation of one in front of a line of law enforcement officers, in a still from Beyoncé Knowles-Carter's "Formation" in her film *Lemonade*. (Parkwood Entertainment, 2016)

Lorna Simpson, *Source Notes, 2019*. Ink and screen print on gessoed fiberglass.

GIs float face down in a battle scene in Spike Lee's *Miracle at St. Anna* (2008), recalling the flooding of Black New Orleans that Lee captured with *When the Levees Broke*.

Black American World War II soldiers stationed in Italy stage a moving portrait of armed Black resistance to Jim Crow and imperialism, in Spike Lee's *Miracle at St. Anna* (2008).

Zana Wilder, a Black woman lawyer for Exxon played by Kerry Washington, defends the Black soldier deserter in Spike Lee's *Miracle at St. Anna* (2008).

Alex, played by Blair Underwood, tells his psychiatrist about exchanging looks with an Iraqi civilian after bombing his village, in *In Treatment*, season 1, episode 7 (2008).

BEING
CONDOLEEZZA

As the tensions between Hezbollah and Israel explode in the Middle East, the death toll rises in Iraq, and nations from North Korea to Iran remain defiant in their pursuit of nuclear weapons, the Bush administration struggles to regain the confidence of both foreign allies and citizens at home. And on the front line is a Black woman. Here in an exclusive interview, ESSENCE's Tatsha Robertson sits down with the secretary of state to ask the questions Black America wants the answers to
PHOTOGRAPHY BY TIMOTHY WHITE

ESSENCE 184 10.2006

An *Essence* feature shows Condoleezza Rice gracefully peering into the near distance while the Lincoln Memorial, a symbol of freedom and the promise of multiracial democracy, looms behind her reflection.

An album filled with pictures of former US secretary of state Condoleezza Rice was found in Muammar Gaddafi's compound on August 24, 2011. This photo appeared on NBC News's website *Photoblog*.

Scandal's Olivia Pope, played by Kerry Washington, caresses the glass case holding the US Constitution.

July, 1982

Dearest June:

Received your letter one evening after having come home from work (yes i got the job, thank-you for your reference) after having redd articles in the Voice regarding the acts of genocide against the Lebanese and Palestinian people—in the name of a jewish state. Who will secure the state of the Lebanese and Palestinians? the ride to work is long, an hour and a half—feel like I'm going out of state—I am reading these articles and feeling such shame—certainly horror but shame that the human race continues such inhumanity upon itself! Some times I wonder what in the world am I doing here in this time and space.... feeling so delicate and tender lately.... I want only pretty silk kimonos, flowers

Letter from Gwendolen "Lil' Bit" Hardwick to June Jordan, 1982. (Courtesy of Schlesinger Library, Radcliffe Institute, Harvard University, Cambridge, MA)

June Jordan in repose at Yaddo in upstate New York. (Courtesy of Schlesinger Library, Radcliffe Institute, Harvard University, Cambridge, MA)

First Lady Nancy Reagan (*right*) and daughter Maureen (*left*) applauding as guests of honor Clara "Mother" Hale (*second from right*) and the Vietnamese-born West Point cadet Jean Nguyen (*second from left*) stand with her.

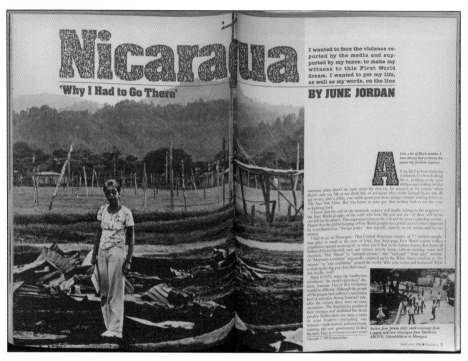

June Jordan, "Nicaragua: Why I Had to Go There," *Essence*, January 1984.

PART II

Insurgent Grammars

4

Scenes of Incorporation; or, Passing Through

A graduating senior idles in a classroom. Spring, pushing up on summer, has firmly established its bloom. It is 1968. It is heated. Smoke almost unnoticeably drifts toward the senior's desk from the row of open windows across the room. Or is the funk of a rotting old world, or what could be the smell of a liquor store in embers, or what could even be the stink of her college president, in effigy, smoldering, simply pressed into the fibers of her tank top? Try as she might, she can't seem to focus her sight on the text in front of her. She is forgetting about reading. She is thinking in every language except English.

Black women's writing refracted the long war on terror's security regime. It reflected the post-1968 shifts in racialization demanded by the changing nature of threat, translating the imperial grammars of Blackness. At the same time, the radical Black feminist grammars that often erupted into the new forms of Black women's writing that emerged in this period *broke* and *broke open* the racial ideologies that tied public security to the often private, and definitively privatized, activities of reading and writing. Through part 2 of this book, I attend to the way Black feminist writing served as the lens that did this crucial breaking. To refract is to cut, as Alexis Pauline Gumbs suggests when she writes, "she was sharp refracted everything"; it is also to magnify.[1] In chapter 5, I argue that June Jordan's work between 1979 and 1985 decimated the imperial grammars of Blackness while inventing new grammars of safety and insurgent expression, and then, in chapter 6, I argue that Black feminist writers after the September 11 attacks undertook this same work of refraction, skewering the grammars of posttraumatic national unity. In this chapter, I want to provide context for chapters 5 and 6 by surveying the scene in which Black feminist writers like Jordan, Alice Randall, Danielle Evans, and Gloria Naylor came to work through the institutions that published, reviewed, taught, challenged, censored, anthologized, and archived their work.

In 1968, the phrases "Afro-American literature," "Black literature," and "Black Aesthetic" were, if not neologisms, invitations to a revolution that would explode all previous definitions of those terms. Rather than refer to a classification that was already in place, these terms were, indeed, attempts to blast a new world from the lavish greens of the US university. For Spillers, 1968 "irrevocably split time into a 'before' and 'after'"; and in retrospect, we can now grasp the central paradox of our lives as Black scholars and, indeed, of the very fields of African American literature and Black studies: that while we enjoy greater and greater access to the means for disseminating creative and intellectual work, the relative enjoyment that structures the Black creative academic's life (or the life of the Black studies program) is contraposed to the general "genocidal circumstance of Black life."[2] While the creative intellectual does not necessarily have to take credit for the gulf between the Black downwardly mobile and the Black upwardly mobile—a gulf that dramatically widened over the post-1968 decades—to establish a "*total perspective* against which the work of the intellectual unfolds" and to "map the terrain anew" remain necessary tasks in fields of study that, despite their rootedness in radical social formations, are saturated by market imperatives.[3] In Spillers's 1994 "The Crisis of the Negro Intellectual: A Post-Date," she exposed how the photogenic Black creative intellectual "lends herself/himself—like candy being taken from a child—to the mighty seductions of publicity and the 'pinup.'"[4] (And that was before digital platforms changed the very nature of intellectual exchange, before you could apply a flattering filter to an image of yourself at work, or of the four or five academic books stacked on your coffee table, and disseminate it instantly to your thousands of friends and followers.)

The "total perspective" of the terrain for Black academic and creative work, which includes the way the long war on terror lubricated the successive racial gendered regimes of late contemporary US power, provides crucial context for the study of contemporary Black women's writing. In what follows, I detail Black women writers' difficult position within the racial regimes of the long war on terror by chronicling their incorporation into mainstream literary culture vis-à-vis the university and the literature industry. I end the chapter by reflecting on the way Black women writers imagine safety beyond state defense, arguing that their invention of insurgent grammars of safety provides us with an analytic through

which we can better understand their work in the contemporary era
beyond the language of genre and generation. As Black women passed
through the institutions that wanted to eat them alive, their writing left
a trail of instructions for how to work in, and how to carve one's way out
of, the belly of the beast.

During the four decades between 1968 and the 2012, texts by and
about Black Americans surfaced in the most unlikely of places to do
the weighty ideological work of building a domestic multicultural consensus to post–Cold War US foreign policy. Texts by Black authors bore
the iconoclastic standard for revolutionary change at the same time as
they were marketed to consumers in the multicultural classroom or
bookshop, or even the daytime talk-show audience, as keys for understanding the other. In other words, the developments in the culture of
Black books at times destabilized but at other times shored up the ideological scaffolding of late–Cold War and post–Cold War US security.
Black texts, that is, played an important role in making the world that
was being made safe for democracy *feel* safe for readers in the liberal
arts classroom. Importantly, discourses within literary studies—the discourse of the race novel or protest novel, for example—have been key
sites for the articulation of official state antiracisms: as Jodi Melamed offers, "Liberal antiracisms have had to repeatedly institutionalize a notion
of literary texts as practical and effective tools that Americans can use
to get to know difference" and have so positioned racism as that which
can "be corrected in the name of liberal-capitalist modernity rather than
as internal to its political and economic structures."[5] If literature in part
bears the responsibility of remaking race, the discourses of Black literary
studies since the incorporation of Black studies in the US academy after
1968 have both served as a site for the radical anticolonial impulses of
antiracism *and* aided the ideological production of the United States as a
globally diverse community. In the context of the simultaneous upward
and downward expansion of life chances for African American communities, that is, literary studies played an important cultural role in
managing the shift to neoliberal multiculturalism at the end of the Cold
War and into the twenty-first century.

To be a Black woman passing through the filtering apparatuses of
cultural power—universities, literary agencies, publishing houses, archives, newspapers and magazines, and television shows—was to ab-

sorb the massive pressure of simultaneous institutional formation and deformation, that is, to bear in one's body the costs of that pressure. My goal here is not to offer a comprehensive history of the conditions that made Black women responsible for the diversity projects of contemporary literature during the decades of the long war on terror, throughout which they were engaged in an internationalist project to permanently destabilize and delegitimize the US state violence that announced itself as counterinsurgency. It is rather to sketch out, through a series of brief scenes or encounters, the stakes of deciphering the radical tendency of what, for lack of a better term, I will continue to call *Black feminist literature*—the work we might gather not as a collection of singular texts by great writers but rather under the banner of a collective project of marshaling the embodied practices of reading, writing, hearing, and performing literature in the interest of abolitionist anticolonial social change—as a passing-through that devastates the desires of the liberal literature teacher. For the promises of individual merit that co-opted radical movements and exhausted the Black woman political organizer were the same pieces of silver that exalted the Black woman writer who inevitably appears on the syllabus as a diversifying "twofer" or, perhaps, as a pressure-release valve for the rage of generations. I wager, then, that the scenes of incorporation that tell the story of Black women's passing through the very fields through which I now pass—Black studies and literature in particular, universities and literary culture in general—might highlight a contradiction at the heart of contemporary Black (literary) studies, at the heart of English, at the heart of this book: that Blackness is as intimate with empire as the reader is with the book on-screen or on her lap, that the Black cultural text is, in other words, a transfer point, a too-short bridge, between the long war on terror's brutal practices of counterinsurgency and its smooth calls of advancement, inclusion, celebrity, and celebration.

Making Use of Being Used

I am plucked, dropped, pounded onto a plastic desert, pushed onto the edge and left on my face for damn near seventy-five minutes. That's long enough to conjure memories of foul-smelling instruments lining through my front half, sometimes determined and head-on, sometimes pillowy,

dreamily, almost nothingly. I am picked up, rifled, and I can tell that the
warm, fat hands want nothing from me. Just pull something out of me,
keep on using me for your shit paper, your requirement, your graduation
nite, your retirement—hell, your mama.

As I wrote in chapter 1, the years of brute repression and absorptive co-optation that followed the 1960s were the very years that Black feminist organizations, activists, and writers heightened their calls for organized, insurgent resistance to racism, colonialism, nuclear armament, and gender violence. Indeed, by 1984, June Jordan had Palestinian liberation, the South African antiapartheid struggle, and socialist struggles in Nicaragua and Grenada in mind when she called out to the "new women" that the previous decade had produced, women "completely uninterested in keeping calm, women entirely prepared to make a scene, to raise a ruckus and to be shrill, if you will."[6] As historians of Black women's organizing and Black feminist activism have argued, the 1970s witnessed the development of Black women's radical and internationalist challenges to racism, sexism, incarceration, unfair labor conditions, sexual and reproductive violence, and other threats to Black women's subjectivity and collective well-being as well as the growth of cultural forms of counter-insurgency in response. Kimberly Springer explains that Black feminist organizations that formed after 1968, such as the Third World Women's Alliance, the National Black Feminist Organization, the Combahee River Collective, and the National Alliance of Black Feminists, articulated expansive visions of liberation amid at least three challenges: (1) the marginalization of Black women's issues in the women's movement and the Black Power movement, (2) the "structural obstacles upheld by racist and sexist theorizing in sociological and public policy literature that alleged a Black matriarchy as responsible for the Black community's ills," and (3) an onslaught of updated stereotypes, from the Mammy to Sapphire, that had the effect of discrediting Black women's antiracist and antisexist work.[7]

In addition to these cultural, ideological barriers, Black feminist organizers and cultural workers encountered the everyday violence that Audre Lorde wrote of when she addressed white feminists' apathy: "You fear your children will grow up to join the patriarchy and testify against you; we fear our children will be dragged from a car and shot down in the street and you will turn your backs upon the reason they are dying."[8] Safety was a weapon wielded against Black female flesh, an entitlement that white feminists could detach from the caged and beaten and impoverished Black people who secured it. So the situation of Black feminist organizing was constrained by the very conditions to which activists addressed themselves.[9] That is, the state left Black women activists vulnerable to the vicissitudes of health care and employment in the postwelfare state and not only failed to protect them from crime, surveillance, sexual violence, and intimate-partner violence but also *originated* those forms of violence. The memoirs and autobiographies of Black feminists of the post-civil-rights era, such as Assata Shakur, Angela Davis, Maya Angelou, and Paule Marshall, read as a catalogue of the unprotection that was the context for Black women's writing, studying, defending, building, and organizing.

At the same time as literature served as a record of state violence and Black women's resistance, Black women's writing bore a self-conscious relationship to the state's *affirmative* relationship to racial, gender, and sexual difference throughout the postwar years. Marshall's 2009 memoir *Triangular Road*, for example, begins with an account of her receiving a letter from the State Department inviting her to accompany her mentor, Langston Hughes, on a cultural tour in 1965. When Marshall accepts the invitation and travels to the State Department for her briefing, she learns that the agency has been tracking her political involvement; she finds in front of her a file divulging her history as an activist in leftist organizations such as American Youth for Democracy and the Association of Artists for Freedom. And there was, she imagines, more: "The extensive file must also have included the transcript of every speech in which I had roundly taken the government to task. Also on record had to be a list of each rally, protest meeting, demonstration, and march I had participated in, including the first-ever joint Civil Rights–Anti-Vietnam War march. . . . As usual, the FBI agents in their London Fog trench coats had been on hand, openly writing down names and taking photographs from the sidelines."[10] When the briefing official makes little mention of the dossier and moves forward with preparation for the tour, Marshall suspects that the government has invited her dissent as proof of a thriving democracy. "The fact that I would be openly critical of [the US government's] policies could well serve as proof that the country was truly

state-sanctioned dissensus

a democracy committed to respecting the First Amendment rights even of its most vocal detractors," Marshall writes. "Thus, Washington might well come out the winner every time I opened my mouth." Marshall embarked on the tour with the intention of "making use of being used."[11] The struggle between Black feminist insurgency and state-sanctioned and state-sponsored surveillance and violence in the age of rights was, in this way, never very distant from the state's affirmative uses of Black expressive culture.

Still, during the post-1968 decades of Black literary professionalization, Black women were writing, anthologizing, teaching, and organizing to keep the literature of Black feminists in circulation in ways that can only be understood as para- or counterinstitutional. Perhaps the best example of this was the 1968–69 struggle for open admissions at the City College of New York, from which June Jordan's theory and practice of Black studies as "Life Studies" emerged.[12] But the years between 1975 and 1984 were a key juncture in this regard. As Barbara Christian put it, "Afro-American women were making public, were able to make public, their search for themselves in literary culture."[13] In now-classic texts like Alice Walker's 1975 "Looking for Zora," Barbara Smith's "Toward a Black Feminist Criticism" (1978), and Barbara Christian's "A Race for Theory" (1987), Black feminism was figured as a lifeline for Black women writers struggling in the US publishing industry. These are the texts that "began to reverse the trends that by 1975 had jeopardized the survival of black studies."[14]

By the early 1980s, the work that Black feminists were doing to make Black women's writing available to students, professors, book clubs, and everyday readers was materializing in what has since come to be called a Black women's literary renaissance. Publishing houses like Random House and Kitchen Table: Women of Color Press were regularly disseminating works by Black women; Robert Hemenway, supported by two NEH grants, published the first authoritative biography of Zora Neale Hurston, which was followed by the 1978 republication of *Their Eyes Were Watching God*; and academic work on Black feminism was finding space in journals such as *Signs*, *differences*, and *Black American Literature Forum*. With the founding of Kitchen Table: Women of Color Press in 1981 and the publication of *All the Women Are White and All the Men Are Black, but Some of Us Are Brave: Black Women's Studies* in 1982 and

Home Girls: A Black Feminist Anthology in 1983, Black literary feminism was at the height of its print activism.

It was during these years of the Black women's renaissance in print culture, in fact, that Marshall, along with June Jordan, Audre Lorde, Vèvè Clark, Alice Walker, and others, organized a collective they called the Sisterhood that would serve as a "clearinghouse" for Black writers. Founded by Jordan and Walker, the Sisterhood was an autonomous organization that changed the course of Black literary history, as Courtney Thorsson argues.[15] In her forthcoming history of the Sisterhood, Thorsson chronicles how the rebirth of Black women's writing from the late 1970s through the 1980s was the result of concerted, collective organizing efforts. While the Sisterhood left no anthologizable, print record of its activity, the members of the organization formed a bridge between the academy, the literary world, and social movements. At one of their early meetings in April in Brooklyn, New York, the group members discussed how they might create more space for Black women's writing in publications like *Essence* and *Ebony*. By April 1977, the Sisterhood had developed a proposal for new publishing ventures—potentially under the auspices of a publishing outfit, Kizzy Enterprises, Inc.—to provide outlets for Black women's writing, to republish out-of-print publications, and to counter the neglect of Black women's writing by publications like *Ebony*, which at the time boasted a monthly circulation of 1.4 million readers.[16] The Sisterhood wanted to force John Johnson, CEO of *Ebony*'s Johnson Publishing Company, to "respond to and encourage new writing from the Black world." This was especially important for the group because Johnson Publishing had recently announced that *Ebony* had "absorbed" the more progressive publication *Black World*.[17]

The Sisterhood's proposal to sustain Black print culture's progressive, pan-African perspective through the inclusion of Black women writers who would challenge the "Antra/Nadinola [fading creams] image of Black women" voiced an objection to mainstream representations of Black women writers, which, whether celebrating their achievements or vilifying their representations of "the Black community," domesticated the most radical impulses in their work.[18] I mean "domesticated" here both ways: the public discourse about Black women's writing often isolated that work from the leftist, often lesbian Black feminist collectives that supplied the context for its production and its reception, *taming* its challenges to white heteropatriarchy; and the same discourse limited the terms of discussion to a national, intraracial frame centering around matters of *home*, specifically, what many readers saw as pathological representations of Black husbands and fathers voiced by pathological, overly masculine women.

In a market that could both expand to absorb the shock of the monstrous collectivity of Black women writing their narratives into public consciousness ("the vivid new fact" that Spillers wrote of in 1985) and sustain charges that Black women writers were dirty launderers—it is worth pointing out that the Sisterhood was formed partly in response to the backlash that Shange received after *for colored girls who have considered suicide / when the rainbow is enuf*—Black women defied the expectations of capitalist niche marketing by creating autonomous publishing units, flipping literary pedagogy upside down, and supporting the extrainstitutional labor of other creative workers. As Alexis Gumbs painstakingly chronicles, this work was built on queer practices of mothering that undermined the *authority* of the state. But again, it was not without its costs in illness and financial precarity.[19] As Loretta J. Ross writes, "Imagine feminists of color in 1981 seeking to explain the complex matrix of domination and oppression we faced under Ronald Reagan's cowboy capitalism, yet feeling invalidated in our communities of color because our militant feminism called attention to sexism, homophobia, and violence. Simultaneously, we were devalued in majority-white feminist circles because we confronted racism, xenophobia, and colonialism in feminist thought and practices."[20]

Black feminist literary activism mounted counterinstitutionalization projects, in effect *making use of being used*, and radically opening the institutions they passed through not only to critique them but also to create anticapitalist, anticolonial, anti-imperial possibilities within and alongside them. These projects led them around and through the beautiful, wasteful factories of knowledge production and creative extraction that secured civil society by "regulating the collocation of the discourses of political power and knowledge" through the bureaucratization of disciplinary study.[21]

Passing Through

We are outside an office on a third floor, in late November 1974. We are up north. It is chilly up in here. We are waiting to meet with a professor, to crowd into her office and pepper her with nonquestions about busing, about sellouts, about the future of the race. Here she comes, speed-tiptoeing down the hall from the bathroom past all of us who've been waiting since the "Afro-American Literature Class" she taught over three hours ago. Her afro is still fresh. She is an open secret. She'll be my homegirl in the not-too-distant future. The sister next to me got the nerve to ask, "Why your heels so loud, professor?" Professor flashes that smile and sings, louder than the heels, "Let the hallowed halls echo to the fact of a woman, a Black woman, passing through!"[22]

English departments took on the burden of universities' incorporative labor and, in that sense, the work of domestication. In particular, the canon wars of the 1980s and 1990s shored up the ideology of liberal multiculturalism, limiting knowledge about racism to a pluralist framework that asserted the primacy of individual and property rights over materialist understandings of race and domination.[23] After the 1968 revolutions that rocked the knowledge and creative industries, literature remained a domain for the practice of freedom. This was especially true for Black women writers and critics, who saw text and live performance as (1) realms for persuasion, in which they could become what Mary Helen Washington dubbed "image-makers,"[24] creating new Black female subjectivities that gave lie to Mammy and Sapphire; (2) material tools for funding the revolution through, for example, benefit readings; (3) creative material around which to gather in the cocreation of antiwar and anti-imperial communities. What we now refer to as the Black women's literary renaissance was an activist literary movement that worked with literary texts as a bridge between a Black internationalism that survived the global assault on Black radicalism and the literary institutions, including English departments, that were commodifying their work.

It should not surprise us that the university has functioned as a primary site for the multiculturalization of a Black literature that posed itself as one definitive answer to the late-capitalist United States' imperial mandate. As Roderick Ferguson compellingly argues, the social movements of the 1960s were vulnerable to institutional solicitation, especially by the university. The US university functioned as an archiving apparatus, housing and logging and cataloguing and getting to know the student movements that developed in tandem with the antiwar, anticorporate, and anticolonial movements that broke through its gates. The university, confronting the student movements, experimented with "courtship, invitation, and acknowledgement" and in turn taught the state and the institutions of finance how to "reduce the initiatives of oppositional movements to the terms of hegemony."[25]

One of the ways this affirmation worked in Black studies and in Black literary studies was by professionalizing and bureaucratizing the study of Blackness. The student movements wanted to replace "alien, useless study" with "life studies," or generate autonomous and student-designed programs of study that would offer courses in Black studies and, and as, revolutionary struggle.[26] Universities, by professionalizing and appropriating the study of Black culture, could create an institutional home for Black studies' radical impulse while reinforcing the very universalist, humanist standards of "excellence" that were now in crisis. Administrators saw Black studies as a threat as well as a "balm to soothe racial tensions"; the most prevalent model of Black studies in contemporary universities was designed by the Ford Foundation's president McGeorge Bundy, who brought the emerging field into his strategy "to restore peace to troubled college campuses."[27] To create a Black studies program was, for many colleges and universities, good defense in the face of the coming demand and, besides that, a way to enhance and diversify the education of white students. Meanwhile, scholars within Black studies programs might have seen their work as the fulfillment of US democratic ideals, or they may have seen it as a contrarian, even revolutionary, force in enemy territory. Radicals like Toni Cade Bambara saw Black studies as an opportunity to abolish the university. "To obtain a relevant, real education, we shall have to either topple the university or set up our own," Bambara wrote, also in the context of the open admissions struggle at City College, in 1969.[28] That same year, John O. Killens, writing with a group of artists that included Ossie Davis, Ruby Dee, Max Roach, James Baldwin, Louis Lomax, and Odetta, reflected on the artist's role in the "Black university." In the inaugural issue of the *Black Scholar*, Killens explained that these artists, having formed the Association of

Artists for Freedom, had organized themselves in defiance of the civil rights consensus. Focused on creating college experiences geared toward "total relevance" to Black liberation struggles, they wanted to establish a Black "Communiversity" and host a Homecoming every week. That Homecoming would call "on the brothers and sisters to come home to their Black commitments from wherever they find themselves, lost as most of us are in this vast quagmire of a white supremacist society."[29] The communiversity, Killens imagined, would make the campus "the very sidewalks of the Black community." In the meantime, on-campus Black studies was a "'make-do' situation."[30]

Black studies was thus a compromise for university administrators and a compromise for radicals. "Incorporation" is the term that best describes this compromise. As Robert Smith chronicled in his 1996 study of the post-civil-rights era, the state responded to the challenge of militant Black radicalism with repression (infiltration, harassment, legal repression, incarceration, murder) as well as with co-optation (the inclusion of more moderate activists or groups in highly visible positions within institutions). Co-optation, Smith pointed out, "is part of the structural adjustment of democratic systems to the claims of new groups for inclusion, integration, or incorporation."[31] Incorporation is an affirmative value, a sign of achievement and legitimacy for activists and administrators alike. It has functioned, indeed, as the value undergirding the discrete processes—*affirmative action, diversity hiring*—that have managed minority difference throughout the postwar era. Universities incorporate minority difference in order to "run difference through its machinery of validation, certification, and legibility" and, in doing so, to generate programs of knowledge that solidify, rather than disrupt, hegemony.[32] Melamed refers to the university's incorporative projects as "restrictive affirmation," counterinsurgency strategies that, during the 1970s, 1980s, and 1990s, focused on disciplining Black and ethnic studies formations so that they would, again, serve to augment rather than detract from the university's core mission to reproduce civil society through the regulation of discourses of political power and knowledge.[33] The birth of Black studies did not spell the end of racial power; it was a "profound moment of danger" that signaled power's "new beginning."[34] What did this rebirth of power mean for Black feminist textuality and its radical future?

Paramilitary Affairs

She came armed with a quote from the book she had read three times last summer, so the legacies and the kids from Choate and Chapin didn't wither her with their perfect grammar. She was affirmative, yeah, but she was action too. Under an oil portrait in the vestibule is where the recruiter found her, and what the recruiter promised was cash for a "summer research opportunity," for an indenture of "transforming the academy." It sounded better than a summer at the Gap.

When Black women writers of the 1970s and 1980s constructed new literary genealogies by, for example, traveling to Hurston's unmarked grave or remarking on the "miracle" of Phillis Wheatley, they asserted a collective sense of literary agency that differed vastly from the individualist rhetorics of "great works." We could see these actions as generative instances of ex nihilo collective preservation: Black women writers "made models of how it is possible to live," in Washington's words, by fashioning new stories of Black life after the 1960s and by bringing out-of-print works into publication.[35] Black feminist writers created new artistic heritages that declared their work's independence from second-wave feminism and Black nationalism. In addition, they called attention to the role of English literature and official English language in the new codes of behavior that were the price for power's affirmation of racial difference in the post-civil-rights era. Neoliberalism, we cannot fail to note, was not simply an economic model; it was foremost "an epistemological structure of disavowal," a habit of knowledge, an ideology that figured racial power as disappearing and that offered "selective protection" in exchange for complicity with its ways of knowing.[36] The neoliberal racial regime sutured "protectable life" to "reproductive respectability," in Grace Hong's words, so that Black feminists' rejection of respectable forms of dress, address, and redress not only challenged the sexism of Black nationalist movements or the racism and classism of mainstream white feminists but also "offer[ed] an analysis of a broad historical process that was incorporating those elements of nationalist and feminist movements into a new modality of power at that very moment."[37] When the poet Carolyn Rodgers, for example, wrote about this invitation to respectability that undergirded the incorporative mode of neoliberalism, she defied the dictates of the "new Black Womanhood":

> they say,
> that i should not use the word
> muthafucka anymo
> in my poetry or in any speech i give
> they say,
> that I must and can only say it to myself
> as the new Black Womanhood suggests
> a softer self
> a more reserved speaking self. they say,
> that respect is hard won by a woman
> who throws a word like muthafucka around

Rodgers's 1969 poem "The Last M.F." calls attention to itself as a form that survives attempts by the "pigs" and the "hunks" and the "negroes" to "destroy our moves toward liberation." Wielding the word "mutha-fucka" eleven times before trading it in for "m.f.," Rodgers's speaker holds onto the curse word as a defiant practice of refusing the new codes of behavior and, perhaps more importantly, as a tool for exposing the counterinsurgent practices that ranged from telling women to be "soft" to police infiltration and agent provocateurism. Whether she says it or not, she cautions, "there's plenty of MEAN muthafuckas out / here trying to do the struggle in and we all know / that none of us can relax until the last m.f.'s / been done in."[38] Rodgers's use of the sanitized, censored version of "muthafucka" is laced with the promise of vengeful self-defense. Whatever she says, the speaker reserves the spirit of a bad muthafucka.

"living into" To write "through" the English language, as Nikki Giovanni referred to the practice of flouting the grammars of incorporation after the 1960s, was not only to preserve the autochthonous forms of Black speech against the staid rules of English; it was also to package the promises of Black liberation in typescript pages and, furthermore, to refract—expose and break open—the intelligence program that was dead set on undermining those very promises.[39] Black feminist criticism was, again, a lifeline for Black feminist writers who were wielding their typewrit-ers in this insurgent literary enterprise that was taking place in ivory-cum-ebony towers as well as in YMCAs, off-campus writers' groups and classes, bookstores, and other locales that hosted noisy gatherings of those for whom "this literature was not so much an object of study" but also, crucially, a "life-saving" tool for community building.[40]

Black feminist writers' work to reinvent literature in the 1970s and 1980s amounted to a revolution that rippled through the Xerox machines of US English departments, through the pages of national newspapers, and through the publishing houses. During this same time, they were experimenting with new iterations of Black internationalism and transnational coalition building that circulated the terms "third-world feminism" and "third-world women" to align US Black feminism with a global struggle for decolonization. Drawing on the Cold War term that was used to refer to the nonaligned nations, feminists of color used the term "third world" to link the struggle for liberation in the United States to a global movement of decolonization.[41] *resituating "third world"*

To be sure, Black feminist experiments with third worldism—both in autonomous organizations and in literature, in an era during which such distinctions, as I just pointed out, were hardly respected—were fraught, especially when disagreements about solidarity with Palestinian liberation emerged. June Jordan charged Audre Lorde and Barbara Smith, for example, with acting in a "wrong and cowardly fashion" when they sent her a position paper condemning her writings in defense of Palestinian liberation. After the 1982 massacre at the Sabra and Shatilah refugee camps in Lebanon, in which right-wing fascists of the Lebanese Maronite Phalange slaughtered over one thousand Palestinian elderly men, women, and children while the Israeli army stood guard, Jordan had written a response to Adrienne Rich that blamed the prominent feminist for signing her name to a statement, coauthored by the Jewish feminist group Di Vilde Chayes, that condemned anti-Zionism as anti-Semitic. That statement, published in July 1982 in the feminist journal *Off Our Backs* and then in October by the New York feminist newspaper *WomaNews*, expressed outrage over anti-imperialist feminists' "insinuation that to fight for Jewish survival is antithetical to working against racism and for Third World liberation."[42] Jordan stridently critiqued Rich; Smith and Lorde, in turn, wrote to express solidarity with the Di Vilde Chayes while chiding Jordan for singling Rich out and "making vicious assumptions" about Rich's politics.[43]

It could have been painful exchanges such as these that Smith was referring to when she wrote, in the introduction to the 1983 collection *Home Girls: A Black Feminist Anthology*, of "those excruciating places where I have abandoned, and been abandoned by, other women, when our anger about our differences seemed insurmountable, and we gave up on each other."[44] Smith encouraged those Jewish women with awareness and sensitivity to "both racism and anti-Semitism" to develop "fruitful alliances" with Black women and encouraged Black women to take account of their anti-Semitism. This was, of course, a recapitulation of the long history of Black-Jewish coalition in freedom struggles in the United States. At the same time, Smith expressed greatest concern over "the responses of other Black women" and questioned "whom it serves when we permit internal hostility to tear the movement we have built apart."[45] As Keith Feldman discusses feminists' dissensus over Palestinian self-determination, he argues that Palestine was an "absent presence" in early-1980s feminist communities; it emerged "as part of an alternative archive of radical women of color feminism" even as Arab and Arab American feminist perspectives were "often registered as spectral at best."[46]

Other attempts at third-world organizing were less fraught: the poet Pat Parker's Black Women's Revolutionary Council hosted workshops on liberation struggles in Puerto Rico, Eritrea, and Palestine; and Black women writers actively organized against South African apartheid, for example, in the organization that Gloria Joseph spearheaded, Sisterhood in Support of Sisters in South Africa (SISA). As Stéphane Robolin points out, Black women writers did not do away with the category of the nation-state, but they "aimed to mitigate its most pernicious power" by seeking forms of relation that could not be accommodated by states and offered new maps of belonging.[47] Leftist internationalism shaped Black women's writing throughout the late–Cold War period, with writers like Alice Childress, Paule Marshall, Toni Morrison, Ntozake Shange, Audre Lorde, Maya Angelou, Toni Cade Bambara, and Rosa Guy directing their prose and poetry against US imperialism. As Cheryl Higashida argues, we should see the "nationalist internationalism" of writers who wrote of US imperial adventures in the Caribbean and Africa as a legacy of the postwar Black Left.[48] She writes, "Despite the fact that it has been diluted, misrepresented, and repressed, the feminism of women writers on the anticolonial Left circulates within and questions dominant U.S. culture while sharing affinities with new directions in African American women's political activism in the twenty-first century."[49]

The postwar university was a stage for the historic meeting between leftist Black feminism and state power; and literary studies was a particularly loaded site for that encounter. For Black feminists who told the story of the university during its decades of structural adjustment in the aftermath of 1968, experiments in knowledge and writing made Blackness, in Fred Moten's terms, a mode of "sensuous theoretical practice" that "celebrates against predatory incorporative worldliness."[50] But those experiments, like the collective experiments in internationalism, did not occur in a vacuum; they occurred within the crucible of a metanarrative of multiculturalism that was rapidly cannibalizing the work of Black women writers, and they took place at the intersections of Black-Jewish and Black-Muslim relations. The 1980s university housed a profound irony: as Black feminism flowered as a literary movement whose primary, if not always welcoming, home was the English department, its most radical critiques of power faced the problem of domestication. What did it mean that when Black women writers opened up Black feminism as an unbounded form of internationalism, their work was being cycled into spectacles of domestic confrontation?[51]

The canon wars made literary studies and its objects sites for the articulation of the long war on terror's practices of counterinsurgency, sites for incorporative labor that put radical knowledge to work in and for the university, in and for the multiculturalist state. Following Laleh Khalili, counterinsurgency might be understood as a military tactic *and* as the core logic of post–Cold War governmentality. New forms of control crystallized as the US government encountered the rising costs of asymmetric warfare against both large militaries and guerrilla opponents. "The theoreticians of these [new] mechanisms of containment, of confinement instead of slaughter, envisioned and advertised their tactics as more human, as more liberal, and ultimately as techniques for socially engineering the people and places they conquered," Khalili argues.[52] US counterinsurgency is population-based: in texts like *The U.S. Army/ Marine Corps Counterinsurgency Field Manual* or David Kilcullen's *The Accidental Guerilla*, counterinsurgency is "armed social work," and the work of the counterinsurgent soldier is to get to know the whole society in which the enemy emerges, to win the hearts and minds of the civilian population, to gain a "holistic, total understanding of local culture" through ethnographic intelligence.[53] It is with this understanding of counterinsurgency—as a knowledge project centered around getting to know the other—that we can apprehend Melamed's claim that the canon wars were, indeed, "deliberate counterinsurgency," with "each side working to limit knowledge about racism to a pluralist framework that takes for granted as antiracist the primacy of individual and property rights over collective and social goals."[54]

Black feminist writers and critics were on the front lines of the counterinsurgency wars that came home to US English departments. They issued sober reminders about literature's role in smoothing multiculturalism's rough edges. As early as 1980, Hazel Carby offered a genealogy of multiculturalism's emergence from discourses of Black deficiency and deprivation in educational policy, pointing out that multicultural educational policy offered itself as the answer to the structural racism in which it was deeply implicated. Carby linked this history to the multiculturalist approach to Black texts: the tendency in literature classrooms was to offer positive representations of Black people as a way of combating racism, to thereby "promote 'racial harmony' by creating an unproblematic understanding of the culture of 'others'" and to "prove that 'Blacks have a culture too.'"[55] The "supermarket" approach to canon disformation, Carby later argued, allowed literature programs to offer increasing "brands and flavors of literature"; but reducing analyses of a society structured in dominance to "questions of representation on a syllabus" only further mystified racialized hierarchy.[56] Black texts in integrated classrooms not only provided faulty ground for racial justice but also provided cover for increasingly rigid immigration laws, police violence, and inequalities in housing and employment.[57] By the time Carby published "The Multicultural Wars, Part One" in 1992, she could reflect on the role that the circulation of Black women's fiction in college classrooms was playing in the state's cultural counterinsurgency: the "Black female subject is frequently the means by which many middle-class white students and faculty cleanse their souls and rid themselves of the guilt of living in a society that is still rigidly segregated," and Black women's writings could now stand in as "fictional substitutes for the lack of any sustained social or political relationships with Black people in a

society that retains many of its historical practices of apartheid in housing and schooling."[58]

Responding to the same concerns, Bambara went so far as to refer to
Black women cultural workers ("bibliophiles, book dealers, independent
press founders, and troops that occupy arts councils") as paramilitaries
in the hostile territory of late-1980s US culture. The "image makers" and
"image resurrectionists" were fighting a "minute to minute battle over
who will define/depict/disseminate"; they were "combatants," even, who
"did not always know that simply keeping the records straight could be
a para-military affair."[59] What was at stake in Bambara's use of the martial metaphor was autonomy: Black women's ability to control the dissemination and interpretation of their own work in light of the "state's
culture-brokers" who "would appropriate our tongues and assign us to
back ward asylums for having the nerve to think we have something
worth saying on our own."[60] This was a battle over voice and dollars:
would Black women's work be controlled and sold and spoken for by
"people who don't know us" or "people who don't wish us well" in a
"crooked society that hard sells amnesia," or could we keep assuming
that "glorious task of speaking the truth in the teeth of literary-cultural-
political-hit-squad bullies who would appropriate our tongues"?[61]
Cheryl Wall called this work to preserve the autonomy of Black women's
truth-telling in the context of inclusion "changing our own words."[62]

If Black women writers and critics were at war in the multicultural
literary marketplace, the war around their words was simultaneous to
the counterinsurgency wars—wars against "terrorism," wars for "freedom," wars in the name of "democracy"—that were pushing through the
university and into live battle theaters in Lebanon, Nicaragua, Grenada,
Puerto Rico, and Iraq. "All cultural texts implicated," scribbled Bambara
in the notes she gathered for a short story tentatively titled "Gulf" (or, alternatively, "Yellow Ribbons") about the 1990–91 Iraq war and the ubiq-
uitous yellow ribbons that were the sign of national unity and faith in
the US military.[63] In particular, terrorism studies grew as an academic
field after 1968 to "explain the resurgence of the seemingly inexplicable,"
and it produced a literature on the psychopathology of terrorists, making foreign-policy studies a critical site for producing the terrorist as a [*orientalism*]
deviant, racialized figure. As Jasbir Puar and Amit Rai clarify, this "figure of the inexplicable" is what haunts "all the civilizational grids that

the Western war machine would deploy in its attempt to 'understand the terrorist psyche.'"[64] University intellectuals created the language through which the multiculturalist US state would understand and justify the "outer wars" against terrorism and the "inner wars" against the racialized poor. The racialization of Islam and the discursive construction of "the Islamic world" drew on the images that were already circulating about Islam in US culture, which were, until the late 1960s, deeply linked to Black American Muslims in the Nation of Islam.[65]

Indeed, the sociological production of Black pathology lubricated the carceral build-up of the post-1968 decades and attached narratives of Black deviance to the imagination of foreign threat, with the trope of the deviant Black mother reproducing the culture of poverty paving the way for consent to more and more militarized protection. As Wahneema Lubiano urged in 1996, "Think of the 'culture of poverty' and its *ethnographic knowledge* as the grease that makes the engine of the United States' racial imagination run more smoothly. Think about how the international circulation of all these narratives forces those of us who are temporarily not in prison, or temporarily not being targeted, but who are concerned about the drug trade's ravaging of our neighborhoods, to participate in the state's disciplinary apparatus, sometimes without our even knowing it."[66] As I pointed out in the introduction, the elite white intellectual and political formation that theorized the 1960s "excess of democracy" as a crisis of governmentality and that demonized Black women as a drain on state resources, figuring public assistance as a racialized gendered threat to national order, was composed of the same thinkers who built the rationale for preemptive war in the so-called new world order.

It was not sociological and foreign-policy discourses alone that justified increased policing domestically and abroad; literature had its role to play as well. Literary texts prepared state managers for their role in erecting the architecture of the war on terror by acquainting them with representations of the racialized dispossessed.[67] Just as Black books in white classrooms symbolically bridged the gap between white Americans and Black Americans after desegregation, texts belonging to the new category of "global literature" would allow readers to have the experience, or at least the fantasy, of "presumptively knowing Arab and

Muslim women and thereby symbolically bridging the gap between their experience and that of the West," thereby stabilizing the neoliberal multicultural narratives of difference and US exceptionalism that justified the Iraq wars and the global regime of counterterrorism that regularized rendition, drone warfare, and touchless torture.[68] In this context, indeed, "all cultural texts [were] implicated," as Bambara feared.

The strange alchemy that turned Blackness from danger to "required academic commodity" transformed Black women's texts into the precious material that, fittingly enough, came to bear golden seals emblazoned "An Oprah's Book Club Selection" or "Winner of the Nobel Prize in Literature" or "Pulitzer Prize for Fiction." The velocity at which this happened is mind-boggling. Barbara Christian worried in her classic 1987 essay "The Race for Theory" that Black women's literature would disappear as *theory* replaced *criticism* as the mark of academic sophistication. Just two years later, she voiced the opposite concern: that Black women's culture had become the prized object of a "critical clamor" that kept it locked into circuits of trade and professional discourse that were doing nothing to counter stereotypes of Black women and were actually making it harder and harder for Black feminist critics to produce "sustained readings" of that very literature.[69] This was bell hooks's concern too.[70] But Bambara took even Black women critics to task for revering the "black woman writer." In 1979, when she was living in Atlanta and developing the Southern Collective of African American Writers, Bambara offered three answers in response to Beverly Guy-Sheftall's question, "Do you think the black woman writer has been treated fairly?" They eviscerated the very notion of "writer":

> I have no idea. It's not something I have any comments on because it's not something I generally think about, that is to say, the black woman writer. We know for sure that any cultural product of black people has not been treated intelligently and usefully by white critics. That's one kind of answer. The fact that a good many black women writers do not get into anthologies that are put together by black men is another kind of answer. The fact that black women critics sometimes approach black women's writing as though they were highly particular and had no connection to group traditions, that's another kind of issue.[71]

The commitment to collective preservation that motivated Bambara's work in culture meant that she would continuously be struggling against the institutions that employed her, even when those institutions were "African American literature" or "Black woman writer." By her account, the rise of the Black woman writer as a category for criticism turned a field of *cultural workers* into a handful of elite *novelists* and occluded the central organizing principle of the Sisterhood and the Southern Collective of African American writers: "Community is the primary reality."[72] She then told Guy-Sheftall that, while she preferred the short-story genre (because "it can creep up on you on your blind side"), she had "come to grips with the nature of publishing" and decided that it was now "shrewd" to finish her novel, the only one she would publish in her lifetime.[73] When she wrote *Those Bones Are Not My Child*, which Toni Morrison edited and published posthumously in 1999, the text exceeded anything that might be understood as the work of a novelist. The text, as Thorsson suggests, overwhelms the reader with Black feminist grammar: sentence fragments, repetition, lists, abbreviations, and conjured-up compound words. This excess makes the "book," if we want to call it that, an ongoing collective project of documentation that narrates the unspeakable and represents the failure of communication that results from surviving the incessant war.[74] *Those Bones* was unincorporable because it sprawled in multiple narratives, collected countless streams of information, defended Black life, and exploded the institution of the American novel.

The critical commodification that was detaching Black feminist writing from the community that produced it was Ann DuCille's concern, too, when she published "The Occult of True Black Womanhood: Critical Demeanor and Black Feminist Studies" in response to the Black woman writer/critic's emergence as "a hyperstatic alterity," a "hot commodity" on the theory market. Writing to Black women academics, DuCille asked, "Are we in danger of being trampled by the 'rainbow coalition' of critics—'Black, white, male, female, artists and academics, historicists and deconstructionists'—that our own once isolated and isolating intellectual labors have attracted to the magnetic field of Black feminist studies?"[75] Further, she asked, "What does it mean for the future of Black feminist studies that a large portion of the growing body of scholarship on Black women is now being written by white feminists and by men whose work frequently achieves greater critical and commercial success than that of the Black female scholars who carved out a field in which few 'others' were then interested?"[76] If cultural texts, and specifically Black women's cultural texts, were implicated in the internal and external wars that the state waged at the height of multiculturalism, they were implicated, too, in the reorganization of literary value and academic labor that made Black women writers and critics at once "sacred texts" and obsolete.[77]

Black feminist writers, as I have noted, dramatically expanded literature's role in representing and defending Black life against the state-produced and state-sanctioned forms of terror that were going so far as to gather literary knowledge into its arsenal of counterinsurgency. This expansion amounted to a "seismic reshuffling of what had been a stacked deck," according DuCille. In her 2017 article reflecting on the way Black women novelists were both celebrated and forgotten in the clamor of the 1990s, DuCille refers to the way Black women writers changed the novel form, in particular: novels like Morrison's 1970 *The Bluest Eye*, she argues, "defied known forms, invented new grammars, upset, inverted, and subverted traditional structures and narrative strategies—the novel, unbound, blackened, feminized, repopulated, and unpunctuated."[78] (This is to say nothing of the experimental poetry and theater that refused written forms altogether.) And yet Black women's craft often went undertheorized. Looking through the articles published in the academic journal *Novel*, DuCille finds the journal all but silent on the Black women's literary renaissance. "I had lived through the arguments and the exclusions," she writes. "But still, coming face to face with *Novel*'s elisions cut me to the core. I felt—feel—stupid, and complicit in the absolute erasure of the discourse I so prize."[79] Reflecting on academia's disappearance of Black women's artistic labor, she reverses course on her earlier work, musing, "What a tunnel I was in, thinking black women writers were such hot stuff, the fetishized commodity every Tom, Dick, and Harriet wanted to consume."[80] But of course, DuCille's assessments of Black women's marketability in "The Occult of True Black Womanhood" were as correct as were her later meditations of the hostility that Black women writers faced, even as their work grew in innovation, in audience, and in economic and cultural impact. That Black women's writing and Black feminist knowledge have prompted equal levels of desire and derision ought simply to alert us to the vicissitudes of the market and the challenges of knowledge production and circulation after the false promise of the multicultural. Bambara spoke, for example, of the reporters who contacted her when Toni Morrison was set to publish *Beloved*, asking her to "offer some personal anecdote" that would make Morrison "more 'human.'"[81] At once enthralled by the rise of a great Black woman writer who had just written her master work and desperate for a way to temper her grandness, the arbitrators of taste scrambled to square the culture market's desire for the products of Black women's collective labor and the allure of the solitary, genius writer. The professionalization of Black literature and literary studies made it possible to cite and celebrate Black women while solidifying the meritocratic values of authorial celebrity and heightening the mystique of the solitary writerly life that was a far cry from the raucous collectivity of, say, the Sisterhood.

Homeground

She is preparing her final lectures for those who came to meet her at her job in search of the salvation, the issue, the irresistible, the revolution, the life to save, my own, the rainbow, the purple, the third world, the womanish, the gardens, the uses, the clearing, the vellum. Her coworkers can't stand what they themselves want, which is her, which is what she brings with her, but before long they'll take her piles and piles of paper, cart them out, store them in unsanctified cartons, and pull them out to display next February. If need be.

Black feminist labor in the academy has been haunted by an anxiety that can hardly be said, even now—especially now—to be unwarranted. That is the anxiety of the market, the anxiety that the objects in which Black feminist theory travels the world are traded on an open market that will, as markets do, with no gravitas whatsoever, sell the image of a multiracial, beneficent society that, quite contrary to the giddy sense of self-congratulation that the very sight of our books invites, will continue to hypercommodify the objects we produce while relying on the tenure denials, breakdowns, and overwork that accompany that production. Ours is the anxiety of incorporation, which, no doubt, is the psychic life of Black feminist literature and criticism in the age of terror.

Still, our complicity in the production of an elite research university system that is invested in the metaphorical and actual wars of our time is not all that we, or the texts we work with, might produce. Black feminist writers moved through and beyond literary texts and institutions to envision, and then to practice, the modes of mutual tending—tending to another, tending to language, tending toward revolution—that did their best to shield Black life from the onslaught of the long war on terror, the latest phase in the incessant war. Attention to the Black feminist modes of defending, holding, and resurrecting Black life in the crucible of empire is one way, perhaps, to do justice to the experiments in Black women's literature that predicted and followed the rise of the national security.

Let us return to Bambara for one last example of how literary texts were points of transfer, not only between radical Black internationalism and the institutions that tried to contain it but also between the impermanent and insecure structures of safety that Black feminist writers were seeking and building. In her review of June Jordan's collection of essays *Civil Wars*, Bambara clarified the context in which Black women were writing. It was winter 1980–81, and Black people were disappearing in Atlanta during what became known as the Atlanta child murders. Opening her review with an account of how she kept her notes on *Civil Wars* in her pocket while she walked through Atlanta in a search party, Bambara writes, "We huddled in doorways trying to keep warm and waited for news. Up and down the block, the conversation was the same: the missing and murdered children of Atlanta, the butchered of Buffalo, the slashed of New York, the stomped of Boston, the stabbed of San Francisco, the snatched of Trenton, the mowed down of Cleveland, the housing projects under siege in New Orleans. Death dogging our steps across the map. The Black Community being disemboweled. At dark, members of the search party finally returned from the woods, but with nothing to report—no clues, no leads, no news." In this bleak landscape where death overwhelms Bambara's movements through space and charts a map of anti-Black terror throughout North America, Bambara sees in Jordan's essays about police violence, life studies, and South Africa a "chilling but profoundly hopeful vision of living in the

USA." In this scene, Black women's literature literally serves the cause of survival: Bambara removes her gloves to arm herself with the masterful word-works that she calls Jordan's "chosen weapons." While Bambara takes up Jordan's armor as she tracks the trail of anti-Black terror running through the 1980s United States, she also reminds readers that Jordan's work issued not from the "relatively safe vantage point the writer's desk affords" but instead "from the danger zone, in the heated thick of things."[82]

literature is (at least) part of the public's library

But as much as writing served the cause of surviving the terrors of late capitalism, it was not enough light in the darkness of that winter. Indeed, Bambara, like Jordan, was at a crossroads, that place that M. Jacqui Alexander refers to when she writes of the 1980s context in which women of color committed to "a personal and epistemic self-reflection out of which feminism has never been the same."[83] Bambara wrote to Jordan later that year to tell her a story of Black communal self-defense as a kind of everyday training. In the letter, Bambara tells Jordan that she was on her way to the airport, on her way to St. Louis, when she and her taxi driver sparked up a conversation about the child murders. The driver turned off the meter while they talked; then they went to a bar and began planning a self-defense organization centered around community training in martial arts. Thinking from these intraliterary and extraliterary sites of what Christina Sharpe imagines as *lateral* or *intramural* care, we end up with a different understanding of contemporary Black women's literary history, one in which the spectacles of intraracial fighting between Black men and Black women are less important than the collective, feminist, craft of living through state regimes of violence and security.[84] Bambara described her coconspirator as "one of them real old timey young brothers raised by . . . older men who hunt and have gold teeth and know how to swing a hammer and take pride in planing a door so it travels smoothly over carpet. Talks real slow and careful like making every syllable count."[85] Security was a craft that one could devote oneself to, a tending aesthetics that could be as interested, all at once, in rescuing Black life and in "making every syllable count." For Bambara, who wrote famously that the Black writer's work was to "make revolution irresistible," the task was to enlist literature not in the work of securing the world we know but rather in the labor of that mode of thought/practice that Jordan called, again, life studies: a daily, collective discipline of rescuing persons from "the amorality of time and science."[86] Life studies, as Jordan imagined, could evacuate the university campus and "the people who feed their egos on the grass, inside the gates," and replace it with a "workable concept of homeground or, as children say in their games, home-safe."[87]

When Black women both served for target practice in the ongoing war against terror and were recruited to carry out that target practice, when Black books exploded in US literary culture and in multicultural classrooms, and just as the Black literary text was up for conscription into the reign of US empire, Black women writers, in prose, poetry, drama, and invented genres like the choreopoem, generated grammars of survival on the other side of terror. Black feminists' outward, extraliterary orientation to print, I want to argue, is the acting out of the press of survival, of unsecured safety, against literary form. With death dogging their movements across maps and across genres, Black feminist writers pressed the craft of surviving the long war on terror against literary form. It is still on students of literature and students of insurgent social movements to study that urgent pressing. In chapter 5, I turn more fully to June Jordan's midcareer projects as examples of the geolinguistic work called forth by this very craft of extraliterary Black feminist insurgency.

5

Perfect Grammar

June Jordan and the Intelligence of Empire

The US government's war against the Black poor, the Black mothers, the Black ill, and the Black radicals after 1968 sounded its rallying cries with linguistic cunning. As the writer and organizer June Jordan wrote in 1972, "The Man has brought the war home, where it's always really been at: sometimes explosive, sometimes smoldering, but currently, as stark, inhuman, and deliberate as the 'perfect grammar' of Nixon's war cries raised, calm as a killer, against the weak, the wanting, and the ones who cannot fight back." To this she added a question: "How will we survive this new—this, to use a standard English term, 'escalated'— phase of white war against Black life?"[1] Jordan's work as a radical writer, activist, city planner, and teacher in the decades of the 1970s and 1980s consistently called attention to the relationships between the state violence leveled at Black people "at home" in US cities and towns and the US-led and/or US-funded invasions and occupations in the Middle East, Latin America, and South Africa. The way her work wrestled with the many arms of US imperialism's broad reach was to return to the elemental forms of language—verb tenses, possessive cases—that built the language of empire and to invent insurgent grammars of survival. From offering primers on the official state language that covered over and covered for the atrocious violence committed by a government that was desperate to recover its authority and to position itself as the world's exemplary democracy, to cataloguing the forms of speech that kept the militant, internationalist energies of Black Power and third-world feminism alive well into the 1980s, Jordan's cross-generic inquiry into the perfect grammars of intelligence and counterinsurgency offered Black text and Black speech patterns up for a radical reclaiming from empire's uses. If the imperial grammars of Blackness translated Black pain into the speech of empire, not just in words but also in gestures and postures of affirmation and empowerment, Jordan's work joined the radical Black feminist project of inventing insurgent grammars.

Jordan was one of the Black feminist cultural workers who passed through the institutions that legitimized the long war on terror. Throughout the post-1968 period, Black feminist writers like Jordan shattered the terms—the very grammars—that articulated the unstable, coproductive relationship between the defiant culture of Black books and the incorporating imperatives of late- to post–Cold War US culture. In this chapter, I analyze the poetry, drama, and nonfiction that June Jordan wrote between 1979 and 1985 as interventions that are deeply attuned to the linguistic work of US public discourses of security and policing and, at the same time, attentive to the ways that Black grammars of resistance and subsistence slant those imperial grammars of empire. Jordan's work over these years articulated Black literary feminism as a code for urgent care, or rather insurgent care, in the era of late Cold War. From 1979 to 1985, Jordan's geolinguistic poetics theorized counterinsurgent intelligence—the intelligence of empire—as the very medium of state violence and offered itself up as a key—an essential tool, a strategy of interpretation, a strategy for practice—to insurgent safety. I refer to this key as Jordan's *postintelligence code.*

[handwritten margin note: the liberal institution reads without a cypher]

Jordan wrote about the perfect grammar of the domestic war against Black people and the wars against independence movements in Latin America, the Middle East, Africa, and Southeast Asia in 1972. She was writing about a "new phase" of white war against Black life exemplified by the post-1968 escalation of surveillance, torture, incarceration, and murder leveled at Black activists and Black everyday people. In her militant Black Power–era writings, Jordan rejected assimilation as a way of surviving that new phase of war. In "White English / Black English: The Politics of Translation," the same essay in which she wrote of the war come home, she identified the Black government worker as a figure who colludes with the violence of counterinsurgent warfare and, at the same time, has the capacity for insurgent translation:

> By now, most Blackfolks—even the most stubbornly duped and desperately light-headed nigger behind his walnut, "anti-poverty" desk—has heard the Man talking that talk, and the necessary translation into Black—*on white terms*—has taken place. Yeah. The Man has made his

standard English speech, his second inaugural address, his budget statements, and ain' no body left who don't understand the meaning of them
words falling out that mouth: In the *New York Times*, February 25, 1973,
Dick Nixon has described the genocide perpetuated by America in Vietnam as "*one of the most unselfish missions ever undertaken by one nation
in the defense of another.*"[2]

Throughout Jordan's writing, the tendency to identify and ridicule
the precise words of liberal democracy's fallacies of protection often
returned to the convention of "White English," where the quotation
marks (around, for example, "anti-poverty") expose the clichés of official
state language. Jordan exposes and redefines a number of terms, from
"efficiency" and "competence," when she is writing about the contemporary university's "deadly, neutral definition of these words," to "foreign
policy," the "Department of Defense," "law and order," or "escalated,"
when she is writing about what she calls the "rhetoric about borders
and national security and terrorism and democracy and vital interests,"
to "balancing the budget," when she is challenging the pretensions of
late capital. In Jordan's radical dictionary, the defining of official terms
is a call to the kind of safety that can only be secured when oppressed
peoples wrest linguistic and material freedom from the Western colonial
powers. Jordan clarified this philosophy of language when she called
for a "purification of terms" in her 1985 address at Columbia University.
There, she asked her audience, "Is it a good thing, is it a noble thing, is
it a mandatory thing that we in the United States of America, arm and
train and feed and clothe and house the 'contras,' the 'freedom fighters?'"
She urged, "Then let us demand of the President of our country, and let
us demand of our Congresspeople, a purification of those terms. Let us
demand that, finally, that, at last, we act to support, to fund, and to arm
and to bolster the true pro-life forces of the world, the true freedom
fighters of South Africa."[3]

Jordan's sociolinguistic interventions extended beyond the genres of
the definition and the redefinition, which appear throughout her work
in quotation marks, to meditations on syntax, grammatical formulations
such as the passive voice, and possessive pronouns. The English language was for Jordan, as it was for other Black Arts poets and Black feminists of the early 1970s, a material that one worked with—one worked

or passed through—to slow the processes of capture and co-optation that US governmental agencies and corporations were implementing to defang the militant movement of Black Power.[4] Ridiculing the man at the Man's "anti-poverty" desk or the "minority businessmen" selling out the dreams of economic autonomy for Nixon's brand of Black Power, Jordan makes Black English the language of survival in an era when liberal reform, especially in the form of inclusion in the corporate work-place or electoral politics, dissimulated the evisceration of Black life under the Nixon-era acceleration of the carceral society. In a moment when, as Manning Marable argues, reform "had supplanted rebellion," Jordan's writings inhabit Black English as the motor of a rebellious mili-tancy that she kept alive through the 1970s and the following decades. Whereas "most Black leaders were now determined to cast their lot with the system that they had for years denounced as racist, in order to gain goods and services for their constituents,"[5] Jordan issued militant threats in the language that she was desperately trying to preserve, the language of survival, Black English: "we gone make you *answer* for this shit";[6] or "it's on";[7] or "what you think would happen if / everytime they kill a Black boy / then we kill a cop?"[8]

Many recent scholars and artists have turned to Jordan as a people's poet, an exemplar of radical poetics whose work enlarges conceptions of Black feminist writing and organizing.[9] This new research has lifted the cloud of quiet that hovered over her work after she published "Apologies to All People in Lebanon," a poem that explicitly defended the human rights of Palestinian peoples, in the *Village Voice* in 1982. My interest here is in the journalism, drama, and poetry she produced between 1979 and 1985, a period when her work crescendoed its militant calls to col-lective defense against the retrenchment of the post-1960s era, deepened an intrahemispheric analysis of police violence and military counterin-surgency, mounted an interhemispheric resistance to counterinsurgency through live poetics, and commandeered Black literary form from the incorporative optics of the liberal literary establishment and the univer-sity. By the end of the 1970s, Jordan's interests in the official language of counterinsurgency and in the militant uses of Black English infused her published work in nonfiction, drama, and poetry with an uncompro-mising politics that would continue to escalate in the ensuing years. By the end of the following decade, the precision of Jordan's sociolinguistics—to be sure, *geolinguistics* is a better term to describe the studies that put language to work to map the violence of counterinsurgency and to plot, too, people's militant resistance to it—would result in the censorship of her most affecting work. As Valerie Kinloch describes, "In the 1980s, the *New York Times* refused to ever again print Jordan's work; her New York City publisher vowed to let her books go out of print; and one of her literary agents removed her from the client list, mainly due to her increasing focus on Palestine."[10]

At the turn of a decade that would witness the decimation of Black urban communities under the surveilling and carceral sweep of the War on Drugs and late–Cold War foreign policies of defense, Jordan articulates Black literary feminism as the radicalization of safety and as the code for urgent, insurgent care. From 1979 to 1985, Jordan's postintelligence code theorized counterinsurgent intelligence as the very medium of state violence and offered itself up as a key—a strategy of interpretation, a strategy for practice—to a different and insurgent safety characterized by watchfulness, internationalist coalition, and mutual tending.

The Whispering Misery and the Ruckus

In 1979, Jordan wrote the first draft of *The Issue*, a play that was performed as a dramatic reading at the New York Shakespeare Festival in 1981. Directed by Ntozake Shange, the play dramatized what Jordan saw as the most critical issue facing Black Americans at the end of the 1970s: police violence. *The Issue* tells the story of a young social movement leader, Lloyd Wilson, who is on the run from police after having issued a threat at a nationally televised press conference: "Every time the police kill a Black kid we'll kill a cop: Every time, from now on."[11] In a flashback in scene 2, Lloyd is a young boy, seated at a kitchen table in his Brooklyn apartment. When his West Indian father asks Lloyd if he has finished his homework and finished reading Shakespeare's *The Merchant of Venice*, Lloyd confesses that he could not understand it. He asks his exacting father, "Can I go outside and play?" His father answers, "Yes, you *can*. But no, you *may not go!*"[12] Mr. Wilson trains his son to be a proper, literate, standard-English-speaking citizen in a small kitchen that is heavy with the weight of the times. As Jordan notes in her stage directions, "Instead of walls/windows, there are *things*."[13] The space of the kitchen, walled off from the world and overflowing with "junk glut," is the site for accumulating the intelligence necessary for proper Black citizenship in an age of rights. This is the very home training, the training in proper citizenship, that Lloyd denounces when he vows revenge after the police murder of a Black teenager. The failure to master Shakespeare portends, then, the failure of assimilation after the civil rights movement and the issue of the militant threat. In Jordan's work in 1979 and in the five years that followed, scenes of domestication and its refusal brought her sociolinguistic analysis of a growing US empire to aesthetic and political concerns about the promise, and the failures, of freedom and democracy in the post-civil-rights United States.

Jordan wrote *The Issue* at a defining moment in her career. Her growth and productivity as a writer during the period between 1979 and 1985 were evident in her multiple publications of poetry, opinion pieces, and news reports. Jordan had spent most of her childhood in Brooklyn and then at sixteen years old enrolled at Barnard College before marrying and moving to Chicago two years later. She then moved back to New York, had a son, and later divorced. In the 1960s, after her divorce, Jordan worked across artistic and political forms while supporting her family as a single mother. She worked as an organizer in Mississippi, where she was mentored by Fannie Lou Hamer, and as a freelance writer. She served as a production assistant for the film *The Cool World* and collaborated with R. Buckminster Fuller on an architectural redesign of Harlem. She published *Who Look at Me*, a volume of ekphrasis poems accompanied by reproductions of paintings, in 1969. By then, she had begun teaching in adjunct positions, first at Connecticut College and then at the City College of New York, where she taught alongside Toni Cade Bambara, Addison Gayle, and others, and in the mid-1970s at Sarah Lawrence and Yale. Jordan published her novel, *His Own Where*, written in Black English, in 1971 and followed that publication with her first collection of nonfiction. She assumed a tenured post at SUNY Stony Brook from 1978 to 1982. Throughout the 1980s and 1990s, she was in residence at several institutions, including Macalester College, the University of Pennsylvania, the University of Wisconsin, and the University of California, Berkeley. In 1989, she moved permanently to Berkeley, where she founded and directed Poetry for the People and taught on the faculty as a professor of Afro-American studies and women's studies.

218 | PERFECT GRAMMAR

She remained in the Bay Area until she died of breast cancer in 2002. As Kinloch describes, Jordan's was a life lived "writing and fighting energetically, and campaigning for universal peace."[14] When Jordan was drafting *The Issue* at the artists' retreat in upstate New York, she was also writing poems that would later be published in the 1980 volume *Passion*, her fourth volume of poetry.

During the late 1970s and early 1980s, Jordan's previous experience as a civil rights activist turned from nonviolent idealism to horror and the militancy that horror invites. At a moment when revolutionaries were becoming race leaders and the most radical energies of Black nationalism were being co-opted and incorporated when not gruesomely punished, Jordan insisted on the continued relevance of self-defense, nationalism, and an ever-expanding critique of state-secured forms of safety. Jordan's publications between 1969 and her death in 2002 proliferated. Considering the sheer volume of nonfiction, poetry, and children's books that she published (twenty-seven in all)—to say nothing of the drama, musical collaborations, and other media that were produced in her extraliterary forms—against the relative paucity of critical scholarship devoted to her at least partially explains the renewed interest in her work in recent years.[15] However, the lack of critical comment on Jordan's work also forces us to confront the limitations of its opposite, for the visibility that Black women's writing generally achieved during what is widely acknowledged as its renaissance in the late 1970s and early 1980s, paradoxically enough, provided the terms by which the academic marketplace and commercial publishing would archive and taxonomize Black women's artistic labor. At times those terms were quite limited. Would Jordan's novel, *His Own Where*, be widely taught in African American literature classes, for example, had it been chosen as an Oprah's Book Club selection?

In the lectures that Jordan delivered about the context for contemporary African American literature to students enrolled in her class at Yale in 1974, she repeatedly took issue with the optimistic master narrative about the emergence of a Black middle class, the narrative of overcoming touted in Black publications like *Ebony*. She sought other explanations for the decline in Black protest and the disappearance of Black protest literature. She told her students that after 1968, "people got scared." She reminded them of "the Cemetery created by the CRE" (the civil rights establishment), "the fate of the Panthers," and "the fate of George Jackson." She referred, too, to drug addiction ("the turning inward of rage"), "the cop-out"—the process of co-optation that appeased and delegitimized revolutionary movements—and multicultural literary culture. With regard to this latter point, she specified that "the new, general American literature eclipsed and pushed out the Afro-American literature of the sixties." The destructive elixir of fear, exhaustion, and mainstream literary success created, in Jordan's words, "the terrible silence that grows" in Black protest literature and in Black American protest culture more generally speaking. From within this field of terrible silence, Jordan provided a key for understanding intelligence and called for the crescendo of the "ruckus," as she called it, of militancy.[16]

Intelligence, broadly conceived, was one of the primary forms that packaged and delivered the retrenchment of the post–world War II Black freedom struggle in the 1968–74 juncture that Jordan was lecturing about. I am using the word "intelligence" to refer to two interrelated developments: (1) the broad culture of *surveillance* that repressed Black internationalist radicalism throughout the 1960s and, especially, after 1968 and (2) the production and careful management of knowledge about antiracist resistance, in part through literacy and literary pedagogy. If "intelligence" names a claim to cognitive capacity, it captures how leftist internationalist activism became knowable to the post-civil-rights world, first, through the brute force of investigation, counterinsurgency, and police violence and, second, through the archiving of the post–World War II social movements. The rise of neoliberalism in response to the 1960s flourishing of social movements and the global economic downturn of the 1970s demanded that the governments of developed nations such as the United States manage dissent ruthlessly. As Keeanga Yamhatta-Taylor explains, the rise of colorblindness shrouded the right-wing resurgence of the 1970s: "The battle in the sixties had legitimized black demands; now that legitimacy had to be rolled back."[17] The counterinsurgent tactics with which official intelligence agencies and police forces experimented on Black radicals would no doubt prove essential in the punitive management of dissent throughout Latin America and the Middle East after 1968.

On the other hand, intelligence functioned as an *affirmative* process of producing consent to this very repression. For Roderick Ferguson, the United States is "the archival nation par excellence," a state that, like an archive of manuscripts, promises to unite a heterogeneous body of work under a single, official narrative of order. After World War II, the rise of a new mode of neocolonial power that was officially affirmative of difference would, in Ferguson's words, "test power's archival flexibility."[18] Just as neocolonial Britain and France were "admitting recently held colonies into the realm of independence," the United States was relating to insurgency through engagement in addition to repression, "invitation rather than wholesale rejection": "The former colonies were thus like documents gathered together into the library of modern nations. As such, these newly minted nations were *consigned* to the location of sovereignty and coordinated according to the ideal of freedom. Yet archiving those former colonies was also a kind of house arrest in which freedom signified genres of subjugation and domiciliation."[19] This *domiciliation* or *house-arresting* of revolutionary formations was, in Ferguson's account, a kind of ingestion and dissection: in the US context, the crisis in capital, combined with the threat to national hegemony posed by the antiracist, feminist, antiwar, and student movements, compelled capital to "feed on" local histories and languages, putting difference to work for profit, while the nation-state worked "with and through the very local, vernacular, and subjugated histories and differences that brought the nation-state to crisis in the first place."[20] The domestication of revolutionary projects, therefore, was a process of getting to *know* difference. That process of managing difference through knowledge projects in corporations, governmental agencies, and universities constituted a different, *informal*, if you will, intelligence-gathering enterprise that had profound effects on literary culture and pedagogy.

The formal intelligence enterprise overwhelmed the revolutionary 1960s and ushered in what June Jordan called the "'seventies' of hidden, whispering misery."[21] The Federal Bureau of Investigation's domestic counterintelligence program (COINTELPRO) was, of course, the most well-known governmental entity tying police beat work and investigation to the agency's objectives of producing intelligence, dispensing counterintelligence, and physically targeting Black Power organizations and activists, or "Black Extremists," as the FBI described them. By eavesdropping, fabricating correspondence to sow dissension within organizations, disseminating propaganda, repeatedly harassing and arresting targeted individuals, deploying infiltrators, fabricating evidence, and orchestrating assassinations, the FBI mobilized the discourse of domestic security to test the boundaries of civil liberties and to all but incapacitate Black radicalism. The FBI's favored intelligence-gathering tactic was to recruit individuals close to targets—neighbors, family members—and convince them to report on the activities of their familiars. This tactic extended the state's power into the innermost chambers of safety, comfort, and political friendship, making strangers of comrades and confidants and inducing a certain implosion from within.

Against the backdrop of this scene of domestication, which I have described more fully in the preceding chapters, Jordan's resignification of domestic space and domestic work is pointed. Against the rise of reform, Jordan's work actually became more militant after the repression of the 1970s. To consider Jordan's geolinguistic code in this context is to encounter her speaking in code and her speaking of code in the years after domestic and global counterinsurgency brought intelligence into the arsenal of hot and cold weaponry that it marshaled against anticolonial movements. Speaking *of* code, Jordan carefully constructs a Black feminist theory of postwar counterinsurgency's imperial grammars, the "code of pacification," as Ranajit Guha refers to it, valorized and ossified by the "prose of counterinsurgency."[22] Speaking *in* code, Jordan inhabits Black English as the language of rebellion: "Let us meet the man talking the way we talk," she writes.[23] In "Black Folks and Foreign Policy," published, indeed, in *Essence* six years after the Sisterhood drew up its plans for *Essence* and *Ebony*, Jordan likened the Reagan-era United States to an antebellum plantation. Originally drafted with the subtitle "Good House Niggers," "Black Folks and Foreign Policy" is an opinion piece on Black Americans' involvement in foreign policy. "Used to be a time when most of us were field niggers," she writes. "Back then hardly any of us stayed up in the Big House, watching de Massa do his thing, throwing salt or arsenic in his soup. But now every last one of us is a house nigger, for a fact. From Brooklyn to Los Angeles, we all stay in the Big House and, what's more, we pays de Massa taxes for our troubles!"[24] The metaphor is less an indictment of Black bourgeois apathy and more a call to militant house/field—or domestic/international—solidarities: Black Americans, she writes, "act as though we think we're on the outside, in the fields, somewhere," but "this Big House belongs to you and me." The fields belong, as Jordan has it, to our cousins:

> The fields beyond belong to the Vietnamese, the Black peoples of Southern Africa, the Palestinians of northern Africa, the brown and Black peoples of Nicaragua—our victim cousins making their way to freedom. And whether they speak Spanish or Xhosa or Arabic, these new field niggers expect the rest of us, here, in the Big House to watch de Massa and to take appropriate care of de massa's soup!
>
> Why don't we do that?

To "take care" of the master's soup was to withdraw sustenance from the plantation economy and to incite rebellion through the precipitating act of poisoning. Jordan's call to internationalist sabotage brings the question of language to the space of the home, bringing Black English-asserted militancy to the glossy pages of *Essence*. As Sarah Haley argues, sabotage can be understood as a radical Black feminist practice and epistemology that confronts state with "the will to break rather than the will to tweak"; sabotage is "the rupture and negation of Western epistemologies of law and order, racial hierarchy, and gendered racial difference and docility."[25]

Delivered at the very end of the June 1983 issue of *Essence*, between a Bronner Brothers advertisement for Super Gro hair cream and a full-page, Dewar's Scotch–sponsored profile of the musician Sherry Winston, "Black Folks and Foreign Policy" was, perhaps, in a basket on your bathroom floor or hidden under the mail piling up on your aunt's kitchen table or under a stack of *Jet* magazines on a shelf in the beauty salon on your corner. There is where it was fulfilling the promise of the Sisterhood, making ruckus and undomesticating the very Black feminist print culture that disappears in narratives of post-civil-rights defeat *and* in stories of Black women's literary success. As I return to *The Issue* in the next section, I would like to return to Lloyd Brown's kitchen table, another, more ephemeral site of undomestication in Black feminist literature.

This Is Brooklyn

June Jordan wrote *The Issue* at Yaddo, a four-hundred-acre retreat center for artists in Saratoga Springs, New York. Funded by Spencer and Katrina Trask and opening its doors to creative residents in 1926, Yaddo lies just southeast of the Saratoga Race Course and just north of the Saratoga National Golf Club. By the time Jordan arrived there in 1979, Yaddo had hosted many well-known poets and novelists—Saul Bellow, James Baldwin, Gwendolyn Brooks, Jacob Lawrence, Truman Capote, Sylvia Plath—as well as been the target of FBI surveillance during the Red Scare. At the campus's center is a forty-five-thousand-square-foot Italian villa with stucco walls and dark-oak furniture. Cherubs carved into sculptures watch over artists at work. The poet in George Parsons Lathrop's 1897 *Yaddo: An Autumn Masque* sings an ode to the inspiriting grounds: What maze of sweet enchantment have I found? / Each footfall here seems lost in rippling sound / Of forest breathings, mingled with the tone / Of brooks that whisper, sigh or laugh, alone / Yet lend their music to my heart's at rest."[26] Tucked between brooks that, as Lathrop had it, actually babbled and the lake where the Mahicans and Iroquois fished for trout and eel, Yaddo was a place for resting and musing and settling. "Do they deliver mail at YADDO?" asked Jordan's confidant E. Ethelbert Miller.[27] Was this safety? Was this any place to be a Black woman, writing? Jordan wrote to the Broadway producer Robert Nemiroff, who had recently written to Jordan asking her to contribute to a forthcoming issue of *Freedomways* devoted to Lorraine Hansberry, that she was completing as much as she could "under these entirely benevolent circumstances."[28]

The Issue is a little-known, unpublished text in Jordan's massive oeuvre, but she saw it as an important artistic and political accomplishment. In the letter she sent to Nemiroff from Yaddo, Jordan informed the producer that she had just finished drafting the three-act play: "I am passionately eager to have someone such as yourself, and someone such as Lloyd Richards, and Harry Belafonte, and other people capable of mounting a first magnitude production read and consider this work, as soon as humanly possible."[29] *The Issue* was eventually performed as a staged reading directed by Jordan's close friend Ntozake Shange and produced by the New York Shakespeare Festival (NYSF). The reading

June Jordan in repose at Yaddo in upstate New York. (Courtesy of Schlesinger Library, Radcliffe Institute, Harvard University, Cambridge, MA)

took place at the Public Theatre in Greenwich Village on April 13, 1981, and featured Morgan Freeman reading the part of Lloyd Brown.[30] Gary Bolling, who had appeared in Shirley Clarke's *Cool World* (1963), a film for which Jordan served as a production assistant, played Lloyd's close friend Meatball. Other actors included Graham Brown, Frances Foster, and Sarah Joseph. This collaboration with Shange was one of many; it was the fruit of a close friendship between two artists who shared political and artistic commitments. By the time Shange wrote to Jordan in a winter 1980 mailgram, "I STILL HAVE YOUR CHRISTMAS PRESENT AND HAVE BEEN TRYING TO CONTACT YOU ABOUT *THE ISSUE*," the two had already worked together as playwrights.[31] In fact, in 1979, she had collaborated with Jordan on a previous Public Theatre production, *In the Spirit of Sojourner Truth*. According to Celeste-Marie Bernier, this earlier collaboration "emerged out of a determination to reject the claim of Michele Wallace's book *Black Macho and the Myth of the Superwoman*," which, as Jordan saw it, denigrated Harriet Tubman and Sojourner Truth and represented them as one-dimensional activists who were sexually undesirable.[32] As Jordan wrote of the collaboration in her 1981 edited collection of essays, *Civil Wars*, the evening of music, song, and poetry that *In the Spirit of Sojourner Truth* staged at the Public Theatre "was the very kind of thing that *Black Macho* declared was nonexistent.[33] Shange had also worked with NYSF to stage her 1979 *Spell #7: Beecher jibara quick magic trance manual for technologically stressed third world people*, a choreopoem that was first workshopped, then staged as a full production, at the Public Theatre. NYSF produced Shange's earlier work as well: *Boogie Woogie Landscapes* in 1978 and *A Photograph: Lovers in Motion* and *Where Mississippi Meets the Amazon* in 1977. While Jordan was finishing her draft of *The Issue* in the North Studio at Yaddo, Shange was working with the Shakespeare Festival again, this time preparing to direct *The Mighty Gents* for the NYSF mobile that toured the five boroughs of New York.[34]

While the collaboration between Shange and Jordan was a felicitous exchange of gifts between friends, Jordan's communication with NYSF intimates that there were some creative differences between her and Joseph Papp, the company's founder and producer, and Gail Merrifield, director of the Play Department. The staged reading of *The Issue* was initially to have taken place on December 8, 1980, and it was canceled.[35] It was rescheduled to appear four months later, but that date fell through as well. In late March 1981, just three weeks before the reading actually took place, Jordan wrote to Merrifield, threatening to withdraw *The Issue* from NYSF. "Throughout this inordinately long saga regarding my play, *The Issue*, a saga more than six months long," she wrote, "I have endeavored to meet with every change and every disappointment in good faith, and with courtesy, and willing respect for the apparently difficult process entailed by the decision to hold a staged reading." The fact that no firm date had materialized represented for Jordan "a pattern that suggests disrespect and/or the judgement that this playwright and her commitment to the work . . . are always to occupy the position of the variable / the postponable." She demanded a meeting to determine a firm date for the reading and informed Papp why she was issuing the ultimatum: "not because I am no longer committed to *The Issue*, but precisely because I am committed to *The Issue*, and to the issues of honor and self-determination raised therein."[36] Within two weeks, there was a firm date, and the reading proceeded on the afternoon of April 13. The correspondence with NYSF that followed indicates that while the company was considering producing the play as a full production, and Jordan completed revisions toward that end, a larger production never materialized. Discussions about the play, which included the generation of a full casting list, dropped off after October 1981.[37]

It was at Yaddo, among the whispering waters and singing trees, that Jordan first drafted a play that begins, indeed, with Black flight to white-owned sanctuary. In act 1, scene 1 of *The Issue*, Lloyd Wilson, Jordan's "fugitive Black man, fugitive Black Leader," wakes up from the nightmare in the upstate country home owned by his white girlfriend's parents. When his girlfriend, Claudia, gestures to the home as a refuge—"here we are, surprise, among the trees"—Lloyd asks, "How come, to be safe, I have to be hiding out with you? How come nobody Black got anything, anything safe?" (act 1, scene 1, pp. 11–12).[38] At Claudia's "harmonious and elegant" kitchen table, "a pristine orderliness rules the room" (act 1, scene 2, p. 18). Here Lloyd tells Claudia about the nightmare he has just had, a nightmare about police war in Brooklyn. "I'm supposed to be home, see: homesafe," he tells her. "Gonna walk on up the block and buy something: milk or bread." The dream of the quotidian domestic life is interrupted when he passes his mother: "this Black woman / skin so thin you don' never want to hug her too hard and she screams at me." The Black mother's scream alerts Lloyd to an attack by "white commandos"; but, Lloyd clarifies, "this ain happening Overseas this ain the News International. This is Brooklyn" (act 1, scene 1, p. 14). The scene of *domesticus interruptus*, polite country kitchen conversation broken by the reality of urban war and broken by the loud indocility of Black English, marks the opening action of *The Issue* with the politics of undomestication that motivated Jordan's writing in the late 1970s and early 1980s. Like Lloyd's dream, *The Issue* collapses the domestic with the international scenes of intelligence, the "inner" and "outer" wars of US counterinsurgency. The play decodes and recodes safety, making its inquiry into the grammars of intelligence the entry point into a larger sociolinguistic analysis of US empire after 1968. To interrogate the perfect grammars of US empire, *The Issue* undomesticates Black radical speech.

The primary site for this undomestication is, fitting enough, the home. *The Issue* is about Lloyd Wilson's struggle with the personal, existential demands of Black leadership. The play begins with Lloyd's surfacing as a fugitive at Claudia's farmhouse. They are joined in the second scene by Kimako, a Black queer woman who also works with the Brotherhood, the organization that Lloyd leads. Kimako gives Lloyd the message that the Brotherhood has asked him to return to Brooklyn following the police killing of a Black teenager, Larry Rhodes, a name that conjures the story of Victor Rhodes, a sixteen-year-old who was beaten by the Hassidic Jewish patrol force in Crown Heights, Brooklyn. (In the play's first draft, the name "Victor" is barely visible under white eraser liquid). Jordan discusses the Rhodes case at length in her 1978 article "In the Valley of the Shadow of Death," which appeared in *Seven Days* and later in Jordan's *Civil Wars*. She writes, "Ten years after the assassination of the Civil Rights Era we, Black people, find ourselves outside the door to the hospital ward where Black life, the very remnant breath of Victor Rhodes, hovers in the shadow of death."[39] *The Issue's* Larry Rhodes, too, is in the valley of death's shadow, languishing in the hospital after being badly beaten by forty vigilantes. After Kimako reveals that the police have made no arrests and that the police attacked protestors at the protest in response to the Rhodes attack, Lloyd decides to return to Brooklyn. Act 2, scene 1, is the scene of incorporation in young Lloyd's kitchen, in which Lloyd learns the language of assimilation that he will eventually refuse.

The final scene, act 2, scene 2, takes place in the church basement where Lloyd is preparing to speak at a protest rally in Brooklyn. Here is where Lloyd must settle his dilemma and decide whether or not to do so with Claudia by his side. This brings the politics of the bedroom and the politics of the kitchen to the public, political stage as Lloyd weighs both the cost of his desire and the cost of assimilation. Jordan hints that these are the very questions for Black leadership in the post-civil-rights era: Will freedom mean freedom *"across the boards,"* as Kimako terms it, the latitude to explore the depths of one's personal, sexual, and metaphysical desires (act 2, scene 2, p. 27)? Will Lloyd step away from the struggle altogether and attend to his family? Will Lloyd walk out of the basement and kneel and offer a statement in favor of nonviolence? Or will Lloyd choose the martyr's way, standing by his defense of self-defense and facing the consequences of certain death at the hands of the police? The play ends with Lloyd's remaining undecided about Claudia (although he has revealed that he wants to marry her) and his opting for the militant's way toward social justice. The play, then, leaves its audience with no safety at all. Lloyd heads out of the basement. He opens the door, a shot rings out, and the curtain falls.

The set and setting of *The Issue* clarify its sociolinguistics of undomestication. The Brooklyn setting scales down the questions of social movement leadership that the play grapples with. In Jordan's notes about a meeting with fellow playwright and *Village Voice* editor Thulani Davis, she writes, "Lloyd is a Brooklyn leader, and *not* National: 'National' means easier to evade/supercede [*sic*] conflicts between the public & the private," whereas "'Brooklyn' means to be honest." Brooklyn is where Lloyd is born and "where he may die," where "he loves, lives, leads, lives, loves," as Jordan says.[40] Given the context of the play's writing and production between 1979 and 1981, when public longing for charismatic civil rights leadership funneled radical social movement energy toward electoral politics and when, on the other hand, the state's fear of effective Black leadership triggered its manipulation of intelligence to police Black radicalism, Jordan's choice to make *The Issue* an inquiry into the nature of post-civil-rights Black leadership attests to her interest in exposing the racial gendered structure of post-civil-rights Black politics. Jordan wanted the play to show how Black social movements restricted the personal lives of leaders like "Douglass, Fanon, Martin" and "how we forgive the dead, evidently, but condemn the living."[41] At the same time, Jordan's play makes the scenario of Black leadership the basis for a larger set of questions about the possibilities for radical safety—for living and loving, for freedom "across the boards"—in an era of the state-coded security of counterintelligent, counterinsurgent warfare in the United States and abroad. That is, instead of making Brooklyn the scene of splendorous charismatic leadership or situating urban space as the new front in a long civil rights battle, Jordan withholds the scene of charismatic performance and instead foregrounds the existential crises that leadership creates against the backdrop of the late-1970s culture of intelligence. Lloyd would like a "A Moment to Breathe," she notes; he would "like to really sit under a tree for a few days."[42]

Brooklyn, crawling with its bloodthirsty police who cover their violence with the perfect grammar of euphemism and passive voice, brings the urgency of sexual politics and social movement metaphysics into intimate reach. The Brooklyn streets are occupied, and the occupying force is set to invade the innermost sanctums of Black life. Lloyd's night-mare at the beginning of the play pictures his son, Roger, walking along a sidewalk on Halsey Street. He is "dressed like Vietcong," Lloyd tells Claudia in Jordan's initial draft. He "got a M-15 weighing down his right arm and he's sweat through the Army fatigues or it's blood / some damn thing" (July 1979 version, act 1, scene 1, p. 14). As Roger shows up in Lloyd's nightmare as a street soldier in the domestic war, Lloyd sees the "white commandos moving in closer every minute": "on my home on my mother on my son." Meanwhile his father, "stubborn sonofabitch," is behind the house prettifying things, "tying up rainworm roses to the sticks of the trellis: tying them up with regular household string and thickfingered knots won't hold too tough and the enemy this close!" (act 1, scene 1, p. 14).

The subsequent October 1979 draft of *The Issue* makes the imagery of domestic warfare even more explicit: it begins with the sounds of sirens playing overhead as a montage flashes images of beaten civil rights activ-ists and Black children killed by police onto a screen. Lloyd's stream-of-consciousness description of the dream suspends the rules of standard English. First, it minimizes the inflection of verb forms by eliminating conjugations of the verb "to be," and, as Shange's work often does, it uses the syntactical innovation of the backslash—something between a comma and a dash—to approximate the rhythm of Black speech pat-terns: "they closing in / thrown a circle around the 'target area' / my own neighborhood and moving forward, roof and stoop and hallways. Even the raggedy backyards got the fuckas coming closer and I'm supposed to be home, see: homesafe: gonna walk on up the block and buy something: milk or bread."[43] In a lengthy passage with multiple subjects—the com-mandos, Lloyd, his son, his parents—often occupying the same run-on sentence, Lloyd is the only subject who occupies the conjugated form of "to be," and even that occupation is often conditional ("I'm supposed to be"). The rendering of the dream in the Black English of Lloyd's stream of consciousness thus unmasks the racial violence of domestic warfare, which proceeded throughout the Cold War, particularly after the 1970s, under the cover of the language of peace.

As Singh argues, racial difference has historically collapsed "dis-courses of crime and war: criminalization of threats to the social order has been accompanied by a consistent militarization of policing strategies and tactics, even as military action has increasingly been justified for the policing of foreign states recast as failed or criminal regime."[44] This collapse of internal policing and foreign war entered a new phase after the urban rebellions in locales as diverse as Watts (1965), Detroit (1967), and Jacksonville (1967). At that point, the architects of US warfare in Vietnam mobilized the counterinsurgency tactics of the quagmire on the home front. As Singh offers, counterinsurgent policing "was imagined as a shift away from large-scale, more violent, less discriminating military intervention."[45] The normalization of counterinsurgent policing, as Jordan was careful to point out over and again, demanded the perfection of state languages of war. In 1982, after the massacre of Palestinians at the Sabra and Shatila refugee camps in Lebanon, Jordan returned to the problem of "official state language." She wrote, "Against official pronouncements such as 'Security measures have been taken,' or "It seems that an incident has taken place inside the camps,' nearly half a million Israelis, after the massacre at Sabra and Shatila, demanded another kind of language: an inquiry into the truth, an attribution of responsibility, a forcing of the powerful into an accountability to the people."[46] Like the Palestinians evacuating the passive voice, Lloyd's nightmare of a Brooklyn under siege counters the grammars of security with the freedom language of Black English.

While the city functions, as I have described, as the site of invasion and existential, grammatical, programmatical interrogation, the interior spaces of the upstate farmhouse and the childhood home surface on Jordan's stage as sites for discursive revision, places where characters decode the "perfect grammar" of empire and send messages of insurgent liberation in the coded language of untamed Black English. The first scene takes place in the bedroom, a space that introduces interracial intimacy, and the dilemmas it creates for Black political leadership, as a central problem. Claudia and Lloyd are lovers who are both committed to Black radical struggle. Throughout the scene, Lloyd expresses his anxiety about Claudia. "You're white so you can't be right," he says (act 1, scene 1, p. 9). Caught between his love for Claudia and his responsibility to the Brotherhood, the organization that he leads, Lloyd alternates between expressing affection toward his girlfriend—when Claudia urges him to get the rifle in case of danger, he responds, simply, "hold me and let me hold you" (act 1, scene 1, p. 8)—and deliberating on the inappropriateness of the love affair. Claudia, for her part, affirms her love for Lloyd and her commitment to the struggle for justice. She points out that when Lloyd went underground after he issued the threat to the police, the Brotherhood asked her to find Lloyd and to help him escape upstate. This scene is longer than it appears in the 1979 drafts; it includes the couple's backstory, revealing that they met a at a book party for *Roots*. At the party, at Princeton, Lloyd was representing the NAACP; his son, Roger, was also enrolled at the university. Claudia was covering the event as a journalist. The effect is a deeper meditation on the personal life of Black leadership. The play, that is, translates public concerns about the future of Black leadership after the "whispering misery" of the 1970s into the intimate lover-to-lover, relative-to-relative discourses about the future of Black safety.

There are two kitchen tables in *The Issue*. Both represent temporary forts in the post-civil-rights war against Black life, shoddy shelters that the play evacuates as it constructs a more militant safety. The second scene of the play opens in the farmhouse kitchen. It is "ivory white with skyblue / pearl gray points of reference: Butcher block table, lemons, large clean windows letting in much light." It as a "Vermeer environment," where, as Jordan initially describes it, there is a "'wall' of windows/screens leading to a patio leading to lawn leading to woods."[47] The stage set recalls the serenity and spaciousness of Yaddo: there are doorways all around, and even the wall is not a wall. In this scene, Kimako provides provisions for Lloyd and Claudia, and the three characters discuss Lloyd's next steps. Jordan's July 1979 draft is clearest in its attempt to demarcate the kitchen as a site of interior, existential inquiry that ultimately undomesticates Black activism. In Jordan's first draft, Kimako tells Lloyd and Claudia of the Rhodes beating and the police riot that follows, using Jordan's convention of placing the euphemisms that cover state terror in quotation marks: "We had what turned out to be a small demonstration at City Hall, to protest the Larry Rhodes' beating and the cops, can you believe them, they showed up, several hundred strong, in a 'counter demonstration' and went ahead and *rioted* [underlined in original]. Broke car windows with their nightsticks. Attacked the people in our group; we have fotos of the cops in action And they held these signs up to the tv cameras: 'ONE OF THEIRS IS BEATEN BUT ONE OF OURS IS *dead*!' The Mayor was and has been 'unavail-

[handwritten margin note: cop violence reframed as riot]

able for comment."[48] Kimako's news heightens the sense of calm order that the kitchen scene conjures. Brooklyn is under siege, but the kitchen offers a bright, wide-open space for the characters to consider their options. Kimako is the queer sexual force that holds this tenuous kitchen-table safety together. Left alone first with Lloyd and then with Claudia, Kimako becomes the object of both characters' desires. Lloyd asks why she and he "never made it," and Claudia reveals that Kimako had recently broken up with her as well as broken with the Sisterhood, an interracial feminist organization. Kimako "had to make a choice" between the struggle for racial justice and her intimate relationship with Claudia because, she says, she had to be responsible to her son. In this scene, the kitchen offers a queer respite from the normative sexual politics of Black social movement leadership. Here the characters literally feed their illicit sexual and political desires: for interracial romance, for lesbian erotics, for a space of quiet beyond the scene of protest.[49] The farmhouse kitchen only serves as a temporary haven for errant, undomesticated desire. By the end of the scene, Lloyd has exited the stage to prepare for his return to Brooklyn, the field of battle.

The other kitchen in *The Issue*, the one where Lloyd sits in his childhood home, spatializes the connection between patriarchy, assimilation, and language. In Jordan's notes after the staged reading of *The Issue*, she includes specific instructions about the play's kitchen scenes: "Make sure the script carries through kitchen sameness from Act I Scene II to Act II Scene I, and table placement of characters."[50] This "sameness" was readily apparent in the early drafts, where, again, Jordan was clearest in her stage directions regarding the kitchen. In the first draft, the kitchen of the Brooklyn brownstone "remains basically the same as described" in the earlier scene. The crucial difference, though, is that the Wilsons' kitchen in Brooklyn lacks the clarity and openness of the farmhouse kitchen. This kitchen is "afflicted by a junk glut: a radio on top of a roto-broiler on top of a utility cart, a toaster on top of the stove: redundancies that give the impression of a spacious kitchen without space."[51] Where there is a wall of windows in Claudia's house, there is a wall of cabinets in Lloyd's childhood home. The doorways, instead of leading the characters to the woods, lead to a cellar, to a screen door, to a hallway. The physical state of the flashback mirrors the political state of the present: just as the brownstone residents are hemmed in by their junk, so are the activists impeded by the "issues," the sexual politics, that are internal to post-civil-rights Black politics.

Young Lloyd is seated at the table when the lights come up on act 2. It is Saturday morning, and Lloyd is coloring in a coloring book depicting Roy Rogers on horseback. The scene mirrors the home training in recitation and self-cultivation that Jordan herself received as a young child. (In her memoir, Jordan reproduces this scene of instruction in the kitchen with many of the details she includes in *The Issue*, including the recitation of *The Merchant of Venice*. When her father sings the praises of Roy Rogers and the settlers, Jordan writes, "I should agree or cheer for 'The Frontier,' but I don't know how.")[52] Lloyd's father, Herb Wilson, enters from the garden, where he has been working, and begins a dialogue with Lloyd. The dialogue in this scene is ironic. Herb ridicules his son's conciliatory manners, mimicking Lloyd's "Yes, sir," with a sarcastic retort: "'Yassuh, yassuh': that all you know how to say to me? You tink this is the army?" (act 2, scene 1, p. 3). But Herb also demands Lloyd's obedience. When he sends Lloyd to do work on *The Merchant of Venice*, he calls him to attention. Jordan's stage directions note, "Mr. Wilson goes over to the boy and, as he gives each instruction, demonstrates what he means, by actually pushing the boy's chin up, pushing back the boy's shoulders, and giving the boy's stomach a light tap" (act 2, scene 1, p. 6). Herb Wilson's project is one of domestication vis-à-vis a defiant brand of assimilation: "And you don' be shuffling, boy. You ain gwine be no run of the mill *negro* sneaking around," he says (act 2, scene 1, p. 6). Mr. Wilson wants to keep his son safe by keeping him off the streets and away from the "*nigga riff raff*" of the streets (act 2, scene 1, p. 9). He has planned to enroll Lloyd in a private boarding school with hopes of sending his son to school with future "Captains of Industry" (act 2, scene 1, pp. 12–13). The literary instruction I just wrote of, then, is a crucial part of a larger pedagogical project aimed at keeping Lloyd safe by cultivating him the way Herb cultivates his garden. In the Wilsons' kitchen, the linguistic and literary mastery that a young Black kid pursues by sweating over his homework on a midsummer's Saturday morning is the answer to the problem of Black premature death. As Mr. Wilson hopes, "He will come out the school like a veritable prince. Among men!" (act 2, scene 1, p. 13).

Literary recitation is key to the pathos of act 2, scene 1. Throughout the scene, Mr. Wilson speaks in West Indian–inflected Black English.

Jordan is careful to detail his accent: "In general, an 'h' at a beginning of a word, is *silent*. And the 'th' combination is pronounced either as a hard 't' sound or as a 'd'" (act 2, scene 1, p. 1). The tendency toward assimilation appears first in Mr. Wilson's instructions to his son. The impulse toward domestication, toward the careful cultivation of proper Black bourgeois citizenship in the age of rights, escalates throughout the scene in the interaction between Mr. Wilson and Mrs. Wilson. Mr. Wilson berates his wife: "You are not me! Look at this. (Meaning the difference between their forearms) You a *Block* wo-mon: A monkey chaser down to you soul. I set you up here, something swell, in this house: Turn it over to you, and what. You wan' tie my hands. You wan' drag me down. You wan' throw that devil child to the streets. . . . You damn Block woman: A mon home suppose be a castle and I have me have to make my own someting to eat! (Outraged) I talk how I want in my own house!" (act 2, scene 1, p. 10). At the height of their argument about Lloyd's schooling, Mr. Wilson knocks his chair to the floor and slaps his wife. In this scene of domestic terror, Mr. Wilson literally beats his wife and son into submission, demanding that they consent to the dominant linguistic and economic order. As Lloyd studies his Shakespeare and Kipling so that he can compete with the children of capitalists, Mr. Wilson praises his own light skin and terrorizes his darker-skinned wife. Now Lloyd uses his literary knowledge to intervene in the domestic drama. Lloyd runs into the room and offers to recite lines from Rudyard Kipling's "If": "'If you can walk with kings . . .' (He forgets. Blinks hard. And then remembers:) 'If you can walk with kings *yet keep the common touch* . . .' (Forgets again, and then remembers:) '. . . why then, you'll be a man, my son!'" (act 2, scene 1, p. 15). This pleases Mr. Wilson, who goes to fetch ice cream for his dutiful son.

Left alone in the kitchen, Mrs. Wilson offers her son a different kind of literary instruction. She tells him, "I wan' that you learn something for me: For all time" (act 2, scene 1, p. 17). Mrs. Wilson reaches for her Bible and, finger to page, reads Psalm 91, pausing so that Lloyd can repeat each line after she reads it. Psalm 91 is a song of safety amid terror: "He who dwells in the shelter of the Most High shall abide under the shadow of the Almighty," reads the Modern English Version. And "You shall not be afraid of the terror by night, nor the arrow that flies by day" (Ps. 91:5). At the end of this scene, a *scene of incorporation* that scripts assimilation as a violent compulsion of West Indian patriarchy in modern Black America, is a second recitation. Whereas the father imposes proper language acquisition through literary instruction, mother and son sit together, embodying the refuge that they conjure and sanctify with each repeated line. This is Lloyd's learning under the protection of and in the interest of a maternal care that exceeds the domesticating energy of the Wilson kitchen. Unlike the homework that Lloyd completes offstage, which offers up literary expertise and linguistic perfection for capitalist acquisition, the biblical recitation is a performance onstage that admits the utter vulnerability of Black life in police-occupied Brooklyn. The practice in memorization that Mrs. Wilson offers against Kipling and Shakespeare can be understood, then, as a practice that undomesticates the kitchen. More than a site for perfecting the false safety of assimilation, the kitchen is place that invites shared vulnerability: a collective entering into the knowledge that, in Jordan's words, "we will not survive by joining the game according to the rules set up by our enemies; we will not survive by imitating the doublespeak/bullshit/nonthink standard English of the powers that be."[53] Because the kitchen is not safe and because the kitchen is not home, Lloyd's search for what Jordan refers to as a "homesafe" will eventually culminate in the issue of the threat that may cost him his life. This threat emerges from this place of shared vulnerability to the violent culture of intelligence after the civil rights era.

The prayer-recitation of protection hangs between the safety of the farmhouse and the danger awaiting Lloyd outside the church basement. In act 1, Lloyd finds refuge in the domestic and then refuses it, leaving the farmhouse and returning to Brooklyn with self-defense on his mind. In act 2, Lloyd passes through the domestic scene of his childhood and ends up in the church basement, where he will prepare for his final reckoning with the police. As the shot rings out at the end of the play, the audience is left wondering if the shelter that Mrs. Wilson and her young son hold between their bodies in the kitchen where they are terrorized is enough to stand up to the nighttime terrors and daytime arrows of present-day Brooklyn, USA.

"Pure Terror for Our Lives"

Between the initial draft of *The Issue* in 1979 and the staged reading at Greenwich Village's Public Theatre two years later, Jordan's work escalated its militant calls to undomestication. The final work undoubtedly bears the imprint of Jordan's own intimate experience with police violence. After she finished drafting *The Issue* at Yaddo, Jordan returned to a Brooklyn that looked a lot like the city of Lloyd Wilson's nightmare. On August 22, a twenty-nine-year-old Puerto Rican man, Luis Baez, was killed by police in his mother's house. Five days later, Jordan participated in a demonstration at the New York Police Department's Seventy-Ninth Precinct police station in Brooklyn. The demonstration was organized by the Black United Front, a coalition of activist organizations that joined together against domestic issues like police violence and foreign-policy issues like the United States' support for Israel and Zionism.[54] Jordan attended the demonstration with two friends, Gwendolen Hardwick, who was then studying drama at NYU, and the writer and activist Alexis De Veaux. The trio arrived at the demonstration in front of the Seventy-Ninth Precinct station, located in the Bedford-Stuyvesant neighborhood, across the street from what was then Tompkins Park. It was around 6:00 p.m. when Jordan, Hardwick, and De Veaux joined the rally with several hundred other protestors (later estimates would number the crowd between one thousand and three thousand).

Later that night, when Jordan was back home, she wrote of the march, which proceeded in pouring rain. It was "a peaceful protest march"; the protestors "marched peacefully from Tompkins Park." The protestors were then attacked by police. First, Jordan remembers, the police approached the protestors from behind and threw bottles from their squad cars; then they advanced toward the protestors with their squad cars. When the police retreated, the protestors regrouped and continued "on a very circuitous route that rather widely circled the precinct's location." The police then rioted. Jordan writes,

> At Marcy Ave and Lexington, we halted and stood quietly in the rain waiting for directions
>   At this point, suddenly, cop cars came from everywhere abruptly flashing lights & roaring sirens and drove directly into the people

We tried to hold our lines but the cars were ploughing directly into bodies

Everyone was screaming with shock & terror

On the hood of the police car closest to my line 2 young Latino brothers were lying—they had jumped on top in order to avoid being run over

Taking cover behind a cement wall, Jordan, Hardwick, and De Veaux crept between two fences and lay still while cops "came out fast, hunting for people." "We lay as still as possible," she writes. "It was pure terror for our lives." The three made it back to Jordan's car and then back home, where Jordan recorded what had happened on a legal pad. "This is all the truth as best I can recollect it at this time, 11:10 P.M.," she wrote. Then she added, "There was absolutely NO provocation from the demonstrators."[55]

After the police raid in Bed-Stuy, Jordan used the word "terror" to describe the relationship between Black people and the police. In a report titled "Black Power in the Police," first drafted on August 29 and probably read aloud at a press conference or rally, she described Black America as "a community of hunted people" and a "neocolonial outpost ruled by the police: a colony in which funerals and grief, fear and the screams of the terrorized consume the energy of our collective spirit, the energy of our collective experience."[56] Jordan became involved in several collective efforts to hold the police department accountable for its terrorist attack on the protestors. In her own recollection of the events, Jordan referred to the August 27 raid as a "savage attack" and referred to this most recent episode in the "ever worsening, and official, contempt and hatred for Black life" as "Old Blues." Turning to the "Heavy Dues" of Black life, she rejected the proposal of an NYPD investigation into the attack: "We know that we ridicule the dead if we will even consider action allegedly to be taken on our behalf by the Mayor / the District Attorney / the Police Commissioner. We know the relationship between these public officials and the patrolman abusing the people on the corner of your block: It is the relationship of the guilty and the damned." Finally she turned to the "Good News," speaking with hope of the possibility of federal intervention in the form of "an exhaustive, Congressional investigation into the New York system of injustice and terror" and speaking

[handwritten margin note: why is Congress exempt from this relationship?]

with even greater buoyancy about "a nationwide turning of attention to this crisis of police violence."[57]

Jordan also went with De Veaux and Hardwick to a press conference at the Puerto Rican Legal Defense Fund, where they worked with other activists to organize a People's Tribunal and submitted a report, along with a recording of the collective testimony presented at that tribunal, to the local news department.[58] The tribunal took place at the Brooklyn Armory on September 7, during which eyewitnesses recorded testimony for the press. There De Veaux read aloud the collective testimony of Black artists and writers, noting that the "intentions of the police were not simply to disperse the demonstrators, but attack, bodily, as many participants as they could."[59] The written collective testimony, "Unprecedented Police Riot in Brooklyn," names Jordan, Hardwick, De Veaux, Jill Nelson, Stanley Kinard, and Amiri Baraka as authors. The authors write of the police riot as an attack, exposing the myth of public safety that rationalized the violence: "the intentions of the police were not simply to disperse the protestors but to attack bodily as many participants as they could." They end the testimony with a list of charges: that the events of August 27 constituted "a full scale police riot," that the mainstream white press was guilty of "criminal negligence, specifically in deserting the marchers at the close of the rally, thereby avoiding witness to and reporting of the police riot which followed," and that the city government was complicit with the racist assault.[60] When they charged the artistic community with shying away from involvement ("We charge with gross negligence those sectors of the Black and white political, artistic, and intellectual community who have refrained from involvement"), they dampened the critique of their first draft, which read, "We charge the blk. [Black] political artistic and intellectual community with gross negligence in their lack of participation in the demonstration and subsequent silence since the police riot which followed."[61]

Jordan's activism in late summer 1979 was something of a dress rehearsal for *The Issue* and a tragic, dramatic reenactment of the problems of state language that she had been writing about since the early 1970s. The demonstration, the attack, and the organizing that followed gave lie to the understatements and silences that filled newspaper coverage of the police raid. On the day following the raid, the *New York Daily News* reported that "5 cops [were] hurt in Bed-Stuy," that the police "skirmished" with the protestors, and that "most of the violence was caused by about 100 youths." The paper reported that the protestors "pelted riot-clad police" and "wrecked a patrol car with cinder blocks." The police officers, passive victims for most of the article, are finally described as charging into the crowd not with their cars but with "swinging nightsticks."⁶²

The August 1979 police riot changed the play that Jordan had just finished drafting upstate. She completed a revision of the play in October 1979. In that version, Kimako's account of the police riot after the demonstration in Brooklyn incorporates details from the Tompkins Park scene. In the earlier version, the protest takes place at City Hall. All of the later drafts move the demonstration to Tompkins Park. Kimako tells Lloyd that the police outside of the Seventy-Seventh Precinct station "drove the police cars fullspeed into the crowd" and that they were "plowing into" the crowd, "straight ahead" (act 1, scene 2, p. 23). The elaboration of the scene of terror recalls Jordan's notes and the collective testimony she wrote with her colleagues: "We had to run for our lives—crawling across the concrete (SHE turns up the palms of her hands so the long scratch marks daubed with iodine can be seen) to get away. We had to *try not to breathe*: they were that close!" (act 1, scene 2, p. 23).

Another change was an audiovisual accompaniment, first introduced in the October 1979 version of *The Issue*. Jordan scripted an introduction to the play that called for an audio track to play sounds of sirens, first singing slowly and then "maddeningly intensif[ying]," holding for nearly an "earsplitting minute and a half" before descrescendoing into "a threatening whine." If the sound here is meant to assault and awaken the theater audience with the ongoing threat of police violence, sound also works to tell the story of hope: intermixed with the siren's whine is the gospel song "Mary Don' You Weep." Jordan added a photograph montage, a "Black and white silent film," as she called it, above this soundtrack. The montage shows images of police violence against Black people—an Alabama state trooper beats a Black man on the ground; Birmingham police hold snarling dogs at the faces of Black protestors; newspaper headlines flash, reading, "Sheriff shoots would-be voter through head" or "Fannie Lou Hamer Pistol Whipped in Overnight Jail." There are also images of Black joy and belonging: the play's main character, Lloyd Wilson, appears in a photograph "holding 3 or 5 year old Black child in one arm, up against his shoulder, while shaking hands and laughing with a crowd of well-wishers" and "longshot of little girl (among her playmates) posing for camera: big smile." The photographs also capture Black militancy: "Waist shot of LLOYD in the middle of a running front line of shouting, muscular Black men, arms raised in the Black Power salutation." The prologue to the play ends with a montage of headlines that normalize, regularize, and euphemize police violence against Black people: "'HONEST MISTAKE' SAY COPS: TEEN, 18, DEAD IN SCHOOL YARD," "BOY, 7, SHOT BY HOLIDAY PATROL," and so on.[63] The sirens blare for a full minute and a half after the images fade. Then the action begins.

Kimako's elaboration of the police raid heightens the play's realist rendering of police violence and announces *The Issue* as a revelation of the violence that official state language dissimulates. In contrast, the dizzying flash of photographs, soundtracked by the discordant sounds of gospel singers and squad cars, achieves the opposite effect: not to reveal that which the audience does not know but to force a disorienting audiovisual confrontation with what the audience knows too well: Black life's quotidian overexposure to the state's machinery of death.

The August 27 police attack also deepened Jordan's commitment to a kind of progressive literary production that maintained a critical relationship to its conditions of production. Less than two weeks after the attack and only two days after the People's Tribunal on Police Violence, Jordan followed Audre Lorde in resigning from the feminist journal *Chrysalis*, citing the Tompkins Park raid as a catalyzing event. Citing what she calls the magazine's "flagrant disregard of the Black woman in America," Jordan conjures the memory of that night of state terror: "Two weeks ago, myself and another Black woman poet and another Black woman artist came within 18 inches of losing our lives inside an unbridled police riot in Brooklyn, N.Y. Our crime: To be Black and breathing on the streets of the 79th precinct. Tell me / show me how your hopelessly academic, pseudo-historical, incestuous, and profoundly optional profoundly trifling profoundly upper middle-class attic white publication can presume to represent our women's culture: the very tissue of our ongoing, tenuous, embattled experience."[64] As Alexis Gumbs writes of this exchange, "If racism slept, unfortunately it doesn't, but if racism slept it would have nightmares about June Jordan."[65] Sent just after

Lorde's resignation from the magazine's position of poetry editor, Jordan's missive to *Chrysalis* unleashed the anger that burned in Brooklyn in fall 1979.[66]

After Jordan's intimate encounter with police repression, the urgency of unmasking the violent work of intelligence surfaced in the connections she noticed—or noticed lacking—between US publishing and Black vulnerability to the weaponry of counterinsurgency. This urgency coincided with a commitment that was perhaps even more pressing for Jordan: to enlist her craft as a writer in an ongoing battle against a US imperialism that produced consent through the dulling daily drone of news about counterinsurgent actions around the globe. If *The Issue* undomesticated post-civil-rights Black political speech by focusing on interpersonal relations and the inner life of Black leadership, the work that followed in Jordan's poetry jumped scale to assert its militancy. Jordan's first collection of nonfiction, published two years later, *Civil Wars: Observations from the Front Lines of America*, attests to this critical priority: "You begin with your family and the kids on the block," she writes, "and next you open your eyes to what you call your people and that leads you into land reform into Black English into Angola leads you back to your own bed where you lie by yourself, wondering if you deserve to be peaceful, or trusted or desired or left to the freedom of your own unfaltering skull. And the scale shrinks to the size of a skull: your own interior cage."[67] As I attend this calibration of scale in Jordan's early-1980s poetry, I return to Jordan's geolinguistics of intelligence.

Can You Say?

The dark-pink lipstick kiss print is still visible at the top of a letter between friends dated July 1982. The dramatist and actress Gwendolen Hardwick writes to the writer and organizer June Jordan, "Received your letter one evening after having come home from work . . . after having read articles in *the Voice* regarding the acts of genocide against the Lebanese and Palestinian people—in the name of a Jewish state. Who will secure the state of the Lebanese and Palestinians? . . . I am reading these articles and feeling such shame . . . that the human race continues such inhumanity upon itself! Some times [*sic*] I wonder what in the world I am doing here in this time and space." Hardwick lists the scenes of destruction that make 1982 New York feel like the end of the world: the poor Black and Latinx folks in the East Bronx and the Lower East Side, police murder in New York, the "British arrogance in the Malvinas," the influx of Haitian refugees to the United States. "And what about the Black South Africans? El Salvador?" she asks. At the end of the litany of assaults, Hardwick includes a few simple notes of care: gratitude for the communication; wishes for a speedy recovery after a recent operation. Then, "I love you," another imprint of lipstick, and then, as if an afterthought: "Happy Birthday!"[68]

We could read Hardwick's opening and closing passion marks as extralingual, labial-lingual pieces of code: the first mark an invitation to communication on terms other than those fossilized in newsprint, an initiation into a time and space that is other than here, and the second mark a haptic benediction, a goodsaying better left unsaid.[69] In this section, a further inquiry into the intelligible and unintelligible code of the long war on terror, I turn from Jordan's 1979 play to two books she published in 1985: a collection of poetry, *Living Room*, and a collection of essays, *On Call*, both of which followed her 1983 trip to Nicaragua. Calling for a purification of terms like "freedom" and "security," Jordan's post-Nicaragua poems and essays joined her earlier work's critique of official state language with her field research on hemispheric counterinsurgency. The internationalization of Jordan's activism and writing in the early 1980s articulated what Zahra Hussein Ali calls "new political mappings" when the grammars of the long war on terror were collapsing the distance between Brooklyn and Beirut, Managua and Pretoria.[70] Jordan's literature was resistance literature; it drew on her long commitment to crafting space, in poetry and in the other genres of writing and organizing she engaged, to train the reader to see the world differently.[71] In a forthcoming book, Meta DuEwa Jones calls this work of retraining through the alchemical processes of literary craft the "afterlove of slavery."[72]

While much of the focus on Jordan's internationalism has centered around her sixth volume of poetry, *Living Room*, particularly its poems about Palestine, scholars have said less about Jordan's *intra*hemispheric study of intelligence and the poetics of revolution. If Jordan's linguistic inquiries into white English and Black English gave way to her undomestication of Black political speech in the 1970s and early 1980s (in

July, 1982

Dearest June:

Received your letter one evening after having come home from work (yes i got the job, thank-you for your reference) after having redd articles in the Voice regarding the acts of genocide against the Lebanese and Palestinian people—in the name of a jewish state. Who will secure the state of the Lebanese and Palestinians? The ride to work is long, an hour and a half—feel like I'm going out of state—I am reading these articles and feeling such shame—certainly horror but shame that the human race continues such inhumanity upon itself! Some times I wonder what in the world am I doing here in this time and space.... feeling so delicate and tender lately.... I want only pretty silk kimonos, flowers

Letter from Gwendolen "Lil' Bit" Hardwick to June Jordan, 1982. (Courtesy of Schlesinger Library, Radcliffe Institute, Harvard University, Cambridge, MA)

The Issue, for example), they also explored revolutionary poetic forms that worked at the limits of language to forge leftist internationalist affiliations between the dispossessed of the Caribbean and of Central and South America, especially Nicaragua.

While Jordan might have celebrated the end of the 1970s "whispering misery" when she spoke of the "resurrection of the spirit" that she was feeling in Brooklyn in 1978, the years between 1979 and 1985 challenged her idealistic resolve.[73] There was the serial murder of twenty-eight Black children and adults in Atlanta between 1979 and 1982. There was Great Britain's bloody defeat of Argentina in the Malvinas War in April 1982, which gave Margaret Thatcher "the political cover she needed to bring a program of radical capitalist transformation to a Western liberal democracy for the first time."[74] There was the massacre of hundreds of thousands of Salvadorans by US-backed and US-trained forces battling the Farabundo Martí National Liberation Front. In December 1981, over 750 civilians in the village of El Mozote were massacred, leaving only one survivor. There was the callous refusal of refugee status for Haitian asylum seekers. There was the US-supported and US-funded genocide of Mayan peasants in Guatemala: between 1981 and 1983 alone, one hundred thousand were executed. There was massacre of Palestinian refugees at the Sabra and Shatila camps in June 1982. There was the US policy of "constructive engagement" with South Africa. There was the US invasion of Grenada in 1983. And, of course, there was that fateful night when Jordan and her dear friend Gwendolen Hardwick crawled on their hands and knees to safety when the Brooklyn police attacked.

Jordan's relationship with Hardwick was one of many intimate political relationships that she forged with activists and artists against this backdrop of early-1980s intelligence (where "intelligence," again, means both repression through the extraction of counterinsurgent knowledge and the affirmative practice of knowledge production). These relationships—with Hardwick and Alexis De Veaux, Sara Miles, Ntozake Shange, Alice Walker, Adrienne Torf, E. Ethelbert Miller, Toni Cade Bambara, Etel Adnan, and others—were based in mutual desires to marshal love, language, and bodily strength in the war between what Jordan called, again, the "*true* pro-life forces" and the US-trained armies and operatives that were experimenting with the techniques of torture, information extraction, mass intimidation, and primitive punishment that would later be unmasked in Guantanamo and Abu Ghraib.[75] Jordan's 1980s poetry and nonfiction provide an insurgent map of all the places Hardwick mentions, and many more besides, where partially aligned or nonaligned Black and indigenous peoples were fighting for freedom throughout the late–Cold War years. Her work develops "a spatial imag- inary for justice that governing language otherwise obscures," as Keith Feldman puts it.[76] This spatial imaginary materialized in her poetry and nonfiction on Palestine, South Africa, and Nicaragua as the very scalar analysis that Jordan referred to in *Civil Wars* when she wrote of all the places one's commitment to one's people leads, from the inside of one's own skull to Angola.

[handwritten margin note: what would this mapping project look like?]

Jordan's internationalist imaginary of justice faced off against the Rea- gan administration's campaign to rid the earth of the threat of commu- nism, a campaign that used the language of democratic idealism to cover for imperial expansion, capitalist plunder, and a sheer thirst to rid the United States of its "Vietnam syndrome." Visiting Nicaragua in the after- math of the Sandinista revolution, during which US-funded counterin- surgents (Contras) were actively staging a brutal assault on Nicaraguan civil society, Jordan went "on call," as she referred to her mission, to can- vas a point of intensity along the itinerary of the long war on terror. Latin America was, at this late–Cold War juncture, a laboratory for the United States' development of "more pragmatic and flexible imperial strategies" that lent authority and might to its rise as a global superpower in the late twentieth century.[77] The region served as a training ground for US for- eign policy and military strategy. Throughout the 1980s, US aggression in Latin America, particularly in the Central American countries of Guate- mala, El Salvador, and Nicaragua, provided the terms for counterinsur- gent rhetoric and warfare that would mature in the latter end of the war on terror. Greg Grandin writes, "The Reagan White House perfected new techniques to manipulate the media, Congress, and public opinion while at the same time reempowering domestic law enforcement agencies to monitor and harass dissidents. These techniques . . . prefigured initiatives now found in the PR campaign to build support for the war in Iraq and in the Patriot Act, reinvigorating the national security state in ways that resonate to this day."[78] During the war in Nicaragua, the CIA director William Casey and the National Security Council's Oliver North funded the Contras through the covert transnational exchange now known as the Iran-Contra scandal. The CIA also funded mercenaries from other Central American countries like Honduras. Suspending the scholarly distance Jordan might achieve by using commas and keeping with the Black feminist punctuation of what I like to call the blackslash, she explained, "Armed and goaded by the CIA, *contra* troops based in Honduras daily invaded Nicaragua border towns: blowing up bridges / burning hospitals / ambushing international press personnel / murdering doctors / blowing up babies and tobacco barns."[79]

US involvement in Central America in the early 1980s revitalized an intelligence industry that was in decline after COINTELPRO formally dissolved in 1971 and after the Senate's investigation of US intelligence agencies in 1975 and 1976.[80] What distinguished Nicaragua as a target in the United States' vicious campaign for hegemony that used Latin America as a laboratory for repression was the discursive scaffolding that the US government erected and the terms—"low-intensity conflict," "freedom fighters," "self-defense"—that made the violent repression of Nicaraguan people palatable to the US public. "The Contras were by no means the first anti-Communist insurgency sponsored by the United States," Grandin writes. "Similar policies had already been attempted in Guatemala in 1954, Cuba in 1961, and in Southeast Asia, Africa, and Afghanistan. But no other insurgency was championed for such a sustained period of time in such idealistic terms."[81]

It is crucial to note, though, that these idealistic terms might be unintelligible if not for the Black female's function as a "national treasury of rhetorical wealth," in Spillers's terms.[82] In the 1985 State of the Union Address, for example, Reagan made the fight for "self-defense" in Nicaragua legible through three figurations of women of color: the redemptive figure of the female Vietnam refugee, the deviant figure of the poor Black mother, and the salvific figure of the elder Black matron. First speaking of the anti-Sandinista forces, Reagan urged Congress to support funding the "freedom fighters" and "continue all facets of our assistance to Central America." "I want to work with you," he said, "to support the democratic forces whose struggle is tied to our own security." Continuing his speech about his "great plans" and "great dreams," Reagan then turned to Jean Nguyen, a Vietnamese immigrant who left Southeast Asia after the Vietnam War. Nguyen "studied hard, learned English, and finished high school in the top of her class"; she was now at

West Point, Reagan said, becoming an "American hero" and somehow redeeming the failed mission in Vietnam. Finally, bringing the speech to a close, Reagan turned to Clara Hale, who founded Harlem's Hale House to care for children in need, especially children addicted to drugs. Reagan went so far as to invite us to Mother Hale's window, to watch her cradle the children who, we might presume, have been abandoned by welfare queens hardly worthy of the "assistance," the tax dollars, that might otherwise find their way to the Central American death squads and mercenaries: "Go to her house some night, and maybe you'll see her silhouette against the window as she walks the floor talking softly, soothing a child in her arms—Mother Hale of Harlem, and she, too, is an American hero."[83]

Reagan offers this image of soothing care and soft whispering to sanitize the dirty war he is asking Congress to authorize. This places Black female *not*-mother *not*-mothering, following Spillers's classic formulation, in a vestibular relation to subjecthood in the grammar book of the neoliberal United States: we must pass through this "marked woman," this "locus of confounded identities," to get to the United States.[84] (*My country needs me*: is that what this American hero was saying to herself as Reagan pointed to her across the chamber floor?) What the Vietnamese student and the Black mother tell us, says Reagan, is that "anything is possible in America if we have the faith, the will, and the heart" and that "history is asking us once again to be a force for good in the world."[85] While Grandin points out that rhetorical flourishes such as these allowed the White House to cast the Soviet Union as the imperialist power against which a revolutionary US force was waging a freedom crusade and that Reagan's speechwriters "turned the tables on those who portrayed America's brutal opposition to third-world nationalism as standing on the wrong side of history," he fails to note how the discursive scaffolding of the Reagan doctrine called on racialized gender difference to signify redemption and to personify the kind of "assistance" that the United States was offering to Central America by way of torture manuals, artillery, guns, and mercenaries.[86] The soldier and the not-quite-mother are the available subject positions for women of color. Contrary to Reagan's claim that the two women whom he hosted were proof that "anything is possible," what Nguyen and Hale signified is that imperial culture had specifically gendered capacities for them: to give life and to take it. Jordan does not disavow the specifi-

First Lady Nancy Reagan (*right*) and daughter Maureen (*left*) applauding as guests of honor Clara "Mother" Hale (*second from right*) and the Vietnamese-born West Point cadet Jean Nguyen (*second from left*) stand with her. (Getty Images)

cally gendered labor of caregiving on which the state's claims to be providing "assistance" relied. Rather, her poetry reclaims Black women's care work as a version of security that privileges interdependence and mutual vulnerability across borders. I will return to this point shortly.

Jordan's analyses of official state language relentlessly expose the racial gendered logics and imagery of state-manipulated terms such as "freedom" "security," "America," and "hero." Discussing the word "safe," for example, she addresses a woman who was interviewed on television after the 1984 vice presidential debate. "She said she would vote for Reagan because she would feel 'safe' with a man," Jordan writes. "Like George Bush." She refers, too, to a woman who "said she felt good about Geraldine [Ferraro] because Geraldine 'stayed calm.'"[87] These are the terms of safety and peace—the code of pacification—that Jordan rejects, that she had been rejecting since after the police attack in Brooklyn. When she writes of the problem with a "safety" that concedes in advance of politics that "no woman is safe in this man's world" and then asks if Ferraro would have been wrong for "becoming furious, indignant, disgusted, and thoroughly impassioned, as she righteously reacted to the lies and the self-absorbed and morbid and patronizing complacencies of Mr. George Bush," she recalled the critiques of state violence that she offered in the essay that she wrote four years earlier after the protest in Brooklyn.[88] In "Civil Wars," she wrote, "This has been the code, overwhelmingly, for the oppressed: that you keep cool and calm down and explore proper channels and above all, that you remain law-abiding and orderly precisely because it is the order of the day that you will beg and bleed, precisely because it is the power of the law of the terrorist state arrayed against you to force you to beg and bleed without acceptable recourse except for dumb endurance or mute perishing."[89] In refusal of this tragic reverence to calm and safety, Jordan reinvents the gendered code of the oppressed and provides a catalogue of New Women, women "completely uninterested in keeping calm, women entirely prepared to make a scene, to raise a ruckus and to be shrill, if you will."[90] The impulse in Jordan's work to identify the grammatical and sociolinguistic forms of pacification and domestication and then eviscerate those terms unifies her work throughout the Reagan years.

Jordan's studies of US empire, honed in close readings of the daily news and in fieldwork in Nicaragua, provided direction for her piercing early-1980s essays, which are collected in *On Call*. "Life After Lebanon," from 1984, for example, begins with a series of affirmative negations, beginning with the phrase "I am not" and then repeating the phrase "I am glad I am not":

> Let me just say, at once: I am not now nor have I ever been a whiteman. And, leaving aside the joys of unearned privilege, this leaves me feeling pretty good: I am glad I am not the whiteman who warns that Nicaragua is next on his evil list and who, meanwhile, starves and terrorizes that country through "covert action." I am glad I am not the whiteman who congratulates El Salvador and who supports South Africa. I am glad I am not the whiteman who lies about Managua and who denies asylum to real freedom fighters opposed to Pretoria. I am glad I am not the whiteman who dyes his hair, wears pancake makeup, and then tries to act like the last cowboy out here surrounded by wild Indians.[91]

Jordan's map of the Reagan frontier emphasizes the indispensability of misinformation ("lies") to the racial gendered regime of violence that constructed white manliness through the late–Cold War conquest of "real freedom fighters" by the made-up actor in the White House. In this same essay, Jordan defines Reagan as an exemplar of this "new manliness," the articulation of white masculinity that was, first, garnered by power's multiscalar predations and, second, justified by the language that at turns euphemized and overstated its assaults. The New Man "preys upon his wife, his children, his Black co-worker, the poor, the elderly, Grenada, Nicaragua, *and he boasts about it.*"[92] The whiteman who warns while starving and terrorizing, then congratulates and supports while massacring, then lies and denies while bombing, then dyes and tries while conquering, now preys while boasting.

Jordan understands this production of late–Cold War white masculinity as a linguistic project that ties the circulation of terms like "safety" and "security" in the deceitful rhetorical flourishes of policy speeches to the understatements and euphemisms that fill news accounts of state violence. In "Problems of Language in a Democratic State," Jordan tracks this connection between high rhetoric and everyday speech in news and opinion shows. Analyzing the overuse of the passive voice in official state language (what she earlier called "White English"), Jordan refers to a news talk show on which the four white men hosting the show spoke in terms like "The Federal Reserve has been forced to raise interest rates" or "It is widely believed . . ." In response, Jordan asks, "Is somebody really saying those words? Is any real life affected by those words? Should we really just relax into the literally nondescript, the irresponsible language of the passive voice? Will the passive voice lead us safely out of the action?"[93] Returning to the specter of perishing, Jordan argues for the elimination of passive voice and the crescendo, again, of shrill ruckus: "We will have to drown out the official language of the powerful with our own mighty and conflicting voices or we will perish as a people."[94]

Hardwick's letter to Jordan was a catalogue of "low-intensity conflict" and proxy war and an inhabitation of the intimate relation that the scene of reading produces between the Black American subject and the devastation caused by US-led and US-funded war in the Middle East, Africa, and Latin America. (It begins, recall, with an account of her reading the *Village Voice* on the way home from work.) The impression of lipstick, as I mentioned earlier, might be read as a coded call to a different intimacy and a different relationship to letters. In that way, we could read

the imprint as the kiss of poetic knowledge placed in risky proximity to
the cartographic project of imperial intelligence. If that poetic knowledge could take on new grammatical and extragrammatical forms, how
would they appear on the page? What would they sound like?

The suite of poems that Jordan offers in *Living Room* and that follow
her 1983 trip to Nicaragua are a study in the new grammatical forms that
she called for in response to the massacres along the Reagan frontier.
Living Room offers a series of six poems "for" Nicaragua and "from" Nicaragua. "Poem for Nicaragua," the first of these, is composed of ten cou-
plets addressed to the country, which is personified with "coffee skin"
and "outlaw lips."[95] The next four poems are gathered as a numbered
series, beginning with "First poem from Nicaragua Libre: *teotecacinte*"
and ending with "Fourth poem from Nicaragua Libre: Report from the
Frontier." The last poem is "Safe," twelve tight lines describing a night
watch on the Río Escondido. In each of these poems, Jordan toggles
or suspends subjects and predicates so that Nicaragua and its people,
the object of malevolent care, exert their force on imperial grammars,
taking over the subjects of narration and narration itself. In "Poem for
Nicaragua," for example, the first three stanzas offer descriptions of the
you addressed in the poem, conceivably the country itself, by offering
subject complements detached from the second-person subject (*you*)
and transitive verb (*are* or *were*):

> So little I could hold the edges
> of your earth inside my arms
>
> Your coffee skin the cotton stuff
> the rain makes small
>
> Your boundaries of sea and ocean slow
> or slow escape possession

The subject of the poem casts a hold over the speaker who could, or
would, "hold" the subject "inside" the speaker's arms. This hold that
the withheld, withholding subject "escap[ing] possession" has on the
speaker who longs to hold the subject surfaces in the truncated verses,
the lines without subjects or transitive verbs. If the subject cannot be

held, they can neither be captured in language. Instead, they are the one who captures, by way of a compulsion, that liberates: "Even a pig would move towards you / dignified from mud," reads the fourth stanza. The first conjugated verb that the poem iterates is the conditional "would" of a hog transcending its earthly ties. The diminution of the subject—a subject "So little," made "small"—conjures a childlike innocence that is later belied by the same subject's "outlaw lips" curled in a snarl and the image of a hand holding a gun: "A pistol calms the trembling / of your fingers." The poem offers an impression of a subject's "slow escape possession" rather than a mimetic account of a subject's appearance. Indeed, the most material, actually concrete, image in this poem, composed of surreal figures, is an image of speech overwhelming the boundaries of civil speech and complete sentences:

> Your inside walls a pastel stucco
> for indelible graffiti:
>> *movimiento del pueblo*
>> *unido*

"Poem for Nicaragua" is addressed to a subject who eludes capture in language, whose *withholding hold* possesses the speaker. The subject is not a figure who appears in or along the dictates of a linear space-time continuum that is implied by conjugations of the transitive verb "to be." Rather, the subject of the poem is imminent, is *among*, a landscape to which that the speaker of the poem can only gesture when she, at last, in the last two stanzas, shows up in the first person:

> I imagine you among the mountains
> eating early rice
>
> I remember you among the birds
> that do not swallow blood.

The entry into *Living Room*'s Nicaragua poems, then, arranges language to withhold the subject of its lines. This withholding challenges the grounds on which Nicaragua would otherwise come to be known through the projects of affirmative incorporation or surveillant repression that I have gathered as two modalities of the late–Cold War project of *intelligence*. All that is knowable about Nicaragua, here, is the indelibility of its people united in self-defense, an indelibility not quite captured by the poem's single Spanish-language stanza, a stanza that is, again, about wayward language's spray-painted defilement of the bounded.

Poems like "Poem for Nicaragua" democratize poetic form. They show the influence of the Nicaraguan poet Ernesto Cardinal, whose poetic *exteriorismo*, Barbara Harlow describes, offers "a documentary account" of the daily revolutionary struggle.[96] If democratic language, for Jordan, could eviscerate the forms of speech that enable Americans' complacent consent to unchecked capitalist expansion, low-intensity warfare, and urban policing, it would appear in poetry as "a reverence for the material world that begins with a reverence for human life," as Jordan wrote in a celebration of the kind of "people's poetry" she identified with Walt Whitman. It would "bear an intellectual trust in sensuality as a means of knowledge"; it would have "an easily deciphered system of reference"; it would embrace "collective voice, and, consequently, emphatic preference for broadly accessible, spoken language"; and it would "match moral exhortation with sensory report." It is this last wish, for a radical democratic poetics that could "tell the truth about this history of so much land and so much blood" by making the demand of the ethical ("moral exhortation") tantamount to the demand of the apparent ("sensory report"), that suffuses the poems on Nicaragua with a sensory detail that eludes photographic intelligence and escapes the frames of liberal democratic regard toward Latin America—the very frames projecting Mother Hale's home in Harlem as the scene of a dirty war authorization, a dirty war's authorization—that, in fact, enabled the Contra war.[97]

The poems that Jordan wrote for and from Nicaragua appeared in print after her visit to Managua and its surrounding areas. In May 1983, Jordan met with Francisco Campbell, the first secretary of political affairs at the Nicaraguan embassy in Washington, DC, who invited her to visit Nicaragua. She then wrote to *Essence* pitching the essay that was eventually published as "Nicaragua: Why I Had to Go There" in the January 1984 issue of the magazine. In her letter to the *Essence* editor Cheryll Greene proposing the trip to Nicaragua, she pitched two different feature story ideas—one on the Black Atlantic-coast community of Nicaragua, focusing on its foodways, music, and dance and telling the story of the 1979 Sandinista revolution through this lens, and one on the revolutionary women of Nicaragua, which would describe "the Nicaraguan women's achievements, crises, programs, self-images, and concepts of womanhood and revolution, both." Jordan included in her letter to Greene a brief history of the revolution and, importantly, the history of revolutionary poetry. Poetry "occupies a preternaturally central and essential place in the life of the Nicaraguan peoples," she wrote. "For example, regular poetry workshops are conducted, and poetry-theatre presentations mounted, throughout the country side [sic], as well as among the militia units right now defending the northern borders of Nicaragua." She asks, "Why is poetry the national language of this country?"[98] In a memo for Campbell, Jordan included a list of traveling companions that included the poets Sara Miles (Jordan's partner), Kathy Engel, Robert Bly, Jim Scully, and Arlene Scully; the *Newsday* editor Les Payne; and the *Freedomways* editor Jean Cary Bond. She coordinated with Campbell to arrange interviews, secured a letter of introduction from the Nicaraguan minister of culture, and planned her June trip. She decided that she would draw on her experience as a photojournalist and take responsibility for the photographs herself, but it is probably the photographer Jonathan Snow, Engel's partner, who took the photograph featured in *Essence*.

When Jordan published *On Call* and *Living Room* two years later, she reclaimed the authorial control that the magazines' editors stripped from her when she submitted her stories on Nicaragua. When she first returned from Nicaragua in summer 1983, she submitted pieces to *Ms.* and the *Village Voice*, then wrote a third piece for *Essence*. By fall, she was still going back and forth with Cheryll Greene, the *Essence* editor, about her essay, "Nicaragua: Why I Had to Go There." At the time, Greene was executive editor and special projects editor for *Essence*. The exchange between Greene and Jordan might even be understood as an extension of the efforts to transform convivial Black feminist bonding into material publishing opportunities that guided collectives like the Sisterhood. As Alexis Gumbs argues, Greene was responsible for creating "transnational black feminist critique in what otherwise would have been a black beauty and lifestyle magazine" during her time there, from 1979 to 1985. She "orchestrated interviews with revolutionary women who were decolonizing African nations, radical conversations between Angela Davis and June Jordan, mind-blowing statements from Lucille Clifton and Toni Morrison, tangible resources for how black women with the weighted privilege of U.S. citizenship could act in solidarity with black women targeted by U.S. imperialism in Haiti, Nicaragua, South Africa, Zimbabwe, and Grenada."[99] For Thorsson, too, Greene worked in a network that stretched through and around the Sisterhood to "to realize a radical abundance of possibility for Black women writers."[100] Urgent to get the essay on Nicaragua to print, Jordan wrote a middle-of-the-night appeal to Greene for more editorial latitude, writing, "I have done several rewrites, by now, as you know. I have now done my best, each time. I do not believe this final best effort will fail your hopes, or the interests of the readers of *Essence* or my love for all First World peoples."[101] The essay appeared as a feature in *Essence* two months later, with Jordan appearing in a photograph of a desolate landscape on a double-page spread. The photograph of Jordan, with shoulders slightly hunched and lips pursed in consternation, serves as a fitting picture of the exhaustion she had reached as a self-described revolutionary writer: "Here in the United States you do get weary, after a while; you could spend your best energies forever writing letters to the *New York Times*," her words read. "But you know, in your gut, that writing back is not the same as fighting back." The *Essence* article, conveying this mix of rage and inspiration, was reprinted in *On Call*. The *Village Voice* published an October 1983 feature titled "Black Power on Nicaragua: 'Leave Those Folks Alone,'" in which Jordan argued that Black people's opposition to the US support for the antirevolutionary forces stemmed from their "disaffection from American 'democracy.'" She called this disaffection "Black realism."[102] *Ms.* did not print any of Jordan's essays on Nicaragua. When Jordan collected her essays on Nicaragua in *On Call*, along with "Life After Lebanon," "South Africa: Bringing It All Back Home," and several other essays addressing US foreign policy, she described the collection this way: "my political efforts to coherently fathom all of my universe, and to arrive at a moral judgement that will determine my future political conduct."[103]

Progressive publishers printed the pieces of Jordan's Nicaragua archive. Thunder's Mouth Press, the progressive imprint of Perseus Books that had recently published Sonia Sanchez's *Homegirls and Hand Gre-*

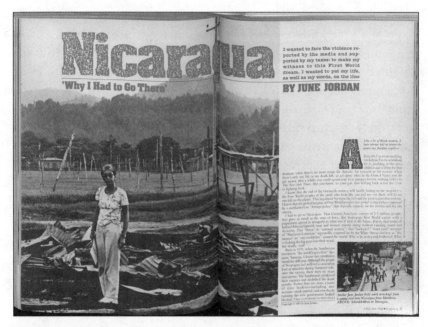

June Jordan, "Nicaragua: Why I Had to Go There," *Essence*, January 1984.

nades (1984) and Jayne Cortez's *Coagulations* (1984), published Jordan's *Living Room*. The nonprofit progressive publisher South End Press published *On Call*, which opens with Jordan's account of her struggle to get her arguments to print. "In a sense, this book must compensate for the absence of a cheaper and more immediate, print outlet for my two cents. If political writing by a Black woman did not strike so many editors as presumptuous or simply bizarre, then, perhaps this book would not be needed. Instead, I might regularly appear, on a weekly or monthly schedule, as a national columnist." She writes here, too, of being "whitelisted" by editors who, as she says, "hide behind 'many of us' who 'have problems' with me. Apparently, there is some magisterial and unnameable 'we' who decided—in the cowardly passive voice—what is 'publishable' or not."[104]

With *On Call* and *Living Room*, Jordan defied the publishing difficulties she faced after her writings on Palestine appeared in print the summer before. In *On Call*, she studies the map of the Reagan frontier and dissects the official state language that justified the bloody counterinsurgency in Nicaragua. Recounting her travel to Managua in "Nicaragua: Why I Had to Go There," a version of the essay that first appeared in *Essence*, Jordan begins with the sarcastic quotation marks that had by then become characteristic of her prose: "I had to go to Nicaragua. That Central American country of 2.7 million people, that place as small as the state of Iowa, that front-page First World nation with a population spread as meagerly as what you'd find in the Sahara desert: that home of Indian/Africa/Spanish women and men mostly doing without running water and electricity. That 'threat' to 'national security,' that 'backyard'/'frontyard' monster of 'Marxism-Leninism' repeatedly conjured up by the White House cowboy as 'the menace' to 'our credibility' around the world?"[105] The truth-telling mission that Jordan undertook was, as she intimates here, a sociolinguistic one and a geographic one; it was a study in the way language arranged the Reagan frontier.

Jordan challenged her readers to examine their assumptions about Central America: "Unless you are careful, you might conclude that Nicaragua is nowhere and that nobody lives there, and so, why not do whatever might cross your imperial mind?"[106] She then writes of the bodily postures of vulnerability that refuse and indict that imperial mind and its ideas of security. Traveling through the Central America to bear witness to the struggle for real democracy, she writes, "This is a journey of harrowing hopscotch. And I feel there is no controlling the odds. Either I leave Nicaragua or I accept the palpably enveloping chances of death. The strain of such ultimate alert tires the body. But as the Sandinistas say, 'the enemy is everywhere.' And as I move among the intricate disasters, as I track through the spreading bloodstain of U.S. Foreign policy, there is no denying *this is the truth of things*."[107] Inside this truth, that the enemy is everywhere, Jordan finds an unlikely temporary refuge in the commons. In this refuge, one does not rest easy; one stalks and tracks the trail of blood that counterinsurgency leaves behind; and one uses one's homegrown paranoia as sustenance.

When Jordan's vehicle runs out of gas, she has to sleep in a public park in Juigalpa. There she is protected until dawn by Sandinistas who patrol the surroundings, watching for watchers. She finds out that the militia patrolling the street is made up of young women who talk and laugh to stay awake while watching for the enemy. One of them tells her, "You see, we never sleep." Jordan writes, "I look at the trusting of her twenty-six year old face. In my mind I flip through images of North

American nuclear weapons and fighter planes and cluster bombs, and I lower my eyes and turn away from her. She cannot imagine the com-plicated, the evil might of this enemy she thinks to deter with laugh-ing young women who must struggle to stay awake."[108] Just after this, a fifteen-year-old boy takes her inside to rest in a police station, and they talk about poetry until dawn. "Even now," Jordan writes, "I can hear Faustino: talking to me, softly, close to the ending of the night," which leads her to ask finally, "How many of these gentle people have I helped to kill just by paying my taxes?"[109]

Jordan's essays in *On Call* challenge readerly assumptions about the benevolence of US foreign policy and invent forms of safety that throw off the conventions of liberal regard for the global dispossessed. This re-fusal of liberal regard is apparent in "Poem for Nicaragua"'s withholding hold. And this inhabitation of the kind of safety that eludes liberal re-gard is apparent in "Safe," in which Jordan's speaker occupies the "edges of deep water possibilities":

> helicopter attack
> alligator assault
> contra confrontations
> blood sliding into the silent scenery

A single conjunction turns this catalogue of danger into a story of inti-macy: the speaker is "cold and wet / but surrounded by five compañeros / in a dugout canoe."[110] The speaker's leaning into this dangerous sur-round, Jordan's leaning into the rocking chair next to Faustino: these are "deep water possibilities" that redraw the map of Reagan's hemisphere.

The poems that follow "Poem for Nicaragua" in *Living Room* heighten Jordan's indictment of North American innocence and her attention to these forms of care amid devastation. In "First Poem from Nicaragua Libre: *teotecacinte*," Jordan reproduces formal elements of "Poem for Nicaragua": the withheld or deferred subject and the second-person address to question "White English" assertions of the righteousness of the Reagan frontier. The poem refers to Teotecacinte, the Nicaraguan village near the border of Honduras where Sandinistas fought against counterinsurgents in mid-June 1983, when Jordan was there on call.

The *New York Times* reported that the Contras, "insurgents," attacked Teotecacinte for eight days before retreating back to Honduras. It reported property damages of over $15 million and noted that eleven tobacco warehouses were burned along with eleven homes.[111] The *Times* represents the invasion of Teotecacinte as a battle between the counterrevolutionaries stationed in Honduras and Nicaraguan rebels and lists only the deaths of 140 contras and 48 Sandinistas, normalizing and distancing violence as an unfortunate, unpreventable, and intrinsic part of third-world existence. It relegates violence "to the recessive picture plane" and "presents the mutilated bodies as merely adjuncts to something larger."[112]

Jordan's poem, surfacing what Ali calls an "aesthetics of memorialization," zooms in on the space that is, in photographic terms, represented aerially in the article. Unlike the *Times'* representation of the battle as a border skirmish far from US soil or US interests, Jordan's second-person address indicts US complacency while refusing the liberal regard of identification. The first stanza offers two questions:

> Can you say Teotecacinte?
> Can you say it,
> Teotecacinte?[113]

The questions first function as a lesson to English speakers, an invitation to North American readers to consider the cost of US-backed war. But whereas the poem first offers up Teotecacinte as the object of speech, the object that might be spoken *by* a US subject, the second iteration of the question makes Teotecacinte the "you," the subject of the address: "Can *you* say it, *Teotecacinte*?" (emphasis added). This revision of the poem's guiding question in the first stanza, which is composed only of these three lines, reveals the poem's interest in both making the suffering of Nicaraguans visible and occluding the terms of that visibility. The speaker addresses, then eclipses, the English-speaking "you."

The second stanza accomplishes this revelation-occlusion by representing the human victim of an artillery attack through a kaleidoscopic gaze that approximates the impressionistic rendering of "Poem for Nicaragua":

> Into the dirt she fell
> she blew up the shell
> fell into the dirt the artillery
> shell blew up the girl

The arrangement of the verses mimics the scene of explosion it is describing. Jordan reverses the rhyme of "fell" and "shell" in the first two lines, placing those words at the beginning of the following two lines. The repetition and rearrangement of the word-phrases "fell," "shell," "into the dirt," and "blew up" throughout these four lines intimate words landing on the page: the poem, like the earth under the girl's feet, is scattered in pieces. Jordan also toggles the subject-verb placement throughout these lines to shatter the language with which she writes of the unsayable destruction in Teotecacinte. The subject follows the preposition in "Into the dirt she fell"; then, in the following line, she becomes the active subject who goes so far as to explode what is exploding her: "she blew up the shell" before "shell blew up the girl." The internal rhyme of "fell"/"well" and "shattered"/"scattered" in this same stanza re-creates the figurative effect of "fell" and "shell," the effect of zooming in on a scene whose destruction is reflected in language:

> the little girl of the little house fell
> beside the well unfinished for water
> when that mortar
> shattered the dirt under her barefeet
> and scattered pieces of her four
> year old anatomy

The use of rhyme throughout the poem mimics children's literature and song. Like nursery rhymes with their iambic meter and their simple rhyme schemes, "First Poem from Nicaragua Libre" attempts something of a primer for its readers. It is teaching an audience how to address—to literally enunciate—Teotecacinte, a town razed by US-sponsored terror. But the internal rhyme destabilizes this very lesson: it is not as simple as it appears; the words are not where they should be, and neither is the girl the words are describing. The poem repeats its question three more times. Its last two stanzas return to the toggling of object and subject that opens the poem:

> Teotecacinte
> Can you say it,
> Teotecacinte?

> Can you say it?

Repeating the question as if teaching a child how to speak, the poem references the young girl's lost vitality and lost innocence. As importantly, it denies the audience the very innocence of liberal regard. If, as Judith Butler suggests, *intelligibility* is "the general historical schema" that founds ← "domains of the knowable" and produces "norms of recognizability" that serve to affirm existing relations of power, Jordan offers a description of death that holds off the liberal consumption of victimhood from a comfortable distance.[114] Instead of asking, "Can you *see* it," the poem asks, "Can you *say* it," inviting readers to iterate their own complicity only to, again and again, destabilize the very *you* to whom the question is posed.

Other poems in *Living Room* develop this interest in picturing and sounding the devastation of the Reagan doctrine in ways that confront the US media's conventions for representing the suffering of Black and brown peoples. As Ali outlines, Jordan's "kaleidoscopic description" of the 1982 invasion of Beirut in *Living Room* "offers the reader the controlled, decelerated rhythm of an attention-giving frame of mind." In "Moving towards Home," for example, Jordan "achieves a somber mood and a powerful, state tempo through the simple, bare, straightforward, yet intense language of parallel short sentences."[115] Throughout *Living Room*, Jordan disrupts the apathy of the North American news consumer while refusing the uninterrogated sympathy that might allow easy consent to the policies of malevolent "assistance" in Central America.

We can see this refusal of both apathy and sympathy in the poems in the "Nicaragua Libre" suite. The third poem, "from Nicaragua Libre: photograph of managua," proceeds as a series of negations and truncations that begin, indeed, from the truncated title (this is the only poem in the four-poem series that lacks a number indicating its placement).

While its conceit is ekphrasis, the speaker of the poem refuses to describe the subject of the photograph that its title refers to:

> The man is not cute.
> The man is not ugly.
> The man is teaching himself
> to read.[116]

The speaker describes the subject of the photograph's actions rather than his appearance; this disallows the perception of a passive victim. What is more, the action being described is an insurgent inhabitation of literacy: "He tracks each word with a finger / and opens his mouth to the sound. / Next to the chair the old V-Z rifle / leans at the ready." In another portrait-not-portrait of domestic life undomesticated, Jordan invites the reader into this home space, promising a "photograph," only to suspend the Manichean scheme of revulsion and paternalism with which readers/viewers might otherwise apprehend suffering. As Ali suggests about "Moving towards Home," Jordan slows the pace of apprehension. In this case, the relaxed tempo invites the reader to notice the domestic details that contradict ideas of Sandinistas as terrorists:

> The dirt of his house has been swept.
> The dirt around the chair where he sits
> has been swept.
> He has swept the dirt twice.
> The dirt is clean.
> The dirt is his dirt.

The shifts in verb tenses describing the man's relating to the dirt and the dirt's relating to the man—from the passive voice "has been swept" to the past perfect "has swept" to the present "is"—describe a would-be tranquil domestic scene becoming active. Importantly, *things* that might escape notice in a photograph are living actants in the poem. While the man "is not," the dirt "is." This attention to the living undomesticability of objects makes visible, if impressionistically, "what might otherwise lie submerged in the flood of media images and the constant cascading of its mundane discourses," as Ali suggests.[117]

Locating the revolutionary vitality that is missing both in daily news accounts of counterinsurgency and in the high rhetorical performances of the president and his officials, Jordan's poems from "Nicaragua Libre" chart a Black feminist geography. Here, visiting with her cousins way down south, Jordan stakes a claim to place that, in Katherine McKittrick's words, is "not naturally followed by material ownership and Black repossession but rather by a grammar of liberation, through which ethical *human*-geographies can be recognized and expressed."[118] (If McKittrick, following Sylvia Wynter, would call these geographies "demonic," Reagan no doubt would have, too.)[119]

The following entry in the "Nicaragua Libre" suite, "Fourth Poem from Nicaragua Libre: Report from the Frontier," returns, presumably, to Teotecacinte and offers a picture, if we can call it that, of another scene of explosion. Its first stanza is a sentence with no subject at all:

> gone gone gone ghost
> gone
> both the house of the hard dirt floor and the church
> next door
> torn apart more raggedy than skeletons
> when the bomb hit
> leaving a patch of her hair on a piece of her scalp
> like bird's nest
> in the dark yard still lit by flowers[120]

In a poem that is an eerie catalogue of what remains after a Goliath's attack on this little village with its little girl, there is a single subject preceding a single verb: "I found." The lines that follow this intimation of discovery continue the catalogue of disaster, pointing to "the family trench empty," later "shards/shreds," later "dead hanging plants," and later, "many dogs lost." The speaker's location of that which cannot be "found," or reconstituted or revitalized, casts the poem into the world of ghosts whose absence presses on the lyric I/eye with the same withhold- *haunting* ing hold I mentioned earlier.

Jordan's Nicaragua essays and poems marshaled the intelligence of touch and the grammars of withholding against the intelligence of surveillance, counterinsurgency, and moderate political reform. Like the marks of rageful love framing Hardwick's letter recalling the protest in Brooklyn and indexing an internationalist passion for justice, Jordan's Nicaragua archive coded messages of insurgent survival in a historical moment when the most powerful weaponry of the West was aimed at what Jordan called "the global lunging of First World peoples into power."[121]

Mood: Imperative

Jordan's work in the late 1970s and early 1980s theorized the long war on terror as a racial gendered regime whose front line was language. Her work at this juncture also sought to "wrench language from the clutches of normalized violence and turn it toward other ends," as Feldman writes.[122] While Jordan decoded the grammars of counterinsurgency, she encoded messages of liberation: in Black English, in undomesticated Black militant speech, and in the withholding morphology of her poems. Of course, Jordan crafted her postintelligence code with a keen eye toward the discourse of counterterrorism and protection of US security interests in the Middle East. As she organized and created in defiance of the "ultimate taboo" of Palestinian self-determination, she applied her analyses of "the male white rhetoric about *borders* and *national security* and *terrorism* and *democracy* and *vital interests*" and she exploded the conventions of political writing and behavior in US literary culture.[123]

These explosions, set off in poems like "Apologies to All the People in Lebanon" and "Moving Towards Home" or in essays like "Life After Lebanon," no doubt contributed to the cloud of silence that has surrounded Jordan's work. In a letter sent after *Living Room* was published, her friend the Lebanese writer Etel Adnan encouraged Jordan not to be derailed by criticism her poetry: "You know that 'Beirut' divides the world in two. It is one of the most untouchable 'taboos' for some. That's why. They never forgive you for thinking that Arabs are human beings. It is the one issue that one doesn't tackle without paying a price." In this same letter, Adnan turns from the grim matter of censorship to the militant pleasure-making that these two might pursue together:

> Let's have fun!
> The city planner in you must love paintings. The human being in you loves Beirut and Manila. The poet in you loves the clouds and the child in

you puts bombs under the police cars when they shoot the wrong people. Let's have fun![124]

Adnan's use of the imperative mood ("let's") infuses the suggestions that Adnan poses—to make art, to dream of freedom, to sabotage the means of police murder—with an air of mischievous play. Like Jordan's suggestion to "take appropriate care of de massa's soup" in "Black People in Foreign Policy," Adnan's flight of imperatives posits an ethic of care that reclaims care from government initiatives and places it in the hands of revolutionary artists and activists: dreamers tending to each other, tending to Beirut and Manila, tending to the dead.

This reorientation of care affirmed Jordan's project of "purifying" the grammars of US empire. Jordan's analysis of the sociolinguistics of the early war on terror inhabited, like Adnan's urging toward mischievous militancy, the imperative mood. Recall that Jordan's address to Columbia Students urged, "let us demand of the President of our country, and let us demand of our Congresspeople, a purification of those terms."[125] The repetition of the imperative "let us" in the address to students, like Adnan's "let's," activates a militant care that draws Manila, Beirut, Brooklyn, Teotecacinte, and Palestine together in a circle of convivial, stubborn intimacy.

Jordan's craft, perfected in trenchant essays and let loose on poetic experiments, posited another kind of intelligence: the kind of live, experimental, extraliterary presence that Barbara Christian, with Jordan and Audre Lorde on her mind, defined as "a tuned sensitivity to that which is alive and therefore cannot be known until it is known."[126] And if it was imperative in 1979, or 1983 or 1985, to locate the grammatical and extragrammatical forms that would interdict the imperial grammars of Blackness that, for example, invited you to cozy up with a Black woman's book so that you could be a better citizen or, for example, called on an aging Black not-mother to smile in assent to Contra war in Nicaragua, it was even more so in the decades to come, when Blackness increasingly circulated throughout visual culture to win favor for the wars in Iraq and, especially after the 9/11 attacks, when Blackness in high places shielded the government from critiques of its imperialist march to unending war. In chapter 6, I analyze how Black women's literature after 9/11 carried this imperative forward.

6

"How Very American"

Black Feminist Literature and the Occult of Paranoia

Nikky Finney's 2011 volume of poetry *Head Off & Split* depicted the culture of emergency of the post-9/11 era with mocking, ironic verse addressing former president George W. Bush's reign of terror, Condoleezza Rice's masterful mastery of the concerto and her shoe shopping during Hurricane Katrina, and the everyday state of emergency that that hurricane revealed Black people of the bayou to be living in. In a series of nineteen sonnets titled "Plunder," Finney uses George W. Bush's cowboy persona as a window into the wars in Iraq and Afghanistan "raging / endlessly on" and, at the same time, to the "hundreds of thousands dead of America," those "1,836 ghosts of Katrina." These are the disasters of the long war on terror, the disasters wrought by a war of conquest reaching its blood-dripping fingers into a new millennium under the cover of multiculturalized nationalism. "How very american," reads Finney's ironic manipulation of the romantic sonnet form. "How very undivided / we are, how we promise on the hide of every / endangered polar bear, on the feather of every / balding eagle."[1]

Two years before *Head Off & Split* was published, the novelist Alice Randall published a Black epic novel about the savage American hope of the new millennium. The novel's protagonist is Hope Jones, a Black woman in Tennessee who is mourning her ex-husband, Abel, a Black CIA spy and conservative Pentagon lawyer who commits suicide in a horse barn where Confederate reenactors are restaging a Civil War battle. As Hope discusses Abel's strange career in counterinsurgency with another of his former lovers, Nicholas, the two stare at a photograph of Hope and Abel and Nicholas, and Nicholas moans, "You've become so— *American.* You and Abel became so American."[2] *Rebel Yell*, like *Head Off & Split*, addresses the September 11 attacks as, more than a cataclysmic moment, a juncture that collocates Black responsibility *for* and Black vulnerability *to* a vicious and voracious state power that sacrifices all forms of human and nonhuman life on the altar of capital in the name of the security of the racialized, gendered ideals of home and homeland.

This is the last chapter in this story of Black women and the culture of empire. As the Negrophobia of law and order, the individualism of multiculturalism and colorblindness, and the millennial romance of postracialism served as the racial logics of the long war on terror, expressive culture and its figurations of Black women legitimated the authority of a government that was increasingly authoritarian and—I hesitate to say— sophisticated in its uses of surveillance, torture, cruise missiles, "rendition," "perpetual detainment," fortified fences and walls, and drones. On this side of terror—the zone of "freedom" and "democracy" made secure by these technologies of war—Black women's writing draws Black gender into the figuration of a new United States and its delusional dreams of personal security, individual aspiration, inclusion, and homeland unity. On the other side of terror, where advancement and progress provide no cover for the terrorist state, Black feminist writers detail both the trajectories of mass destruction and the means of collective preservation. The latter was the case even and especially through the high war on terror, when the government's calls to racial unity and the performance of pretty, brown-skinned "government men" and government women were at their Blackest and most beautiful.[3] Again, this is not to suggest that there are bad Black women writers who serve as mouthpieces for the state and good Black women writers who are the state's radical critics. It is rather to suggest that the contradictions shaping the terrain for Black women's writing frustrate approaches to contemporary Black literature that would see it as either an unsullied site of resistance or, on the other hand, damned to complicity.

If *intimacy* is the name for the reproductive relations of the bourgeois home and its possessive individuals, and even for the "monstrous" forms of subjection and confinement that "aren't acknowledged to be horror" within the bourgeois home, it is also a heuristic, as Lisa Lowe suggests, for observing "the historical division of world processes into those that develop modern liberal subjects and modern spheres of social life, and those processes that are forgotten, cast as failed or irrelevant because they do not produce 'value' legible within modern classifications."[4] Black women's intimacy with empire makes the project of discerning the line between "this side" and "the other side" of terror not a study of good politics or bad politics but rather a study of the terrain of power on which such distinctions are made. In this final chapter, then, I extend the map of that terrain. I argue that Black feminist writers of the early twenty-first century—Alice Randall, Danielle Evans, and Gloria Naylor—exposed imperial culture's delusions of omnipotence and its fears of destruction ("imperial paranoia" is the term Anne McClintock uses to describe the social psychopathology of late empire) while also figuring Black feminist paranoia as a form of occult knowledge in the service of collective preservation.[5] Black feminist paranoia has real effects—it could destroy careers, it could permanently delay perfectly good books—so instead of romanticizing it, I want to inhabit its suspicions of closure. When Black feminist literature's encounter with incorporative power left it nowhere to go, I argue, Black feminist writers crafted livable realities on the other side of terror. Whether those realities were made warm and cozy by critique or made barely livable by constant watchfulness, they exposed Blackness's "very American" intimacy with empire as a problem for contemporary students of Black culture and our abiding interests in genre and generation.

If generic innovation and generational shifts do not fully serve to explain the formations of postmodern, post-soul, post-Black Black literature—and in fact yield categorizations that only serve to occlude the uncanny collisions between the war on terror and Black culture that I wrote of in chapter 1—I advocate a different approach to the common, open text of Black women's writing, an approach to literature focused on the continuities between the terrorist regimes of the state and Black literary culture and pedagogy. That is, if Americanness now partly gains its coherence in *the imperial grammars of Blackness*—the linguistic and cultural codes turning the irreconcilability of Blackness and Americanness into a gory parody—the narrative and lyrical language with which Black writers approach this new problematic give shape to contemporary Black literature in ways we have yet to fully comprehend. This chapter is about both that failure of comprehension and the literature that exposes it.

As I discussed in chapter 1, what we have come to call "9/11" by shorthand was not a cataclysmic shift but rather a catalysis, a moment of crystallization and intensification in which existing codes of race, nation,

and safety came together to direct public narratives of US global dominance and destiny. In the years since the 9/11 attacks on the World Trade
Center and the Pentagon, African American literature has been marked
by a peculiar confluence between the shifts in racialization that occurred
after the end of the Cold War, with the multiculturalization of counterterrorism, and the transformations in the US political economy of
reading that were occasioned by, among other things, the exorbitant rise
and then the precipitous decline of megabookstores like Borders and
Barnes and Noble, the marketing phenomenon of Oprah's Book Club,
the increase in the celebrity of African American authors such as Toni
Morrison, and the negotiations of postracial and post-Black discourse
in public discussions of Black authorship. This convergence—between
racial power and literary consumerism, between disaster, power, and
money—is acutely apparent in those texts that position the September
11 attacks as a definitive moment that changed the direction of racial discourse in the United States. While I analyze such texts—narrative fiction
such as Randall's *Rebel Yell* and Danielle Evans's short story "Someone
Ought to Tell Her There's Nowhere to Go"—to argue that their feminist critiques of the long war on terror lay bare the intimacy between
its modes of subjection and Black culture's means to success, I end the
chapter by analyzing Gloria Naylor's paranoid memoir *1996*, a memoir
that altogether refuses the aspiration and success that Randall and Evans
are so critical of.

Making *Gender*ations

Contemporary Black women's writing cannot be understood in the terms
of generic innovation and generational identity, such as "post-soul" or
"post–civil rights," that have often served as however-useful analytics for
their interventions. To understand how Black literature reflects changes
in the nature of racial power after the turn of the millennium, we will
have to follow critics like Margo Crawford, Evie Shockley, Meta Jones,
Carter Mathes, and GerShun Avilez in refusing narratives of break that "post-"
posit contemporary innovation against the supposed strictures of the
Black Arts Movement.[6] While studies of millennial Black culture have
detailed the historical context for innovations of the post-soul generation and "post-Black" artists—deindustrialization, Reaganomics, the

War on Drugs—we have yet to grasp the impact that the long war on terror has had on notions of Blackness in the popular and literary spheres and, perhaps more importantly, the way Black authors' understandings of violence, counterinsurgency, and torture are at the core of its significations on history, aesthetics, and race.

While postracialism came to serve as the racial logic that lubricated the political rationalities of counterterrorism and neoliberalism, post-Blackness emerged as the name for the innovations in Black expressive culture after the 1970s. Terms like "post-soul," "post-Black," "post-liberated," and "new Black" have named the diverse and innovative expressive culture of those Black Americans who came of age in the wake of the Black Power and Black Arts movements. The generation(s) of Black artists who came of age after the civil rights movement and Black Power rejected the aesthetic and political strictures of earlier decades in favor of "troubling" Blackness, "worrying" Blackness.[7] By the end of 1980s, the appearance of terrain-shifting essays like Greg Tate's "Cult-Nats Meet Freaky-Deke" and Trey Ellis's "The New Black Aesthetic" were celebrating the artistic freedom of Black writers, musicians, and visual artists and also documenting a certain recognition that demographic and political shifts in the neoliberal United States—the production of a sizable Black middle class and mounting intraclass tensions in what could no longer be called "*the* Black community"—was affecting ideas about art and politics. Stuart Hall related in 1992's "What Is This 'Black' in Black Popular Culture?" that the differences within and among Black communities throughout the African diaspora prompted him to speak of "the end of the innocence of the Black subject or the end of the innocent notion of an essential Black subject," but he also noted "that this end is also a beginning," arguing that artists such as Isaac Julien were now able to open up representations of Blackness to a proliferation of "different kinds" of Black subjectivities.[8] The experiments of the 1990s cast Black arts in an "expanded field of Blackness," enlarging all of what Black could signify.[9] Mark Anthony Neal's definitive work on the post-soul era used the term "post-soul" to mark a generational shift pioneered by "those folks, artists and critical thinkers, who live in the fissures of two radically different social paradigms; folks born between the 1963 March on Washington and the [*Regents of the University of California v.*] *Bakke* case, children of soul, if you will."[10] The shift from soul to post-soul, like the end of innocence that Hall announced, was an end and a beginning, the end of essentialist understandings of Blackness inherited from the lexicons of civil rights and Black Power and Black art's initiation into the world of proliferating intraracial difference.

Throughout the first two decades of the millennium, Black writers and artists experimented with the preface "post-." In Thelma Golden's introduction to the catalogue for *Freestyle*, the well-known exhibition of twenty-eight artists mounted at the Studio Museum in Harlem in spring 2001, she uses the term "post-Black" to refer to "artists who were adamant about not being labeled as 'Black' artists, though their work was steeped, in fact deeply interested, in redefining complex notions of Blackness."[11] In *The Grey Album: On the Blackness of Blackness* (2012), Kevin Young rejects the term "post-Black" but embraces what it signifies for Golden: experiments with and redefinitions of Blackness. "Blackness is not something I wish to be beyond or past; it is still ever-present and remains unavoidable, and more important, pleasurable," Young writes. "More than post-Blackness, I am concerned with pre-Blackness—what made and makes up Blackness."[12] Bertram Ashe's introduction to *African American Review*'s Winter 2007 special issue on the post-soul aesthetic declared the "end of the beginning" of the post-soul aesthetic, looking back on the post–Black Arts decades to identify the issues that post-soul artists take up: "the peculiar pains, pleasures, and problems of race in the post–Civil Rights movement United States; the use of nontraditionally Black cultural influences in the work; and the resultant exploration of the boundaries of Blackness."[13] In 2011, Evie Shockley's collection of poems *The New Black* offered in Shockley's "ode to Blackness" an image of Blackness that in many ways parallels Ashe's assessment of the post-soul:

> I see the light
> at the end   of you   the beginning[14]

Terms like "post-Black," "post-soul," "post-liberated," and "new Black" thus gathered diverse artistic and political impulses into critical-aesthetic categories that defied genre and that attempted to preserve the spirit of experimentation and play that characterized much of the work under discussion.

Since the scholarship on these various "posts" emerged over the decade that witnessed the election of Barack Obama as the United States' first Black president and increased public talk of the United States becoming a postracial society, it became increasingly important to distinguish the post-Black and the post-soul from the postracial. Now when artists and critics speak of post-Blackness or the post-soul, they do so with important qualifications and clarifications. But the historical conditions of possibility for the emergence of post-Blackness—the expansion of a Black middle class, the widening influence of Black popular culture, increasing openness toward Black queer subjects and formations within Black communities—are the same conditions for the production of postracialism. That is, if Black culture producers invested in the opening up of racial signification to the play of difference, state and capital invested in this same aperture for their own ends. This was particularly the case after the 9/11 attacks realigned racial difference and security. As Herman Gray argues, the "connection between the promise of seeing more diversity in media and post-9/11 attacks on the United States links the regulatory role of race and difference with the discourse of homeland security and global terrorism," with Blackness now serving as the face of global capital necessitating securitization.[15] There are, then, at least *three* new Blacks: (1) the "new Black" who is so named for assuming the marginal position once presumed to be especially reserved for Black people (as in "Arab is the new Black" or "Gay is the new Black"); (2) the new Black so named for breaking out of those strictures—heteronormativity, masculinism, and so on—associated with the civil rights and Black Power movements; and (3) that shining figure, that exceptional Black man or woman, who signifies the multicultural promise that is the soul of US governmental power in high places.

Throughout the 1960s, 1970s, and 1980s, Black feminists predicted, nurtured, and advanced the post-civil-rights critiques of racial essentialism based in manly literary value that often suffused the rhetoric of the Black Arts Movement, the critiques that would become commonplace not only in Black feminist discourse but, more importantly for us, throughout critical discussions of African American literature, in the decades of new Blackness that followed. Curiously, in Black men's novels about Black male writers—Michael Thomas's *Man Gone Down*, Trey Ellis's *Platitudes*, Paul Beatty's *The White Boy Shuffle*, Percival Everett's

Erasure—the end of the Black subject's innocence occasions not only a writerly crisis but also a sexual crisis, a phallic crisis occasioned by the deconstruction of Blackness by Black feminist activists and thinkers but also, conceivably, by the success of Black women writers in the popular and academic spheres. Thomas, for example, represents the protagonist's father and his generation, and the civil rights model of masculine leadership, as "toothless and impotent."[16] In Ellis's *Platitudes*, DeWayne Wellington, an author writing a novel about a Black comic-book nerd, struggles against Isshee Ayam, a Black feminist writer who writes in vernacular. In *Erasure*, Everett's protagonist, a writer of literary fiction, struggles in a literary marketplace that celebrates Black women writers like Juanita Mae Jenkins, the author of the bestselling novel *We's Lives in Da Ghetto*. In both of these latter novels, the heterosexual male protagonist conquers through sexual conquest a literary anxiety that is conflated with his gender-sexual anxiety. We can hear the echo of Robert Staples's now infamous 1979 screed against Black women writers.[17] We can hear the echo of the comment that Ishmael Reed made in 1977, referred to in Barbara Smith's well-known "Toward a Black Feminist Criticism"— "Maybe if I was one of those young *female* Afro-American writers that are so hot right now, I'd sell more [books]"—in the novels that emerged two decades later.[18] We can hear the echo of Stanley Crouch charging Toni Morrison with "no serious artistic vision or real artistic integrity" or calling Morrison's definitive 1987 masterpiece *Beloved* a fraud.[19] Thus, not only can the post-soul/post-Black be understood as a post–Cold War historical-aesthetic phenomenon that developed in parallel to the shift from liberal multiculturalism to neoliberal multiculturalism or color-blindness; it might also be more properly understood as, more than a generational shift, a series of generational gender-sexual *crises*.

Surfacing in the midst of these *gender*ational crises, 9/11, itself a rupture in patrilineal endowment—what Paul Anker calls "a perceived menace to paternity" betraying "American ineptitude, or the disavowed truth of late imperial impotence and failure"—is cast in contemporary African American literature as an event that brings into focus the post-civil-rights fractures within and between Black American subjects and communities and, to some extent, between Black Americans and oppressed peoples of color around the world.[20] Post-9/11 Black feminist literature reflects the peculiar convergences, the troubling intimacies, of Black aesthetic practice and postracialism while also breaking them open and apart; this is the work of *refraction* that texts like Alice Randall's 2009 novel *Rebel Yell*, to which I now turn, effect to expose the shared historical conditions between post-Blackness and postracialism and to recast those historical conditions within a longer history of Black intimacy with state-sanctioned terror and state-sponsored projects of counterterror. To posit that work of exposure as the heart of contemporary Black feminist literature is to refuse the "posterizing" narrative of Oedipal rupture and innovation and to privilege, instead, the continuities in Black feminist writing throughout the long war on terror.

This Side of Terror

As Randall's *Rebel Yell* opens, a Black American spy and Pentagon lawyer remembers the trauma of the 1963 church bombing in Birmingham, Alabama, that killed four young girls and brought the terror of the Black freedom struggle home to hearts all over the country. In the flashback, a young Abel Jones III mourns his babysitter while the mother of one of the four girls admonishes him against civil rights activism and sets him on a lifelong course of paranoid antiterror that will shape him as the fictional caricature of post-9/11 Black complicity with US empire, a CIA spy turned Pentagon lawyer who spends his days "pars[ing] the crazy definitions and distinctions that allow for Abu Ghraib."[21] "Don't you forget these men," the grieving mother tells him. "These Black men, and these big white Birmingham mules, these men. They used you children to fight this war. Negro men were tired of what we all had to suffer and they sent our babies to die" (10). Writing civil rights history as a war on innocent children that gives way to a vicious cadre of Black antiterrorists, *Rebel Yell* connects the social movement battles of the 1960s to the post-9/11 wars in Iraq and Afghanistan. The novel figures Black intimacy with state terror and counterinsurgency not as an accident or aberration but as a formal and thematic necessity.

Throughout the long war on terror, the image of Black agents of counterterror has become necessary for the redemptive understanding of the homeland. The fiction of a States "united" against terror makes not only thinkable but in some sense irresistible the end of African American literature as a record of Black suffering and national division. African American literature in the 9/11 complex of counterterror, consumerism, and Black empowerment thus marks the confluence of a collective writerly reinvention of Black literature and a state demand for the postracial. It is in the context of the post-9/11 convergence of the national-security state and Black political progress in US civil society, as Jared Sexton suggests, that "*institutionalized* Black complicity with the structures of white supremacy" takes on the ruse of Black masculinity dressed up as police power in US visual culture.[22] The route out of the old "color line" canon into an African American literature of the now is, then, through a second blood-stained gate; and imperial *counter*terror, not terror, is constitutive of this new African American literature. After 9/11, that is, "African American literature," as a field of cultural expression and knowledge production, uneasily carries the trace of Blackness's incorporation into a hegemonic field of identification called "African American literature," which corresponds with other similar identifiers— "African American citizen," "African American soldier," "African American president"—to reorganize, remake, and reassemble Black writing through, first, a resurrection of and, second, a reckoning with the ghosts of civil rights. This reconstitution is on the one hand a reparation, a necessary repositioning of the legacy of antiracist struggle for the present that ruptures the hegemonies of gender and class that have scripted the master narrative of the civil rights movement. But the reconstitution of African American literature after 9/11, in addition to sifting through the histories of post–World War II struggles against colonialism and white supremacy to make sense of the present, also turns on the figuration of intimate estrangement from those struggles, the throwing off of civil rights, Black Power, and anticolonial imperatives and the taking up of a tortured and torturing intimacy with state power, an intimacy imagined through fictional and poetic engagements with historical figures such as Condoleezza Rice, Barack Obama, and Colin Powell and through the depiction of literary characters who bear the weight of post-civil-rights anxieties about their agency for state terror after the "successes" of civil rights and the "successes" of a state whose carceral and surveillance apparatuses depend not only on Black objects of scrutiny and discipline but also Black *subjects* of the same. These are those characters who violate ideals of intraracial solidarity while making their way into our African American literature classrooms: Edward Jones's Black slave owner Henry Townsend, Aaron McGruder's antagonistic Uncle Ruckus, Charles Johnson's antihero Chaym Smith, Alice Randall's Black Confederate Abel Jones III.[23]

If post-9/11 African American literature transcended racial protest— or transposed it into the grammars of imperial achievement—within the *post*-postwar cultural complex, we have to theorize both African American resistance to *and* African American intimacy with the violence of empire as thematically and formally constitutive of post-9/11 Black expressive culture. In this context, Alice Randall's *Rebel Yell* draws an unorthodox line between Black protest and Black involvement in and responsibility for the war on terror. Rather than figuring complicitous Black subjects as aberrant, deluded, self-hating Uncle Toms, Randall's novel presents them as the beloved sons and daughters of civil rights, the ones who were not killed in combat, the ones who went to Ivy League schools, the ones one who not only work in the White House but may indeed be lurking in, passing in, Black spaces: barbershops, Black colleges, bars, soul-food restaurants. *Rebel Yell* is a fitting follow-up to Randall's first two novels, *The Wind Done Gone*, a parody of *Gone with the Wind*, and *Pushkin and the Queen of Spades*, a story of a Vanderbilt University Black Russian-literature professor struggling to reconcile her son's choice to marry a white Russian exotic dancer. *Rebel Yell* weds Randall's postmodern irreverence to her commitment to recasting Black cultural forms as diverse as soul food, poetry, and hair grease. In its chronicles of conservative cosmopolitanism abroad and down-home comfort in the US South, the novel imagines Black imperial agency as an unlikely outcome of the violence of the 1960s and as a structure of feeling to be laid to rest with post-soul tenderness.

Abel Jones III, the fallen ex-husband of the protagonist of Randall's *Rebel Yell*, is the son of a civil rights activist who grows up to be a CIA spy in the Philippines in the 1980s, takes a Foreign Service assignment in Martinique in the 1990s, and becomes White House special advocate to the Pentagon just in time for 9/11. The novel opens when he collapses from an asthma attack at a restaurant called the Rebel Yell, a dinner theater that stages Confederate reenactments. After he dies, the novel follows the attempts of his ex-wife, Hope, to retrace the footsteps from the Pentagon in the 2000s back to Abel's childhood in 1960s Nashville, where he is the son of a well-known rights crusader and heir to Black

Atlantic literary fame. The reader learns, for example, that the "day Abel was born, sweet tucked deep in the dark South, Langston Hughes . . . typed a little poem in his celebration. In Paris, Richard Wright received three different postcards and a letter shouting the good news" (14). The attempts to reconstruct the life of this disinherited messiah of civil rights politics and culture begins when Abel's ex-lover Nicholas visits his ex-wife, Hope, after the funeral. As the two former lovers forge an unlikely alliance and sit sipping Gentleman Jack, Nicholas "took out a stack of photographs and laid them down on the table as if he were playing eccentric solitaire, three rows of three. The pictures—photographs—were disturbing and familiar. Naked men, dogs, leashes, piles of bodies, simulated sex acts, a uniformed smiling soldier, hoods, framed in a neat white border" (152). Placing before Hope nine photographs of prisoners at Abu Ghraib, Nicholas confesses that he fears he recognizes in them Abel's "signature." Reproducing the images as photographs—"not beaming from a computer screen or glossy in a magazine"—accomplishes the novel's task of bringing Black responsibility for racist violence, along with the images, "closer, alarmingly close," and at the center of the novel's attempts to reconstruct Abel's life narrative from civil rights to the war on terror (153). Gazing at another photograph, this one of Abel "standing in front of a flag—what looked to be his official White House or Pentagon portrait"—Hope is finally able to "put it all together. September eleventh. Waterboarding. Guantánamo, Abu Ghraib. Abel" (92). Nicholas and Hope's reunion is thus an attempt to reconfigure the pieces of Abel's life, and this anchors the novel's attempts to reconstitute Black identity through its proximity to security and national identification—and, by extension, to global counterinsurgency—after the post–World War II social movements.

The surfacing of the Abu Ghraib photographs in *Rebel Yell* captures the novel's fascination with the racial-sexual life of counterterrorism. Nicholas's recognition of Abel's signature in the photos ties the dead man's racial shame to his fascination with torture. As Nicholas later reveals to Hope, Abel "lusted for recognition like he lusted for big-bosomed white-skinned centerfold ladies" (300). The specter of Abel's touch in the scenes depicted in the photographs and on the photographs themselves is the mysterious, ghostly force that coheres the split plot of this post-civil-rights epic, tying Abel's humiliating emasculation by white supremacists to his drive toward physical, political, and sexual domination as a spy and government operative. As Jasbir Puar argues, the US exceptionalism that grounds performances of counterterrorism after 9/11—such as the performances of sexual domination in the images of torture at Abu Ghraib—attaches sexual competition to the trajectories of counterterrorism such that the Orientalist production of the terrorist identifies terrorism as a form of queer deviance in need of correction and, at the same time, frames the United States as a liberal homeland in which various forms of gender and sexual queerness are permitted and normalized. This normalization reproduces the value of whiteness, "disaggregat[ing] U.S. national gays and queers from racial and sexual others, foregrounding a collusion between homosexuality and American nationalism that is generated by both national rhetorics of patriotic inclusion and by gay and queer subjects themselves: homonationalism."[24] And if the torture at Abu Ghraib was productive within the imperial modalities of US warfare—it was meant to "coercively produce the Arab subject and the Arab mind," not just to shame or humiliate—in *Rebel Yell*, it brings Abel's imperial paranoia into view as a racial-sexual crisis linking US racial slavery to post-9/11 security practice.[25] When Hope remembers the frustration and anger that Abel feels when he reads that deserting Confederate soldiers in the Civil War were punished with "thirty-nine lashes and a brand on the cheek," she wonders if Abel had "translated that indignity into new sets of gestures, gestures he could misuse at Guantánamo and Abu Ghraib?" (233). This, the question that drives the novel, brings the sexual life of the Confederacy into articulation with the sexual life of the war on terror, with Abel serving as the unlikely "modern-day Black Confederate" who masterminds state violence in order to overcome the abjection of his childhood in 1960s Nashville. It is, indeed, his *lust for recognition,* for the conferral of humanity, that compels him from one side of terror to the other.

Inhabiting the psychological complex of paranoia—what Anne McClintock refers to as "fear and impotence oscillating dangerously alongside omnipotence"—Abel experiences terror as both generational breach and intimate encounter.[26] His thirteenth birthday is the episode that the novel cites as the primal scene of this breach-encounter. As an army of civil rights activists—husbands, wives, students, schoolkids—celebrates Abel's birthday in the Jones's Nashville home, white supremacists set fire to a cross on the front yard. Spooked, Abel pees his pants and feels, along with the others, "the shame of all the dark, the pale-dark, and the hard-dark people around him; a shame intensified for the presence of a white witness to their humiliation" (296). Singling out Abel's white friend Ben as the bearer of the white gaze that consumes Black humiliation, the novel tells this story as a clash of masculinities, a spectacle of castration after which neither Big Abel nor Little Abel is ever the same. As the cross stands erect in the yard, Big Abel attempts to extinguish the fire with the garden hose only to find it slashed. Big Abel's limp, disfigured garden hose, Little Abel's regression to soiling his pants, and the absurd image of a six-foot-tall, thirteen-year-old "Little Abel" finding refuge in police power as he is scooped up into the arms of a white cop draw together the novel's matrix of racialized debasement, sexual competition, and refuge in national security. Describing Abel's flight to two white policemen, Randall writes, "Mistaking their disinterest for courage, he ran to stand in the sheltering space he imagined between their two bodies. The larger of the two men lifted him into his arms and cradled him like a baby" (297). As Abel clings to the police, Big Abel promises his son a beating that will convince him that he has nothing to fear but the father himself. Big Abel does not beat Abel as he promises; rather, the novel relates in second person the scene of breach and intimate touch between father and son, the breach-encounter that actualizes the novel's preoccupation with the transition from civil rights to the war on terror. "Your eyes are mirrors," Randall writes. "You try to imagine what someone opening the door would see. You stand close together, face-to-face, toes touching. You look up into the daddy's face. . . . You see him and he sees how you see him: smaller than the policemen, smaller than the firemen, smaller than Ben's father. . . . You come undone and he comes with you" (361). And then, "You are ashamed of him. The breach is a reciprocal bond" (362). Aida Levy-Hussen argues that the novel "may imply a broader cultural ambivalence about the stature of authority that accrued to male leaders of the black bourgeoisie as self-designated representatives for an illusory black unity" and that this ambivalence manifests itself in the novel as the two Abels' "trifecta of aggression, love, and loss."[27] This not only tempers what Levy-Hussen calls "civil rights idealism," a "collectivizing self-story, a political affect, a personal ideal, and an itinerary for political action," but also figures the intimacy between generations as the very ground of a Black imperial agency that must be accounted for.[28]

What connects the cross-burning at the birthday party to the photos from Abu Ghraib is Abel's "signature," the mark of his arrival at legibility within a political order secured by and structured in violence, a legibility won by the performance of masculine bodily integrity designed at once to subdue and control femininity and to project deviant femininity onto the Arab/Muslim other. The cross-burning is a scene of visual subjection that locks Abel into his lifelong quest for a proper viewing, that lust for recognition that lands him in the Pentagon. The effect of the terror in Nashville is reflected in Abel's keen awareness of being visually apprehended by two subjects he desires: Ben, his white friend, and Sonia, a young Black woman from the Joneses' extended family. Ben, the "white boy," Abel's best friend, symbolizes that world beyond Abel's Black Nashville enclave that his coming of age entitles him to: first, the birthday party "felt significant, as if he was leaving his cradle friends behind and joining something bigger, the company of men, the world his white classmate Ben had been ushered into at the temple off Harding Road" (285). Sonia is a beautiful young woman, older than Abel but younger than his parents, Abel's former babysitter, who symbolizes the erotic allure of Black upward mobility and intraracial gender hierarchy. Abel's father encourages Sonia's enrollment at the University of Tennessee because "he wanted to torture Chattanooga with her existence. A fresh Black beauty just off the farm, whose daddy was a lawyer and whose uncle was a judge and who was wholly unavailable to white men. Big Abel wanted the white boys, he wanted the white men, to see this, to know this. . . . He wanted Chattanooga to see Sonia, and want Sonia, and not have Sonia" (289). Big Abel's lust for recognition materializes as a drive to make Sonia an object of desire and therefore torture. Little Abel, too, positions Sonia as a coordinate in the triangulation of his lust for recognition by white power, here represented by Ben. He wanted "to let Ben see, again, just how pretty she was" (293). Interrupting this scene that projects the lustful desire to be seen through the manipulation of the Black woman's body as an object of white gazing is the cross-burning that culminates in castration and infantilization: Abel with slashed hose and soiled pants, cradling in the arms of a police man. Caught limp and powerless rather than possessing and powerful, Abel's response is to fetishize the seeing, penetrating power of the state.

   That Randall's narrator likens Abel's lust for recognition to his passion for white skin emphasizes the racial shame that subtends Abel's imperial paranoia, which plays out throughout *Rebel Yell* as an attachment to the Confederacy. When Abel visits Arlington National Cemetery on a high-school field trip, he reluctantly follows his classmates to the Confederate Memorial. Sculpted by the Jewish Confederate army sergeant Moses Ezekiel and unveiled in 1914, the sculpture surfaces in *Rebel Yell* to expose the gendered texture of Abel's signature—his performance of legibility vis-à-vis torture—and his erotic attachment to military power. Heading toward the memorial with his white classmates, who want to pay tribute to the Confederate ancestors they claim are memorialized at Arlington, Abel "had refused to make his displeasure known. He wouldn't be scared off any acre or inch of the place. He would stick in the middle of the group. He would blend in, until he could safely vanish" (136). Abel's need to blend in with his white classmates quickly turns into a desire to stand out, to be exceptional, when his blending in is made impossible by the appearance of the figure of the female Black servant in the sculpture. Here is the source of Abel's shame: "The mammy had made Abel wince. Then he had seen the soldier—seen the soldier and known in that moment that he was to be a soldier" (136). Like the thirteen-year-old who clings to the police officer on his front lawn, Abel sees in the weapon-bearing, uniformed agent of the state the promise of bodily integrity, as the standing refusal of a Blackness that is feminized: prone or bowing, violated, penetrated, heavy-laden, overcome. Rejecting the civil rights model of masculine leadership, the model that was violated by the penetrating wood on the front lawn of his childhood home, Abel visits the Pentagon after leaving Arlington Cemetery and decides to make a life "inside the five-sided fortress" (136). Defense, then, is an arena of racial-sexual fortification in which Abel, *able*, acts out a drive to overcome that primal scene of abjection, the scene of the limp phallus, the penetrated ground, the soiled underpants.

   Abel tells the story of his thirteenth birthday as a story of a rape rather than "utter and tender, complete and mutual defeat" (362). The shame of mutual defeat that both locks Big Abel and Little Abel together—toe to toe, eye to eye—and splits them apart will become, in Abel's journey from Nashville to Harvard to Manila to Martinique to the Pentagon, expressed as what McClintock calls "imperial déjà vu," that is, a "deep and disturbing doubleness with respect to power" constituted by, at the same time, "deliriums of absolute power and forebodings of perpetual threat."[29] Through the hearsay flashback, the scenes of terror at the hands of white supremacy keep suspended the question of how this son of civil rights royalty becomes an agent of imperial torture and detainment. It is the novel's construction of imperial paranoia as the outcome of civil rights, then, that asks us to situate it in the cultural work of the long war on terror, as a novel that resurrects the terror of the civil rights and post-civil-rights years to make sense of its own reinvocation and its own splitting apart. That is, the image of Abel and Abel coming together and splitting apart in Abel's room on the night of his birthday is an analogue for a contemporary African American literature that is at once converging and diverging, beginning and ending, clinging to the nation and desperately fleeing it.

Abel is both heir to racialized subjection (object of terror) and beneficiary of incorporation into a US citizenship secured by torture (subject of terror). On this side of terror, Abel's signature marks the Abu Ghraib photographs. On the other side of terror, the paramedics who show up to the Rebel Yell horse barn to administer aid to Abel when he undergoes an asthma attack recognize him as Abel Sr.'s son and withhold the oxygen that would save his life. There is a structural tension between the novel's attempts to render the Black conservative son of civil rights as exception, as deviant, and the attempt to rationalize him, to claim him as a member of a clan, a wayward son. This tension splits the plot between the heritage narrative—composed by the archival retrieval exercises that make this an epic historical novel—and the counterterror narrative, the story of the way the US security state enlists exceptional Black men and women in spite of and against history. The genealogies that Randall offers for Able and Hope "worry the line" of Black tradition, to use Cheryl Wall's generative formulation. When the quest to recover origins is thwarted, Black feminist texts classically use nonempirical forms—memory, dreams, ritual, music, "sometimes a family photograph," but more often "an intangible representation"—to construct genealogies that do not adhere to linear conventions or heteroreproductivity. "A worried line is not a straight line," Wall insists.[30]

In the case of *Rebel Yell*, the heritage narrative could not be less straight. On one hand, Abel is an aberration, a child so badly damaged by white-supremacist violence during the civil rights era that he becomes the embodiment of imperial paranoia. On the other hand, Abel holds a history of Black conservatism that becomes visible through Randall's excessive assembling of genealogical facts, which reclaims earlier Black conservatives, from the Black Confederates to Booker T. Washington, and, at the same time, splinters any possible explanation for Abel's tragic love affair with discipline and punishment. This simultaneous coming together and splitting—the suturing to *and* disavowing of Black cultural specificity through the tracking of bizarre genealogies that span the United States, Europe, and Pacific Rim—is expressed, too, in the image of Abel and Hope, in another photograph from Nicholas's jacket pocket. In a picture taken on their honeymoon, "Abel and Hope had found themselves side by side, but [Abel] was moving in one direction, toward the large world, and [Hope] was moving in the other, toward the South" (169). This image of the marriage as an untenable convergence and splitting mimics the unities and fractures of post-9/11 Black narrative, which sets the cultural retrieval exercises (such as Randall's beautifully rendered descriptions of Black epicurean delights such as Prince's hot chicken or Hope's sweet potato biscuits with blackberry jam) uneasily beside the material forces demanding the representation of Black men and women criminalizing, detaining, and torturing. The split plot marks out two competing geographies of Abel's life. Readers follow him, for example, to Manila, where he lives on a military base and guards the Marcoses during the People Power Revolution; it is here where Abel, young CIA spy, learns the technologies of antiterror. But readers also follow Hope to the house of Abel's grandmother down home in Nashville, a "haven of Black, well-salaried people" (74).

When Hope wonders if Abel had "*translated*" Confederate military practice into "new sets of gestures, gestures he could misuse at Guantanamo," the novel identifies Abel as a subject of imperial grammar who updates the codes of racial subjection and counterterror. The reader learns through the friends whom Hope surveys after Abel's funeral that his job in the Pentagon was to "parse the crazy definitions that allow for Abu Ghraib" (62), to "[parse] 'perpetual detainment'" (216). If Abel's job is to decide which forms of torture are permissible by attending to definitions in international law, he brings to that legal-linguistic work an intense investment in the safety of defense. By the end of the novel, Hope recognizes with chagrin that it "had leavened something in Abel's spirits to move from 'I am not safe' to 'We are not safe' to 'No one is safe'" (319). Abel's translations of nineteenth-century white supremacy into torture in the war on terror and, here, of the first-person singular subject of insecurity to the first-person plural to the third-person indefinite mark safety as a zone of home and homeland protection. Abel translates the scene of a civil rights masculinity overcome with humiliation into the imperial grammars of Blackness, those maneuvers in language that tie the racial subject's *having been overcome* and, importantly, *having overcome* to the nation's drive to overcome terror itself. At Abel's funeral, one of Abel's friends remembers Abel's lifelong work of translating anti-Black terror into anti-Arab counterterror as a gothic labor of those who survived what they were not meant to survive. Abel, like his lover, Randall's Condoleezza Rice–ish national security adviser, Aria Reese, "was raised in a time and place of terror, a place of bombings and shootings, a place of funerals and wakes, a place of police dogs and fire hoses turned toward children, a land red with the blood of the recently slaughtered, a place where wedding bells didn't ring" (52). If Aria Reese chooses "to infect the nation with the anxieties of Black children who came of age in a time of terror when the war at home rocked their churches," so too does Abel's signature, the signature that authorizes Guantanamo and Abu Ghraib, serve to animate the fiction of state safety in grammars of pain, vengeance, and overcoming (53). In this way, *Rebel Yell* probes the relationship between Black authorship and the war on terror, surveying how, as Cynthia Young suggests in her work on contemporary narratives of Black American masculinity and the war on terror, "Black abjection secures national absolution" in a "narrative rehearsal of the lethal necropolitics that defines our contemporary moment."[31]

But the gothic safety that Abel authors and seals with his signature—his signature on the photographs, his signature on "perpetual detainment"—is only one form of safety in Randall's novel. There is also the safety of the surround, which is also, of course, no safety at all, no fortress at all, but rather "the life that surrounds it," the "common beyond and beneath—before and before—enclosure."[32] The taste of "luscious plenty" or the smell of the holiday eats that Hope's great-aunts teach her to cook. Or the revelation that Hope has when she realizes at the repast after Abel's funeral, heading into the basement of his grandmother's house, "There was a God in heaven. Mo Henry was pouring drinks" (76). Soul food and soul drink in *Rebel Yell* set sensation off on wayward paths, back down home and before: before and before the security of both home and homeland:

> Not having Thanksgiving on calendar Thanksgiving and doing all the cooking herself were tribute to her aunties, long dead, who, working as domestics, had often been obliged to cook for strangers and serve strangers on the fourth Thursday in November. The aunts had moved their family holiday to Wednesday and Hope, in solidarity, had kept hers there—except for the years she had been married to Abel. Drinking (cases of champagne and sparkling cider) and eating, mainly turkey (roasted, smoked, fried, and confit), continued into the early hours of Thursday morning, when a second round of sweet potato pie baked into a crust of homemade gingersnaps was served. Later on Thanksgiving Day, just before noon, Hope served a less elaborate but still big breakfast—egg casserole, twisted bacon, and blueberry crepes, all recipes the aunts had perfected working in other folks' kitchens. Only then would the hunters, laden with sack snacks, extra spiced almonds, and man-bought provisions, leave for Michigan.
>
> "Thank you for the luscious plenty," one tipsy old lady had gasped, most earnestly, just after midnight one Thanksgiving morning after getting so high and tired she couldn't remember what she was supposed to say. (35)

What does the feel of ginger sweet melting into warm potato on your tongue want from the reader of a novel that begins with a death in a horse barn and ends with the messianic appearance of none other than Barack Obama, who gives Abel the glimpse of a "new happily ever after" that inspires him to give up his own life (363)? The novel's diverging geographies of post-civil-rights Black life make Abel's form of security an errant outcome of anti-Black terror that meets its antithesis in, first, the aunties and their culture of plenty and, second, dubiously, Obama and the culture of liberal reform.

Randall's *Rebel Yell* is a post-Bush-era epic novel that draws together the homegrown terrorism of the Ku Klux Klan with the directives of global counterterrorism, charting a shaky course from civil rights to the Pentagon and laying the wayward son of civil rights to rest in the safety promised by both old-time Black folkways and Obama's liberal reform agenda. Like so many other African American texts that absorbed the shock of the Bush administration's foreign policies of preemption and domestic policies of incapacitation and abandonment, *Rebel Yell* interrogates Black intimacy with state-sanctioned terror and state-sponsored projects of counterterror in a way that refracts those projects, making them visible, cutting through them and breaking them open. As I turn to Danielle Evans's 2010 collection of short fiction *Before You Suffocate Your Own Fool Self*, I want to stress that the energies of Black radical feminism that have throughout the long war on terror worked at unraveling the violence on which fictions of homeland rest continue to surface precisely in Black women's writing of the twenty-first century. We can track this surfacing—a certain eruption that ends up being the corruption of US literary patriotism—in the literature's investigations into the racial-sexual life of counterterrorism.

Nowhere to Go

The short stories in Danielle Evans's 2010 collection bring the poetics of the early phase of the long war on terror into conversation with early twenty-first-century narratives of Black female risk and vulnerability. Like *Rebel Yell*, *Before You Suffocate Your Own Fool Self* measures the price that Black women pay for the United States' preemptive war against terror. Exposing safety as a racial gendered set of prescriptions, the story "Someone Ought to Tell Her There's Nowhere to Go" ushers the energy of radical Black feminist critique into the story of a Black veteran's return to the United States after a tour in Iraq, querying the fiction of multicultural *homeliness* through which *homeland security* gains its coherence. Published in 2010, Evans's work of short fiction joins the other stories in *Before You Suffocate* in interrogating Black girls' and women's vulnerability to both interracial and intraracial forms of violence.

That Evans's short-story collection borrows its name from Donna Kate Rushin's "The Bridge Poem" emphasizes its connection to feminist-of-color critiques of the violence that the Black or brown woman is asked to bear for the nation, and the nation within a nation. Rushin's poem served as the preface for *This Bridge Called My Back*, the 1981 collection that was something like an inhabitation, an in-dwelling, of internationalist feminist consciousness. Importantly, Frances Smith Foster pointed out in her contemporaneous review of *This Bridge* that the volume was not a "literary gem" or an "intellectual challenge" or "even a clear communication from voices previously unheard," that it was rather a "testimony and a witnessing that the definitions of freedom change but the struggle continues."[33] If the *This Bridge* anthology surfaced at the onset of neoliberalism, it was a text that captured not the strength and coherent legibility of political statements but, as Foster insists, the *vulnerability* and *precarity* of the woman of color in the era in which "equal opportunity" was supposed to provide cover. Rushin writes,

> I am sick
> Of having to remind you
> To breathe
> Before you suffocate
> Your own fool self[34]

In these lines, quoted at the beginning of Evans's *Before You Suffocate*, the illness that Rushin writes of, the illness of the translator, is a disease of the postrevolutionary period, during which Black women like Rushin were asked to mediate between constituencies and bear the marks of political progress. The pressure to become public, to become known, to become a basis for "becoming hip," pushes Rushin's speaker to refuse explanation vis-à-vis translation:

> I explain my mother to my father my father to my little sister
> My little sister to my brother my brother to the white feminists
> The white feminists to the Black church folks the Black church folks
> To the Ex-hippies the ex-hippies to the Black separatists the
> Black separatists to the artists the artists to my friends' parents . . .
>
> Then
> I've got the explain myself
> To everybody
>
> I do more translating
> Than the Gawdamn UN

The refusal to translate that "The Bridge Poem" imagines to be the performance of Black feminist consciousness opens onto the larger project of *This Bridge* and the project of radical feminist internationalism that, in contrast to that work of low translation between domestic constituencies or those acts of high translation at the "Gawdamn U.N.," ruins the imperial grammars of Blackness through which notions of neoliberal progress in the post-civil-rights era gain their coherence.

This Bridge's version of "The Bridge Poem" names and frames *Before You Suffocate Your Own Fool Self*. Given how Evans's collection plots Black women's sexual and social vulnerability against the backdrop of early twenty-first-century discourses of safety, the impression of its two epigraphs—seven lines from "The Bridge Poem" and two lines from Lorde's "Between Ourselves" ("I do not believe our wants / Have made all our lives holy")—historicizes early-millennial Black literary production within the longer period in which Black women mobilized text against the market demand for easily consumable objects of difference, in ways that disorganized the imperial grammars of Blackness. This is the period that included, of course, Jordan's withholding in her Nicaragua poems and Bambara's inquiry into the language of security in *The Salt Eaters*.

Before You Suffocate's works of short fiction are stories of what Frances Beale called "double jeopardy" multiplied to the nth degree, stories that expose the violence that both brings Black girls and Black women into national narratives of freedom and progress and constructs Black women's being as the unprotected, unprotectable situation that makes those narratives, *as* narratives, possible.[35] In the first story, "Virgins," two girls come of age in late-1990s Mt. Vernon, New York. Tupac has just died, it is early fall, and Erica and Jasmine are discovering the banality of sexual violence. Erica, the protagonist-narrator, remembers, "My first kiss was with a boy who'd said he'd walk me home and a block later was licking my mouth. The first time a guy had ever touched me—like touched me there—I was eleven and he was sixteen and a lifeguard at the city pool. We'd been playing chicken and when he put me down he held me against the cement and put his fingers in me."[36] The scene of play turns to violation and unprotection; this is what coming of age, or *progress,* is. Erica identifies her friend Michael as her and her best friend's protector—"Michael kept people like that out of our way" (6)—

and, at the story's climax, she calls Michael for help when she runs out of an apartment in the Bronx where she and Jasmine have absconded with four older men from a nightclub. Later that night, Michael's brother advances on Erica, and she realizes, "There was no such thing as safe, only safer; that this, if it didn't happen now, would happen later but not better. I was safer than Jasmine right now, safer than I might have been" (25). "Virgins" grounds the question of safety, the question of so much lofty public discourse at the turn of the millennium, in the body that exposes safety as a fiction. Likewise in "Snakes," the mixed-race protagonist is terrorized by her white grandmother and cousin. She muses, "We are safe, with our families, until we are not."[37] It is *Before You Suffocate's* work at the scenes of Black female insecurity that makes its connection to late-1970s and early-1980s Black feminism available as an interruption of the imperial grammars of Blackness.

Much of the fourth short story in the collection, titled "Someone Ought to Tell Her There's Nowhere to Go," a story about an Iraq War veteran who was released because of PTSD, takes place at an unlikely, or perhaps totally predictable, site for a war story: a shopping mall. When George, called Georgie, home from the war, begins babysitting his ex-girlfriend's five-year-old daughter, he begins to pretend that he is her father, and he treats her to days out at Glitter Girl, a shop that caters to young girls by selling dolls, clothes, and even spa treatments. Just as late-1970s Black feminist texts like Shange's *for colored girls who have considered suicide / when the rainbow is enuf* sympathized with the figure of the returning veteran while calling attention to the cost Black women at home pay for US wars abroad, "Nowhere to Go" brings the returning vet into Evans's narratives of Black women's vulnerability to sexual and discursive violence even as it emphasizes the vet's vulnerability to, and agency for, state violence. Georgie's fantasy of marrying Lanae and becoming father to her daughter, Esther, compels him to perform the fantasy of domestic contentment and fatherly protection; he weaves together a narrative of war heroism and patriarchal protection that exposes the grammars of homeland while also exposing various forms of homelessness under the surface of the war-on-terror fantasy. Esther and Georgie spin a tale for the sales attendant at Glitter Girl, telling her that Georgie is Esther's father and a war hero, and Georgie later convinces Esther to weave the same tale into a video that she enters into a contest to win tickets to a live concert at the shop. The fiction of fatherhood, in this case, comes to stand in for national narratives of the war against terrorism after 9/11, which, too, were constructed through the grammars of home: "I ask you to live your lives and hug your children," George W. Bush counseled in his address to the nation on September 20, 2001, as he declared war against Al Qaeda. In "Nowhere to Go," Georgie, as a miniature or representative of George W., coauthors the fiction of homeland: "And when she started the first time, it wasn't even a lie, really. *Hi Glitter Girl*, she began, all on her own, *for a whole year while he was away in Iraq, I missed my Daddy.* OK, so he wasn't her father, but he liked to think she *had* missed him that much."[38]

The war story that Georgie and Esther create to win the video contest wholly makes over Georgie's experience in Iraq. Georgie's mission in Iraq is to produce intelligence by "knock[ing] on strangers' doors in the middle of the night, hold[ing] them at gunpoint, and convinc[ing] them to trust him" (94). One night he encounters two "pretty girls" with big black eyes and sleepy baby-doll faces; when he returns the next night, they are "lying there, throats slit, bullets to the head, blood everywhere but parents nowhere to be found" (95). After the two girls are murdered because Georgie's company extracted information from their parents, Georgie is haunted by them. He becomes "jumpy and too spooked to sleep," and one day he misidentifies another girl on the street as one of the girls who are haunting him. Her running away from him after Georgie shakes her and commands her to tell him why she has been playing dead prompts George's comrade to ask, "The fuck you think she's running to so fast, anyway? Someone ought to tell her there's nowhere to go" (98).

When Georgie retells this story through Esther's video, he refashions himself as the patriarchal war hero from the United States who serves the cause of freedom and enlightenment in the Muslim third world:

Esther didn't doubt for a second that he had a heroic story to tell. He closed his eyes.

"Two girls," he said, finally. "A girl about Mindy's age. She was missing her two front teeth. And her little sister, who she loved a lot. Some bad men wanted to hurt them, and I scared off the bad men and helped them get away."

"Where'd they go then?"

"Back to their families," he said. He opened his mouth to say something, but nothing came out. "Start the movie over," Esther said. "I'm going to say that too." (107–8)

The video fantasy ties the fantasy of familial wholeness and domestic contentment in both the United States and Iraq to the larger fantasy of the United States' imperative to bring the people of Iraq into a proper familial relation. The Iraqi girls are figures for the homelessness that sustains Georgie's fantasy of homeland bliss in "Nowhere to Go."

Georgie's denial is familiar in the culture of the long war on terror. It is similar to the fighter pilot's guilt in *In Treatment*, which I discussed in chapter 2; guilt substitutes for the rebellion or for the desertion that has a long history in the wars of empire. It is similar, too, to the denial of the Korean War veteran in Toni Morrison's novel *Home*, who conspires with the narrator to depict himself as a valiant family man who rescues his sister from the home of a savage eugenicist in order to conceal the fact that he killed a young North Korean girl who offered a sexual favor to him in a bargain for a rotten piece of fruit she finds among the US soldiers' garbage. "*I have to tell the whole truth,*" Morrison's protagonist finally says as he confesses to the narrator. "*I lied to you and I lied to me.*"[39] For Morrison's Frank Money and Evans's George, the homecoming that the veteran projects as a work of salvation aimed at young Black women is really penance for the blood on his own hands. Coming "home" is not an act of recovery or salvation; it is the beginning of an unreconcilable reckoning with the vet's intimacy with imperial warfare.

Underneath the veneer of Georgie's benevolent care as Esther's babysitter is the force of violence; that violence requires Georgie's ongoing denial. When Georgie first deploys to Iraq, Lanae ends their brief love affair, opting out of the sentimentality of the army-wife position. "I'm not waiting for you to come home dead," she tells him. But Georgie "didn't believe for a second that she was really through with him this time" (86). When Georgie returns from the war, he finds Lanae cohabiting with Georgie's old friend Kenny. The day Georgie returns from the war, he sits on his mother's sofa watching television, being drawn into those cultural forms of denial: the talk show, the soap opera. The suburban quiet of the mother's home estranges Georgie. The house's "bright robin's egg blue of the paint" is "cheerful in a painfully false way"; its "surfaces were all coated with a thin layer of dust"; and he realizes "it had been a long time since he heard silence" (89). His immediate flight from the pastel-colored, feminine domestic space of the mother to Lanae's apartment, where he attempts the rekindling of the affair, is an act of denial that refuses Lanae's rejection of wartime patriarchy and seeks to correct his patriarchal displacement by re*handing* Lanae ("It bothered him to think of Kenny putting his hand on her that way" [89]). We can hear Georgie's denial in the screech of the brakes as he speeds through town on a mission to forget the girls murdered in Iraq and become father, become whole. The brakes "screeched every time he stepped on them," and Georgie wonders only if "he should have asked his mother how the car was running" (90). Later, when he goes to Glitter Girl, Georgie "*told himself* he was there to talk to the manicure girl, pick up a little present for Esther" (104). What Georgie tells himself throughout the story tends toward a denial of the creeping, stalking force of the unhoused veteran, the would-be war hero with nowhere to go.

With "Nowhere to Go," Evans unravels a common narrative of Black fatherly protection in the Iraq. As I discussed in chapter 2, the representation of the Black returning vet as the perennial missing father returning to redeem the pathological Black family is what Wahneema Lubiano calls "the U.S. state at its ugliest and most subtle" when she refers to the way "the Gulf War and the military's exploitation of a racially, economically, and politically oppressed group is costumed into a Black father's doing his duty for his country and his daughter."[40] When Georgie offers to babysit for Esther, he turns the national fantasy of dominance back onto itself: "They were always going places that encouraged fantasy. Chuck E. Cheese's, where the giant rat sang and served pizza. The movies, where princesses lived happily ever after. The zoo, where animals that could have killed you in their natural state looked bored and docile behind high fences. Glitter Girl, Esther's favorite store in the mall, where girls three and up could get manicures, and any girl of any age could buy a crown or a pink T-shirt that said ROCK STAR. What was a pretend family relationship, compared to all that?" (98). Those "animals that could have killed you in their natural state" are the force of freedom caged within the domestic writ large, and Georgie brings his own complicity in securing the homeland into articulation with his fantasy of home, pretending familial protection while the nation pretends protection in Iraq.

The Black feminist grammar of "Nowhere to Go" refracts the language of this contrapuntal security narrative. The recommendation that Georgie's fellow soldier makes after Georgie sends a young Iraqi girl fleeing—"Someone ought to tell her there's nowhere to go"—is an expression that exposes the futility and devastation of the landscape of occupied Iraq and the silent disregard hovering under the veneer of the culture of innocence in the United States. The living, fleeing Iraqi girl in "Nowhere to Go" stands in for the more than 165,000 civilians who were killed in Operation Iraqi Freedom, which began in 2003 and officially ended in 2011, the year after *Before You Suffocate* was published. The plot here hangs on the modal verb "ought," which normally works in the positive sense to recommend or advise: you ought to eat your vegetables. The irony of the Iraq War itself—that gap between its stated mission of freedom and the lived reality of occupation—and the aporias within the national narrative of the war are captured in the silence that accompanies the modal verb in Evans's story.

> Once, in the daytime, he thought he saw one of the dead girls, bold as brass, standing outside on the street they were patrolling. He went to shake her by the shoulders, ask her what she'd been playing at, pretending to be dead all this time, but he'd only just grabbed her when Ramirez pulled him off of her, shaking his head, and when he looked back at the girl's tear-streaked face before she ran for it like there was no tomorrow, he realized she was someone else entirely. Ramirez put an arm around him and started to say something, then seemed to think better of it. He looked down the road at the place that girl had just been.
>
> "The fuck you think she's running to so fast, anyway? Someone ought to tell her there's nowhere to go." (97–98)

The "ought" that drops into the air between Georgie and the girl-ghost who runs away eviscerates the modal verb as a positive recommendation and brings it into narration as, rather, the failure of speech to secure anything like freedom. This *turning* of the verb is what I am signaling as the resurfacing and redrafting of Black feminist grammars in Evans's work.

Recall, for example, what the lady in orange says about the Vietnam-veteran beau willie brown in Shange's *for colored girls*:

> & he'd get up to make coffee, drink wine, drink water/ he
> wished one of his friends who knew where he waz wd come by
> with some blow or some shit/ anythin/ there waz no air/[41]

As Nadine Knight observes, Shange was one of many Black feminist writers of the 1970s whose revolutionary worldviews were shaped by anti–Vietnam War activism. Not only did Black feminist literature dissent to the war; it also critiqued how Black women were expected to provide care for the veterans who were returning, helping them return to civilian life "with grievously inadequate (social) services for veterans."[42] The 2010 revision of *for colored girls* reimagines beau willie as a veteran of the Iraq War who brings the violence of the war home:

> beau waz sweatin terrible/ member in Basra
> beatin on Crystal/ & he cdnt do no more with the table n chairs/.[43]

This, like the earlier version of the choreopoem, "communicates how the suffocating force of state violence constricts the domestic sphere," as Soyica Colbert suggests.[44] The fractured memory of Iraq, signified by the broken speech that also gestures to the war as a mission of phallic recovery, of phallic (re)membering in Basra ("member in" for "remembering"), erupts into *for colored girls* as the deadly force of the father returning to claim his rightful place at the head of the family at all costs. Beau willie's wish for escape by way of narcotics, and his insistence on a kind of fatherly protection that articulates itself as the violent rejection of home as he drops Crystal's children from the fifth-floor window, brings Evans's modal "ought" into articulation with Shange's simple past-tense "stood" and "cd." Evans's narrative of the veteran's return brings Black feminist critiques of the long war on terror into empire's fable of fatherly protection, interrogating Black intimacy with state-sanctioned terror and state-sponsored projects of counterterror in a way that refracts those projects of patria as fatherspace.

After Georgie's lie is exposed, he makes one last attempt to assume the role of husband-father. As Lanae sends him away, the story ends in the dark silence of the unanswered question that recalls the scene of devastation in occupied Iraq. "I think you need to go for a while," says Lanae. "Where?" George asks. Then George "kept standing there, long after the porch light went off, not so much making an argument as waiting for an answer" (112). One could make an argument about structural irony here: the Black returning vet shares the condition of homelessness and dispossession with the young Iraqi girls. But I want to suggest that rather than create a sympathetic picture of Arab-Muslim humanity, "Nowhere to Go" refuses the ground of enlightened identification between occupier and occupied—literally going dark when the reader expects Georgie's "moment of truth"—and instead opens up grammar itself to expose counterterrorism as a racial gendered regime based in the fictions of home that demand the continued extraction of Black women's affective and manual labor.

The "ought" here is of course uttered in the shadow of the *conditional* language of the war on terror. To return to Jodi Kim's elaborations of imperial temporality, the logic of preemption "relies on a metaleptic substitution in which Iraq comes to stand in for al-Qaeda and its action and on a *proleptic 'preemption'* of future attacks against the United States."[45] The grammar of preemption is the future-perfect tense. *Will have done, could have done, would have done*: these grammatical formulations are the basis for what Brian Massumi calls "potential politics" based on conditional statements that cannot be proven wrong.[46] The future perfect belongs to the security planner, true, but it also belongs to the counter-planner. As Avery Gordon notes, the future perfect is the utopian tense, the grammar through which we give voice to what we see as the future ingresses into the present, the grammar for apprehending the utopian on the margins of the here and now. Utopians "will have known what is possible today, yesterday, tomorrow."[47] But speculation is not on offer in "Nowhere to Go"; Evans's nowhere is atopian rather than utopian. The modal "ought" in the story does not recover but rather slants, or breaks, the conditional grammar of imperial temporality. Where there might be instruction or moralizing, there is silence. Where there might be identification and protection, there is failure. Where there might be catharsis, there is anticlimax. The silence that ends "Nowhere to Go" leaves Evans's protagonist unmoored, without the protection that he pretended in Iraq. Evans's silence might be understood as an insurgent grammar of survival, one that speaks Lanae's and Esther's carrying on behind the closed door, not under the pretended protection of a warrior patriarch but rather in shared vulnerability: a care*less*ness. This is the other side of terror.

Interestingly enough, "Nowhere to Go" refuses the cathartic tale of Shange's beau willie brown. If there is no tragic end for Georgie, there is no cleansing or healing for Lanae either. This holding off of Black women's empowerment of course asks us to reconsider the translation work that we expect Black women's texts to perform and forces us to reckon with the fact that the Black literary text, caught in the nexus of war, institutionality, and the epistemologies of multiculturalism, *also* has nowhere to go. In light of, or perhaps in the darkness of, a world that increasingly demands Black intimacy with power on this and on the other side of terror—and surely those two sides dwell as much within the contemporary Black scholar as much Du Bois's "two unreconciled strivings" do—Black feminist literature asks us to be keenly attuned to how projections of US empire onto and through the face of Blackness have shifted the very ground on which we teach, think, and write.[48]

A Black woman and her daughter are locked behind a closed door, where the existing grammars of protection cannot reach, or describe, or know, them. Is this a desired end? To consider the end of Danielle Evans's 2010 short story "Nowhere to Go" as a template for Black feminist forms of unsecured safety based in self-defense or horizontal affiliation is to return to where we began, with Bambara's Velma Henry and her experiments in vitality that enact, conjure, and perform the world we want right inside, in the ruins of, or just above the world we are given. The nowhere that Lanae and Esther—could-be casualties in the war come home—occupy at the end of Evans's story is not the nowhere that Gloria Wade-Gayles writes of in her 1984 study of Black women's fiction. Writing of characters like Ann Petry's Min in *The Street*, Toni Morrison's Pauline Breedlove in *The Bluest Eye*, and the "sad, lonesome girls" of Alice Walker's *The Third Life of Grange Copeland*, Wade-Gayles considers these characters pessimists "who know that their lives are hostage to forces over which they have little control," or ghost-walkers "on a treadmill, 'going nowhere immediate.'"[49] Instead, the stasis at the end of "Nowhere to Go" is the vestibule where defense becomes offense. Here Lanae and Esther take up the space of endurance and, possibly, the posture of defense, where such a posture manifests itself not as ability or strength or the stance or dance of pugilist but rather as a quiet "bodying forth" of survival. The interior is the stage for what Kevin Quashie refers to as a "dynamic and ravishing" inner life that, while not apolitical, "is a stay against the dominance of the social world."[50] On that stage, to assume the posture of defense is to hold out, to take cover in the margins, and so to outlive the terror of late empire. Such is the posture that Gloria Naylor's protagonist assumes in the 2005 paranoid memoir *1996*.

Perfect Cover

From where I sit, no one exemplifies the contradictions of being the subject of Black writerly success and the object of US counterinsurgency better than Gloria Naylor. In this final section, I want to turn to Naylor's *1996* to excavate the Black feminist ways of knowing and being that lie beyond the reach of existing grammars of protection. Proposing that *1996*'s protagonist, Naylor herself, offers us a portrait of a woman who has paid a high price for refusing to perform the (reluctantly) accepted models of Black writerly excellence, I offer that Naylor's paranoia is, more than a psychological pathology or even a social psychological effect of living in an empire, an occult form of knowledge that offers the writer a position from which to assess and survey, and potentially interrupt, the ongoing assault of security culture. In contrast to Abel's imperial paranoia in Randall's *Rebel Yell*, which manifests itself as a campaign to reconstitute the national phallus after 9/11, Naylor's Black feminist paranoia is an insurgent mode of study that refuses state-secured safety while inviting its alternatives.

1996, an account of Naylor's year-long residency on St. Helena Island in Beaufort County, South Carolina, was her last work. That year, something broke, and broke open, in Gloria Naylor. It was a break that had been scored decades earlier, when Naylor, set to graduate high school when Martin Luther King Jr. was assassinated on that Memphis balcony, paused on her fast track to college and joined the Jehovah's Witnesses. "After the assassination," Naylor said in a 1983 interview, "one of my teachers in high school cried in front of the class and said, 'You know there's a cancer spreading in this country and I want you to go home and think about what that means.' I went home and I did that. And I said, the cancer's not only in this country, that cancer is in the world."[51] Refusing the pull of professionalization and joining the occult practice of alternative Black religiosity, Naylor worked as a switchboard operator in New York through the early 1970s before traveling to North Carolina and Florida as a full-time minister. She left the ministry and attended Medgar Evers College, then Brooklyn College, where she completed *The Women of Brewster Place*, her most well-known work.

This section of this book should really be about Naylor's master work, *Sapphira Wade*, which she started writing in earnest in 1996. But *Sapphira Wade* is the book she never wrote, the one she held onto because there was no safe place for her to write, or even imagine, after 1996. Gloria Naylor rose to literary fame after the publication of *The Women of Brewster Place*, which won a National Book Award for First Novel in 1983, the same year *The Color Purple* won the National Book Award for Fiction, and was adapted seven years later for a television miniseries produced by Oprah Winfrey. The miniseries, like the adaptations of other Black feminist texts, allowed the novel to find a wider and more diverse audience and, in the process, blurred the lines between collective, insurgent Black feminist critique and a privatized, compensatory Black women's empowerment narrative.[52] Naylor followed *Brewster Place* with *Linden Hills*, a lyrical novel that likened the anxiety and alienation of the residents in its titular Black middle-class enclave to the circles of hell. She published *Mama Day*, which introduced the character of Sapphira Wade, the Senegalese captive who gains the insurgent ground, in 1988. She followed with *Bailey's Cafe* and a collection of short stories in 1995. After that, she planned to write a full-length novel about Sapphira Wade.

Sapphira Wade had been Naylor's companion and muse for twenty years, and she was to be the subject of Naylor's seventh novel: the "kick-ass" novel, "the cornerstone."[53] Naylor later wrote to her friend Julia Alvarez, "I believe that she has guided me all these years; protected me when I couldn't protect myself. And I have tried to protect her: that's why I put away all of my material in 1996 and wrote *The Men of Brewster Place*."[54] She did extensive research in Norway and West Africa toward the novel she eventually put away. As Suzanne Edwards and Trudier Harris point out in their introduction to a partial draft of "Sapphira Wade," published by *Callaloo* in 2019, the 131 handwritten pages that Naylor included in the papers she donated to Sacred Heart University chronicled the early life of Bascombe Wade, the Norwegian property owner from whom Sapphira mysteriously obtains her land in *Mama Day*.[55] Sapphira Wade does not appear in the pages she donated. If it was Naylor's intention to keep Sapphira safe after the "1996 experience" she endured, that intention persisted.[56] In May 1996, she told the interviewer Michelle C. Loris that she had designed and built a beautiful garden in South Carolina and that it reaffirmed her belief in "creativity and in life," that she had planted perennials because it would be her retirement home, and that she was writing. She had left by the end of the following month, and when she spoke with Loris at the end of the year, she told her "that it was not yet time for *Sapphira Wade*" and that she had moved on to *The Men of Brewster Place*.[57]

In 1996, Naylor sat paralyzed in her study, unable to write for fear that the computer she was writing on was being hacked, that the room she was writing in was bugged, that the voices she was hearing calling her a bitch and telling her to kill herself were not coming from inside her own head (as *they* wanted her to believe) but rather were being projected through her bedroom wall by a microwave sonic device. Naylor was convinced that the National Security Agency, working with the Drug Enforcement Agency and the Anti-Defamation League, was targeting her with a comprehensive program of surveillance and intelligence experimentation. If her "fictionalized" memoir is to be believed, Naylor was one of many Black women who crossed the line between the terror of anti-Black racism and the terror of the contemporary security regime. "I'm going to come out of this and I'm glad that I grew up a black woman in America. Anything less than that proving ground would have probably sent me to the nuthouse over this a long time ago," she wrote to Alvarez.[58] The "1996 experience" was what Nadine Naber might call an "internment of the psyche," a paralysis caused by the "sense that one might be under scrutiny—by strangers, hidden cameras, wiretaps, and other surveillance mechanisms of the security state," a normal response to the ways that "U.S. imperial structures took on local form" through the post-1945 decades.[59]

Naylor opens and closes her memoir *1996* with identical sentences: "I didn't want to tell this story. It's going to take courage. Perhaps more courage than I possess, but they've left me no alternatives. I am in a battle for my mind."[60] More than it is a work of fiction, *1996* is a work

of Black feminist paranoia. Paranoia is traditionally defined as a pathological condition in which one's behavior is driven by exaggerated or
unfounded fears of harm. But paranoia might also be defined as an epistemological position—a position from which one advances a theory of
knowledge—that both exaggerates and euphemizes threat to further the
political project of anticolonialism. In 1996, paranoia, as occult knowledge, blurs the line between fact and fiction. The text alternates between
first-person past-tense narration (e.g., "I began working on the plans for
my garden layout in my gardening journal" [21]) and the third-person
omniscient narration that tracks the agents who are tracking Naylor
(e.g., "What Dick Simon wants is for Gloria Naylor to just go burn in
hell" [78]). Naylor has purchased a house on the island of St. Helena, off
the coast of South Carolina, and moves there with two goals: to write
a book and to grow her first vegetable garden. These plans are foiled
when she has repeated arguments with her neighbor, a Jewish woman
who accuses Naylor of calling her a "Jew bitch" (28). When Naylor accidentally kills the woman's cat, the neighbor enlists her brother, who
works for the NSA, to watch Naylor, who is now suspected of running
an illegal drug operation. The surveillance escalates quickly: first they
watch her, then they bug her; they move into the house next door; then
they poison her garden; they steal her computer by getting a friend to
betray her; then, finally, they undertake a noise campaign that makes
it impossible for her to rest or write. When Naylor leaves St. Helena
and returns to her Brooklyn apartment, they continue their campaign,
just because they can, just because they have not driven her to madness
or suicide yet. Now they escalate again: they send coded messages via
microwave into her bedroom at night so that she might think it is her
own voice she hears saying, "I'm a bitch. I should just kill myself. I hate
Jews" (100). What they want is for Naylor to behave as the governed, to
admit that they are in control and to keep hidden the seams of their—of
power's—shoddy operation. "If she's on the run, keep her on the run,"
they say. "When she sees there's nowhere left to go, they wouldn't have
to crumble her. She'd crumble on her own" (81). As she persists in watching the watchers, Naylor activates the strength to keep fighting them.
The fight—the flight—drives her to the one place where she cannot hear
their voices or feel their watching eyes: the public library. There she sits
to compose the story that, we are told, we have just finished reading.

Black femininity in *1996* is the terrain on which surveillance applies itself. It is also the ground from which Naylor launches her campaign of counterveillance. The first half of the memoir centers around the way the NSA operation disrupts what would otherwise be the banal routines of traditional feminine homemaking. Naylor refers to her house as her "own little Eden," and as she juxtaposes the work of cultivation to that of contemplation, she genders that labor (10). When she moves into her Sea Islands house, she tells readers, "I would sit at a folded table in the sunroom that gave me a view of the water, drinking my morning coffee in a pink mug that said, 'Hers,' in blue lettering" (11). Later she refers to the same writing table repositioned on the second floor, which grants her a view of the garden she plants as well as the street traffic that picks up once the Anti-Defamation League enlists the congregants of a local synagogue to conduct ongoing surveillance of the property. The postures of writerly repose—of sitting at the window of a sparsely furnished Victorian with a pink mug that marks the gender of its owner even more clearly in the absence of its implied counterpart (a mug marked "His")—alternate with postures of active construction in a brief account of Naylor's Eden before its fall. Naylor restores the greenhouse, plants seeds, nurses seedlings, hauls manure and soil from Walmart, and writes in her gardening journal. For a flash, this is Naylor's Tinker Creek, her Walden Pond, her room of one's own. "I wonder how many people actually get the chance to act out their fantasies," she writes. "I was one of them, and can say the feeling is one of complete and utter peace" (13). While Naylor's dream cannot be reduced to a fantasy of bourgeois writerly solitude—as Naylor scholar Maxine Montgomery suggests, Naylor understood domestic space as "cultured, gendered space," as "a highly symbolic signifying system bound with vexed issues of racial sovereignty and literary authority"—*1996* suggests that her insurgent domesticity is a problem for those around her.[61] As Naylor works at both projects of cultivation, trying to make her way in the world as a Black woman writer and homesteader, her work invites the paranoia of her neighbor and the policing of Black gender that is at the heart of the surveillance campaign, that is perhaps at the heart of every US surveillance campaign.

If the aberrations of Black gender are the very essence of threat, the state's surveillance apparatus is the phallic, penetrating corrective force.[62] As Naylor embarks on her gardening and writing projects, she inadvertently kills her neighbor's cat, aptly named Orwell, who has been turning her beloved garden into a litterbox. Naylor writes in the self-consciously fictional mode to speculate about why the crazy cat lady would enlist her brother, a high-ranking NSA official, to monitor her movements and eventually tap her home and phone lines. Eunice is a lonely, needy woman who is the foil for her orderly and self-sufficient brother. About the siblings, the third-person omniscient narrator reveals, "They are both unmarried and childless. All they've had is each other since their parents' tragic car accident. [Dick Simon, the brother, has] tried to be there for his sister, to reassure her, to tell her that she still has someone to lean on, that someone is still left in the world to love her. But Eunice has a void in her life that no one's love can fill. She's worse than the bottom. She is a bottomless pit that sucks in all you have to give and berates you for not giving more" (28). Eunice lives on St. Helena unprotected by a patriarch; she turns to her brother, and he and his technology serve as prosthetics for the figure of the husband or father.

Naylor meanwhile functions as a kind of Black femme surplus. A garden to be fertilized, a "hers" with no "his," she is a foil for Eunice's neurosis. As one agent thinks, "She is a woman alone, for God's sake. She has no organization behind her, no friends to help" (52). That Naylor represents the feminine surplus that the state must police is reinforced by the fact that, throughout the surveillance and mind-control campaign, the NSA agents repeatedly refer to Naylor as a witch or bitch. "Ding dong, the witch is dead," they say when they make like they are poisoning her water line (61). She is a "lying witch," they say when they hear her telling her friends about how she is being followed (77). When the agents, getting increasingly angry about Naylor's ability to expose the seams of their surveillance operation, begin using a computer program that transmits microwave messages directly to Naylor's brain to simulate an internal dialogue that she is having with herself, she writes, "I remember I was watching Mel Gibson's 'Braveheart' for the fifteenth time when the first thought came to me: *I am a bitch.* It seemed to have just floated up from the bottom of my mind. . . . *I am the worst bitch in the world. I want to kill myself*" (99). And then the agents, angrier still that Naylor has discovered that they have moved in next door and are transmitting messages into her brain, program their computer to say, "*Face it, bitch. You need to kill yourself*" (115). The repeated and increased use of the word "bitch" throughout the second half of the memoir signals the NSA's interest in marking Naylor's aberrant femininity as cause for the continued invasions of her privacy.

The operation begins with a simple enough aim: to watch the woman who is suspect because she is a feminine subject living in excess of patriarchy—again, a hers with no his, a witch or bitch with a garden that finally flourishes wildly. One agent gives up on the operation when he realizes that Naylor's is a "harmless life" (81). But the operation escalates because Naylor's paranoia actually exposes the fragility of the agents' power to know. "I knew, as I sat in front of that computer for hours, that I wasn't crazy. I knew that I would never tell myself to commit suicide. That I wouldn't call myself a bitch from morning to night. And if I wasn't doing it, who was?" (118). Initially ignorant of the surveillance operation, she gradually takes over the position of surveyor, writing down the license-plate numbers of the cars that follow her, asking a friend at the CIA to do something about the men following her, pointing out every car that follows her. The more she knows, the more they have to know. When they use brain-wave technology—called synthetic telepathy—to read her mind, they marvel, "Imagine the intelligence possibilities of being able to read someone's mind. . . . It's a world without secrets" (112). *1996* marks this power to know as sexual-gender violence. The surveillance is carried out by college-age agents called "the Boys," whose homosocial world is built on their ability to penetrate Naylor's bedroom, computer, garden, and thoughts. "The Boys sit transfixed before the small computer screen." And "Paulo can't help himself. . . . A tingling occurs at the bottom of his stomach. To be inside of someone's mind has to be the sexiest thing in the world. There was nowhere left on earth to go, no new frontiers" (119). *1996* refers to the state's operation as "the ultimate rape" (121). Naylor's ability to decipher the operation is in turn understood as a violation. The NSA director, aptly named Dick Simon, "is feeling a growing hatred for this woman who has even now invaded his dreams. Hating her is easier than hating himself for letting her matter" (78).

If Naylor's paranoia operates as a counterveillant force, exposing the agents' power to know and in turn precipitating the increasingly violent forms of watching and penetrating that they undertake to punish and correct her, *1996* holds paranoia out to the reader, too, as one risky way of growing intimate with the state. The form of the memoir induces a kind of paranoia. As Claudine Raynaud writes in one of the scant scholarly pieces on *1996*, the novelistic parts of the memoir that speculate on the mental disposition of the spies undermine "the veracity of the first-person account. The autobiographical thus comes under suspicion," and the abrupt transitions between what the reader thinks is *real* and what can only be *speculated* produce a kind of groundlessness.[63] Naylor "may have invented a new genre" to issue a warning about a democracy that could see "a certain type of writing (Naylor's)" as a threat.[64]

Adding to the cloud of mystery surrounding *1996* is Naylor's archive of correspondence. Letters from friends intimate that something went terribly awry on St. Helena—"I was horrified at the reasons you had to leave South Carolina," one friend writes, and another laments Naylor's move back to New York "because of the problems in South Carolina." But the letters in her files also belie the vision that Naylor paints of a woman alone: a letter from three "sistah-friends" thanks Naylor for the "beautiful experience" of their recent visit, and one mentions a recent visit and encloses pictures.[65] That Naylor insists in interviews that she is telling the truth about the surveillance but omits these visits from friends in the memoir reinforces, first, that Naylor's first-person account is an exercise in self-ownership and, second, that the forms of care that she keeps hidden from readerly view hold an archive of the counterveillance operation that Naylor undertakes to track the state's invasions into her private life. To be clear, I believe the story Naylor tells. I believe that state agencies used her as a test case for surveillance technologies, including electromagnetic field brain stimulation. But whether the memoir tells the "truth," or whether I believe it, is less significant than how its toggling between the autobiographical and the fictional invites the reader to become suspicious (paranoid?): watchful for the cracks in the narrative's surface. This is, indeed, the kind of watching that drives Naylor to the conviction that the work of the state is to monitor, control, and punish (not to protect) and that this monitoring, controlling, and punishing extends to the tools with which she reads and thinks and writes. The narrative's incitement to the reader's watchfulness arms the reader as a cowatcher with Naylor. *1996* is less a book than an invitation, an incitement, a condemnation.

The counterveillance that Naylor manifests, up to and including the book in our hands, is knowledge of state violence cited with shaky empirical evidence produced by a Black woman with natural hair and a house full of books, which means that it is, by nature, illicit. Is it Naylor who is paranoid or the neighbor who obsesses over the Black woman obsessing over her spring garden? Or is it the brother who obsesses over what the Black woman sitting with her manuscript knows? Paranoia ceases to function in 1996 as a psychoanalytic category when the psychoanalyst whom Naylor visits discovers bugs in his office, realizes that Naylor is telling him the truth, and effectively pronounces her free of schizophrenia. In light of the memoir's defense of its own truth claims, paranoia comes to function as a heuristic for white supremacy, on the one hand, and as a form of occult knowledge, on the other, where "occult," from the Latin *occultus*, means not only covered or concealed, as in a secret not divulged, as with magic, but also saved, as in saved up, stored up, stored up beyond the range of understanding. Naylor changes her relation to state power in what she refers to in interviews as her "1996 experience" or her "battle for [her] mind" when she reorients her relation to knowledge. Instead of completing her dream of writing the "big book" that she goes to St. Helena to write, she backs away from producing the novel as a bourgeois object of taste and retreats from the private and proprietary to the public and transparent. "My only peace from the voices," she writes, "was in the library" (121). And "whenever I walked up those vast steps to the main branch of the Brooklyn Public Library, I felt like I was getting out of slavery and moving toward my freedom" (127). Like the fugitive slave narrative, 1996 imagines literacy as the motor of abolition. But unlike the fugitive slave narrative, the authenticating documents do not serve to enlighten or to awaken one to necessity of Black freedom. Rather, the addenda to 1996—a list of websites managed by other victims of mind-control experimentation, the text of a lawsuit alleging that the NSA's domestic intelligence program uses EMF brain stimulation for remote neural monitoring, and a survey of evidence regarding mind-control experimentation—are not calls to concrete political action so much as they are invitations to paranoia as an occult form of knowledge.

As Naylor tells Ed Gordon in an NPR interview, she writes the book in part to validate paranoia as a form of knowledge, as, indeed, a theory or approach to knowledge about state violence:

GORDON: But let me play the devil's advocate, Gloria. There are going to be people who are going to say, just based on what you just said, why would the government follow you? What interest would they have? Etcetera, etcetera. Here's a woman who's just simply, underline, paranoid.

GLORIA: Well, what I can say to them is this: it's the same thing that happens when a child is abused by a trusted adult. Now, that child will go to some parents. . . . They will be believed by some of the parents. Some of the parents will never believe that Uncle George could be doing these things to their little girl. So, it's either that you're gonna believe me, or you're not going to believe me, and I couldn't worry about that.[66]

Naylor's analogy between a young girl's molestation and "the ultimate rape" of 1996 calls attention to the violence of state surveillance as gender-sexual expression of post-1945 power. Perhaps more importantly, it testifies to her vision of the book as a call to the very paranoid expression of Black femininity that gets her ejected from her garden and, thinking in the terms Alice Walker set out, her *mother's* garden: Is this the work of an *artist*, even in the radically expanded definition Walker offers?[67] Paranoid Black femininity is not the work of the artist, but it is perhaps one version of what Simone Browne calls <u>undersight</u> or *dark sousveillance, an epistemology* that "plots imaginaries that are oppositional" by repurposing the tools of social control.[68] Watch Naylor watching the watchers and plotting her escape from the would-be Eden, where she lives across the street from an old plantation:

The Coffin Point plantation house and my house sat on the water; there was nothing beyond us. There was a small amount of traffic from the oyster factory further down McTeer Drive, but it was only evident in the evenings when the trucks, carrying the day's work, were leaving. On a busy day I would sit in my study and see one car every two or three hours. In March, I was seeing three or four cars every hour and it was always the same pattern. A car would come up Coffin Point Road, turn left on McTeer Drive, cruise to the end, turn around, and drive back out. (42)

In her flight from the private to the public, Naylor turns this dark sous-veillance to a paranoid, militant politics: "I AM IN A BATTLE FOR MY MIND," she writes in all caps.

With *1996*, published by Third World Press nine years after the mind-control experiments, Gloria Naylor moved from the mainstream of the postwar literary world to the fringe of US knowledge production reserved for self-published books about UFOs or the Illuminati or racial conspiracy theories.[69] But if Naylor's occult knowledge of the state's sophisticated intelligence technology can be situated alongside the work of other Black women writers of the long war on terror, who expose the limits of state intelligence and take up positions of careful watching, we might begin to understand how the vocation of writing—and the physical space or *scape* of writing—invites paranoia while mapping sites of public tending and programming bodily postures of care in public. In these places and postures, one does not rest easy. One stalks and tracks the trail of blood that counterinsurgency leaves behind; one gets besides one's mind; and one uses paranoia as sustenance.

Studying, teaching, and writing about the relationship between Black women and the state of incessant war demands a kind of Black feminine/feminist paranoia of this sort: the sort that thinks about the writer in public space not only as a cause for celebration but as a fringe subject making unlikely, often unheard, calls for collective defense in the era of COINTELPRO, of the War on Drugs, of Iran-Contra, of the USA PATRIOT Act. This, indeed, is the sort of Black feminist paranoia that gives Black women in the postwar writerscape, Black women like Naylor and Jordan, Shange and Bambara, Randall and Evans, over to both unbridled success and unparalleled marginalization. And then, the margins provide perfect cover for our night watches.

Afterword

The imperial grammars of Blackness are the structures of communication that translate Black pain and Black thriving into the speech of ←
US empire: not just words and phrases but gestures of affirmation and
empowerment that weave Black aspiration into national delusions of
domination. Throughout the late twentieth and early twenty-first centuries, fantasies, images, narratives, slogans, and trinkets of Black women's
freedom and achievement—in the chambers of Congress, on T-shirts
and buttons, uniformed on street corners and offshore, on the stages of
festivals and world meetings, and everywhere you can imagine—served
as prosthetics for an empire desperate for multicultural representation
as the sign of its righteousness and the ground of its tenuous authority.
Black women writers and critics and foreign service officers and enter-
tainers had a role to play in legitimizing power, in restoring order, no less
than enlisters and university presidents and national security advisers.
Black feminist literature—and by this I mean to refer not to the singular
"great works" that make up the syllabus for the successive regimes of
liberalism but the open, insurgent, actively mass-authored text, the *radically different text for a female empowerment*—also had a role to play in
throwing the safety secured through militarized control into perpetual
crisis. The intimacy between Black women and US empire is a mirror
for the inescapable intimacies between Black liberalism and Black radicalism, between Black literature's ascent and its dissent. These pages are
my endeavor to take those intimacies, which shape my own labor conditions, as a productive prompt for framing the contemporary period in
African American literature.

Around the same time that it became customary to think of our time
as continuous with the time of slavery, that it became possible, if not
customary, to think of African American literature as a cultural compromise with Jim Crow segregation that had outlived its narrow mission,
that it was conceivable to be a serious writer in the tradition of African

American letters and not write a book about slavery, that it became inconceivable to be a serious Black theorist without considering oneself a slave, that one could hear the Black president promise to "put more boots on the border" so many times that it would give one nightmares about bloodied black boots on brown dirt: this was when my father dropped a November 2010 book review from the *Washington Post* in my lap. It was a review of Alice Randall's *Rebel Yell*, a novel that featured a Black man protagonist who was an heir to civil rights royalty and who traded that heritage to be a member of the neoconservative elite that redefined security in the late twentieth century. I spent the next several years following the tracks laid down by that novel: the trails between the domestic police state and the global security regime, between repression unto death and affirmation unto life, between writing and carving new possibilities out of a dying world. The tracks, I discovered, were in my hands: in my course numbers and course descriptions, in the novels I taught, in the smiling packages being dropped on my doorstep day by day. Black books and the worlds around them were not the only places where US empire gathered legitimacy, but they were not exempt from its seductions of success and stability.

Rebel Yell ends with a fantasy of Black political redemption that now seems fantastically quaint. The son of civil rights who survives the terror of Bloody Sunday and cradles his imperial dreams of torture at the foot of a Confederate monument dies in peace, even as he is suffocated by white EMTs, because a dazzling senator's eighteen-minute speech at the 2004 Democratic National Convention has just laid out a less wretched path to safety. The happily ever after that Randall's protagonist imagined was not an end; it was a conjuncture between racial regimes. When Barack Obama, then a first-term senator from Illinois, promised, "there's not a liberal America and a conservative America, there's the United States of America," it was the height, and the limit, of the alliance between Black liberalism's tendency to exploit US patriotism for its race-relations agenda and Black radicalism's urgency toward a liberation that would be secured through working-class militancy. What followed the peak, with Obama's election four years later, was a descent: the Democratic Party immediately began to suffer massive losses; Obama conceded to incremental reforms, and while he dampened his predecessor's antiterrorism bluster, he extended Bush's executive war powers, expanded surveillance, deported two and a half million people, and oversaw nearly six hundred drone strikes that killed hundreds of civilians. The racial regime that followed Obama-era postracialism is the one of the present, a regime that no longer functions to pass off structural inequities as race-neutral but openly promises that anti-Black violence will benefit from the unchecked endorsement of the executive power Obama helped to salvage. Meanwhile, the charge of terrorism is still so easily tossed about to delegitimize Black radicalism as Black Lives Matter gains mainstream support, and Black aspiration remains entangled with the seductions of US unity and safety. Today's most visible Black woman elected official earned her reputation as a tough-on-crime prosecutor who crusaded to save young girls from human trafficking. (She's *"for law and order,"* a headline proclaimed; "ENOUGH IS ENOUGH!" read a campaign mailer whose cover image was a shirtless brown man holding a revolver and throwing a gang sign.)

In positing Black feminist literature as a radical body of labor that predicted, theorized, and combated the long war on terror and, at the same time, presenting it as a body of labor that, in light of literature and literary criticism's own embeddedness within that very war, is insufficient to the task of ending that still-unending war, I share many contemporary scholars' reservations about scholarly critique as the answer to social problems and suspicions of collectivist politics. Still, the urgency toward an insecure safety that has motivated Black feminist literature—again, not as a collection of texts but as a social world—is an urgency that I also share. That Black women's writing since the 1970s surge in radical Black feminist print culture has produced itself in excess of the professionalizing, individualizing tendencies of literary culture is a testament to the productive potential of that urgency. When Ntozake Shange designed the performance of *for colored girls*, recall, she began with the demand that it be moveable and changeable, that the ladies in colors continually open up the question of what it means to be a woman of color, that performances build on each other and yet keep unresolved the choreopoem's founding "metaphysical dilemma," and that, in the end, the performances become the very antithesis to words on the page. When Shange's lady in brown pleads in that unforgettable line for "someone, anyone" to "sing a black girl's song," "to bring her out to know herself / to know you," then, the kind of embodied knowledge *embodiment speech sound* she was imagining was always already at odds with the print form of the text that we now will have lived and taught and written with for the past forty-five years.[1] How do we bring the colored girl "out" of the text in order to know her? Is knowing her what the text even wants, given the very *out*ness that Shange posited as the ontological position of bein colored and bein a girl?[2]

To know Black women's writing differently requires a new understanding of Black women's complicity with power. It is too simple to say that salacious narratives of Black women in bed with power are racist and sexist; it is more accurate to say they draw on a reservoir of ready associations of Black women with selling out radical politics. Throughout this book, therefore, I have used "intimacy" as a term that better aligns with the full range of positions that Black women occupied throughout the long war on terror. Where "intimacy" invokes an alarming closeness that might call one's attention to where one's desire is lodged, that might prompt the at once deeply internal and necessarily collective work of dislodging and redirecting the aspiration for achievement within the given terms of order, "complicity" summons judgment and the false promise of political sanctification. When June Jordan invoked the old plantation metaphor, with its pure revolutionary "field Negroes" and its sellout "house Negroes," to address the predicament of the Black Americans who were reading *Essence*, her point was not to condemn her readers for their complicity in waging imperial war in Latin America and North Africa, to suggest that complicity was a choice or a tool they could apply, say, as an image editor applied an airbrush. Complicity with empire was the very ground of the radical's work, and the challenge was to imagine, bravely but unromantically, all that friends and lovers and cousins and coconspirators and soup-poisoners could do on that ground. In her original draft, Jordan wrote of her mother and grandmother, who cleaned white people's houses "real good" but "kept their eyes on another house, one that would be as big as the whole world, and as safe as a pair of arms, and full of family come to freedom."[3] Like Gloria Naylor's "other place," the insurgent ground she writes of in *Mama Day*, the Black feminist grounds of radical safety is not so far off. It is not a fantastic place in another world; it is the right-now place on the margins of this world. It is the other side of terror, where the constant practice of watching for the opportunity to break the system of subjection is also a constant practice of complicity in the fullest sense: to be folded together in a *complex* of impurities, as *accomplices* and *companions*, until we can bring ourselves out.

I began this book because I wanted to figure out how to work differently. Could I teach without the easy narratives of generations, breaks, and progress that I was recycling even though I knew they were shortcuts? Could I sit on another Black History Month committee or suffer through another equity training with live actors performing parodies of watercooler "microaggressions"? Could I write without the comfort of ✓ ideological purity? Could I teach *Beloved* one more time and deny that the short leap from "You your best thing" to "Live your best life" was a maneuver I was expertly trained to help students perfect, the joys of our classroom "deconstructions" notwithstanding? Could I do my job without making Jeff Bezos richer? When I could no longer work with the pretense or even the hope of clean hands, beginning this book was like scrubbing desperately at my fingers. Satisfying. Cool. As I conclude this book, the work I do is constitutively different, but not in the ways I dreamed. With the fantasy of clean hands both more palpable and more useless than ever—the COVID-19 pandemic has claimed the lives of 555,000 people at the time of this writing, with Black people dying at two and a half times the rate of white people—the uses to which Black feminist literature was put during the racial regimes of multiculturalism and postracialism are still with us. The worldwide rebellion to racial capitalism that hastened in 2020, not only because of the coldblooded murders of George Floyd, Breonna Taylor, and Ahmaud Arbery but also because of the decades of organizing by Black feminists and other feminists of color, led many an academic department to circulate statements that only slightly differed from the statements of shops and corporations that filled their consumers' inboxes, to shine a virtual spotlight on antiracist literature and those of us who teach it, to redesign curricula, and to host mandatory workshops on Black Lives Matter and antiracist pedagogy. In this context, I can only hope that the stories I have told in this book help to temper the idealism of an official antiracism that is ╱ more vocal than ever and sharpen the tools of sabotage, the tools of our collective preservation.

ACKNOWLEDGMENTS

I cannot remember if this book started that day my dad dropped that review of *Rebel Yell* in my lap or the time I rode out to the naval recruiter's office with my cousin or the time I got in an argument with my sister's godfather about why I was not proud of Condoleezza Rice. It is impossible to individuate the ontological totality out of which this book materializes and to which it is addressed, but I nevertheless want to acknowledge the gracious, flexible, brilliant company that has made it possible.

This work follows from a commitment that I learned from Wahneema Lubiano, whose work taught me that one part of our job as cultural workers is to decipher the power of the state to provide metaphors for explaining how the world works, to go where the state's presence is most dangerous because it is most unnamed. I hope I have succeeded well enough to show her influence and my gratitude. This work is richer and more coherent because of Avery Gordon, an impossibly sharp thinker, teacher, and interlocutor, and the gift of her painstaking interventions in this particular text, and Grace Hong, an infinitely generous reader, intellectual, and friend. The work is furthermore shaped by my studies of and sometimes with the other great teachers whose work has provided me with a lifelong syllabus: Toni Cade Bambara, Lindon Barrett, Hazel Carby, Angela Davis, Ruth Wilson Gilmore, Alexis Gumbs, Saidiya Hartman, June Jordan, Robin D. G. Kelley, Fred Moten, H. L. T. Quan, Cedric Robinson, Hortense Spillers, Mary Helen Washington, and the great Cheryl Wall.

Eric Zinner was a very patient and thoughtful editor. My thanks to him and to the whole staff at NYU Press. Fellowships from the Radcliffe Institute of Advanced Study, the Rutgers Center for Historical Analysis, and the UC Center for New Racial Studies were essential in providing space for collaboration and time for writing. Holly Smith and Kassandra Ware of the Spelman College Archives, Suzanne Edwards and the Gloria

Naylor Archive Project at Lehigh University, and the archivists at the Arthur and Elizabeth Schlesinger Library on the History of Women in America, the New York Public Library for the Performing Arts, and the library at Sacred Heart University aided me in working with the material that really tells the story here.

I was fortunate not to have had to write in solitude. Thank you to the Formation, the Black Feminist Think Tank, the Claremont Cartel, the Famosity Crew, the Louis Place community, and the Townies for providing all the tight spaces and right nourishments for "life studies." Thanks to Nadia Colburn and the intuitive writers, my long-distance writing friends Lara Bovilsky and Beth Buggenhagen, and the Tuesday- and Thursday-morning writing groups at Rutgers.

My colleagues and students at UC Riverside inspired, changed, and educated me. I appreciate the patience and generosity of Alex Alston, Sarah Buckner, Ashon Crawley, Jennifer Doyle, Regis Fox, Laura Harris, Jennifer Hughes, Jodi Kim, Mariam Lam, David Lloyd, Nick Mitchell, Jennifer Morgan, Keenan Norris, Vorris Nunley, Jas Riley, Dylan Rodrí-guez, John Rufo, Sarita See, Setsu Shigematsu, and Alexander Sterling. My colleagues at Rutgers have likewise provided a most inspiring atmo-sphere for working together. Deep thanks and love to Kim Butler, Akissi Britton, Brittney Cooper, Vanessa Crawford, Lavaisa Ezell, Zaire Din-sey Flores, Nicole Fleetwood, Marisa Fuentes, Kali Gross, Lena Ham-mam, Derek Jablonski, Douglas Jones, Jeffrey Lawrence, Carter Mathes, Imani Owens, Adrianne Peterpaul, Zelda Ralph, Stéphane Robolin, Evie Shockley, Carol Spry, Michelle Stephens, Rebecca Walkowitz, Maurice Wallace, Deborah Gray White, and Omaris Zamora and to the graduate students who nurtured this book with their insights. My thanks is again, most of all, to Cheryl A. Wall, who lovingly built so many of the shel-ters in which we are so fortunate to gather and who taught me so much about our common project.

At the Radcliffe Institute, Quito Swan supplied a writing partnership and an encyclopedic knowledge of the radical Black world, plus jokes, while Steffani Jemison enlivened and continues to breathe joy into ev-erything I know about the expression of human strength and potential. The valuable feedback from and camaraderie with Amahl Bishara, Sha-ron Bromberg-Lim, Julie Guthman, Rebecca Haley, Francoise Hamlin, Shireen Hassim, Sophie Hochhäusl, Sharon Marcus, Adela Pinch, Judy

Vichniac, Chad Williams, Patricia Williams, Leah Wright Rigueur, and the other fellows helped me deepen the questions I was asking and the stories I was trying to tell.

In addition to my NYU readers, Carter Mathes, Fred Moten, Sherie Randolph, Sherene Seikaly, and Courtney Thorsson read the manuscript in its entirety. Each of their humbling, careful responses brought nuance and depth to my reflections. The feedback from other readers—Kandice Chuh, Deb Vargas, Sarah Haley, and Chris Freeburg—did the same. Ricardo Bracho was a meticulous and brilliant editor and interlocutor. Meta DuEwa Jones was an inspiring and instructive collaborator and friend. Comparing notes, exchanging drafts, and sharing laughs with Randi Gill-Sadler was essential to this work and my soul.

I am grateful to Jordan Villegas, my research partner who burrowed into many delightful rabbit holes with me, and to Amelia Cruz and Maithreyi Ravula, who stepped in as research assistants at the end of the process.

The conversations I have had in invited talks, conference panels, bars, and living rooms have left their hopefully visible imprints on each page of this book. I hope that this list serves as some small measure of my deep gratitude to Marlon Bailey, Stephen Best, Darius Bost, Jennifer Brody, Daphne Brooks and her homework assignments, Simone Browne, Dennis Childs, Soyica Colbert, Margo Natalie Crawford, Allison Curseen, Sohail Daulatzai, Gina Dent, Aaron DeRosa, Kirstie Dorr, Dawn Durante, Jonathan Eburne, Amy Elias, Sarah Falo, Rod Ferguson, Julius Fleming, James Ford III, Ernest Gibson III, Dayo Gore, Yogita Goyal, Kai M. Green, Allia Griffin, C. A. Griffith, Beverly Guy-Sheftall, Donna Akiba Harper, Molly Hiro, Gordon Hutner, Candice Jenkins, E. Patrick Johnson (thank you for that *Donahue* DVD!), Gaye Theresa Johnson, Ronak Kapadia, Sara Clarke Kaplan, Kara Keeling, Jenny Kelly, Robin D. G. Kelley, Laurie Lambert, Marisol LeBrón, Aida Levy-Hussen, Stephanie Li, Natasha Lightfoot, Lisa Lowe, Alex Lubin, Jacqueline Mattis, Nadine Mattis, Jarvis McInnis, Charles McKinney, Mireille Miller-Young, Nancy Mirabal, Shaundra Myers, Nadine Naber, Jennifer Nash, Zita Nunes, Hayley O'Malley, Robert Patterson, Donald Pease, Therí Pickens, Laura Pulido, Kevin Quashie, Leigh Raiford, my work wife Sherie Randolph, Shoniqua Roach, Cynthia Spence, L. H. Stallings, Patricia Stuelke, Ula Taylor, Lisa Thompson, Emily Thuma, Dennis Tyler,

Bryan Wagner, Cally Waite, Kenneth Warren, Robyn Wiegman, Tiffany Willoughby-Herard, Ivy Wilson, Lisa Ze Winters, Ken Wissoker, and Cynthia Young.

For twenty years now, Christopher Freeburg has supplied daily doses of the hard questions, provocations, assignments, laughter, and wisdom that make for a truly transformative friendship. Shana Redmond has been my coconspirator in work and play, the one who reminds me constantly of what is really real. Sarah Haley has been a cherished friend who pushes me to think bigger and to write from the freest place within.

My families sustained me over the life of this book. I cannot imagine this work without the abiding soul-friendship of Preeti Bone, Tanya Huelett, Rhon and James Manigault-Bryant, Maylei Blackwell, and our families. I appreciate the confidence and good cheer of Grant Micks, James Philip, William Cogdell, Virginia Grise, Mari Infante, and the Edwardses, Vargases, Moten-Harrises, Guridy-Paredezes, Decenas, Chuh-Greens, Vasquez-Amatos, Bridgeforths, Halls, Maclins, Ogdens, Skeltons, and Wyatts.

Hampton Edwards would have read this book from cover to cover and given me his notes while shuffling through CDs in the basement and pouring way too many glasses of wine. Here's another one for you, Daddy. Eileen Edwards is a constant source of strength, wisdom, courage, and humor. Elise Edwards managed to continually offer wisdom, spiritual guidance, and accountability with radiant, unflappable grace.

Deb Vargas walked every step of this book's journey with me, following its path to that wintery place, making space for me to write (as always), listening to every story and believing in the best of it/me. She is my true partner, my song, and my life's love. Maceo Alexander Vargas Edwards was the most welcome distraction and the most patient teacher of all. You two have made the greatest sacrifices to make this work possible, and I hope that my empty hands opening to our future are thanks enough. Or at least a good start.

NOTES

INTRODUCTION

1. On why 1968 was the year that "irrevocably split time around it into a 'before' and 'after,'" Hortense J. Spillers notes the assassinations of Martin Luther King Jr. and Robert Kennedy and the beginning of a long succession of Republican presidencies that witnessed only a brief break under Jimmy Carter. Spillers, "Crisis of the Negro Intellectual," 68.

2. Bambara, *Salt Eaters*, 17. Subsequent references to this source are cited parenthetically in the text.

3. Spillers, "Cross-Currents, Discontinuities," 249.

4. G. Brooks, *Maud Martha, a Novel*, 80.

5. There are too many studies to list here. I am particularly indebted to M. J. Alexander, *Pedagogies of Crossing*; Alsultany, *Arabs and Muslims in the Media*; Atanasoski, *Humanitarian Violence*; Daulatzai, *Black Star, Crescent Moon*; Jamal and Naber, *Race and Arab Americans before and after 9/11*; Kaplan and Pease, *Cultures of United States Imperialism*; McAlister, *Epic Encounters*; and Melamed, *Represent and Destroy*.

6. Browne, *Dark Matters*, 8.

7. Puar, *Terrorist Assemblages*, 3.

8. As Neda Atanasoski offers, US militarism is an instantiation of imperialism that is based in humanitarian ethics, as narratives that rationalize military aggression, in contrast to idealizing a "world without communism," project a world where religious and racial freedom reign. See Atanasoski, *Humanitarian Violence*. See also Amar, *Security Archipelago*. On the way the advanced phase of neoliberalism produces insecurities about the decline of US empire that in turn call forth "exceptional citizens" who can save a no-longer-exceptional state, see Grewal, *Saving the Security State*.

9. Shaundra Myers, for example, writes that authors like Erna Brodber responded to the nationalization of Black politics by rethinking the federal project of integration. The practice of "Black ellipsis," a withholding of the "short" civil rights movement (1954–68) from the narrative frame, allowed Black writers to "resist incorporation into the dominant national narrative" of inclusion and to turn readers' attention to a "once thriving diaspora community of resistance." Myers, "In the Absence of Integration," 231–32.

10. Jordan, "White English / Black English," 62.

11. Lorde, "Equal Opportunity," 16.
12. Lorde, "Learning from the 60s," 139.
13. The studies that have most profoundly shaped my understanding of security in the terms of feminist of color critique are Naber, *Arab America*; Ritchie and Mogul, "In the Shadows of the War on Terror," 175; C. Kaplan, *Aerial Aftermaths*; Kapadia, *Insurgent Aesthetics*; Cainkar, *Homeland Insecurity*; Camp and Heatherton, *Policing the Planet*; Dayan, *Law Is a White Dog*; Grewal, *Saving the Security State*; Harlow, "Drone Imprint"; Amar, *Security Archipelago*; Hernández, *Migra!*; Browne, *Dark Matters*; Willoughby-Herard, "(Political) Anesthesia or (Political) Memory," 24. Many of the texts I write of in the following pages are examples of these experiments in changing what protection means. But I am also thinking here of Virginia Grise's work, which privileges collective self-defense over self-care. Grise, *Your Healing Is Killing Me*.
14. Davis, *Angela Davis*, 63.
15. Masco, *Theater of Operations*, 2.
16. Masco, *Theater of Operations*, 26; Naber, *Arab America*, 61.
17. Camp, *Incarcerating the Crisis*, 5. On the way the political elite criminalized the freedom struggle as a way of recovering from the defeat of Jim Crow, see Weaver, "Frontlash."
18. Gilmore, *Golden Gulag*, 24.
19. Davis, *Abolition Democracy*, 118. See also Michelle Alexander, *New Jim Crow*.
20. Mitchell, *Carbon Democracy*.
21. McAlister, *Epic Encounters*, 33.
22. Davis, "Reflections," 89.
23. Davis, 89, 95.
24. Hartman, *Scenes of Subjection*, 4, 42.
25. Hartman, 116.
26. Haley, *No Mercy Here*, 189.
27. Haley uses this term to analyze the way that convict leasing and the chain gang were brutal forms of exploitation and extraction that extended the (un)gendering project of racial slavery, solidifying "the position of the black female subject outside of the normative category 'woman.'" Haley, 57. Beth Richie's study of antiviolence policy and the building of the United States as a "prison nation" shows how increased criminalization and incarceration depend on "the ability of leaders to create fear (of terrorism or health-care reform); to identify scapegoats (like immigrants or feminists); and to reclassify people as enemies of a stable society (such as prisoners, activists, hip-hop artists)." Richie, *Arrested Justice*, 3. This scapegoating means that Black women who experience male violence are more likely to be criminalized than protected.
28. The history of state-sanctioned torture through government bodies like the CIA is useful here, but I am also referring to the history of policing and incarceration as torture. See McCoy, *Question of Torture*; Shaylor, "It's like Living in a Black Hole,"

416; Bukhari, *War Before*; Ritchie, *Invisible No More*; Bliss, "Black Feminism Out of Place"; James, *Shadowboxing*; James, *New Abolitionists*.

29. Ritchie, *Invisible No More*, 69.
30. National Press Club, "Luncheon with Secretary of Defense Donald Rumsfeld."
31. Jelly-Schapiro, *Security and Terror*.
32. Daulatzai, *Black Star, Crescent Moon*; Rana, *Terrifying Muslims*; Rana and Rosas, "Managing Crisis."
33. Hong, *Death beyond Disavowal*, 32.
34. Edwards, "Sex after the Black Normal."
35. Said, *Culture and Imperialism*, 291–92.
36. Said, 292.
37. Kaplan and Pease, *Cultures of United States Imperialism*.
38. D. Brooks, *Bodies in Dissent*, 8.
39. Randall, *Rebel Yell*, 32.
40. I am moved by Stephen Best's theory of the melancholic historicism in Black studies as "a kind of crime scene investigation in which the forensic imagination is directed toward the recovery of the 'we' at the point of 'our' violent origin," with racial slavery serving as the origin for the imagination of Black collective identity. Best privileges an idea of Black selfhood "grounded in a kind of lost black sociality" rather than melancholic historicism. Best, *None like Us*, 21–22.
41. Avery Gordon uses the phrase "something more powerful than skepticism," from Bambara's *The Salt Eaters*, to refer to Bambara's utopian philosophy and aesthetics. In Bambara's fiction, Gordon finds not the utopianism of the blank page or the clean slate but rather "a different type of anticipatory consciousness . . . oriented toward the future, but not futuristic; that is to say, it doesn't treat the future as either an off-world escape or a displaced fetish." A. Gordon, *Hawthorn Archive*, 41.
42. Rice, *No Higher Honor*, 301.
43. Rice, 302.
44. Browne, *Dark Matters*, 22–23.
45. Baraka, "Black Art" (1965), in *Selected Poetry*, 105–6.
46. On anti-Blackness as the general atmosphere of Black being, see Sharpe, "The Weather," chapter 4 in *In the Wake*. On Black social life as the "register of black experience that is not reducible to the terror that calls it into existence but is the rich remainder, the multifaceted artifact of black communal resistance and resilience that is expressed in black idioms, cultural forms, traditions, and ways of being," see Williamson, *Scandalize My Name*, 9.
47. Lorde, "Litany for Survival," 31–32.
48. Robinson, *Black Marxism*, 168.
49. Levy-Hussen, *How to Read African American Literature*, 95–96.
50. Freeburg, *Black Aesthetics and the Interior Life*, 4.
51. Quashie, *Sovereignty of Quiet*, 6.
52. Best, *None like Us*, 6–7.

53. Spillers, "Mama's Baby, Papa's Maybe," 68.
54. Spillers, "Crisis of the Negro Intellectual," 114. For Spillers, the outcome of the "the thought-object-become-an-object-of-capital," the alchemy of Black studies' marketability, meant that more often than not, the Black studies model of the early 2000s was designed around "the strong line of gender" separating male heads of programs from the women who took on the social reproductive labor of reproducing the field. If that is no longer (necessarily) the case, it seems to me still useful to question the difference that Black class mobility within our profession and around it has made for a larger scene of imperial power.
55. Rodríguez, *Forced Passages*, 70.
56. In Jenkins's foundational study of Black women's literature, she identifies the salvific wish as a specific iteration of uplift ideology that "limits its focus to fostering black domestic and sexual respectability" as a way to save Black people from anti-Black terror. This most often involves surveilling and policing girls and women "precisely because the black female body has so often been characterized by whites as the sole source of black intimate or domestic irregularity." Jenkins, *Private Lives, Proper Relations*, 125–26.
57. DuCille, "Of Race, Gender, and the Novel," 381.
58. See Edwards, *Charisma*; Patterson, *Exodus Politics*
59. Mathes, *Imagine the Sound*, 149.
60. My reading of Bambara's novel is informed by the many foundational studies of her work, especially the essays collected in Linda Janet Holmes and Cheryl A. Wall's edited volume *Savoring the Salt*. See also Holmes's biography, *Joyous Revolt*. Avery Gordon's teaching and writing on Toni Cade Bambara also had a deep impact on my thinking. Gordon usefully situates Bambara within a multicultural radical tradition of utopian thought that offers "stories of living otherwise with the degradations and contradictions of exploitation, racism, and authoritarianism." A. Gordon, *Hawthorn Archive*, 40.
61. Thorsson, *Women's Work*, 40.
62. Spillers, "Crisis of the Negro Intellectual," 68.
63. Wall, "Toni's Obligato," 34.
64. See, for example, Griffin, "Textual Healing."
65. Thorsson, *Women's Work*.
66. Morrison, *Beloved*, 288.
67. Freeburg, *Black Aesthetics and the Interior Life*, 21.
68. See, for example, Hong, *Death beyond Disavowal*; Dillon, *Fugitive Life*; Bliss, "Black Feminism Out of Place"; Ferguson, *Aberrations in Black*; Ferguson, *Reorder of Things*.
69. Jenkins, *Private Lives, Proper Relations*, 20.
70. While the safe harbor of Islam offers women of color a place for forgetting "that they are targets of physical, emotional, and psychological violence," Chan-Malik offers, it "ultimately owes its existence to the dehumanizing forces of racism,

sexism, poverty, and white supremacy: the very catalysts of the safe harbor's creation." Chan-Malik, *Being Muslim*, 34.

71. You can consider this an answer to Christina Sharpe's generous invitation to "think (and rethink and rethink) care laterally, in the register of the intramural, in a different relation than that of the violence of the state." Sharpe, *In the Wake*, 20.

1. INFORM OUR DREAMS

1. In a study of the colonial archives of the Netherlands Indies, Ann Laura Stoler studies the fabrication of colonial authority through the "epistemic practice" that made the Enlightenment, contrary to its label as the Age of Reason, an age of unreason (*déraison*) in which the emotional stuff of disdain, fear, contempt, and envy "were as much the grammar of rule as anything else," were indeed "instantiations and performances of relations of power, judgments, and interpretations of the social and political world." Stoler, *Duress*, 229.

2. Jordan, "Black Studies," 48.

3. Lorde, *Sister Outsider*, 214.

4. I follow Stefano Harney and Fred Moten in conceptualizing *study* as a speculative, social intellectual practice undertaken in the undercommons of, in defiance of, the university. See Harney and Moten, *Undercommons*.

5. For Spillers, the body of the captive "brings into focus a gathering of social realities as well as a metaphor for *value* so thoroughly interwoven into their literal and figurative emphases that distinctions between them are virtually useless;" and the ruling episteme "remains grounded in the originating metaphors for captivity and mutilation." See Spillers, "Mama's Baby, Papa's Maybe," 68.

6. Spillers, "Crisis of the Negro Intellectual," 114.

7. Melanie McAlister discusses the demonstration as captured by ABC's nightly television show *America Held Hostage*. See McAlister, *Epic Encounters*, 212–13. It was of course Paul Robeson who made "Go Down, Moses" one of the most recognizable sounds of Black liberation in the twentieth century. As Shana L. Redmond argues, in Robeson's hands, songs like "Go Down, Moses" were fundamental to the transnational Black and working-class movements that "galvanized the rebellion of entire nations" by the mid-twentieth century. Redmond, *Everything Man*, xiv. June Jordan wrote of the Black Nicaraguan revolutionary painter who in 1983 begged her to send a recording of Paul Robeson singing "Let My People Go," asking her, "Do you think I have a future? Do we [Nicaraguans] have a future?" Jordan, "Nicaragua," *Essence*, 110.

8. Adelman, "Cakewalk in Iraq."

9. Alex Lubin notes that Obama's June 4, 2009, address at Cairo University depicted the United States as an exceptional democracy to emulate, with his own embodiment as the country's first Black president shoring up the fiction that slavery and Jim Crow were mere "moments of divergence from the values of the liberal state," while he performed a definitive amnesia with regard to US imperialism in the

Middle East and the war on terror's targeting of Arab and Muslim Americans within the United States. Lubin, *Geographies of Liberation*, 1–3.

10. C. Young, "Black Ops," 36, emphasis added.

11. Robinson, *Black Movements in America*, 123. Robinson offers a particularly cogent discussion of the paradox that resulted from wartime activism on the Black left and in the mainstream civil rights movement. While Black radicalism migrated to trade unions and other forms of labor activism in the urban manufacturing centers, Black liberalism was "on the ascendancy" during the patriotic period of the war and in the immediate years afterward (123). During the 1950s and 1960s, Robinson explains, these two tendencies within Black activism approached each other; liberalism exploited patriotism and discourses of national unity to push official antiracism to its limits, while radical activists "insinuated" liberation politics "into working class militancy" (123). Both tendencies were "retarded by a vigorous right-wing political and cultural countermovement," first surfacing in early–Cold War anticommunism and later "reconfiguring" that anticommunism into the racially coded discourse of law and order (124). See chapter 6, "The Search for Higher Ground."

12. Dudziak, *Cold War Civil Rights*, 9. See also Plummer, *In Search of Power*; Iton, *In Search of the Black Fantastic*; Redmond, *Anthem*; Borstelmann, *Cold War and the Color Line*; Anderson, *Eyes off the Prize*.

13. Quoted in Dudziak, *Cold War Civil Rights*, 204.

14. Crozier, Huntington, and Watanuki, *Crisis of Democracy*, 114.

15. Crozier, Huntington, and Watanuki, 114.

16. Huntington, *Political Order in Changing Societies*, 397.

17. Crozier, Huntington, and Watanuki, *Crisis of Democracy*, 80.

18. Crozier, Huntington, and Watanuki, 75, 102.

19. United States Department of Labor, *Case for National Action*, 12.

20. Huntington, "Clash of Civilizations?," 26, 32.

21. Robinson, *Terms of Order*, 22.

22. Robinson, *Black Movements in America*, 123–24.

23. On the self-crafted subject of recognition as the figure for a "cultural politics of diversity" that sacrifices social, economic, and cultural restructuring in exchange for recognition and visibility as outcomes, see Gray, "Subject(ed) to Recognition."

24. Robinson, *Forgeries of Memory and Meaning*, xii.

25. Robinson, xiii.

26. Melamed, *Represent and Destroy*, 7.

27. Melamed, 31.

28. Omi and Winant, *Racial Formation in the United States*, 112.

29. On the Cold War as a global race war, see Kim, *Ends of Empire*. On the Cold War's redefinition of the totalitarian threat *as* communism and the history of anti-Black terror as "an unacknowledged mode of totalitarian domination," see Rasberry, *Race and the Totalitarian Century*, 10–11.

30. Keeling, *Witch's Flight*, 74.

31. Keeling, 75.

32. Jordan, "White English / Black English," 64.

33. Robert Smith wrote in 1976 that the "incorporation" or "cooptation" of the Black freedom struggle by mainstream political institutions undermined the capacity for effective organizing against structural inequality; he argued that "Blacks have lost the capacity to effectively press their demands on the system and . . . the system has consequentially responded to their demands with symbolism, neglect, and an ongoing pattern of cooptation. Consequently, Black politics has become largely irrelevant." R. Smith, *We Have No Leaders*, 21. More recently, Cedric Johnson went so far as to blame the Black Power movement for this irrelevance, arguing that its "ethnic politics" were predicated on "elite entreaty, racial self-help, and incremental social reforms." Cedric Johnson, *Revolutionaries to Race Leaders*, xxiii. These evaluations are consistent with Richard Iton's analysis of how Black politics in the post-civil-rights era were premised on a certain repression of transgressive interiority or the "fantastic" elements of earlier Black organizing. Iton, *In Search of the Black Fantastic*.

34. Weaver, "Frontlash," 238.

35. Sugrue, *Origins of the Urban Crisis*.

36. Camp, *Incarcerating the Crisis*, 55.

37. Camp, 56.

38. Singh, *Race and America's Long War*, 61; Camp, *Incarcerating the Crisis*, 53.

39. Singh, *Race and America's Long War*, 67.

40. Singh, 58.

41. Shakur, *Assata*, vii.

42. Gilmore, *Golden Gulag*, 25.

43. Rodríguez, *Forced Passages*, 21. See also Rodríguez, *White Reconstruction*.

44. I am drawing here on Richie's analysis of the mainstream antiviolence movement, which failed Black women as it "left unchallenged the structural racism, the imposition of gender roles, the assumptions of heteronormative sexuality, and America's persistent invisibility of class inequality in the analysis . . . presumably as a strategy to win continued support from an increasingly conservative state." Richie, *Arrested Justice*, 159.

45. See Churchill, "To Disrupt, Discredit and Destroy."

46. Davis, *Angela Davis*, 227.

47. Davis, 234.

48. Davis, *Abolition Democracy*, 108. See also Dayan, *Law Is a White Dog*.

49. Cunningham, *There's Something Happening Here*, 182.

50. I have found Quito Swan's painstaking research on Black Power's global roots and global reach instructive. Most recently he has defined Black Power as "a global, black internationalist, anti-colonial, inherently Pan-African, and revolutionary movement that sought political, economic, and cultural self-determination from systems of white hegemony . . . even when these systems were represented by black heads of state." Swan, "Caveat of an Obnoxious Slave," 53. See also Swan,

"The Empire Strikes Back: The Government's War against the Berets," chapter 9 in *Black Power in Bermuda*; and Swan, *Pauulu's Diaspora*, 16.

51. See for example Randolph, *Florynce "Flo" Kennedy*. I am also indebted to the important studies of Black women's leftist activism in the decades preceding the 1970s, which likewise refuse narratives of Cold War quiescence. See Gore, *Radicalism at the Crossroads*; McDuffie, *Sojourning for Freedom*; Blain, *Set the World on Fire*; Blain and Gill, *To Turn the Whole World Over*.

52. Knight, "Can You Kill," 123.

53. Knight, 126.

54. Toni Cade Bambara, "From *The Vietnam Notebooks*," 107. For Holmes's detailed account of Bambara's trip, see Holmes, "From Atlanta to Vietnam," chapter 5 in *Joyous Revolt*, 77–94.

55. Cheryl Higashida notes how Black feminist internationalism situated historical materialism as the guiding framework for building alliances between the postwar Black Left and struggles for independence in Latin America and the Caribbean. In the introduction to the January 1975 issue of the Black Left journal *Freedomways* devoted to Black women's internationalism, for example, Higashida writes, "the editors hailed 'our heroic sisters of Africa and Latin America, of Asia and especially Vietnam' in the name of internationalizing 'Black women's 'special struggle' for economic, political, and social equality." Higashida, *Black Internationalist Feminism*, 14.

56. McAlister, *Epic Encounters*, 187.

57. Vitalis, "Aramco World," 153.

58. Bsheer, "Counter-revolutionary State."

59. Gelvin, *Modern Middle East*.

60. Quan, *Growth against Democracy*, 9.

61. Mitchell, *Carbon Democracy*, 139.

62. McAlister, *Epic Encounters*, 110–15.

63. Seikaly, "Politics of Hope."

64. Seikaly, "How I Met My Great-Grandfather," 9; Seikaly, *Men of Capital*, 6.

65. Seikaly, "Politics of Hope."

66. Mitchell, *Carbon Democracy*, 186–87.

67. Daulatzai, "Protect Ya Neck," 136.

68. Lubin, *Geographies of Liberation*, 119.

69. Lubin writes, "Palestine has been a laboratory for a bilateral U.S./Israeli security industry that has shaped Israel's approach to the 'problem' of Palestinians *and* the U.S.'s approach to the 'problem' of the urban black poor": both populations were seen as "surplus populations beyond economic inclusion and therefore were viewed as potential threats" throughout the 1990s and 2000s (152). It is important to recognize here that Arab and Black are not mutually exclusive categories and that scholars of and in the Middle East have intensified work on Blackness and anti-Blackness in the Middle East and North Africa. The pioneering work of Eve Troutt Powell is crucial in this regard. See Powell, *Different*

Shade of Colonialism; and Powell, *Tell This in My Memory*. See also El Hamel, *Black Morocco*; Pettigrew, "Histories of Race, Slavery, and Emancipation"; Mamdani, "Introduction."

70. See Cooper, *Beyond Respectability*, 132–33.
71. See the full text of the speech at Watergate.info, "Barbara Jordan."
72. Cooper, *Beyond Respectability*, 133.
73. Cooper compares Jordan to Shirley Chisholm, for example, who drew on contemporary Black feminists such as Frances Beal and Toni Cade Bambara to fuse electoral activism to radical Black feminism. Cooper, 133. I am also thinking of Ida Wells-Barnett, who took on the dangerous work of organizing and writing passionately to end lynching, holding the nation to its stated values of democracy and freedom, while pushing the limits of Black respectability politics. See Giddings, *Ida*, 3.
74. Edwards, "Sex after the Black Normal," 142.
75. Morrison, *Paradise*, 217.
76. Cooper, *Beyond Respectability*, 27.
77. Gilmore, *Golden Gulag*, 109. See also Murch, "Crack in Los Angeles"; Michelle Alexander, *New Jim Crow*; Lubin, *Geographies of Liberation*.
78. Murch, "Crack in Los Angeles," 166. See also Michelle Alexander, *New Jim Crow*; Ritchie, *Invisible No More*.
79. Rana, *Terrifying Muslims*, 53.
80. Quan, *Growth against Democracy*, 154–55.
81. Reagan, "Inaugural Address"; McAlister, *Epic Encounters*, 201.
82. Quoted in Wills, *First War on Terrorism*, 68.
83. Quoted in Wills, 80–81.
84. Klein, *Shock Doctrine*, 170.
85. Byrne, *Iran-Contra*.
86. Grandin, *Empire's Workshop*, 86.
87. Mitchell, *Carbon Democracy*, 216.
88. Quoted in McAlister, *Epic Encounters*, 236.
89. AP News, "U.S. Service Casualties in Gulf War."
90. McAlister, *Epic Encounters*, 237–38.
91. On the effects of the UN sanctions, see Mitchell, "McJihad," chapter 8 in *Carbon Democracy*; Zahra Ali, "Women, Gender, Nation, and the Ba'th Authoritarian Regime (1968–2003)," chapter 2 in *Women and Gender in Iraq*.
92. The "Punishing Saddam," covered by correspondent Lesley Stahl, was an argument that sanctions in Iraq hurt children while leaving Iraq's leadership unaffected. *60 Minutes*, aired May 12, 1996, on CBS.
93. Quan, *Growth against Democracy*, 157.
94. Antoon, *Corpse Washer*.
95. On the shift from the Cold War model of unilateral anticommunist containment to the "New World Order" model of multilateral, coalitional, UN-supported intervention, see Morales, "US Intervention and the New World Order." On military

multiculturalism, see McAlister, *Epic Encounters*; Widener, "Seoul City Sue and the Bugout Blues."

96. Naber, *Arab America*, 25.
97. M. J. Alexander, *Pedagogies of Crossing*, 95.
98. M. J. Alexander, 95.
99. McAlister, *Epic Encounters*, 259.
100. See Robin Kelley's useful summary of Bill Clinton's legacy in "After Trump."
101. Lorde, "Equal Opportunity," 16.
102. Shakur, *Assata*, 50–51.
103. Dillon, *Fugitive Life*, 7.
104. Jordan, "Nicaragua," *Essence*.
105. Marshall, *Triangular Road*, 11.
106. Rankine, *Don't Let Me Be Lonely*, 91.
107. Sexton, *Amalgamation Schemes*, 51. See also Ibrahim, *Troubling the Family*.
108. Gilroy, *Against Race*, 21.
109. Marable, *Race, Reform and Rebellion*, 234.
110. Swarns, "Racism Walkout."
111. Falcón, *Power Interrupted*, 114.
112. Naber, *Arab America*, 251.
113. Quoted in Falcón, *Power Interrupted*, 6.
114. Marable, *Race, Reform and Rebellion*, 241.
115. Marable, 240.
116. A. Kaplan, *Anarchy of Empire*, 1. See also Sohail Daulatzai's prehistory of Blackness's alignment with security, which argues that the "carceral logic and captive power that has historically been forged around Blackness in the United States not only makes legible this new merging threat [of 'terror'], but it also becomes the template for the exporting of this prison regime to the colony in the 'War on Terror.'" Daulatzai, "Protect Ya Neck," 136.
117. Singh, "Racial Formation," 284.
118. Ong, *Buddha Is Hiding*, 9.
119. Kumar, "National Security Culture," 2167.
120. Kumar, 2170.
121. Harvey uses this term to describe capitalist empire as "a contradictory fusion" of imperialism's drive to command a discrete territory and a "diffuse political-economic process in space and time in which command over and use of capital takes primacy." Harvey, *New Imperialism*, 26.
122. McClintock, "Paranoid Empire," 53.
123. Naber, *Arab America*, 252.
124. McClintock, "Paranoid Empire," 56–57. As Joseph Masco argues, what began as an international response to the attacks by Al Qaeda "evolved into an American vision of planetary engagement that is astonishingly productive and wide-ranging—constituting simultaneously a new geopolitics and a new domestic social contract." Masco, *Theater of Operations*, 194.

125. Lugo-Lugo and Bloodsworth-Lugo, "Black as Brown," On the history of the border patrol as a system targeting "Mexican Browns," see Hernández, *Migra!*

126. Here I am drawing on Nadine Naber's description of the "multiple, shifting, and contradicting lenses" through which Arabs and Arab Americans came to be seen as they entered the terrain of "visibility" through processes of both exclusion and inclusion. See Naber, introduction to *Race and Arab Americans*, 5. Junaid Rana, too, explains how during the war on terror, "the process of racialization simply incorporated new forms of racial demonization and policing based in older histories of racism." Rana, *Terrifying Muslims*, 65. Rana and Gilberto Rosas further argue that the combination of the US state's needs for accumulation and securitization during the war on terror "intensified preexisting forms of state power" that were "informed by preexisting social hierarchies of racial, gender, and sexual politics." Rana and Rosas, "Managing Crisis," 223.

127. Rana and Rosas explain that in post-9/11 period, US Orientalist projections of the Muslim "have taken on significantly global and multiracial meanings. The Muslim as a racialized figure gains specific meanings as Wars on Terror are taken abroad, and simultaneously brought home." Rana and Rosas, "Managing Crisis," 225.

128. Browne, *Dark Matters*, 152.

129. Kapadia, *Insurgent Aesthetics*, 68; Masco, *Theater of Operations*, 197.

130. O'Hagan, "9/11."

131. Mahmood, "Secularism, Hermeneutics, and Empire," 335.

132. Puar, *Terrorist Assemblages*, xvi.

133. Ridley, "Manifesto of Ascendancy."

134. Ellis, "New Black Aesthetic," 233; Charles Johnson, "End of the Black American Narrative," 323; Chiles, "Their Eyes Were Reading Smut."

135. Bayoumi, *This Muslim American Life*, 207. On postraciality as the *deletion* of the racial referent, which endows the white racial subject with an ethical position vis-à-vis the history of racial violence, see Rodríguez, "Goldwater's Left Hand."

2. THE IMPERIAL GRAMMARS OF BLACKNESS

1. O'Brien, "How to Pitch the Military When a War Drags On?"

2. Gilroy, *Against Race*, 21.

3. In chapter 4, "The Tangle of Pathology," Moynihan writes, "Given the strains of the disorganized and matrifocal family life in which so many Negro youth come of age, the Armed Forces are a dramatic and desperately needed change: a world away from women, a world run by strong men of unquestioned authority, where discipline, if harsh, is nonetheless orderly and predictable, and where rewards, if limited, are granted on the basis of performance." United States Department of Labor, *Case for National Action*, 42.

4. I use the term "disidentifications" in the way that José Esteban Muñoz intended, to signal the cultural work of minoritarian subjects "whose identities are formed in response to the cultural logics of heteronormativity, white supremacy, and misogyny." Muñoz, *Disidentifications*, 5.

5. Rasberry, *Race and the Totalitarian Century*, 44.

6. The presence of Black soldiers in Europe during and after World War II has had a significant, if not as widespread, impact on the development of US film. The career of Ninety-Second Infantry captain John Kitzmiller, who was cast in the Italian neorealist Luigi Zampa's 1947 *Vivire in pace / To Live in Peace*, when the director heard him laugh and offered him a role on the spot, is an example. Kitzmiller became the first Black man to win best actor at Cannes and is best known for his appearance as James Bond's sidekick in 1962's *Dr. No*. See Giovacchini, "John Kitzmiller."

7. Cripps and Culbert, "Negro Soldier," 637.

8. Marriott, *On Black Men*, 77.

9. Marriott, 75.

10. Fanon, *Black Skin, White Masks*, 108.

11. Marriott, *On Black Men*, 75.

12. McBride, *Miracle at St. Anna*, i.

13. Carolan, *Transatlantic Gaze*, 85.

14. Quoted in Carolan, 102.

15. Hargrove, *Buffalo Soldiers in Italy*, 49.

16. A. Gordon, *Hawthorn Archive*, 192.

17. Fleetwood, *Troubling Vision*, 12.

18. Walcott, "Sea Is History," 137.

19. Moten, "New International of Insurgent Feeling."

20. M. J. Alexander, *Pedagogies of Crossing*, 243–45.

21. Lubiano, "Imagining Alliances," 447.

22. Lubiano, "Black Nationalism and Black Common Sense," 251.

23. Bush, "Address to the Nation."

24. C. Young, "Black Ops," 36.

25. C. Young, 45.

26. Daulatzai, *Black Star, Crescent Moon*, xvii.

27. Daulatzai, xvii.

28. Daulatzai, xvii.

29. See McAlister, "Military Multiculturalism in the Gulf War and After, 1990–1999," chapter 6 in *Epic Encounters*; Widener, "Seoul City Sue and the Bugout Blues," 78.

30. Stacy Takacs shows how television shows about counterterrorism drew on conventions of hero construction; drawing women and people of color into those conventions "renovated these traditions to suit the new, more expansive conception of national identity underwriting this War on Terrorism." Takacs, *Terrorism TV*, 68.

31. Wilderson, *Red, White and Black*, 110.

32. A. Gordon, *Hawthorn Archive*, 189–90.

33. Gordon points out that the US military recruits with the "false promises of good easy money, of affordable housing, free healthcare, and subsidized pricing for consumer goods, of portable education and skills training, of a life safe from satu-

ration policing and prison, and most notably, the promise of avoiding war and killing itself." These false promises matured with the RMA, the so-called revolution in military affairs, which privileged technological superiority and military asymmetry to the degree that it could claim it was "waging war without casualties." A. Gordon, 190.

34. Population Reference Bureau, "Army Recruitment Goals Endangered."

35. Parry and Solomon, "Behind Colin Powell's Legend."

36. C. Young, "Black Ops," 42.

37. M. Gordon, "Fighting in Panama."

38. United States Office of Deputy Assistant Secretary of Defense for Equal Opportunity and Safety Policy, *Black Americans in Defense of Our Nation*, 5.

39. Lubiano, "Like Being Mugged by a Metaphor," 73–74.

40. Singh, "Racial Formation," 285.

41. Singh, 298.

42. Brock and Jealous, "Lessons of September 11.

43. Omi and Winant use Gramscian terms to differentiate between a racial war of maneuver, in which oppressed peoples struggle for territory and autonomy, and a racial war of position, which, "predicated on political struggle," confronts the racial state on institutional and cultural fronts. Omi and Winant, *Racial Formation in the United States*, 81.

44. "Alex: Week 1."

45. Fanon, *Black Skin, White Masks*, 217, 109.

46. Fleetwood, *Troubling Vision*, 23.

47. C. Young, "Black Ops," 49.

48. "Alex: Week 2."

49. For Junaid Rana, the process of racialization after 9/11, when the discourse of counterterror intensified the racialization of Islam, "simply incorporated new forms of racial demonization and policing based in older histories of racism. In this moment, 'the Muslim' emerged as a category of race that was policed through narratives of migration, diaspora, criminality, and terror." Rana, *Terrifying Muslims*, 65–66.

50. For Judith Butler, "grievability is a presupposition for the life that matters." J. Butler, *Frames of War*, 15. Grievability is prescribed by war photography; this is where the state actively shapes "the field of representability" (72) in order to determine whose life can be grieved and, therefore, who is recognizable within the category of the human.

51. On the scenario of discovery as a loose script that "simultaneously constructs the wild object and the viewing subject—producing a 'we' and an 'our' as it produces a 'them,'" see D. Taylor, "Scenarios of Discovery: Reflections on Performance and Ethnography," chapter 2 in *Archive and the Repertoire*.

52. J. Butler, *Frames of War*, 64.

53. J. Butler, 98.

54. J. Butler, 94.

55. For Warren, Blackness is metaphysics' means of objectifying and projecting the terror of nothingness; it thus has function without being. See Warren, *Ontological Terror*.

56. Marriott, *On Black Men*, 212.

57. On precariousness as a generalized condition of the post-9/11 world, see J. Butler, *Frames of War*; J. Butler, *Precarious Life*.

58. C. Young, "Black Ops," 49.

59. K. Thompson, "Unusual 'Treatment.'"

60. For Nicole Fleetwood, the Fanonian moment is a "racial primal scene in which the black subject comes into self-knowing through the traumatic recognition of another's eyes" and is, indeed, "the inaugural moment for writings on black visual culture and studies of race and subjectivity." Fleetwood, *Troubling Vision*, 23.

61. Poole, *Vision, Race, and Modernity*, 15.

62. Wallace, *Constructing the Black Masculine*, 31.

63. Wallace, 139.

64. Melamed, "Spirit of Neoliberalism," 2–3.

65. Melamed, *Represent and Destroy*, 42.

66. United States Office of Deputy Assistant Secretary of Defense for Equal Opportunity and Safety Policy, *Black Americans in Defense of Our Nation*, 2.

67. For Gramsci, Kara Keeling explains, "good sense is that part of common sense that might be elaborated into a conception of the world that is critical and coherent and thus capable of elevating to leadership the collective it consolidates." Keeling, *Witch's Flight*, 22.

68. S. Johnson, *I'm Still Standing*, 1. Subsequent references to this source are cited parenthetically in the text.

69. J. Butler, *Frames of War*, 83.

70. On the noble grunt in US films depicting the Vietnam War, see Sturken, *Tangled Memories*, 102–7. See also Takacs, *Terrorism TV*.

71. Sturken, *Tangled Memories*, 104.

72. Sturken, 106.

73. Mahmood and Hirshkind, "Feminism."

74. Alsultany, *Arabs and Muslims in the Media*.

75. Wanzo, *Suffering Will Not Be Televised*, 41.

76. On the memoir as a form for tracking disillusionment rather than romantic images of war, see Harari, "Martial Illusions."

77. Wanzo, *Suffering Will Not Be Televised*, 4–5.

78. Wanzo, 6, emphasis added.

79. Lubiano, "Imagining Alliances," 447.

80. Finney, "Florissant." My thanks to Carter Mathes for drawing my attention to this arresting work.

81. Singh, *Black Is a Country*, 13.

82. J. Hall, "Long Civil Rights Movement," 1234.

3. "WHAT KIND OF SKEEZA?"

1. I. Young, "Logic of Masculinist Protection," 15.
2. Spillers, of course, uses this term to refer to the "national treasury of rhetorical wealth" that accumulates "layers of attenuated meanings" for Black gender. Spillers, "Mama's Baby, Papa's Maybe," 65.
3. Baraka, *Somebody Blew Up America*, 46.
4. Appy, "Introduction," 3.
5. Importantly, as Lisa Yoneyama points out, to refer to the period after the fall of the Berlin Wall with the temporal marker "post–Cold War" risks a geographic provincialism, as the division of Korea and the fact that Russia and North Korea have not signed full-fledged peace treaties with Japan signals that what "appears to be history's telos . . . might more appropriately be understood as a structural cessation, a moment of rupture in the way we live through the continuing post–World War II / Cold War Order." Still, this was an "epistemic rupture," Appy suggests, and one that Rice helped to engineer. Yoneyama, *Cold War Ruins*, 5.
6. Grewal, *Saving the Security State*, 59.
7. Grewal, 21.
8. Robertson, "Being Condoleezza," 185.
9. Arnott, "In the Ruins of Gadhafi's Lair."
10. McClintock, "Paranoid Empire," 63.
11. Daulatzai, *Black Star, Crescent Moon*, xvi. On the way Black political thought has been shaped by Afro-Arab alliances and the way US domestic and foreign policies have aimed to limit such alliances, see also Lubin, *Geographies of Liberation*.
12. That Blackness functions as "the face of a U.S. empire in a state of permanent war with the Muslim Third World" while retaining its associations with criminality, pathology, and deviant sexuality is evident in the history of jokes and speculations about Rice's love affair with George W. Bush and about her being a lesbian as much as it is betrayed by the August 2011 stories about the raid on Gadaffi's compound. Daulatzai, *Black Star, Crescent Moon*, xiii.
13. Rice, *No Higher Honor*, 703.
14. Weiner, "More Horrendously Creepy Details."
15. Lakoff, "Preparing for the Next Emergency," 252.
16. Massumi, "National Enterprise Emergency," 158.
17. Lakoff, "Preparing for the Next Emergency," 263.
18. Masco, *Theater of Operations*, 37.
19. Massumi, "National Enterprise Emergency," 175.
20. Puar, *Terrorist Assemblages*, 9.
21. Puar, 39.
22. Massumi, "National Enterprise Emergency," 176.
23. In Mbembe's crucial revision of Foucault's theory of biopower, the sovereign divides the population between "those who must live and those who must die," but under conditions of *necropower*, "sovereignty means the capacity to define who

matters and who does not, who is *disposable* and who is not." Mbembe, "Necropolitics," 17, 27.

24. Foucault, *Security, Territory, Population*, 45.
25. Lakoff, "Preparing for the Next Emergency," 254.
26. Massumi, "National Enterprise Emergency," 156.
27. Massumi, 155.
28. Massumi, "Fear," 36.
29. A. Gordon, "Work of Corporate Culture," 3.
30. Kim, *Ends of Empire*, 8.
31. Angelou, *Singin' and Swingin'*, 128.
32. Davies, "Con-Di-Fi-Cation," 395.
33. Edwards, "Tuning into Precious."
34. Ryan and Haslam, "Glass Cliff."
35. Kulich, Ryan, and Haslam, "Political Glass Cliff," 90.
36. Puar and Rai, "Monster, Terrorist, Fag," 122.
37. K. Brown, "All They Understand Is Force," 443.
38. Melamed, *Represent and Destroy*, 42.
39. Cohen, *Boundaries of Blackness*, 69.
40. Cohen, 69.
41. Robinson, *Black Marxism*, 167.
42. Cohen, *Boundaries of Blackness*, 69.
43. Gilroy, *Against Race*, 23.
44. "Opportunities at the CIA," 42.
45. "Opportunities at the CIA," 43.
46. J. Brown, "Human Project," 122.
47. J. Brown, 123–24.
48. Sexton, "Ruse of Engagement," 39.
49. Rice, *Extraordinary, Ordinary People*, 392. Subsequent quotations from this source appear parenthetically in the text.
50. Melamed, *Represent and Destroy*, 19.
51. Lowe, *Intimacies of Four Continents*, 50.
52. Payne and Green, introduction to *Time Longer than Rope*, 1.
53. Payne and Green, 1.
54. Dudziak, *Cold War Civil Rights*, 14.
55. McKinstry and George, *While the World Watched*, 57.
56. Rice, *No Higher Honor*, xvii. Subsequent quotations from this source appear parenthetically in the text.
57. Daulatzai, *Black Star, Crescent Moon*, xviii.
58. Foucault, *Security, Territory, Population*, 19.
59. Foucault, 19, 21.
60. Kim, *Ends of Empire*, 109.
61. L. Thompson, *Beyond the Black Lady*, 7.
62. *Democracy Now!*, "Angela Davis."

63. Holland, *Erotic Life of Racism*, 108.
64. On the massive rise of torture scenes on prime-time network television, see Hajjar, *Torture*.
65. Daulatzai, "To the East, Blackwards," 60.

4. SCENES OF INCORPORATION; OR, PASSING THROUGH

1. Gumbs, *Spill*, 29.
2. Spillers, "Crisis of the Negro Intellectual," 70.
3. Spillers, 70, 67.
4. Spillers, 73.
5. Melamed, *Represent and Destroy*, 15.
6. Jordan, "Life After Lebanon," 80.
7. Springer, *Living for the Revolution*, 21.
8. Lorde, "Age, Race, Sex, and Class," 119.
9. See Threadcraft, *Intimate Justice*, 20.
10. Marshall, *Triangular Road*, 7.
11. Marshall, 7.
12. Three years earlier, the City University of New York had established the SEEK (Search for Elevation, Education, and Knowledge) Program as a bridge program for incoming Black and Puerto Rican students. Jordan taught in the SEEK program alongside Audre Lorde, Barbara Christian, Toni Cade Bambara, Adrienne Rich, and others.
13. Christian, "But What Do We Think We're Doing Anyway," 6.
14. Gates, *Loose Canons*, 92–93.
15. Thorsson, "Sisterhood."
16. I am referring to the minutes of the February and May 1977 meetings contained in June Jordan's Papers. Folder 3, Box 101, June Jordan Papers, 1936–2002, Schlesinger Library, Radcliffe Institute, Harvard University, Cambridge, MA (hereafter cited as Jordan Papers), 10. The 1.4 million figure is what *Ebony* reported in its feature "Backstage" (27).
17. Meeting notes, April 10, 1977, Folder 17, Box 22, Jordan Papers.
18. Proposal written and submitted by VèVè Clark at the April 10, 1977, meeting, Folder 17, Box 22, Jordan Papers.
19. Gumbs writes eloquently of the choices that writers like Lorde, Jordan, and Alexis De Veaux made to express their accountability to their communities "against the norms of capitalism," noting that the consequences of these choices "are part of the narrative that punishes Black women for creating products and processes that exceed and disrupt the narrative that rebirths inequality in economic terms." Gumbs, "We Can Learn to Mother Ourselves," 195–96.
20. Ross, preface to *Revolutionary Mothering*, xiii.
21. Judy, *(Dis)Forming the American Canon*, 17.
22. Writing in 1974 of her teaching at Yale, Jordan writes of her exercises in sartorial excess: "There I encountered every traditional orthodoxy imaginable so that, as a

kind of flamboyant affirmation, rain or shine, I made myself wear high heels. Let the hallowed halls echo to the fact of a woman, a Black woman, passing through!" Jordan, "Notes toward a Black Balancing," 85. I am thinking of the Black woman's passing through as an analogue for the larger movement of passing through that Black studies enacts. See Fred Moten, for example, on the way Black studies invites "another world while passing through this one, graphically disordering the administered scarcity from which Black studies flows as wealth." Moten argues, "The cultivated nature of this situated volatility, this emergent poetics of the emergency in which the poor trouble the proper, is our open secret." Moten, "Black Op," 2.

23. Melamed, *Represent and Destroy*, 35.
24. As Mary Helen Washington wrote in 1974, one important way of breaking the cycle of reacting to negative representations of Black women or "fingering old wounds" was to study the images Black women produce in print. "We have myth- and image-makers of our own. . . . They have moved us another step toward self- definition, toward peoplehood," she wrote. Washington, "Black Women Image Makers," 10–11.
25. Ferguson, *Reorder of Things*, 4, 7.
26. Jordan, "Black Studies."
27. Rooks, *White Money / Black Power*, 66.
28. Bambara, *"Realizing the Dream of a Black University,"* 18.
29. Killens, "Artist and the Black University," 32.
30. Killens, 36.
31. R. Smith, *We Have No Leaders*, 20.
32. Melamed, *Represent and Destroy*, 31.
33. I draw my understanding of the modern university's function as a regulating ap- paratus from Judy, *(Dis)Forming the American Canon*.
34. I am referring here to Stuart Hall's comments on the rapid institutionalization of US cultural studies as a moment of "extraordinarily profound danger." Hall worried that institutionalization put pressure on academics to make critical intel- lectual work financially viable, to produce their work "while looking over their shoulders at the promotions stakes and the publication stakes, and so on." Worse, he noted, the rise of deconstructionist theories of power led to an "overwhelming textualization of cultural studies' own discourses," in which power functioned as a "floating signifier which just leaves the crude exercise and connections of power and culture altogether emptied of any signification." S. Hall, "Cultural Studies," 285–86.
35. Washington, introduction to *Black-Eyed Susans*, xxxii.
36. Hong, *Death beyond Disavowal*, 7.
37. Hong, 23.
38. Rodgers, "The Last M.F.," in *Songs of a Black Bird*, 37.
39. Giovanni, "My House."
40. Christian, "But What Do We Think We're Doing Anyway," 10.

41. The use of "third world" to capture the internationalism of the impulse toward Black women's literary and political autonomy has of course been uneven and fraught. Jordan wrote in her prefatory note to *On Call*, for example, "Given that they were first to exist on the planet and currently make up the majority, the author will refer to that part of the population usually termed Third World as the First World." Jordan, *On Call*, iv. See also D'Souza, "Early Intersections."
42. The statement in *Off Our Backs* was a reaction to Women Against Imperialism, a Bay Area collective that formed in 1981. Beck et al., "What Does Zionism Mean?," 21.
43. Lorde, "Black Women / Jewish Women."
44. B. Smith, introduction to *Home Girls*, xl.
45. B. Smith, xlvi.
46. Feldman, *Shadow over Palestine*, 207, 195.
47. Robolin, *Grounds of Engagement*, 171. See Robolin's larger account of Sisterhood in Support of Sisters in South Africa as part of a larger antiapartheid movement in Black politics and, importantly, as articulating a Black feminist geography that refuses the territoriality of both state and nationalist movements.
48. Higashida, *Black Internationalist Feminism*, 156.
49. Higashida, 162.
50. Moten, "Blackness," 27.
51. See, for example, the well-known issue of the *Black Scholar* titled "The Black Sexism Debate."
52. Khalili, *Time in the Shadows*, 3.
53. Khalili, 47.
54. Melamed, *Represent and Destroy*, 135.
55. Carby, "Multiculture," 223–24.
56. Carby, "Canon," 238–39.
57. Carby, "Multiculture," 222.
58. Carby, "Multicultural Wars," 249.
59. Bambara, "Community."
60. Bambara.
61. Bambara.
62. Wall, "Introduction," 10–11.
63. Bambara, "Gulf."
64. Puar and Rai, "Monster, Terrorist, Fag," 125.
65. Crucially for Chan-Malik, "the lives and labors of Black Muslim women critically underwrite and inform ways of being Muslims among a new generation of U.S. American Muslims, specifically in the ways that Islam has been at once lived as a religious identity, a political stance, and an expression of racial and gendered agency in the twenty-first century." Chan-Malik, *Being Muslim*, 19.
66. Lubiano, "Like Being Mugged by a Metaphor," 73–74.
67. Melamed, *Represent and Destroy*, 159.
68. Melamed, 161.

69. Christian, "But What Do We Think We're Doing Anyway," 18. This essay was first presented at the "Changing Our Own Words" symposium organized by Cheryl A. Wall in 1989, an auspicious moment for taking stock of the rising interest in Black women's work. It is collected in the volume that followed the conference. See Wall, *Changing Our Own Words*.

70. Recall the story hooks tells about a Friday night out with white colleagues in a small college town. Her colleagues are silent when Hooks is assaulted with the word "nigger" but then erupt into raucous laughter when they enter a bakery and "point to a row of gigantic chocolate breasts complete with nipples . . . seeing no connection between this racialized image and the racism expressed in the entry way." Here, the vestibular role of the Black female academic is to triangulate and sanitize white liberal indulgences in the racialized sexual play invited by Black women's performances in popular culture. hooks, *Black Looks*, 61.

71. Guy-Sheftall, "Commitment," 7.

72. Bambara, "Community."

73. Guy-Sheftall, "Commitment," 12–13. Even though Bambara reversed course two years later, revealing to Kay Bonetti that she cared little for the financial promise of the writerly enterprise and wrote *The Salt Eaters* because her short story was simply getting longer and because her editor, Toni Morrison, greatly encouraged her to write it, her earlier sentiments about the labor of writing a novel for a novel-oriented market might help us appreciate the pressures that writers like Bambara faced during this historical juncture. See Bonetti, "Interview with Toni Cade Bambara."

74. Thorsson, "They Could Be Killing Kids Forever!"

75. DuCille, "Occult of True Black Womanhood," 592.

76. DuCille, 597.

77. DuCille, 591.

78. DuCille, "Of Race, Gender, and the Novel," 381.

79. DuCille, 381.

80. DuCille, 385.

81. Bambara, "Lecture."

82. Bambara, "Chosen Weapons," 40.

83. M. J. Alexander, *Pedagogies of Crossing*, 9.

84. Sharpe, *In the Wake*, 20.

85. Toni Cade Bambara to June Jordan, January 1981, MC 513, Folder 12, Box 28, June Jordan Papers, 1936–2002, Schlesinger Library, Radcliffe Institute, Harvard University, Cambridge, MA.

86. Bambara, "Capitalismo."

87. Jordan, "Black Studies," 48–49.

5. PERFECT GRAMMAR

1. Jordan, "White English / Black English," 64.

2. Jordan, 62.

3. Jordan, "Address to the Students of Columbia University," 121.
4. Giovanni, "My House."
5. Marable, *Race, Reform and Rebellion*, 145.
6. Jordan, "White English / Black English," 65.
7. Jordan, foreword to *Civil Wars*, xiv.
8. Jordan, "Poem about Police Violence," 86.
9. See, for example, Gumbs, "We Can Learn to Mother Ourselves"; Gumbs, "Your Mother"; Harb, "Naming Oppressions, Representing Empowerment"; Zahra A. Hussein Ali, "Aesthetics of Memorialization"; Wall, *On Freedom and the Will to Adorn*; Lubin, *Geographies of Liberation*; Camp, *Incarcerating the Crisis*; Feldman, *Shadow over Palestine*. Most recently, Randi Gill-Sadler has argued that Jordan's critique of Black American tourism invites readers to "resist neoliberal seductions of exceptionalism and leisure and reach for new language and genres that reckon with the contradictions and potentials of various Black mobilities." Gill-Sadler, "Confronting Myths," 249.
10. Kinloch, *June Jordan*, 162.
11. June Jordan, *The Issue*, July 1979 (Yaddo), Plays, Folder 2, Box 74, June Jordan Papers, 1936–2002, Schlesinger Library, Radcliffe Institute, Harvard University, Cambridge, MA (hereafter cited as Jordan Papers), 10.
12. Jordan, 38.
13. Jordan, 10 (stage directions for act 2).
14. Kinloch, *June Jordan*, 58–59.
15. This is not to suggest that Jordan was not celebrated or appreciated as a poet in her lifetime. It is rather to suggest that as students of her work, we are still catching up to her enormous output.
16. Handwritten lecture notes, 1974, Folder 12, Box 76, Jordan Papers.
17. K.-Y. Taylor, *From #BlackLivesMatter to Black Liberation*, 54. For an analysis of the way the racialism of the decades before the 1960s laid the groundwork for federal law enforcement policy, resulting in a "vast carceral archipelago," see Murakawa, *First Civil Right*, 127.
18. Ferguson, *Reorder of Things*, 21.
19. Ferguson, 21.
20. Ferguson, 26.
21. Jordan, "In the Valley of the Shadow of Death," 159.
22. Guha, "Prose of Counterinsurgency," 59.
23. Jordan, "White English / Black English," 68.
24. Jordan, "Black Folks and Foreign Policy," 162. In the original draft, Jordan elaborates on the metaphor, writing of her mother and grandmother, who cleaned houses "real good" but "kept their eyes on another house, one that would be as big as the whole world, and as safe as a pair of arms, and full of family come to freedom." Jordan, "Black People and Foreign Policy: Good House Niggers," February 6, 1983, Folder 27, Box 58, Jordan Papers.
25. Haley, *No Mercy Here*, 200.

26. Lathrop, *Yaddo*, 1.
27. E. Ethelbert Miller to June Jordan, June 5, 1979, Folder 9, Box 38, Jordan Papers.
28. June Jordan to Bob Nemiroff, July 22, 1979, Folder 6, Box 21, Jordan Papers.
29. Jordan to Nemiroff.
30. The records of the New York Shakespeare Festival contain the complete cast and production list, along with the final script, for the reading on April 13, 1981. The list includes Jordan as playwright, Shange as director, and Liz Holloway as stage manager. Folders 7 and 8, Box 3-255, New York Shakespeare Festival Records, *T-Mss 1993-028, Billy Rose Theatre Division, New York Public Library for the Performing Arts, New York, NY (hereafter cited as NYSF Records).
31. Ntozake Shange to June Jordan, mailgram, January 8, 1980, Folder 7, Box 43, Jordan Papers.
32. Bernier, *Characters of Blood*, 240. This was, in Bernier's account, a radical reimagining of Black female heroism whose experimental form challenged "straightforward memorializations" of Black activism (242).
33. Jordan, "Notes toward a Black Balancing," 163.
34. In a letter to Jordan, stage manager Liz Holloway describes this production as "fabulous and easily the best mobile Joe Papp [director of NYSF] has ever sent out." Liz Holloway to June Jordan, July 21, [1979], Folder 7, Box 23, Jordan Papers.
35. Letters from both E. Ethelbert Miller and Ntozake Shange in the June Jordan Papers referred to the December 8 reading: Ntozake Shange to June Jordan, postcard, December 1980, Folder 7, Box 43; E. Ethelbert Miller to Jordan, December 1, 1980, Folder 10, Box 38. Subsequent correspondence suggests that it was postponed: Miller asks two months later, for example, "What's going on with your play?" Miller to Jordan, February 5, 1981, Folder 11, Box 38, Jordan Papers.
36. See Folder 21, Box 2-33, NYSF Records.
37. Jordan's October 3, 1981, cover letter to Gail Merrifield noted all of the changes in the rewrite she had attached. The NYSF play report, written by Bill Hart and dated August 1981, lists some of the play's virtues but notes that it seemed too "simplified and broken down." Hart lamented, "We do not sufficiently experience [Lloyd Brown's] decisiveness and courage because it's not adequately tested for us theatrically. Also, the consequences are not heroically or tragically inevitable here and it's like we're going to have to see the movie to find out what happens to him." Folder 21, Box 2-33, NYSF Records.
38. Unless otherwise noted, all of the page numbers subsequently cited parenthetically in the text refer to the final script archived by the NYSF, with the most recent revisions dated April 12, 1981. Folder 7, Box 2-33, NYSF Records.
39. Jordan, "In the Valley of the Shadow of Death," 152.
40. June Jordan, "*The Issue*: Notes on Conference with Thulani 4/26/81," Folder 6, Box 74, Jordan Papers.
41. Jordan.
42. Jordan.

43. June Jordan, *The Issue—*A Play in Two Acts, October 1979, Plays, Folder 4, Box 74, Jordan Papers, 13.

44. Singh, *Race and America's Long War*, 129.

45. Singh, 63.

46. Jordan, "Problems of Language in a Democratic State," 34.

47. Jordan, *The Issue*, July 1979 (Yaddo), n.p. (act 1, scene 2).

48. Jordan, 21.

49. I am drawing on Kevin Quashie's illuminating discussion of Black culture and politics, where he defines quiet as "the full range of one's inner life." Quashie, *Sovereignty of Quiet*, 6.

50. Jordan, "*The Issue*: Notes on Conference with Thulani 4/26/81."

51. Jordan, *The Issue*, July 1979 (Yaddo), n.p. (act 2, scene 1).

52. Jordan, *Soldier*, 66. See pp. 64–70 for Jordan's account of her father's instruction.

53. Jordan, "White English / Black English," 6.

54. The same day of the protest at the Seventy-Ninth Precinct station in Brooklyn, for example, the Black United Front staged a demonstration at the Israeli consulate. As Rev. Herbert Daughtry stood at the microphone, an activist held a sign reminding demonstrators, "ZIONISM=RACISM," with a line below reading, "declared the united nations." King, "Black Unit, PLO Align."

55. June Jordan, notes, August 27, 1979, Folder 1, Box 59, Jordan Papers.

56. June Jordan, "Black Power and the Police," August 31, 1979, Folder 1, Box 59, Jordan Papers.

57. Jordan.

58. Memo to Robert Knight, WBAI News Dept., September 8, 1979, Folder 1, Box 59, Jordan Papers.

59. June Jordan, Gwendolen Hardwick, Alexis De Veaux, Jill Nelson, Stanley Kinard, and Amiri Baraka, "Unprecedented Police Riot in Brooklyn: A Collective Testimony," Folder 1, Box 59, Jordan Papers.

60. Jordan et al.

61. Jordan et al.

62. Daly, Perez, and Sutton, "1,000 Protest Killing of Baez," 5.

63. Jordan, *The Issue—*A Play in Two Acts, October 1979, n.p. (prologue).

64. June Jordan to the editors of *Chrysalis*, September 10, 1979, copied to Audre Lorde, Adrienne Rich, Alexis De Veaux, Gwendolyn Hardwick, Patricia Jones, and Barbara Smith, Folder 6, Box 21, Jordan Papers.

65. Gumbs, "Your Mother."

66. Lorde had written to Jordan on September 4, enclosing a copy of her letter of resignation and telling Jordan, "The magazine's position concerning the work and struggle of Black and Third World Women has deteriorated steadily." Audre Lorde to June Jordan, September 4, 1979, Folder 9, Box 36, Jordan Papers.

67. Jordan, foreword to *Civil Wars*, xiii.

68. Gwendolen Hardwick to June Jordan, July 1982, Folder 4, Box 34, Jordan Papers.

69. I am moved by Calvin Warren's definition of Black care as code: a "network of strategies and practices entailing the circulation, communication, and sharing of the non-sense hieroglyphic," as an "essential practice of attentiveness" whose aim it is to "provide form and send it forth." Warren, "Black Care," 45.

70. Zahra A. Hussein Ali, "Aesthetics of Memorialization"; Harb, "Naming Oppressions, Representing Empowerment"; Feldman, *Shadow over Palestine*; Gill-Sadler, "Diasporic Dissonance."

71. Barbara Harlow uses the term "resistance literature" to describe the writing produced in the context of anticolonial resistance movements. Resistance poets rewrite national history; they have a "historicity of their own and a claim to an autonomous, self-determining role on the contemporary staging grounds of history." Harlow, *Resistance Literature*, 33.

72. M. Jones, "June Jordan's Primer for Looking."

73. Jordan, "In the Valley of the Shadow of Death," 159.

74. Klein, *Shock Doctrine*, 170.

75. Jordan, "Address to the Students of Columbia University," 121.

76. Feldman, *Shadow over Palestine*, 208.

77. Grandin, *Empire's Workshop*, 15.

78. Grandin, 6.

79. Jordan, "Nicaragua," *On Call*, 65.

80. Headed by Idaho senator Frank Church, the Senate Select Committee to Study Governmental Operations with Respect to Intelligence Activities—known subsequently as the Church Committee—investigated the US intelligence communities. Established by Church to investigate the 1973 assassination of Chilean president Salvador Allende, it sought to balance intelligence and security needs. It led to the 1977 Foreign Intelligence Surveillance Act prohibiting the warrantless government surveillance of US citizens, including the use of wiretaps.

81. Grandin, *Empire's Workshop*, 117.

82. Spillers, "Mama's Baby, Papa's Maybe," 65.

83. Reagan Library, "President Reagan's State of the Union Address."

84. Spillers, "Mama's Baby, Papa's Maybe," 65. For Spillers, *cultural vestibularity* is the place of the broken Black flesh that serves as the entry point into the settler-slave colony of North America. Importantly, writing of the enslaved female who bears offspring, Spillers is careful to note that the "matriarchy" that so repulsed Moynihan and his colleagues "actually *misnames* the power of the female regarding the enslaved community": first because the enslaved female had no claim as a parent and second because "'motherhood' is not perceived in the prevailing social climate as a legitimate procedure of cultural inheritance" (78). My point here is to call attention to Hale as a *not*-mother who is *not* mothering, both because to be a mother mothering would be impossible in the symbolics of Reagan's speech and the larger field on which it took place and because Reagan praises Hale for being the antidote to the stereotypes of illegitimate Black female parenting that he perpetuated (when, for example, he coined the term "welfare queen").

85. Reagan Library, "President Reagan's State of the Union Address."
86. Grandin, *Empire's Workshop*, 82.
87. Jordan, "Life After Lebanon," 79.
88. Jordan, 79.
89. Jordan, "Civil Wars," 183.
90. Jordan, "Life After Lebanon," 80.
91. Jordan, 77.
92. Jordan, 78, emphasis added.
93. Jordan, "Problems of Language in a Democratic State," 31.
94. Jordan, 36.
95. Jordan, "Poem for Nicaragua," 25–26. All subsequent quotations from the poem refer to this source.
96. Harlow, *Resistance Literature*, 73.
97. Jordan, "For the Sake of People's Poetry," 14.
98. June Jordan to Cheryll Greene, May 24, 1983, Folder 10, Box 21, Jordan Papers.
99. Gumbs, "Spelling Soul," 136.
100. Thorsson, "Sisterhood."
101. June Jordan to Cheryll Greene, October 13, 1983, with a 3:45 a.m. time stamp, Folder 10. Box 21, Jordan Papers.
102. Jordan, "Black Power on Nicaragua," 24.
103. Jordan, introduction to *On Call*, 2.
104. Jordan, 1, 3.
105. Jordan, "Nicaragua," *On Call*, 65.
106. Jordan, 78.
107. Jordan, 72.
108. Jordan, 73.
109. Jordan, 74, 75.
110. Jordan, "Safe," 32.
111. "Nicaragua Reports Rebel Defeat," A8.
112. Zahra A. Hussein Ali, "Aesthetics of Memorialization," 616.
113. Jordan, "First Poem from Nicaragua Libre," 27–28. All subsequent quotations from the poem refer to this source.
114. J. Butler, *Frames of War*, 7.
115. Zahra A. Hussein Ali, "Aesthetics of Memorialization," 613.
116. Jordan, "From Nicaragua Libre," 30. All subsequent quotations from the poem refer to this source.
117. Zahra A. Hussein Ali, "Aesthetics of Memorialization," 617.
118. McKittrick, *Demonic Grounds*, xxiii.
119. McKittrick.
120. Jordan, "Fourth Poem from Nicaragua Libre," 31. All subsequent quotations from the poem refer to this source.
121. Jordan, "Nicaragua," *On Call*, 65.
122. Feldman, *Shadow over Palestine*, 216.

123. Jordan, "Life After Lebanon," 82.
124. Etel Adnan to June Jordan, March 25, [1985], Folder 8, Box 28, Jordan Papers.
125. Jordan, "Address to the Students of Columbia University," 121.
126. Christian, "Race for Theory," 62.

6. "HOW VERY AMERICAN"

1. Finney, "Plunder," 25, 31, 23.
2. Randall, *Rebel Yell*, 84.
3. This is a reference to Gwendolyn Brooks's description of the monied men at the Foxy Cats Club in her 1953 novel *Maud Martha*, the "good-looking" "government men" that were "rich and suave" (80).
4. Lowe, *Intimacies of Four Continents*, 18. On intimacy and possessive individualism, see Berlant, *Intimacy*. On intimacy as the conditions of violation and confinement "refused and/or transmitted from one generation to the next" among postslavery subjects, see Sharpe, *Monstrous Intimacies*, 3.
5. McClintock, "Paranoid Empire," 51.
6. Crawford, *Black Post-Blackness*; Shockley, *Renegade Poetics*; Avilez, *Radical Aesthetics*; M. Jones, "String of Grace"; Mathes, *Imagine the Sound*.
7. For a sample of the many significant works in which these terms circulate, see George, *Buppies, B-Boys, Baps & Bohos*; Elam and Jones, *Methuen Drama Book of Post-Black Plays*; Neal, *Soul Babies*; Kim et al., *Freestyle*; Crawford, *Black Post-Blackness*.
8. S. Hall, "What Is This 'Black' in Black Popular Culture?," 32.
9. Copeland, *Bound to Appear*, 71.
10. Neal, *Soul Babies*, 3.
11. Golden, introduction to *Freestyle*, 14.
12. K. Young, *Grey Album*, 283.
13. Ashe, "Theorizing the Post-Soul Aesthetic," 611.
14. Shockley, *New Black*, 11–12.
15. Gray, "Subject(ed) to Recognition," 774.
16. Thomas, *Man Gone Down*, 110.
17. Staples, "Myth of the Impotent Black Male."
18. Domini, "Roots and Racism," 20. Quoted in B. Smith, "Toward a Black Feminist Criticism," 136.
19. Streitfeld, "Author Toni Morrison Wins Nobel Prize."
20. Anker, "Allegories of Falling and the 9/11 Novel," 464.
21. Randall, *Rebel Yell*, 62. Subsequent references to this source are cited parenthetically in the text.
22. Sexton, "Ruse," 39.
23. E. Jones, *Known World*; "Garden Party"; Charles Johnson, *Dreamer*.
24. Puar, *Terrorist Assemblages*, 39.
25. J. Butler, *Frames of War*, 126.
26. McClintock, "Paranoid Empire," 69.
27. Levy-Hussen, *How to Read African American Literature*, 124.

28. Levy-Hussen, 101.
29. McClintock, "Paranoid Empire," 51.
30. Wall, *Worrying the Line*, 9, 13.
31. C. Young, "Black Ops," 54, 56.
32. Harney and Moten, *Undercommons*, 17.
33. Foster, "Struggle Continues," 134.
34. Rushin, "Bridge Poem," *This Bridge Called My Back*, xxi–xxii. All subsequent quotations from the poem refer to this edition. When Rushin published "The Bridge Poem" in her own collection, she heightened the enjambment to mimic the translator's running out of breath: "Sick / Of having / To remind you / To breathe / Before you / Suffocate / Your own / Fool self." Rushin, "Bridge Poem," *Black Back-Ups*, 33–35.
35. Beal, "Double Jeopardy," 109–22.
36. Evans, "Virgins," 5. Subsequent quotations from the story are cited parenthetically in the text.
37. Evans, "Snakes," 51.
38. Evans, "Someone Ought to Tell Her There's Nowhere to Go," 107. Subsequent quotations from the story are cited parenthetically in the text.
39. Morrison, *Home*, 133.
40. Lubiano, "Imagining Alliances," 448.
41. Shange, *for colored girls* (1997), 55.
42. Knight, "Can You Kill," 128.
43. Shange, *for colored girls* (2010), 81.
44. Colbert, "A Woman's Trip: Domestic Violence and Black Feminist Healing in Ntozake Shange's for Colored Girls," 240.
45. Kim, *Ends of Empire*, 109.
46. Massumi, *Ontopower*, 12.
47. A. Gordon, *Hawthorn Archive*, 27.
48. Du Bois of course refers to "double-consciousness" as the definitive condition of the modern American Negro. "One ever feels his two-ness," he writes, "an American, a Negro: two souls, two thoughts, two unreconciled strivings" Du Bois, *Souls of Black Folk*, 3.
49. Gayles, *No Crystal Stair*, 128, 117.
50. Quashie, *Sovereignty of Quiet*, 6.
51. Goldstein, "Talk with Gloria Naylor," 4.
52. On the Black feminist adaptation, see Edwards, "Tuning into Precious."
53. Giovanni and Naylor, "Conversation," 1404.
54. Gloria Naylor to Julia Alvarez, April 3, 2001, Folder 1, Box 40, Gloria Naylor Archive, Sacred Heart University Library, Fairfield, CT.
55. Edwards and Harris, "Gloria Naylor's 'Sapphira Wade.'"
56. Giovanni and Naylor, "Conversation," 1398.
57. Naylor's correspondence suggests that she had left by June 30. Gloria Naylor, "Personal Correspondence," June 30, 1996, Box 7, Gloria Naylor Archive, Sacred Heart

University Library, Fairfield, CT; Felton and Loris, "Human Spirit Is a Kick-Ass Thing," 150.

58. Naylor to Alvarez, April 3, 2001.

59. Naber, *Arab America*, 40.

60. Naylor, *1996*, 3. Subsequent quotations from the novel are cited parenthetically in the text.

61. Montgomery, *Fiction of Gloria Naylor*, xxi.

62. For GerShun Avilez, the novel's representations of Naylor's gendered work also critique the gendered prescriptions of Black nationalism. See Avilez, *Radical Aesthetics*.

63. Raynaud, "Hearing Voices," 143.

64. Raynaud, 157.

65. Michael to Gloria Naylor, June 30, 1996; Gloria to Gloria Naylor, August 7, 1996; and Rona Reynolds, Catherine C. Flowers, and T to Gloria Naylor, May 29, 1996, all in Folder 16, Box 7, Gloria Naylor Archive, Sacred Heart University Library, Fairfield, CT.

66. National Public Radio, "1996."

67. Walker, *In Search of Our Mothers' Gardens*.

68. Browne, *Dark Matters*, 21.

69. Indeed, John Jackson mentions *1996* in a catalogue of racial paranoia, noting that Naylor is "hardly the only prominent African American famous for linking paranoia and race." Jackson, *Racial Paranoia*, 105.

AFTERWORD

1. Shange, *for colored girls* (1997), 4.

2. Shange's lady in yellow confesses that "bein alive & bein a woman & bein colored is a metaphysical / dilemma/I havent conquered yet." But the defiant, improvisatory performance of this impossible ontology begins earlier, when the ladies situate themselves outside ("outside chicago," "outside detroit," and so on). Shange, 45, 5.

3. June Jordan, "Black People and Foreign Policy: Good House Niggers," February 6, 1983, Folder 27, Box 58, June Jordan Papers, Schlesinger Library, Radcliffe Institute, Harvard University, Cambridge, MA.

BIBLIOGRAPHY

Adelman, Ken. "Cakewalk in Iraq." *Washington Post*, February 13, 2002. www.washingtonpost.com.

Alexander, M. Jacqui. *Pedagogies of Crossing: Meditations on Feminism, Sexual Politics, Memory, and the Sacred*. Perverse Modernities. Durham, NC: Duke University Press, 2005.

Alexander, Michelle. *The New Jim Crow*. New York: New Press, 2012.

"Alex: Week 1." *In Treatment*. HBO Video, January 29, 2008.

"Alex: Week 2." *In Treatment*. HBO Video, February 5, 2008.

Ali, Zahra. *Women and Gender in Iraq: Between Nation-Building and Fragmentation*. Cambridge: Cambridge University Press, 2018.

Ali, Zahra A. Hussein. "Aesthetics of Memorialization: The Sabra and Shatila Genocide in the Work of Sami Mohammad, Jean Genet, and June Jordan." *Criticism* 51, no. 4 (2009): 589–621.

Alsultany, Evelyn. *Arabs and Muslims in the Media: Race and Representation after 9/11*. Critical Cultural Communication. New York: NYU Press, 2012.

Amar, Paul. *The Security Archipelago: Human-Security States, Sexuality Politics, and the End of Neoliberalism*. Social Text Books. Durham, NC: Duke University Press, 2013.

Anderson, Carol. *Eyes off the Prize: The United Nations and the African American Struggle for Human Rights, 1944–1955*. Cambridge: Cambridge University Press, 2003.

Angelou, Maya. *Singin' and Swingin' and Gettin' Merry like Christmas*. New York: Bantam, 1977.

Anker, Elizabeth. "Allegories of Falling and the 9/11 Novel." *American Literary History* 23, no. 3 (2011): 463–82.

Antoon, Sinan. *The Corpse Washer*. New Haven, CT: Yale University Press, 2013.

Anzaldúa, Gloria, and Cherríe Moraga, eds. *This Bridge Called My Back: Writings by Radical Women of Color*. Watertown, MA: Persephone, 1981.

AP News. "U.S. Service Casualties in Gulf War." April 4, 1991. https://apnews.com.

Appy, Christian G. "Introduction: Struggling for the World." In *Cold War Constructions: The Political Culture of United States Imperialism, 1945–1966*, edited by Christian G. Appy, 1–8. Amherst: University of Massachusetts Press, 2000.

Arnott, David. "In the Ruins of Gadhafi's Lair, Rebels Find Album Filled with Photos of His 'Darling' Condoleezza Rice." NBC News, January 2, 2014. http://photoblog.nbcnews.com.

Ashe, Bertram. "Theorizing the Post-Soul Aesthetic: An Introduction." *African American Review* 41, no. 4 (2007): 609–23.

Atanasoski, Neda. *Humanitarian Violence: The U.S. Deployment of Diversity*. Difference Incorporated. Minneapolis: University of Minnesota Press, 2013.

Avilez, GerShun. *Radical Aesthetics and Modern Black Nationalism*. Urbana: University of Illinois Press, 2016.

"Backstage." *Ebony*, May 1977.

Bambara, Toni Cade. "Capitalismo." Box 3, Toni Cade Bambara Papers, Spelman College Archives, n.d.

———. "Chosen Weapons: June Jordan's 'Civil Wars.'" *Ms.* 9, no. 10 (1981): 40.

———. "Community." Box 3, Toni Cade Bambara Papers, Spelman College Archives, n.d.

———. "From *The Vietnam Notebooks*." In *Savoring the Salt: The Legacy of Toni Cade Bambara*, edited by Linda Janet Holmes and Cheryl A. Wall, 105–7. Philadelphia: Temple University Press, 2007.

———. "Gulf." Box 3, Toni Cade Bambara Papers, Spelman College Archives, n.d.

———. "Lecture: Loving/Hating Black Women Writers: Sexual Politics and the Black Community (c. 1988)." Box 4, Toni Cade Bambara Papers, Spelman College Archives, n.d.

———. *"Realizing the Dream of a Black University" & Other Writings, Part I*. Lost and Found, The CUNY Poetics Document Initiative; Ser. 7, No. 2. New York: Center for the Humanities, the Graduate Center, The City University of New York, 2017.

———. *The Salt Eaters*. Vintage Contemporaries. New York: Vintage Books, 1992.

Baraka, Amiri. *Selected Poetry of Amiri Baraka / LeRoi Jones*. New York: Morrow, 1979.

———. *Somebody Blew Up America and Other Poems*. St. Martin, Caribbean: House of Nehesi, 2003.

Bayoumi, Moustafa. *This Muslim American Life: Dispatches from the War on Terror*. New York: NYU Press, 2015.

Beal, Frances. "Double Jeopardy: To Be Black and Female." In *The Black Woman: An Anthology*, edited by Toni Cade Bambara, 109–22. New York: Washington Square Press, 2005.

Beck, Evelyn T., Nancy K. Bereano, Gloria Z. Greenfield, Melanie Kaye, Irena Klepfisz, Bernice Mennis, and Adrienne Rich. ". . . What Does Zionism Mean?" *Off Our Backs* 12, no. 7 (1982): 21.

Berlant, Lauren. *Intimacy*. Chicago: University of Chicago Press, 2000.

Bernier, Celeste-Marie. *Characters of Blood: Black Heroism in the Transatlantic Imagination*. Charlottesville: University of Virginia Press, 2012.

Best, Stephen Michael. *None like Us: Blackness, Belonging, Aesthetic Life*. Theory Q. Durham, NC: Duke University Press, 2018.

"Black Sexism Debate, The." Special issue, *Black Scholar* 10, nos. 8–9 (1979).

Blain, Keisha N. *Set the World on Fire: Black Nationalist Women and the Global Struggle for Freedom*. Philadelphia: University of Pennsylvania Press, 2018.

Blain, Keisha N., and Tiffany Gill. *To Turn the Whole World Over: Black Women and Internationalism*. Urbana: University of Illinois Press, 2019.

Bliss, James. "Black Feminism Out of Place." *Signs: Journal of Women in Culture and Society* 41, no. 4 (2016): 727–49. https://doi.org/10.1086/685477.

Bonetti, Kay. "An Interview with Toni Cade Bambara." In *Conversations with Toni Cade Bambara*, 30–48. Literary Conversations Series. Jackson: University Press of Mississippi, 2012.

Borstelmann, Thomas. *The Cold War and the Color Line: American Race Relations in the Global Arena*. Cambridge, MA: Harvard University Press, 2001.

Brock, Roslyn, and Benjamin Jealous. "The Lessons of September 11." NAACP, September 11, 2011. www.naacp.org.

Brooks, Daphne. *Bodies in Dissent: Spectacular Performances of Race and Freedom, 1850–1910*. Durham, NC: Duke University Press, 2006.

Brooks, Gwendolyn. *Maud Martha*. Chicago: Third World, 1993.

———. *Maud Martha, a Novel*. New York: Harper, 1953.

Brown, Jayna. "The Human Project." *Transition*, no. 110 (2013): 121–35. https://doi.org/10.2979/transition.110.121.

Brown, Keith. "'All They Understand Is Force': Debating Culture in Operation Iraqi Freedom." *American Anthropologist* 110, no. 4 (2008): 443–53. https://doi.org/10.1111/j.1548-1433.2008.00077.x.

Browne, Simone. *Dark Matters: On the Surveillance of Blackness*. Durham, NC: Duke University Press, 2015.

Bsheer, Rosie. "A Counter-revolutionary State: Popular Movements and the Making of Saudi Arabia." *Past & Present* 238, no. 1 (February 1, 2018): 233–77. https://doi.org/10.1093/pastj/gtx057.

Bukhari, Safiya. *The War Before: The True Life Story of Becoming a Black Panther, Keeping the Faith in Prison and Fighting for Those Left Behind*. New York: Feminist Press at the City University of New York, 2010.

Bush, George W. "Address to the Nation from Atlanta on Homeland Security." Atlanta, GA, November 8, 2001. *Public Papers of the President of the United States: George W. Bush (2001, Book II)*. Accessed December 18, 2017. www.govinfo.gov.

Butler, Judith. *Frames of War: When Is Life Grievable?* London: Verso, 2009.

———. *Precarious Life: The Powers of Mourning and Violence*. London: Verso, 2004.

Butler, Octavia E. *Parable of the Sower*. New York: Four Walls Eight Windows, 1993.

———. *Parable of the Talents*. New York: Seven Stories, 1998.

Byrne, Malcolm. *Iran-Contra: Reagan's Scandal and the Unchecked Abuse of Presidential Power*. Lawrence: University Press of Kansas, 2014.

Cainkar, Louise. *Homeland Insecurity: The Arab American and Muslim American Experience after 9/11*. New York: Russell Sage Foundation, 2009.

Camp, Jordan T. *Incarcerating the Crisis: Freedom Struggles and the Rise of the Neoliberal State*. Oakland: University of California Press, 2016.

Camp, Jordan T., and Christina Heatherton. *Policing the Planet: Why the Policing Crisis Led to Black Lives Matter*. London: Verso, 2016.

Carby, Hazel V. "The Canon: Civil War and Reconstruction." In *Cultures in Babylon*, 237–44. London: Verso, 1999.

———. "Multiculture." In *Cultures in Babylon*, 219–29. London: Verso, 1999.

———. "The Multicultural Wars, Part One." In *Cultures in Babylon*, 245–55. London: Verso, 1999.

Carolan, Mary Ann McDonald. *The Transatlantic Gaze: Italian Cinema, American Film*. Albany: SUNY Press, 2014.

Chan-Malik, Sylvia. *Being Muslim: A Cultural History of Women of Color in American Islam*. New York: NYU Press, 2018.

Chiles, Nick. "Their Eyes Were Reading Smut." *New York Times*, January 4, 2006. www.nytimes.com.

Christian, Barbara. "But What Do We Think We're Doing Anyway: The State of Black Feminist Criticism(s) or My Version of a Little Bit of History (1989)." In *New Black Feminist Criticism, 1985–2000*, edited by Gloria Bowles, M. Giulia Fabi, and Arlene Keizer, 5–19. Urbana: University of Illinois Press, 2007.

———. "The Race for Theory." *Cultural Critique* 6 (Spring 1987): 51–63.

Churchill, Ward. "'To Disrupt, Discredit and Destroy': The FBI's Secret War against the Black Panther Party." In *Liberation, Imagination, and the Black Panther Party: A New Look at the Panthers and Their Legacy*, edited by Kathleen Cleaver and George Katsiaficas, 78–116. New York: Routledge, 2001.

Cohen, Cathy J. *The Boundaries of Blackness: AIDS and the Breakdown of Black Politics*. Chicago: University of Chicago Press, 1999.

Colbert, Soyica Diggs. "A Woman's Trip: Domestic Violence and Black Feminist Healing in Ntozake Shange's for Colored Girls." In *Black Cultural Production after Civil Rights*, edited by Robert J. Patterson, 225–47. Urbana: University of Illinois Press, 2019.

Cooper, Brittney C. *Beyond Respectability: The Intellectual Thought of Race Women*. Women, Gender, and Sexuality in American History. Urbana: University of Illinois Press, 2017.

Copeland, Huey. *Bound to Appear: Art, Slavery, and the Site of Blackness in Multicultural America*. Chicago: University of Chicago Press, 2013.

Crawford, Margo Natalie. *Black Post-Blackness: The Black Arts Movement and Twenty-First-Century Aesthetics*. New Black Studies Series. Urbana: University of Illinois Press, 2017.

Cripps, Thomas, and David Culbert. "'The Negro Soldier' (1944): Film Propaganda in Black and White." *American Quarterly* 31, no. 5 (1979): 616–40.

Crozier, Michel, Samuel P. Huntington, and Jōji Watanuki. *The Crisis of Democracy: Report on the Governability of Democracies to the Trilateral Commission*. Triangle Papers 8. New York: NYU Press, 1975.

Cunningham, David. *There's Something Happening Here: The New Left, the Klan, and FBI Counterintelligence*. Berkeley: University of California Press, 2004.

Daly, Michael, Miguel Perez, and Larry Sutton. "1,000 Protest Killing of Baez; 5 Seized; 5 Cops Hurt in Bed-Stuy." *New York Daily News*, August 28, 1979.

Daulatzai, Sohail. *Black Star, Crescent Moon: The Muslim International and Black Freedom beyond America*. Minneapolis: University of Minnesota Press, 2012.

———. "Protect Ya Neck: Muslims and the Carceral Imagination in the Age of Guantánamo." *Souls* 9, no. 2 (March 2011): 132–47.

———. "To the East, Blackwards: Bandung Hopes, Diasporic Dreams, and Black/ Muslim Encounters in Sam Greenlee's *Baghdad Blues*." *Souls* 8, no. 4 (December 1, 2006): 59–74. https://doi.org/10.1080/10999940601057358.

Davies, Carole Boyce. "'Con-Di-Fi-Cation': Black Women, Leadership, and Political Power." In *Still Brave: The Evolution of Black Women's Studies*, edited by Stanlie M. James, Frances Smith Foster, and Beverly Guy-Sheftall, 392–412. New York: Feminist Press, 2009.

Davis, Angela Y. *Abolition Democracy: Beyond Empire, Prisons, and Torture*. New York: Seven Stories, 2005.

———. *Angela Davis—an Autobiography*. New York: Random House, 1974.

———. "Reflections on the Black Woman's Role in the Community of Slaves." *Massachusetts Review* 13, nos. 1–2 (1972): 81–100.

Dayan, Colin. *The Law Is a White Dog: How Legal Rituals Make and Unmake Persons*. Princeton, NJ: Princeton University Press, 2011.

Democracy Now! "Angela Davis: We Owe It to People Who Came before Us to Fight to Abolish Prisons." Accessed July 6, 2020. www.democracynow.org.

Dillon, Stephen. *Fugitive Life: The Queer Politics of the Prison State*. Durham, NC: Duke University Press, 2018.

Domini, John. "Roots and Racism: An Interview with Ishmael Reed." *Boston Phoenix*, April 5, 1977, 20.

D'Souza, Aruna. "Early Intersections: The Work of Third World Feminism." In *We Wanted a Revolution: Black Radical Women, 1965–85, New Perspectives*, edited by Catherine Morris and Rujeko Hockley, 73–95. Brooklyn, NY: Brooklyn Museum, 2018.

Du Bois, W. E. B. *The Souls of Black Folk*. Chicago: McClurg, 1903.

DuCille, Ann. "The Occult of True Black Womanhood: Critical Demeanor and Black Feminist Studies." *Signs* 19, no. 3 (1994): 591–629. https://doi.org/10.1086/494914.

———. "Of Race, Gender, and the Novel; or, Where in the World Is Toni Morrison?" *Novel* 50, no. 3 (November 1, 2017): 375–87. https://doi.org/10.1215/00295132-4194984.

Dudziak, Mary L. *Cold War Civil Rights: Race and the Image of American Democracy*. Politics and Society in Twentieth-Century America. Princeton, NJ: Princeton University Press, 2000.

Edwards, Erica R. *Charisma and the Fictions of Black Leadership*. Difference Incorporated. Minneapolis: University of Minnesota Press, 2012.

———. "Sex after the Black Normal." *Differences* 26, no. 1 (2015): 141–67. https://doi.org/10.1215/10407391-2880636.

———. "Tuning into Precious: The Black Women's Empowerment Adaptation and the Interruptions of the Absurd." *Black Camera* 4, no. 1 (2012): 74–95. https://doi.org/10.2979/blackcamera.4.1.74.

Edwards, Suzanne M., and Trudier Harris. "Gloria Naylor's 'Sapphira Wade': An Unfinished Manuscript from the Archive." *African American Review* 52, no. 4 (Winter 2019): 323–40.

Elam, Harry Justin, and Douglas A. Jones, eds. *The Methuen Drama Book of Post-Black Plays.* London: Methuen Drama, 2012.

El Hamel, Chouki. *Black Morocco: A History of Slavery, Race, and Islam.* African Studies. New York: Cambridge University Press, 2013.

Ellis, Trey. "The New Black Aesthetic." *Callaloo* 12, no. 1 (Winter 1989): 233–43.

———. *Platitudes.* Boston: Northeastern University Press, 2003.

Evans, Danielle. "Snakes." In *Before You Suffocate Your Own Fool Self*, 27–64. New York: Riverhead Books, 2010.

———. "Someone Ought to Tell Her There's Nowhere to Go." In *Before You Suffocate Your Own Fool Self*, 87–112. New York: Riverhead Books, 2010.

———. "Virgins." In *Before You Suffocate Your Own Fool Self*, 1–26. New York: Riverhead Books, 2010.

Everett, Percival. *Erasure.* Minneapolis: Graywolf, 2011.

Falcón, Sylvanna M. *Power Interrupted: Antiracist and Feminist Activism inside the United Nations.* Seattle: University of Washington Press, 2016.

Fanon, Frantz. *Black Skin, White Masks.* New York: Grove, 1991.

Feldman, Keith P. *A Shadow over Palestine: The Imperial Life of Race in America.* Minneapolis: University of Minnesota Press, 2015.

Felton, Sharon, and Michelle C. Loris. "The Human Spirit Is a Kick-Ass Thing." In *Conversations with Gloria Naylor*, edited by Maxine Lavon Montgomery, 138–50. Jackson: University Press of Mississippi, 2004.

Ferguson, Roderick A. *Aberrations in Black: Toward a Queer of Color Critique.* Minneapolis: University of Minnesota Press, 2004.

———. *The Reorder of Things: The University and Its Pedagogies of Minority Difference.* Difference Incorporated. Minneapolis: University of Minnesota Press, 2012.

Finney, Nikky. "Florissant." Response Systems Panel, January 7, 2014, https://responsesystemspanel.whs.mil.

———. "Plunder." In *Head Off & Split: Poems*, 23–32. Evanston, IL: TriQuarterly Books / Northwestern University Press, 2011.

Fleetwood, Nicole R. *Troubling Vision: Performance, Visuality, and Blackness.* Chicago: University of Chicago Press, 2011.

Foster, Frances Smith. "The Struggle Continues." *Callaloo* 18 (1981): 132–34.

Foucault, Michel. *Security, Territory, Population: Lectures at the Collège de France, 1977—78.* New York: Springer, 2007.

Freeburg, Christopher. *Black Aesthetics and the Interior Life.* Charlottesville: University of Virginia Press, 2017.

"Garden Party, The." *The Boondocks.* Cartoon Network, November 6, 2005.

Gates, Henry Louis, Jr. *Loose Canons: Notes on the Culture Wars.* New York: Oxford University Press, 1993.

Gayles, Gloria Jean Wade. *No Crystal Stair: Visions of Race and Sex in Black Women's Fiction*. New York: Pilgrim, 1984. http://archive.org/details/ nocrystalstairviooogayl.

Gelvin, James L. *The Modern Middle East: A History*. 4th ed. Oxford: Oxford University Press, 2015.

George, Nelson. *Buppies, B-Boys, Baps & Bohos: Notes on Post-Soul Black Culture*. New York: HarperCollins, 1992.

Giddings, Paula. *Ida: A Sword among Lions: Ida B. Wells and the Campaign against Lynching*. New York: Amistad, 2008.

Gill-Sadler, Randi K. "Confronting Myths of Exceptional, Black Leisure Travel: Teaching June Jordan's 'Report from the Bahamas' in the Contemporary Classroom." *Feminist Formations* 32, no. 1 (2020): 244–51. https://doi.org/10.1353/ff.2020.0021.

———. "Diasporic Dissonance: Black Women's Writing, the Caribbean, and U.S. Empire." Unpublished manuscript, n.d.

Gilmore, Ruth Wilson. *Golden Gulag: Prisons, Surplus, Crisis, and Opposition in Globalizing California*. Berkeley: University of California Press, 2007.

Gilroy, Paul. *Against Race: Imagining Political Culture beyond the Color Line*. Cambridge, MA: Harvard University Press, 2000.

Giovacchini, Saverio. "John Kitzmiller, Euro-American Difference, and the Cinema of the West." *Black Camera* 6, no. 2 (2015): 17–41. https://doi.org/10.2979/ blackcamera.6.2.17.

Giovanni, Nikki. "My House." In *My House*, 67–69. New York: Morrow, 1972.

Giovanni, Nikki, and Gloria Naylor. "Conversation." *Callaloo* 23, no. 4 (2000): 1395–1409.

Golden, Thelma. Introduction to *Freestyle: The Studio Museum in Harlem*, edited by Christine Y. Kim, Franklin Sirmans, Thelma Golden, and Hazma Walker, 14. New York: Studio Museum in Harlem, 2001.

Goldstein, William. "A Talk with Gloria Naylor." In *Conversations with Gloria Naylor*, edited by Maxine Lavon Montgomery, 3–6. Jackson: University Press of Mississippi, 2004.

Gordon, Avery F. *The Hawthorn Archive: Letters from the Utopian Margins*. New York: Fordham University Press, 2017.

———. "The Work of Corporate Culture: Diversity Management." *Social Text* 44 (Autumn 1995): 3–30.

Gordon, Michael R. "Fighting in Panama: The Chief of Staff; Vital for the Invasion: Politically Attuned General." *New York Times*, December 25, 1989. www.nytimes.com.

Gore, Dayo F. *Radicalism at the Crossroads: African American Women Activists in the Cold War*. New York: NYU Press, 2011.

Grandin, Greg. *Empire's Workshop: Latin America, the United States, and the Rise of the New Imperialism*. The American Empire Project. New York: Metropolitan Books, 2006.

Gray, Herman. "Subject(ed) to Recognition." *American Quarterly* 65, no. 4 (2013): 771–98.

Grewal, Inderpal. *Saving the Security State: Exceptional Citizens in Twenty-First-Century America*. Next Wave. Durham, NC: Duke University Press, 2017.

Griffin, Farah Jasmine. "Textual Healing: Claiming Black Women's Bodies, the Erotic and Resistance in Contemporary Novels of Slavery." *Callaloo* 19, no. 2 (1996): 519–36. https://doi.org/10.1353/cal.1996.0049.

Grise, Virginia. *Your Healing Is Killing Me*. Pittsburgh: Plays Inverse, 2017.

Guha, Ranajit. "The Prose of Counterinsurgency." In *Selected Subaltern Studies*, edited by Gayatri Chakravorty Spivak, 44–84. New York: Oxford University Press, 1988.

Gumbs, Alexis Pauline. "Spelling Soul: For Cheryll Y. Greene." *Souls* 18, no. 1 (March 14, 2016): 135–43. https://doi.org/10.1080/10999949.2016.1162612.

———. *Spill: Scenes of Black Feminist Fugitivity*. Durham, NC: Duke University Press Books, 2016.

———. "We Can Learn to Mother Ourselves: The Queer Survival of Black Feminism 1968–1996." PhD diss., Duke University, 2010.

———. "Your Mother: June Jordan and the Orchestration of Anger." *Little Black Book* (blog), October 5, 2009. http://thatlittleblackbook.blogspot.com.

Guy-Sheftall, Beverly. "Commitment: Toni Cade Bambara Speaks." In *Conversations with Toni Cade Bambara*, 3–19. Literary Conversations Series. Jackson: University Press of Mississippi, 2012.

Hajjar, Lisa. *Torture: A Sociology of Violence and Human Rights*. New York: Routledge, 2013.

Haley, Sarah. *No Mercy Here: Gender, Punishment, and the Making of Jim Crow Modernity*. Justice, Power, and Politics. Chapel Hill: University of North Carolina Press, 2016.

Hall, Jacquelyn Dowd. "The Long Civil Rights Movement and the Political Uses of the Past." *Journal of American History* 91, no. 4 (2005): 1233–63. https://doi.org/10.2307/3660172.

Hall, Stuart. "Cultural Studies and Its Theoretical Legacies." In *Cultural Studies*, edited by Lawrence Grossberg, 277–86. New York: Routledge, 1992.

———. "What Is This 'Black' in Black Popular Culture?" In *Black Popular Culture*, edited by Gina Dent and Michele Wallace, 21–33. Seattle: Bay, 1992.

"Happy Birthday, Mr. President." *Scandal*. ABC, December 6, 2012.

Harari, Yuval Noah. "Martial Illusions: War and Disillusionment in Twentieth-Century and Renaissance Military Memoirs." *Journal of Military History* 69, no. 1 (2005): 43–72.

Harb, Sirène. "Naming Oppressions, Representing Empowerment: June Jordan's and Suheir Hammad's Poetic Projects." *Feminist Formations* 26, no. 3 (December 19, 2014): 71–99. https://doi.org/10.1353/ff.2014.0035.

Hargrove, Hondon B. *Buffalo Soldiers in Italy: Black Americans in World War II*. Jefferson, NC: McFarland, 2003.

Harlow, Barbara. "The Drone Imprint: Literature in the Age of UAVs." *Race & Class* 60, no. 3 (January 1, 2019): 59–72. https://doi.org/10.1177/0306396818810988.

———. *Resistance Literature*. New York: Methuen, 1987.

Harney, Stefano, and Fred Moten. *The Undercommons: Fugitive Planning and Black Study*. New York: Minor Compositions, 2013.

Hartman, Saidiya V. *Scenes of Subjection: Terror, Slavery, and Self-Making in Nineteenth-Century America*. New York: Oxford University Press, 1997.

Harvey, David. *The New Imperialism*. Oxford: Oxford University Press, 2003.

Hernández, Kelly Lytle. *Migra! A History of the U.S. Border Patrol*. Berkeley: University of California Press, 2010.

Higashida, Cheryl. *Black Internationalist Feminism: Women Writers of the Black Left, 1945–1995*. Urbana: University of Illinois Press, 2011.

Holland, Sharon Patricia. *The Erotic Life of Racism*. Durham, NC: Duke University Press, 2012.

Holmes, Linda Janet. *A Joyous Revolt: Toni Cade Bambara, Writer and Activist*. Women Writers of Color. Santa Barbara, CA: Praeger, 2014.

Holmes, Linda Janet, and Cheryl A. Wall, eds. *Savoring the Salt: The Legacy of Toni Cade Bambara*. Philadelphia: Temple University Press, 2007.

Home of the Brave. Directed by Mark Robson. Produced by Stanley Kramer and Robert Stillman. Screen Plays Corp., 1949.

Hong, Grace Kyungwon. *Death beyond Disavowal: The Impossible Politics of Difference*. Difference Incorporated. Minneapolis: University of Minnesota Press, 2015.

hooks, bell. *Black Looks: Race and Representation*. Boston: South End, 1992.

Huntington, Samuel P. "The Clash of Civilizations?" *Foreign Affairs* 72, no. 3 (1993): 22–49. https://doi.org/10.2307/20045621.

———. *Political Order in Changing Societies*. 1968. Reprint, New Haven, CT: Yale University Press, 2006.

Ibrahim, Habiba. *Troubling the Family: The Promise of Personhood and the Rise of Multiracialism*. Difference Incorporated. Minneapolis: University of Minnesota Press, 2012.

Iton, Richard. *In Search of the Black Fantastic: Politics and Popular Culture in the Post-Civil Rights Era*. Oxford: Oxford University Press, 2008.

"It's Handled." *Scandal*. ABC, October 3, 2013.

Jackson, John L. *Racial Paranoia: The Unintended Consequences of Political Correctness: The New Reality of Race in America*. New York: Basic Civitas, 2008.

Jamal, Amaney A., and Nadine Christine Naber. *Race and Arab Americans before and after 9/11: From Invisible Citizens to Visible Subjects*. Arab American Writing. Syracuse, NY: Syracuse University Press, 2008.

James, Joy. *The New Abolitionists: (Neo) Slave Narratives and Contemporary Prison Writings*. Philosophy and Race. Albany: SUNY Press, 2005.

———. *Shadowboxing: Representations of Black Feminist Politics*. New York: St. Martin's, 1999.

Jelly-Schapiro, Eli. *Security and Terror: American Culture and the Long History of Colonial Modernity*. Berkeley: University of California Press, 2019.

Jenkins, Candice Marie. *Private Lives, Proper Relations: Regulating Black Intimacy*. Minneapolis: University of Minnesota Press, 2007.

Johnson, Cedric. *Revolutionaries to Race Leaders: Black Power and the Making of African American Politics.* Minneapolis: University of Minnesota Press, 2007.

Johnson, Charles. *Dreamer.* New York: Scribner, 1998.

———. "The End of the Black American Narrative." *American Scholar* 77, no. 3 (Summer 2008): 32–42.

Johnson, Shoshana. *I'm Still Standing: From Captive U.S. Soldier to Free Citizen—My Journey Home.* New York: Simon and Schuster, 2010.

Jones, Edward P. *The Known World.* New York: Amistad, 2004.

Jones, Meta DuEwa. "June Jordan's Primer for Looking." Chapter 2 in "Black Alchemy: Writers and Artists Map Diaspora." Unpublished ms.

———. "The String of Grace: Renovating New Rhythms in the Present-Future of Poetry and Music." In *Furious Flower: Seeding the Future of African American Poetry*, edited by Joanne V. Gabbin and Lauren K. Alleyne, 211–25. Evanston, IL: Northwestern University Press, 2019.

Jordan, June. "An Address to the Students of Columbia University during Their Anti-Apartheid Sit-In." In *On Call: Political Essays*, 117–22. Boston: South End, 1985.

———. "Black Folks and Foreign Policy." *Essence*, June 1983.

———. "Black Power on Nicaragua: 'Leave Those Folks Alone.'" *Village Voice*, October 4, 1983.

———. "Black Studies: Bringing Back the Person." In *Civil Wars: Observations from the Front Lines of America*, 45–55. New York: Simon and Schuster, 1981.

———. "Civil Wars." In *Civil Wars*, 178–88. Boston: Beacon, 1981.

———. "First Poem from Nicaragua Libre: *teotecacinte*." In *Living Room: New Poems*, 27–28. New York: Thunder's Mouth / Persea Books, 1985.

———. Foreword to *Civil Wars*, ix–xiv. Boston: Beacon, 1981.

———. "For the Sake of People's Poetry." In *On Call: Political Essays*, 5–15. Boston: South End, 1985.

———. "Fourth Poem from Nicaragua Libre: Report from the Frontier." In *Living Room: New Poems*, 31. New York: Thunder's Mouth / Persea Books, 1985.

———. "From Nicaragua Libre: photograph of managua." In *Living Room: New Poems*, 30. New York: Thunder's Mouth / Persea Books, 1985.

———. "In the Valley of the Shadow of Death." In *Civil Wars*, 150–62. Boston: Beacon, 1981.

———. Introduction to *On Call: Political Essays*, 1–4. Boston: South End, 1985.

———. "Life After Lebanon." In *On Call: Political Essays*, 77–85. Boston: South End, 1985.

———. "Nicaragua: Why I Had to Go There." *Essence*, January 1984.

———. "Nicaragua: Why I Had to Go There." In *On Call: Political Essays*, 65–75. Boston: South End, 1985.

———. "Notes toward a Black Balancing of Love and Hatred." In *Civil Wars*. Boston: Beacon, 1981.

———. *On Call: Political Essays.* Boston: South End, 1985.

———. "Poem about Police Violence." In *Passion: New Poems, 1977–1980*, 86–89. Boston: Beacon, 1980.

———. "Poem for Nicaragua." In *Living Room: New Poems*, 25–26. New York: Thunder's Mouth / Persea Books, 1985.

———. "Problems of Language in a Democratic State." In *On Call: Political Essays*, 27–36. Boston: South End, 1985.

———. "Safe." In *Living Room: New Poems*, 32. New York: Thunder's Mouth / Persea Books, 1985.

———. *Soldier: A Poet's Childhood*. New York: Basic Civitas, 2000.

———. "White English / Black English: The Politics of Translation." In *Civil Wars*, 59–73. Boston: Beacon, 1981.

Judy, Ronald A. T. *(Dis)Forming the American Canon: African-Arabic Slave Narratives and the Vernacular*. Minneapolis: University of Minnesota Press, 1993.

Kapadia, Ronak K. *Insurgent Aesthetics: Security and the Queer Life of the Forever War*. Durham, NC: Duke University Press Books, 2019.

Kaplan, Amy. *The Anarchy of Empire in the Making of U.S. Culture*. Cambridge, MA: Harvard University Press, 2002.

Kaplan, Amy, and Donald E. Pease. *Cultures of United States Imperialism*. New Americanists. Durham, NC: Duke University Press, 1993.

Kaplan, Caren. *Aerial Aftermaths: Wartime from Above*. Next Wave. Durham, NC: Duke University Press, 2017.

Keeling, Kara. *The Witch's Flight: The Cinematic, the Black Femme, and the Image of Common Sense*. Durham, NC: Duke University Press, 2008.

Kelley, Robin D. G. "After Trump." *Boston Review*, November 15, 2016. http://bostonreview.net.

Khalili, Laleh. *Time in the Shadows: Confinement in Counterinsurgencies*. Stanford, CA: Stanford University Press, 2013.

Killens, John O. "The Artist and the Black University." *Black Scholar* 1, no. 1 (November 1, 1969): 61–65. https://doi.org/10.1080/00064246.1969.11414453.

Kim, Christine Y., Franklin Sirmans, Thelma Golden, and Hazma Walker, eds. *Freestyle: The Studio Museum in Harlem*. New York: Studio Museum in Harlem, 2001.

Kim, Jodi. *Ends of Empire: Asian American Critique and the Cold War*. Critical American Studies Series. Minneapolis: University of Minnesota Press, 2010.

King, Martin. "Black Unit, PLO Align: JDL Replies." *New York Daily News*, August 28 1979.

Kinloch, Valerie. *June Jordan: Her Life and Letters*. Women Writers of Color. Westport, CT: Praeger, 2006.

Klein, Naomi. *The Shock Doctrine: The Rise of Disaster Capitalism*. New York: Picador, 2008.

Knight, Nadine. "'Can You Kill': Vietnam, Black Power, and Militancy in Black Feminist Literature." In *Black Cultural Production after Civil Rights*, edited by Robert J. Patterson, 119–38. Urbana: University of Illinois Press, 2019.

Kulich, Clara, Michelle K. Ryan, and S. Alexander Haslam. "The Political Glass Cliff: Understanding How Seat Selection Contributes to the Underperformance of Ethnic Minority Candidates." *Political Research Quarterly*, July 17, 2013. https://doi.org/10.1177/1065912913495740.

Kumar, Deepa. "National Security Culture: Gender, Race, and Class in the Production of Imperial Citizenship." *International Journal of Communication (Online)* 11 (2017): 2154–77.

Lakoff, Andrew. "Preparing for the Next Emergency." *Public Culture* 19, no. 2 (2007): 247–71.

Lathrop, George Parsons. *Yaddo: An Autumn Masque*. Privately printed, 1897. ProQuest Literature Online. Accessed December 29, 2020.

Levy-Hussen, Aida. *How to Read African American Literature: Post–Civil Rights Fiction and the Task of Interpretation*. New York: NYU Press, 2016.

Lorde, Audre. "Age, Race, Sex, and Class: Women Redefining Difference." In *Sister Outsider: Essays and Speeches*, 114–23. Berkeley, CA: Crossing, 2007.

———. "Black Women / Jewish Women—Openings for Dialogue." November 9, 1982. Box 3, Folder 1.1.063, Audre Lorde Papers, Spelman College Archives.

———. "Equal Opportunity." 1986. In *Our Dead Behind Us: Poems*, 16–18. New York: Norton, 1994.

———. "Learning from the 60s." In *Sister Outsider: Essays and Speeches*, 134–44. Berkeley, CA: Crossing, 2007.

———. "Litany for Survival." 1978. In *The Black Unicorn: Poems*, 31–32. New York: Norton, 1995.

———. *Sister Outsider: Essays and Speeches*. Berkeley, CA: Crossing, 2007.

Lowe, Lisa. *The Intimacies of Four Continents*. Durham, NC: Duke University Press, 2015.

Lubiano, Wahneema. "Black Nationalism and Black Common Sense: Policing Ourselves and Others." In *The House That Race Built: Original Essays by Toni Morrison, Angela Y. Davis, Cornel West, and Others on Black Americans and Politics in America Today*, edited by Wahneema Lubiano, 232–52. New York: Vintage Books, 1998.

———. "Imagining Alliances." In *Talking Visions: Multicultural Feminism in Transnational Age*, edited by Ella Shohat, 444–51. New York; Cambridge, MA: New Museum of Contemporary Art and MIT Press, 1998.

———. "Like Being Mugged by a Metaphor: Multiculturalism and State Narratives." In *Mapping Multiculturalism*, edited by Avery Gordon and Christopher Newfield, 64–75. Minneapolis: University of Minnesota Press, 1996.

Lubin, Alex. *Geographies of Liberation: The Making of an Afro-Arab Political Imaginary*. The John Hope Franklin Series in African American History and Culture. Chapel Hill: University of North Carolina Press, 2014.

Lugo-Lugo, Carmen R., and Mary K. Bloodsworth-Lugo. "Black as Brown: The 2008 Obama Primary Campaign and the U.S. Browning of Terror." *Journal of African American Studies* 13 (2009): 110–20.

Mahmood, Saba. "Secularism, Hermeneutics, and Empire: The Politics of Islamic Reformation." *Public Culture* 18, no. 2 (2006): 323–47.

Mahmood, Saba, and Charles Hirshkind. "Feminism, the Taliban and the Politics of Counterinsurgency." Fathom Archive. Accessed December 12, 2019. http://fathom.lib.uchicago.edu.

Mamdani, Mahmood. "Introduction: Trans-African Slaveries Thinking Historically." *Comparative Studies of South Asia, Africa, and the Middle East* 38, no. 2 (2018): 185–210.

Marable, Manning. *Race, Reform and Rebellion: The Second Reconstruction and Beyond in Black America, 1945–2006.* 3rd ed. Basingstoke, UK: Red Globe, 2007.

Marriott, David. *On Black Men.* Edinburgh: Edinburgh University Press, 2000.

Marshall, Paule. *Triangular Road: A Memoir.* New York: BasicCivitas Books, 2009.

Masco, Joseph. *The Theater of Operations: National Security Affect from the Cold War to the War on Terror.* Durham, NC: Duke University Press, 2014.

Massumi, Brian. "Fear (The Spectrum Said)." *Positions: East Asia Cultures Critique* 13, no. 1 (July 26, 2005): 31–48.

———. "National Enterprise Emergency: Steps toward an Ecology of Powers." *Theory, Culture & Society,* December 9, 2009. https://doi.org/10.1177/0263276409347696.

———. *Ontopower: War, Powers, and the State of Perception.* Durham, NC: Duke University Press, 2015.

Mathes, Carter. *Imagine the Sound: Experimental African American Literature after Civil Rights.* Minneapolis: University of Minnesota Press, 2015.

Mbembe, Achille. "Necropolitics." *Public Culture* 15, no. 1 (2003): 11–40.

McAlister, Melani. *Epic Encounters: Culture, Media, and U.S. Interests in the Middle East since 1945.* Rev. ed. American Crossroads. Berkeley: University of California Press, 2005.

McBride, James. *Miracle at St. Anna.* New York: Riverhead Books, 2002.

McClintock, Anne. "Paranoid Empire: Spectres from Guantánamo and Abu Ghraib." *Small Axe* 28 (2009): 50–74.

McCoy, Alfred W. *A Question of Torture: CIA Interrogation, from the Cold War to the War on Terror.* The American Empire Project. New York: Metropolitan Books, 2006.

McDuffie, Erik S. *Sojourning for Freedom: Black Women, American Communism, and the Making of Black Left Feminism.* Durham, NC: Duke University Press, 2011.

McKinstry, Carolyn, and Denise George. *While the World Watched: A Birmingham Bombing Survivor Comes of Age during the Civil Rights Movement.* Carol Stream, IL: Tyndale House, 2013.

McKittrick, Katherine. *Demonic Grounds: Black Women and the Cartographies of Struggle.* Minneapolis: University of Minnesota Press, 2006.

Melamed, Jodi. *Represent and Destroy: Rationalizing Violence in the New Racial Capitalism.* Difference Incorporated. Minneapolis: University of Minnesota Press, 2011.

———. "The Spirit of Neoliberalism: From Racial Liberalism to Neoliberal Multiculturalism." *Social Text* 24, no. 4 (Winter 2006): 2–24.

Mitchell, Timothy. *Carbon Democracy: Political Power in the Age of Oil*. London: Verso Books, 2011.

Montgomery, Maxine Lavon. *The Fiction of Gloria Naylor: Houses and Spaces of Resistance*. Knoxville: University of Tennessee Press, 2010.

Morales, Walter Queiser. "US Intervention in the New World Order: Lessons from Cold War and Post-Cold War Cases." *Third World Quarterly* 15, no. 1 (March 1994): 77–101.

Morrison, Toni. *Beloved*. New York: Random House, 1987.

———. *Home*. New York: Knopf, 2012.

———. *Paradise*. New York: Knopf, 1997.

Moten, Fred. "Blackness." In *Keywords for African American Studies*, edited by Erica R. Edwards, Roderick A. Ferguson, and Jeffrey O. G. Ogbar, 27–29. New York: NYU Press, 2018.

———. "Black Op." *PMLA* 123, no. 5 (2008): 1743–47.

———. "New International of Insurgent Feeling." Palestinian Campaign for the Academic & Cultural Boycott of Israel, November 7, 2009. www.pacbi.org.

Muñoz, José Esteban. *Disidentifications: Queers of Color and the Performance of Politics*. Minneapolis: University of Minnesota Press, 1999.

Murakawa, Naomi. *The First Civil Right: How Liberals Built Prison America*. Oxford: Oxford University Press, 2014.

Murch, Donna. "Crack in Los Angeles: Crisis, Militarization, and Black Response to the Late Twentieth-Century War on Drugs." *Journal of American History* 102, no. 1 (June 1, 2015): 162–73. https://doi.org/10.1093/jahist/jav260.

Myers, Shaundra. "In the Absence of Integration: Working in and against Nation in Erna Brodber's Louisiana." *African and Black Diaspora: An International Journal* 8, no. 2 (July 3, 2015): 230–44. https://doi.org/10.1080/17528631.2015.1027333.

Naber, Nadine. *Arab America: Gender, Cultural Politics, and Activism*. New York: NYU Press, 2012.

———. Introduction to *Race and Arab Americans before and after 9/11: From Invisible Citizens to Visible Subjects*, edited by Amaney A. Jamal and Nadine Christine Naber, 1–45. Arab American Writing. Syracuse, NY: Syracuse University Press, 2008.

National Press Club. "National Press Club Luncheon with Secretary of Defense Donald Rumsfeld." February 2, 2006. www.press.org.

National Public Radio. "'1996': Under the Watchful Eye of the Government." January 23, 2006. www.npr.org.

Naylor, Gloria. *Mama Day*. Illustrated ed. New York: Vintage, 1989.

———. *1996*. Chicago: Third World, 2005.

———. *The Women of Brewster Place*. New York: Viking, 1982.

Neal, Mark Anthony. *Soul Babies: Black Popular Culture and the Post-Soul Aesthetic*. New York: Routledge, 2002.

Negro Soldier, The. Directed by Stuart Heisler. Produced by Frank Capra, US War Department, Special Services Division, and US Army Signal Corps. Milestone Films, 1944.

"Nicaragua Reports Rebel Defeat." *New York Times*, June 15, 1983.

O'Brien, Timothy L. "How to Pitch the Military When a War Drags On?" *New York Times*, September 25, 2005. www.nytimes.com.

O'Hagan, Sean. "9/11: Time for a New Black Power Movement." *The Observer*, August 18, 2002. www.theguardian.com.

Omi, Michael, and Howard Winant. *Racial Formation in the United States: From the 1960s to the 1990s*. 2nd ed. New York: Routledge, 1994.

Ong, Aihwa. *Buddha Is Hiding: Refugees, Citizenship, the New America*. Berkeley: University of California Press, 2003.

"Opportunities at the CIA." *Black Collegian* 38, no. 2 (February 2008): 40–43.

Parry, Robert, and Norman Solomon. "Behind Colin Powell's Legend—My Lai." *Consortium News* (blog), March 17, 2018. https://consortiumnews.com.

Patterson, Robert J. *Exodus Politics: Civil Rights and Leadership in African American Literature and Culture*. Charlottesville: University of Virginia Press, 2013.

Payne, Charles M., and Adam Green. Introduction to *Time Longer than Rope: A Century of African American Activism, 1850–1950*, edited by Charles M. Payne and Adam Green, 1–9. New York: NYU Press, 2003.

Pettigrew, Erin. "Histories of Race, Slavery, and Emancipation in the Middle East." *Mediterranean Politics* 25, no. 4 (2020): 528–36. https://doi.org/10.1080/13629395.2018.1564508.

Plummer, Brenda Gayle. *In Search of Power: African Americans in the Era of Decolonization, 1956–1974*. Cambridge: Cambridge University Press, 2013.

Poole, Deborah. *Vision, Race, and Modernity: A Visual Economy of the Andean Image World*. Princeton Studies in Culture/Power/History. Princeton, NJ: Princeton University Press, 1997.

Population Reference Bureau. "Army Recruitment Goals Endangered as Percent of African American Enlistees Declines." Accessed June 30, 2020. www.prb.org.

Powell, Eve M. Troutt. *A Different Shade of Colonialism: Egypt, Great Britain, and the Mastery of the Sudan*. Colonialisms. Berkeley: University of California Press, 2003.

———. *Tell This in My Memory: Stories of Enslavement from Egypt, Sudan, and the Ottoman Empire*. Stanford, CA: Stanford University Press, 2012.

Puar, Jasbir K. *Terrorist Assemblages: Homonationalism in Queer Times*. Durham, NC: Duke University Press, 2007.

Puar, Jasbir K., and Amit S. Rai. "Monster, Terrorist, Fag: The War on Terrorism and the Production of Docile Patriots." *Social Text* 20, no. 3 (2002): 117–48.

Quan, H. L. T. *Growth against Democracy: Savage Developmentalism in the Modern World*. Lanham, MD: Rowman and Littlefield, 2012.

Quashie, Kevin Everod. *The Sovereignty of Quiet: Beyond Resistance in Black Culture*. New Brunswick, NJ: Rutgers University Press, 2012.

Rana, Junaid Akram. *Terrifying Muslims: Race and Labor in the South Asian Diaspora*. Durham, NC: Duke University Press, 2011.

Rana, Junaid Akram, and Gilberto Rosas. "Managing Crisis." *Cultural Dynamics* 18, no. 3 (2006): 219–34.

Randall, Alice. *Pushkin and the Queen of Spades*. Boston: Houghton Mifflin, 2004.

———. *Rebel Yell: A Novel*. New York: Bloomsbury, 2009.

———. *The Wind Done Gone*. Boston: Houghton Mifflin, 2001.

Randolph, Sherie M. *Florynce "Flo" Kennedy: The Life of a Black Feminist Radical*. Gender and American Culture. Chapel Hill: University of North Carolina Press, 2015.

Rankine, Claudia. *Don't Let Me Be Lonely*. St. Paul, MN: Graywolf, 2004.

Rasberry, Vaughn. *Race and the Totalitarian Century: Geopolitics in the Black Literary Imagination*. Cambridge, MA: Harvard University Press, 2016.

Raynaud, Claudia. "Hearing Voices, Battling for Her Mind: Gloria Naylor's 1996." In *Entre Apocalypse et Rédemption: L'écriture de Gloria Naylor / Writing in between Apocalypse and Redemption: Gloria Naylor's Fiction*, edited by Suzette Tanis-Plant, Claudine Raynaud, and Emmanuelle Andres, 000–000. Paris: Editions L'Harmattan, 2010.

Reagan, Ronald. "Inaugural Address, January 20, 1981." Ronald Reagan Presidential Foundation and Institute. Accessed December 1, 2020. www.reaganfoundation.org.

Reagan Library. "President Reagan's State of the Union Address to the Congress and the Nation, February 6, 1985." YouTube, March 11, 2016. www.youtube.com/watch?v=mnbQc9NHXJM.

Redmond, Shana L. *Anthem: Social Movements and the Sound of Solidarity in the African Diaspora*. New York: NYU Press, 2013.

———. *Everything Man: The Form and Function of Paul Robeson*. Durham, NC: Duke University Press, 2021.

Rice, Condoleezza. *Extraordinary, Ordinary People: A Memoir of Family*. New York: Crown, 2010.

———. *No Higher Honor: A Memoir of My Years in Washington*. New York: Crown, 2011.

Richie, Beth. *Arrested Justice: Black Women, Violence, and America's Prison Nation*. New York: NYU Press, 2012.

Ridley, John. "The Manifesto of Ascendancy for the Modern American Nigger." *Esquire*, November 30, 2006. www.esquire.com.

Ritchie, Andrea J. *Invisible No More: Police Violence against Black Women and Women of Color*. Boston: Beacon, 2017.

Ritchie, Andrea J., and Joey Mogul. "In the Shadows of the War on Terror: Persistent Police Brutality and Abuse of People of Color in the United States." *DePaul Journal for Social Justice* 1, no. 2 (April 1, 2008): 175–250.

Robertson, Tatsha. "Being Condoleezza." *Essence*, October 2006, 184–89.

Robinson, Cedric J. *Black Marxism: The Making of the Black Radical Tradition*. Chapel Hill: University of North Carolina Press, 2000.

———. *Black Movements in America*. New York: Routledge, 1997.

———. *Forgeries of Memory and Meaning: Blacks and the Regimes of Race in American Theater and Film before World War II*. Chapel Hill: University of North Carolina Press, 2007.

———. *The Terms of Order: Political Science and the Myth of Leadership*. Chapel Hill: University of North Carolina Press, 2016.

Robolin, Stéphane Pierre Raymond. *Grounds of Engagement: Apartheid-Era African American and South African Writing*. New Black Studies Series. Urbana: University of Illinois Press, 2015.

Rodgers, Carolyn M. *Songs of a Black Bird*. Chicago: Third World, 1973.

Rodríguez, Dylan. *Forced Passages: Imprisoned Radical Intellectuals and the U.S. Prison Regime*. Minneapolis: University of Minnesota Press, 2005.

———. "Goldwater's Left Hand: Post-raciality and the Roots of the Post-racial Racist State." *Cultural Dynamics* 26, no. 1 (March 1, 2014): 29–51. https://doi.org/10.1177/0921374013510800.

———. *White Reconstruction: Domestic Warfare and the Logics of Genocide*. New York: Fordham University Press, 2020.

Rooks, Noliwe M. *White Money / Black Power*. Boston: Beacon, 2006.

Ross, Loretta J. Preface to *Revolutionary Mothering: Love on the Front Lines*, edited by Mai'a Williams, Alexis Pauline Gumbs, and China Martens, xiii–xviii. Oakland, CA: PM Press, 2016.

Rushin, Kate. "The Bridge Poem." In *The Black Back-Ups: Poetry*, 33–35. Ithaca, NY: Firebrand Books, 1993.

———. "The Bridge Poem." In *This Bridge Called My Back: Writings by Radical Women of Color*, edited by Gloria Anzaldúa and Cherríe Moraga, xxi–xxii. Watertown, MA: Persephone, 1981.

Ryan, Michelle K., and S. Alexander Haslam. "The Glass Cliff: Evidence That Women Are Over-represented in Precarious Leadership Positions." *British Journal of Management* 16, no. 2 (2005): 81–90. https://doi.org/10.1111/j.1467-8551.2005.00433.x.

Said, Edward W. *Culture and Imperialism*. New York: Knopf, 1993.

Seikaly, Sherene. "How I Met My Great-Grandfather: Archives and the Writing of History." *Comparative Studies of South Asia, Africa and the Middle East* 38, no. 1 (May 1, 2018): 6–20. https://doi.org/10.1215/1089201x-4389931.

———. *Men of Capital: Scarcity and Economy in Mandate Palestine*. Stanford, CA: Stanford University Press, 2015.

———. "The Politics of Hope: 1967 and Beyond." Middle East Research and Information Project, June 9, 2017. https://merip.org.

Sexton, Jared. *Amalgamation Schemes: Antiblackness and the Critique of Multiracialism*. Minneapolis: University of Minnesota Press, 2008.

———. "The Ruse of Engagement: Black Masculinity and the Cinema of Policing." *American Quarterly* 61, no. 1 (March 2009): 39–63.

Shakur, Assata. *Assata: An Autobiography*. Westport, CT: Lawrence Hill Books, 1987.

Shange, Ntozake. *for colored girls who have considered suicide / when the rainbow is enuf: a choreopoem*. 1975. New York: Scribner, 1997.

———. *for colored girls who have considered suicide / when the rainbow is enuf: a choreopoem*. 1975. Trade pbk. ed. New York: Scribner, 2010.

Sharpe, Christina. *In the Wake: On Blackness and Being.* Durham, NC: Duke University Press, 2016.

———. *Monstrous Intimacies: Making Post-Slavery Subjects.* Durham, NC: Duke University Press, 2010.

Shaylor, Cassandra. "'It's like Living in a Black Hole': Women of Color and Solitary Confinement in the Prison Industrial Complex. (Symposium: Women in Prison)." *New England Journal on Criminal & Civil Confinement* 24, no. 2 (1998): 385–416.

Shockley, Evie. *The New Black.* Middletown, CT: Wesleyan University Press, 2011.

———. *Renegade Poetics: Black Aesthetics and Formal Innovation in African American Poetry.* Contemporary North American Poetry Series. Iowa City: University of Iowa Press, 2011.

Singh, Nikhil Pal. *Black Is a Country: Race and the Unfinished Struggle for Democracy.* Cambridge, MA: Harvard University Press, 2004.

———. *Race and America's Long War.* Oakland, CA: University of California Press, 2017.

———. "Racial Formation in an Age of Perpetual War." In *Racial Formation in the Twenty-First Century,* edited by Daniel HoSang, Oneka LaBennett, and Laura Pulido, 277–301. Berkeley: University of California Press, 2012.

Smith, Barbara, ed. *Home Girls: A Black Feminist Anthology.* New York: Kitchen Table / Women of Color Press, 1983.

———. Introduction to *Home Girls: A Black Feminist Anthology,* xxi–lviii. New Brunswick, NJ: Rutgers University Press, 2000.

———. "Toward a Black Feminist Criticism." In *African American Literary Theory: A Reader,* edited by Winston Napier, 132–46. New York: NYU Press, 2000.

Smith, Robert Charles. *We Have No Leaders: African Americans in the Post–Civil Rights Era.* Albany: SUNY Press, 1996.

Soldier's Story, A. Directed by Norman Jewison. Produced by Norman Jewison, Patrick Palmer, and Ronald L. Schwary. Screenplay by Charles Fuller. Columbia Tristar Home Video, 1999.

Spillers, Hortense J. "The Crisis of the Negro Intellectual: A Post-Date." *Boundary* 2 21, no. 3 (1994): 65–116. https://doi.org/10.2307/303601.

———. "Cross-Currents, Discontinuities: Black Women's Fiction." In *Conjuring: Black Women, Fiction, and Literary Tradition,* edited by Marjorie Pryse and Hortense J. Spillers, 249–61. Bloomington: Indiana University Press, 1985.

———. "Mama's Baby, Papa's Maybe: An American Grammar Book." *Diacritics* 17, no. 2 (1987): 64–81.

Springer, Kimberly. *Living for the Revolution: Black Feminist Organizations, 1968–1980.* Durham, NC: Duke University Press, 2005.

Staples, Robert. "The Myth of the Impotent Black Male." *Black Scholar* 2, no. 10 (June 1, 1971): 2–9. https://doi.org/10.1080/00064246.1971.11431050.

Stoler, Ann Laura. *Duress: Imperial Durabilities in Our Times.* Durham, NC: Duke University Press, 2016.

Streitfeld, David. "Author Toni Morrison Wins Nobel Prize." *Washington Post*, October 8, 1993. www.washingtonpost.com.

Sturken, Marita. *Tangled Memories: The Vietnam War, the AIDS Epidemic, and the Politics of Remembering*. Berkeley: University of California Press, 1997.

Sugrue, Thomas J. *The Origins of the Urban Crisis: Race and Inequality in Postwar Detroit*. Princeton Studies in American Politics. Princeton, NJ: Princeton University Press, 1996.

Swan, Quito J. *Black Power in Bermuda: The Struggle for Decolonization*. New York: Palgrave Macmillan, 2010.

———. "Caveat of an Obnoxious Slave: Blueprint for Decolonizing Black Power Studies from the Intellectual Governors of White Supremacy.(Essay)." *Journal of Pan African Studies* 6, no. 2 (2013): 53–71.

———. *Pauulu's Diaspora: Black Internationalism and Environmental Justice*. Gainesville: University Press of Florida, 2020.

Swarns, Rachel L. "The Racism Walkout: The Overview; U.S. and Israelis Quit Racism Talks over Denunciation." *New York Times*, September 4, 2001. www.nytimes.com.

Takacs, Stacy. *Terrorism TV: Popular Entertainment in Post-9/11 America*. Lawrence: University Press of Kansas, 2012.

Tate, Greg. "Cult-Nats Meet Freaky-Deke." *Village Voice Literary Supplement*, December 1986. www.villagevoice.com.

Taylor, Diana. *The Archive and the Repertoire: Performing Cultural Memory in the Americas*. Durham, NC: Duke University Press, 2003.

Taylor, Keeanga-Yamahtta. *From #BlackLivesMatter to Black Liberation*. Chicago: Haymarket Books, 2016.

Thomas, Michael. *Man Gone Down*. New York: Black Cat, 2007.

Thompson, Kevin. "Unusual 'Treatment' Offers Nightly Choices from Couch." *Palm Beach Post*, January 28, 2008.

Thompson, Lisa B. *Beyond the Black Lady: Sexuality and the New African American Middle Class*. Urbana: University of Illinois Press, 2009.

Thorsson, Courtney. "The Sisterhood: Black Women's Literary Organizing." Unpublished manuscript, 2020.

———. "'They Could Be Killing Kids Forever!': The Atlanta Child Murders in African American Literature." *African American Review*, forthcoming.

———. *Women's Work: Nationalism and Contemporary African American Women's Novels*. Charlottesville: University of Virginia Press, 2013.

Threadcraft, Shatema. *Intimate Justice: The Black Female Body and the Body Politic*. New York: Oxford University Press, 2016.

United States Department of Labor. *The Case for National Action: The Negro Family*. Washington, DC: Government Printing Office, 1965.

United States Office of Deputy Assistant Secretary of Defense for Equal Opportunity and Safety Policy. *Black Americans in Defense of Our Nation*. 3rd ed. Washington, DC: Department of Defense, 1985.

Vitalis, Robert. *America's Kingdom: Mythmaking on the Saudi Oil Frontier.* Stanford, CA: Stanford University Press, 2006.

———. "Aramco World: Business and Culture on the Arabian Oil Frontier." In *Counternarratives: History, Contemporary Society, and Politics in Saudi Arabia and Yemen,* edited by Madawi Al-Rasheed and Robert Vitalis, 151–81. New York: Palgrave Macmillan, 2004.

Walcott, Derek. "The Sea Is History." *Selected Poems,* 137–39. New York: Farrar, Straus and Giroux, 2014.

Walker, Alice. *In Search of Our Mothers' Gardens: Womanist Prose.* San Diego: Harcourt Brace Jovanovich, 1983.

Wall, Cheryl A., ed. *Changing Our Own Words: Essays on Criticism, Theory, and Writing by Black Women.* New Brunswick, NJ: Rutgers University Press, 1989.

———. "Introduction: Taking Positions and Changing Words." In *Changing Our Own Words: Essays on Criticism, Theory, and Writing by Black Women,* edited by Cheryl A. Wall, 1–15. New Brunswick, NJ: Rutgers University Press, 1989.

———. *On Freedom and the Will to Adorn: The Art of the African American Essay.* Chapel Hill: University of North Carolina Press, 2019.

———. "Toni's Obligato." In *Savoring the Salt: The Legacy of Toni Cade Bambara,* 27–42. Philadelphia: Temple University Press, 2007.

———. *Worrying the Line: Black Women Writers, Lineage, and Literary Tradition.* Chapel Hill: University of North Carolina Press, 2005.

Wallace, Maurice O. *Constructing the Black Masculine: Identity and Ideality in African American Men's Literature and Culture, 1775–1995.* Durham, NC: Duke University Press, 2002.

Wanzo, Rebecca Ann. *The Suffering Will Not Be Televised: African American Women and Sentimental Political Storytelling.* Albany: SUNY Press, 2009.

"War and Peace." *A Different World.* NBC, January 10, 1991.

Warren, Calvin L. "Black Care." *Liquid Blackness* 3, no. 6 (December 2016): 36–49.

———. *Ontological Terror: Blackness, Nihilism, and Emancipation.* Durham, NC: Duke University Press, 2018.

Washington, Mary Helen. "Black Women Image Makers." *Black World* 23, no. 10 (1974): 10–18.

———. Introduction to *Black-Eyed Susans: Classic Stories by and about Black Women,* ix–xxxii. Garden City, NY: Anchor Books, 1975.

Watergate.info. "Barbara Jordan: Speech on Impeachment." July 25, 1974. http://watergate.info.

Weaver, Vesla M. "Frontlash: Race and the Development of Punitive Crime Policy." *Studies in American Political Development* 21, no. 2 (2007): 230–65. https://doi.org/10.1017/S0898588X07000211.

Weiner, Juli. "More Horrendously Creepy Details about Qaddafi's Condoleezza Rice Obsession." *Vanity Fair,* October 2011. www.vanityfair.com.

Widener, Daniel. "Seoul City Sue and the Bugout Blues: Black American Narratives of the Forgotten War." In *Afro Asia: Revolutionary Political and Cultural Connections between African Americans and Asian Americans*, edited by Fred Wei-han Ho and Bill Mullen, 55–87. Durham, NC: Duke University Press, 2008.

Wilderson, Frank B. *Red, White and Black: Cinema and the Structure of U.S. Antagonisms*. Durham, NC: Duke University Press, 2010.

Williamson, Terrion L. *Scandalize My Name: Black Feminist Practice and the Making of Black Social Life*. New York: Fordham University Press, 2016.

Willoughby-Herard, Tiffany. "(Political) Anesthesia or (Political) Memory: The Combahee River Collective and the Death of Black Women in Custody." *Theory and Event* 21, no. 1 (January 2018): 259–81.

Wills, David C. *The First War on Terrorism: Counter-Terrorism Policy during the Reagan Administration*. Lanham, MD: Rowman and Littlefield, 2003.

Yoneyama, Lisa. *Cold War Ruins: Transpacific Critique of American Justice and Japanese War Crimes*. Durham, NC: Duke University Press Books, 2016.

Young, Cynthia. "Black Ops: Black Masculinity and the War on Terror." *American Quarterly* 66, no. 1 (2014): 35–67.

Young, Iris Marion. "The Logic of Masculinist Protection: Reflections on the Current Security State." *Signs* 29, no. 1 (2003): 1–25. https://doi.org/10.1086/375708.

Young, Kevin. *The Grey Album: On the Blackness of Blackness*. Minneapolis: Graywolf, 2012.

INDEX

Abu Ghraib torture, 127, 138, 274, 276–286
The Accidental Guerrilla (Kilcullen), 201–202
Adelman, Kenneth, 39
Adnan, Etel, 244
affirmative action, co-optation of Black studies and, 196
Africa, US counterinsurgency in, 59, 200
African American literature: compromise in, 309–310; definitions of, 17–18; Jordan's analysis of, 218–219; nationalism in, 282–286; popular culture and, 12; post-9/11 trends in, 275–286; September 11, 2001 attacks and, 71–72, 269. *See also* Black feminist literature; Black men's literature
African American Review, 271
Against Race (Gilroy), 70
Albright, Madeleine, 64, 154
Alexander, Khandi, 152
Alexander, Marissa, 27
Alexander, M. Jacqui, 4, 65, 103, 210
Ali, Zahra Hussein, 242, 259, 261
All the Women Are White and All the Men Are Black, but Some of Us Are Brave: Black Women's Studies, 191–192
Alsultany, Evelyn, 127
Alvarado, Donna M., 119
Alvarez, Julia, 298
Anderson, Marian, 146
Angelou, Maya, 146, 190, 200
anti-Black terrorism: Black military visuality and, 91–98; Rice's understatements of, 158; state-sanction apparatus for, 13–14

anti-communism: military buildup linked to, 62; race discourse and, 40–42
anti-violence movement, Black women and, 325n44
anti-war movement: Black feminists and, 50–51, 294; racialization of terror and, 47–48; suppression of Black empowerment and, 41
anti-Zionism, Black activists and, 56, 199
Antoon, Sinan, 64
Antwone Fisher (film), 89, 106
"Apologies to All the People in Lebanon" (Jordan), 215–216, 264–265
Appy, Christian, 135
Arabian American Oil Company, 52–53
Arab-Israeli War of 1967, US imperialism and, 54–57
Arab-Muslims: Blackness and, 78–80, 329n126; Black radicalism and, 56–57, 138–139, 201, 337n65; criminalization of, 59–60; sympathetic portrayals of, 127
Arab Spring, in Rice's memoirs, 167–168
armed Black resistance, racialization of terror and, 45–46
Army Wives (television series), 106
Ashcroft, John, 166
Ashe, Bertram, 271
Assata: An Autobiography (Assata), 67–68
assimilation: in Jordan's The Issue, 233–235; US imperial ideology of, 41
Association of Artists for Freedom, 195–196

Black Power movement, racialization of terror and, 48

"Black Power on Nicaragua: 'Leave Those Folks Alone'" (Jordan), 255

Black Radical Congress, 70

Black Scholar, 195

Black Skin, White Masks (Fanon), 111

Black soldier: in Black feminist literature, 289–292; multicultural military mythology and, 130–131; in visual culture, 102–107

Black speech, Black feminist literature and, 198–208

Black studies: Black feminist literature and, 194–196; Black life in context of, 186–188; corporate appropriation of, 195–196; passing through metaphor in, 335n22

Black United Front, 236, 341n54

Black university, Black literature and, 195–196

Black women: Black feminist literature's representations of, 336n24; black militarism and, 81–84; contemporary state power and, 146–153; counterinsurgency impact on, 56–57, 66–67; in politics, 58–68, 130; in popular culture, 151–153; public trust and role of, 57; state violence against, 58–68; surveillance of, 57, 75–76

Black Women's Revolutionary Council, 50, 200

Black World, 192

Blanchard, Terence, 92–93

Bland, Sandra, 27

Bloodsworth-Lugo, Mary, 74

The Bluest Eye (Morrison), 207, 296

Bolling, Gary, 224

Bond, Jean Cary, 254

Boogie Woogie Landscapes (Shange), 225

Botha, P. W., 41

The Boundaries of Blackness: AIDS and the Breakdown of Black Politics (Cohen), 149

"The Bridge Poem" (Rushin), 286–288

British Petroleum, 53

Bromley, Sue, 150

Brooks, Daphne, 11

Brown, Graham, 224

Brown, Jayna, 150–151

Brown, Keith, 148

Browne, Simone, 16, 75

browning of America, Latinx perspectives on, 74

Buffalo Soldiers, 85

Bukhari, Safiya, 27, 179

Bumpurs, Eleanor, 27

Bundy, McGeorge, 195–196

Bush, George H. W., 63, 65; Rice and, 154

Bush, George W., 37–38, 290; election of, 70–71; in Finney's poetry, 266; imperial grammar in speeches of, 37–38; Iraq War and, 64; Rice and, 154, 160–168

Bush, Mary Kate, 156

Bush Doctrine, 162–164

Butler, Judith, 114, 122, 331n50

Butler, Octavia, 20, 80

BYP 100, 31

Callaloo (journal), 298

Camp, Jordan, 46–47

Campbell, Francisco, 253–254

carbon democracy, 7–8

Carby, Hazel, 202–203

Cardinal, Ernesto, 253

Caribbean: Jordan's activism involving, 244–264; US counterinsurgency in, 59, 200

Carter, Jimmy, 60

Casey, William, 62, 245–246

Central America and South America: Jordan's writing on, 244–264; US imperialism in, 61–63, 245–248

Chan-Malik, Sylvia, 30–31, 337n65

Chayes, Di Vilde, 199

Childress, Alice, 200

Chiles, Nick, 78

ABOUT THE AUTHOR

ERICA R. EDWARDS is Associate Professor of English at Rutgers University–New Brunswick, where she holds the Presidential Term Chair in African American Literature. She is the author of *Charisma and the Fictions of Black Leadership*, which was awarded the Modern Language Association's William Sanders Scarborough Prize. She is the coeditor of *Keywords for African American Studies*, published in 2018 by NYU Press.